City University
Library Information Services
Cass Learning Resource Centre

ufdl

THE CYRIL KLEINWORT L
RESOURCE CENT
106 Bunhill Row, London EC1Y 8TZ
Telephone: 020 7040 8787

This book must be returned or renewed on or before the last date stamped below.

FINES ARE CHARGED ON OVERDUE BOOKS

15 ~~JUL~~ 2014

EXPERIENCING ORGANISATIONS
New Aesthetic Perspectives

Ian W. **King** and **Jonathan Vickery**

LIBRI PUBLISHING

First published in 2013 by Libri Publishing ■ Copyright © Libri Publishing ■ Authors retain copyright of individual chapters ■ The right of Ian W. King and Jonathan Vickery to be identified as the editors of this work has been asserted in accordance with the Copyright, Designs and Patents Act, 1988 ■ ISBN 978 1 907471 55 1 ■ All rights reserved. No part of this publication may be reproduced, stored in any retrieval system or transmitted in any form or by any means, electronic, mechanical, photocopying, recording or otherwise, without the prior written permission of the copyright holder for which application should be addressed in the first instance to the publishers. No liability shall be attached to the author, the copyright holder or the publishers for loss or damage of any nature suffered as a result of reliance on the reproduction of any of the contents of this publication or any errors or omissions in its contents ■ A CIP catalogue record for this book is available from The British Library ■ Cover and page design by Helen Taylor ■ Printed in the UK by Information Press Ltd.

Libri Publishing, Brunel House, Volunteer Way, Faringdon, Oxfordshire SN7 7YR

Tel: +44 (0)845 873 3837

www.libripublishing.co.uk

PHOTOGRAPHS
INDEX OF TITLES:

All photographs © by Chris Poulson.

Cover image: *The career climb as seen from the Top* (Hotel Nordica spiral staircase Reykjavík, March 2005). Nikon D100 1/160 at $f/6.7$. Nikon 24.0-50.0mm $f/3.3$-4.5. ISO 500.

Contents page: *London Offices a la Mondrian* (2010). Nikon D3. 1/250th sec at $f/5.6$. Focal length 135mm. Lens 18.0-200 mm $f/3.5$-5.6. ISO 2000.

Introduction: *Redundancy – Departure: National Gallery of Victoria, Melbourne* [NGV International] (2006). Nikon D200. 1/320 sec at $f/7.1$ 28.0-200.0 mm zoom. Focal length 66mm. ISO 500.

Chapter one: HANDS *Magic touch – Guangdong Museum of Art* (Guangzhou 2010). Nikon D3. 1/40 sec at $f/3.5$. 18.0-200.0 zoom. Focal length 18mm. ISO 4000.

Chapter two: *Art or Capital – International Gallery courtyard* (Melbourne, 2006). Nikon D200. 1/250 sec at $f/8.0$. 18.0 – 200.0 $f/$ 3.5-5.6 zoom. Focal length 28mm. ISO 100.

Chapter three: *Lehman Bros – The Pillars of Wall St. 2009* (14 May 2010). Nikon D3. 1/1600 sec at $f/20$. 8.0 – 200.0 $f/$ 3.5-5.6 zoom. Focal length 90mm. ISO 1250.

Chapter four: *Happy Chinese Capitalism* (22 Oct 2010). Guangzhou, China. Nikon D3. 1/640 sec at $f/13$. 18.0-200.0 mm zoom. Focal length 65mm. ISO 1000.

Chapter five: *Hands at Work: Los Angeles County Fair*, USA. (2009) Nikon D100. 1/20 sec at $f/4$. 70.0-300.0 mm zoom. Focal length 190mm. ISO 1600.

Chapter six: *Ah, but the Design! – Albequerque, N.M.* (2010). Nikon D3. 1/200 sec at $f/5.3$. Focal length 95mm. ISO 500.

Chapter seven: *The Evolution of Management* (2007) On the Thames, London. [Classical, modern, post-modern] Nikon D100. 1/4000 sec at $f/4.5$. Focal Length 130mm.

Chapter eight: *Glass Ceiling* (2002). The City, London. 14 Sept 2002 Nikon D100. 29mm. 1/250 $f/9.0$ ISO auto.

Chapter nine: *Corner Offices* (2001). 9 Aug 2001. Nikon D100. 1/2500 sec at $f/6.7$. 70 - 300mm zoom. 300mm. ISO 1600.

Chapter ten: *Art Budgets* [interior San Diego Museum of Art. Note torsos of photographer and partner above the midline and their feet and calves below the "waterline".] (2010). 11 April 2010. Nikon D3. 18.0 – 200mm $f3.5$-5.6. 1/30 sec at $f/5.6$. 170mm. ISO3200. Colour adjustment with Photoshop.

Chapter eleven: *Comparing Bonuses* (Melbourne, 2006). NikonD200. 1/750 sec at $f/14$. Lens 28.0-200.0 mm $f/3.5$-5.6 ISO 500.

Chapter twelve: *Footpath art by out of work artist* (Melbourne, 28 Nov 2006). Nikon D200. 28.0-200.0 $f/3.5$-5.6. 1/125 sec at $f/5.6$ ISO 400. Focal length 200mm.

Conclusion: *World View from Auto* (2001). San Francisco 17 Aug 2001. Nikon D100. 1/640 sec at $f/5.6$. ISO400 Lens 70-300 mm $f/40$-5.6.

CONTENTS

1   Introduction

15   CHAPTER ONE
        De-familiarising Organisations
        Ian W. King

33   CHAPTER TWO
        The Sense-Making of the Senses – Perspectives on Embodied *Aesthesis* & Aesthetics in Organising & Organ-isations
        Wendelin M. Küpers, and the Senses

57   CHAPTER THREE
        Peripheral Awareness and the Business of Strategy
        Robert Chia and Robin Holt

87   CHAPTER FOUR
        Thinking through Design – Processes and Tools for Knowledge Sharing in Organisations
        Bob Robertson

103   CHAPTER FIVE
        The Relational Art of Leadership
        Steven S. Taylor and Barbara A. Karanian

117   CHAPTER SIX
        Organisational Topophilia: the Countryside and Aesthetic Pleasure at Work
        Samantha Warren

137   CHAPTER SEVEN
        Design Thinking as Multi-epistemic Intelligence in Organisations
        Robert M. Bauer and Ward M. Eagen

157   CHAPTER EIGHT
        Aesthetics and the Spaces of Organisational Life
        Jonathan Vickery

177 CHAPTER NINE
Researching the Aesthetics of Organisation
Alberto Zanutto and Enrico Maria Piras

193 CHAPTER TEN
POEM'E': Effectively Managing 'Engagement'
Nuno Guimarães-Costa and Miguel Pina e Cunha

205 CHAPTER ELEVEN
Masters of Business Art: Visiting Art and Business in Europe 2000-2005
Pierre Guillet de Monthoux

223 CHAPTER TWELVE
Becoming or Process: What Future for Aesthetic Discourse in Organisations?
Antonio Strati

249 CONCLUSION
The New Landscape of Organisational Life
Ian W. King and Jonathan Vickery

263 Contributors

268 References

INTRODUCTION

Human life can be characterised as a movement within and between various organisations, from domestic life to education to work to civil associations and cultural activities, to public and state institutions. The term 'organisation' can stand for just about anything from an anthill upwards towards a multi-national conglomerate. Organisations, however simple, emerge and are sustained through concerted *organising* – which involves particular forms of knowledge, communication and management. Even the same types of organisation develop radically different structures, hierarchies, protocols and behaviours, management and leadership. They are never wholly predictable, and develop through responding to the minutiae of local issues as much as their own markets or constituencies, all the while always moving in the broader field of the global economy. This book, in purposively general terms, addresses *the way we think (and engage/experience with) organisations:* we discuss *how* we think, what concepts we use, what assumptions we maintain, our aspirations and what we hope organisations will be for us.

In the diverse chapters that make up our volume, we consider both the entity of the organisation along with the activities that make that entity what it is – what we call 'organisational life'. The concept of 'life' here is both ambiguous and significant, as it acknowledges the way that organisations are so often set up to repress, discipline and control in ways that do not enhance a sense of 'life'. Moreover, there are 'human' (bodily, emotional, imaginative) realms of experience that we need, and need organisations to facilitate and develop. The basis of this need may be ethical or existential, or to do with the nature of the human body, but what is sure is that our experiences of organisations are more often than not life-denying rather than life-generating. This book therefore looks at organisational life from a set of questions circulating around a broader concern for 'life', the 'human', and the unfolding of a human subject's powers of perception, expression and articulation. This we generally define in terms of *aesthetic experience*, something, of course, normally associated with art or culture.

In this book, aesthetic experience is defined in many different ways – as embedded in communication, as a mode of cognition, as design thinking or design process, as spatial movement, as a psychological condition of strategic thinking, as response to visual imagery, as a form of politics or an art business. The *aesthetic* is a concept that has a long philosophical history. Through our many chapters, 'aesthetic' refers to the senses and perceptual faculties, our powers of visual discrimination, corporeal awareness and various modes by which we apprehend the sensory environment. The term 'experience' can refer to visual observation, participation or interaction, reflection and interpretation, immersion in sensory environments, or a specific function of self-consciousness.

This book therefore involves new ways of re-thinking the nature of organisation – particularly reflecting on our *methods* of thinking and researching (which are often by way of received wisdom, habitual or unconscious). It offers a range of ideas, perspectives, and theories that help us reflect on the fundamental dynamics of organisational life as a distinct realm of experience, emotion and perception. Organisation – like the market – is not wholly logical, or accessible to common forms of rational thought, to be confirmed by statistics. It works by feeling, interpersonal interaction, vision, spatial awareness, intuition and also communication and the clash of ideas or ideals.

The concept of the aesthetic in this book is re-formulated with each chapter, that is, with a different aspect of organisation under discussion. We do not appeal to a philosophical orthodoxy – this book is for those who wish to explore the subject without being directed or ushered surreptitiously into a school of academic thought. Our focus necessarily has one foot firmly planted within empirical settings. A central objective of this volume is to promote a form of research-informed writing that is not contained by self-referential academic debates (valuable as they are), but is more intellectually oriented and accessible to the world outside, more reliant on the intellectual experience, curiosity and independence of the writer. From an academic standpoint, therefore, we have deliberately avoided established forms of research content, like lists of references, methodology sections, data analysis, exegesis or complex argumentation. Our framework is general, addressing big issues, promoting re-thinking on a broad conceptual level, which we intend to be accessible to a broad and even eclectic audience.

In the last twenty years we have witnessed the emergence of fantastically successful and sophisticated entrepreneurial organisations, super-complex multi-site global corporations, international internet-based or virtual organisations, extraordinary international NGOs, global media groups, an international 'art world', and indeed mysterious and ever troubling mobile terrorist networks. Organisations in their form, structure and management have become diverse and are constantly adapting to new technologies as they are shifting and to globalised fields of capital and commerce. And yet, the dominant corporations and institutions that dominate global markets are still working with many outdated concepts and theories on the nature of 'organisation' (and some are resistant to new concepts and theories on the nature of 'organisation', suspecting that they could impede their corporate success).

'Success' (and the strategic imperatives of competitive advantage and financial performance in which it is embedded) is a relative term, often misleading and self-destructive, whose end can mean misery for a lot of people just as it brings great rewards for others. Certain forms of success can, and often do, subvert the very economic sustainability that organisations presuppose will follow their central performance indicators. What has become clear, at least since the economic crisis beginning in 2006, is that the orthodoxies of strategic organisational management and their success-driven policies have been put into question, not just by academics or the usual critics of big business, but by the corporate establishment itself, and even by the national political elites that have gained so much by past corporate hegemonies over the social lives of their nation states. Yet it would be naive to think there are easy 'alternatives', not least in the contested and often random maelstrom of art and culture. But a lot of re-thinking is now going on, using art and culture as models of thought, mechanisms of reflection, frameworks for critique, and a means with which to penetrate the concealed or embedded processes and dynamics of organisational life. This book is part of a move to develop alternatives to the reigning orthodoxies.

We aim to engage anyone who is professionally concerned with the nature (and future) of organisations – not simply as profit-making production, or public-service providers, but as incubators of alternative life-forms, media of cultural thought, expression and communication, generative of long-term social reproduction. The recent global economic crisis is in many ways a failure at the level of the organisation – where powerful organisations, from corporations to local government, became the 'rogue' element in social life. The recent economic crisis revealed the permeability and fragile ecology of even the largest and most rigid organisations (for example, banks), and how the stability of even homogenous and mechanical administrative systems is relative to the perceptions, experiences, intuitions and aspirations of their executive and even junior employees or members. Much of the financial chaos was not constituted by actual shifts in the coordinates of economic variables, but by 'feelings', hunches, imagined scenarios, expectations and sublimated fears of brokers and financial operatives. The global stock markets of course are driven by, and dissolve under, the *imagination* of their operatives and clients – where the mental projection of future possibility reaches a point of no-contact with the 'real' economy.

This book is written by a group of people who have all been discussing the role of art and aesthetics in organisations and management practice for the last ten years or more – at various events, conferences, exhibitions, in restaurants and other social spaces across many different countries. The chapter authors are all university academics, but all have either worked in industry, consultancy, or are still active in creative practice of one form or another. Ian King worked in the theatre and then the music business before returning to university life; Jonathan Vickery was an artist, then designer and writer. It is the chasm and conflict between the worlds of theory and research, and of practice and actual organisations, which motivate this book. The amount of specialist scientific and academic research on organisation and management published in the last twenty years is remarkable, as is its lack of proportionate impact on the general shape and structure of industry and business itself. Apart from industry journalism and 'guru' consultancy, there are few direct means of interchange between the worlds of academic research and organisational practice.

The origins of this book are one such attempted means of interchange, called The Aesthesis Project. Over the course of some years, the project involved all the authors in this book, in international conferences – in London, Paris, Krakow and Banff (Canada) – and a published journal called *Aesthesis*, from which some of these chapters were taken (albeit rewritten, extended or updated). The project involved bringing together for dialogue on key fundamental issues in organisation and its management managers, consultants, artists, writers and media professionals, and academics and researchers.

The Aesthesis Project was developing its global (and high-cost!) aspirations throughout 2007 when the so-called global credit crunch made a swift impact. What was interesting was the way 'reactions' emerged, along with sudden and shifting frameworks of value and priority, preceding any substantive economic change. The sudden movement in the 'psychological' modus operandi of markets and their management impacted public as well as private sectors, in reaction to what was then (and to some degree still is) an unknown quantity. This for us underlined the significance of aesthetic modes of experience – in the forms of anticipation, imagination of unprecedented outcomes, emotionally driven response and expression of an environment in flux. The aesthetic surely has a dark, pathological dimension, particularly where felt vulnerability and perceived insecurity are involved. In 2008-9 in the UK and USA, many large organisations, without substantive economic reason, began shedding staff and long-term employees, targeting others with new reviews and assessments, then attenuating terms and conditions. In all could be witnessed new forms of corporate paranoia, where imagined catastrophic failure, fear of what could not be seen nor anticipated, apparitions of enemies within or without, quickly generated 'other'-denying forms of self-interest as accepted executive modus operandi. The corporate 'imaginary' has many demons, which routinely provoke self-destructive un-corporate behaviour (if, classically, corporate life is grounded in cooperation, trust, loyalty, the integrity of individual occupation, and so on).

During these last few years it has become apparent to us that the radical instability and uncertainty of outcomes mean a necessary realignment of organisational priorities. Organisations need to be able to cultivate two areas of neglected activity. First, they need to increase their self-knowledge as a means of managing their 'experiential' dimension (or what in the above context might be called their 'aesthetic unconscious': how they react and respond to unknown, imagined or forecasted outcomes). And second, they need to be able to construct broader, theoretically informed frames of reference for interpreting and combating the new panoply of paranoid corporate behaviours. Further, as some of our contributors in this volume suggest, the myopic and telescopic forms of vision that so consolidated the nature of corporate strategy and its management in the 1980s and after, needs to be supplanted by a hyperopic vision. This would entail a re-focusing or re-positioning of visual attentiveness, where the horizon and space beyond is clear, but tasks at hand are more 'blurred' – demanding different viewpoints, open to shifts in understanding, resisting first impressions. The shift from the detail to the broader view, from the short-term strategic objective to medium-or long-term historical development, will not just be desirable but a matter of survival.

This volume therefore attempts to be broad in its vantage point on organisational life, and accessible enough to be read by professionals and those working in organisations and willing to increase their certain capacity for reflective thinking, or interrogation of the philosophical and social assumptions that animate organisational management. The old certainties provided by strategic formulae, economic stats and their 'hard' data, ever increasing patterns of consumption, are no longer sure in quite the same self-evident way.

Many of the authors of this book now teach management, business, or what is called 'Organisation Studies' [OS]. The latter is a growing subject in business and management schools, out of which has emerged a small but growing and voracious group of researchers in 'organisational aesthetics'. This volume sits comfortably within this congenial and cosmopolitan sub-field, and we as editors have in turn been inspired by its openness and exploratory approach, catering for our own involvement in art and cultural practice. Organisational aesthetics is an interdisciplinary engagement with the dynamic realms of overlapping experience which make up the organisation as a living (social, cultural and political) entity – and the research of which necessitates a dialogue with artists, curators and critics, as much as sociologists, continental philosophers and political theorists.

However, we need to acknowledge at the outset the formative texts that have acted as exemplars, provocations and sites of discussion for us, and from which we have ventured into new avenues of thought. Pasquale Gagliardi's edited volume, *Symbols and Artifacts: Views of the Corporate Landscape* (1990), opened up a new horizon for the studied understanding of organisations. Coming after a decade of corporate investment in visual design, brand and advertising communications, Gagliardi's edited work was indicative of a new opening field of systematic study – looking at the critical role of artifacts (the material culture of organisations, with their strategically designed interiors and diverse range of objects), along with the symbolic systems they formed, their embedded cultural codes, the phenomenon of cultural identity and the expressive behaviours they generated. From that moment, it became clear that the 'organisation' was a potentially enormous field for aesthetic, cultural, and sociological as well as anthropological research.

The 1990s witnessed substantial financial and industrial expansion, and with it the corporate world's willingness to take risks and invest in 'creative' activity, and not simply in their branding and marketing communications. New integrated design consultancies and entrepreneurial professors (particularly in the US) inspired new approaches to workplace design, team and project work, production processes, the 'creative' or 'experience' economy, made more immediate by the rise of the internet and mobile communications through this decade. Graphic design, architecture, spatial design, brand design, design photography, all became stock in trade to the most modest organisations, private and public, radically changing attitudes, behaviours, environments and even strategic management methods. The development of organisational research must to some degree be placed in this context, particularly as by the turn of the year 2000 this context had generated a stream of popular business and management gurus proclaiming the salvific power of creativity, offering time and again completely to transform strategic, management or organisational thinking.

In some ways Antonio Strati's book *Organization and Aesthetics* in 1999 became a seminal reference point for the new decade just as Gagliardi's was for the previous one. It was soon joined by another edited collection, Stephen Linstead and Heather Höpfl's *The Aesthetics of Organization* (2000), which notably opened organisation studies to younger interested onlookers in sociology, art history and cultural studies. Within three years another volume of collected essays made a similar impact and has become a similar long-term resource – Adrian Carr and Philip Hancock's Art and *Aesthetics at Work* (2003). The specific contribution of the latter was to frame a series of central questions in organisation studies within the critical traditions of European social thought, particularly post-Frankfurt School social theory. The 'field' of organisational aesthetics has become diverse in subjects as well as theoretical frameworks, yet has forged a disciplinary identity through its participation in associations like the Standing Conference on Organizational Symbolism (SCOS) and the European Group for Organization Studies (EGOS) and through prodigious amounts of published research in major journals like *Culture and Organisation, Tamara: Journal of Critical Postmodern Organisation Science, Organisation* and *Organisation Studies.*

From the last few decades there are countless texts that could be quoted, many have an essential role in the growing corpus of aesthetic investigations, still being generated by authors like Vincent Dégot, Ralph Bathurst, Josef Chytry, Robert Austin, Steve Taylor, Nick Nissley, Daved Barry, Jonathan Schroeder, Janet L. Borgerson, Niina Koivunen, Klaus Harju, Barbara Karanian, Anne-Britt Gran, Arja Ropo, Stefan Meisiek, Ralph Kerle, Nancy Adler, Hérve Colas, Andrew Rowe, Brigitte Biehl, Per Darmer, Louise Grisoni, Jane James, Beatrice Rossi, Jennifer Lawn, Peter Pelzer, Timon Beyes, Terry Brown, Kathy Mack, Barbara Loftus, Claire Jankelson, Boris Ewenstein, Laura Verdi, Jennifer Whyte, and compelling art practice by Anna Scalfi, Florence Kutten, Navid Nuur, Nicholas Pope, Colin Halliday and Mikael Scherdin.

One major issue that has been addressed by organisational aesthetics researchers in the last decade is the way mainstream business and management education and research takes the large commercial corporation as its archetype, or dominant model of 'organisation'. In the face of the hegemonic power of this model of the corporation for public, political or cultural organisations (hospitals, universities and even churches) have been modeled or model themselves on it. The historically informed research of Guillet de Monthoux has revealed a range of prodigious and effective organisational forms, from art movements and art projects to unique institutions like opera houses. Apart from his influential creative output in various research projects, peripatetic lectures, films and articles, his book *The Art Firm: Aesthetic Management and Metaphysical Marketing* (2004) expanded the conceptual breadth of 'organisation' as a subject, foregrounding many issues in management and marketing as internal to the very concept of organisation.

Beginning with this issue – the corporation as dominant organisational model – the rest of the issues broached in this volume are as follows:

- What method? We re-think the way we investigate, analyse and interpret organisations (and the philosophical or social implications of the methods we employ).
- What is knowledge of organisations? Organisations are sites of knowledge production, are media of knowledge, and also knowledge-embedded environments. Yet traditional sources suggest a quite different position and their relationship to our understanding of meaning demands careful consideration.
- What is the organisational subject? How do we understand the human person as an organisational being, an embodied being whose senses are active, being formed by and forming organisational environments?
- What is the organisation as an environment? How do we assess the spaces of organisation and the design of those spaces? What different lines of inquiry open up if we consider the organisation as designed space, or a space for design?
- How do we assess the organisation as a site of experience? Here we consider the various forms of perceptual awareness and vision of the people who work within particular office environments.
- How can the organisation serve as a platform for creativity and critical thinking? Here we underscore the need to formulate non-standardised models of management, of leadership, and of the fundamental disposition of workers or employees.

Before each chapter we offer a brief introduction that defines its distinct subject, approach and purpose. In addition, both as a frontispiece and coda to every chapter, there is the photography of Chris Poulson. For us, Chris's photography demonstrates the realisation through an image of the necessity to look anew – if you like to de-familiarise yourselves with traditional expectations and bathe in the form of potentiality.

Ian King and Jonathan Vickery

ACKNOWLEDGEMENTS

We wish to convey our warm thanks to the following people:

To Libri Publishing for being receptive to what began as an unusual publication project, then remaining committed through its various permutations, and then being adventurous in thinking about its audience and market.

To Jane Malabar, who was the capable and multi-skilled administrator for the Aesthesis Project. She contributed much more than administration, however, acting as troubleshooter and problem-solver. Through her consistent oversight, she was a pillar of stability around which we all frantically worked.

Dr Ceri Watkins of Essex Management Centre, another central member of the original team. Ceri played a role in managing The Aesthesis Project (and the journal), particularly the administration of the international conferences. This volume to that degree reflects his specific contribution.

To Hannah Jamieson Vickery, as design consultant and technical back-up throughout the duration of the Aesthesis Project and beyond.

To Stephen Linstead, as one of the original Art of Management and Organisation conference pioneers.

To the advisory board of the *Aesthesis* journal, who included Dawn Ades, Daved Barry, Jo Caust, Pierre Guillet de Monthoux, Laurie Heizler, Nick Nissley, Antonio Strati and Steve Taylor. It is in the new online journal of *Organizational Aesthetics* (OA), led by Steve Taylor, that *Aesthesis* has found a second life.

To Chris Poulson, emeritus professor of management and photographer of organisational life (extraordinaire). Chris's portfolio of photographs featured throughout this book are here as an expression of his generosity and selfless goodwill as much as his phenomenal travelling and distinctive creative style.

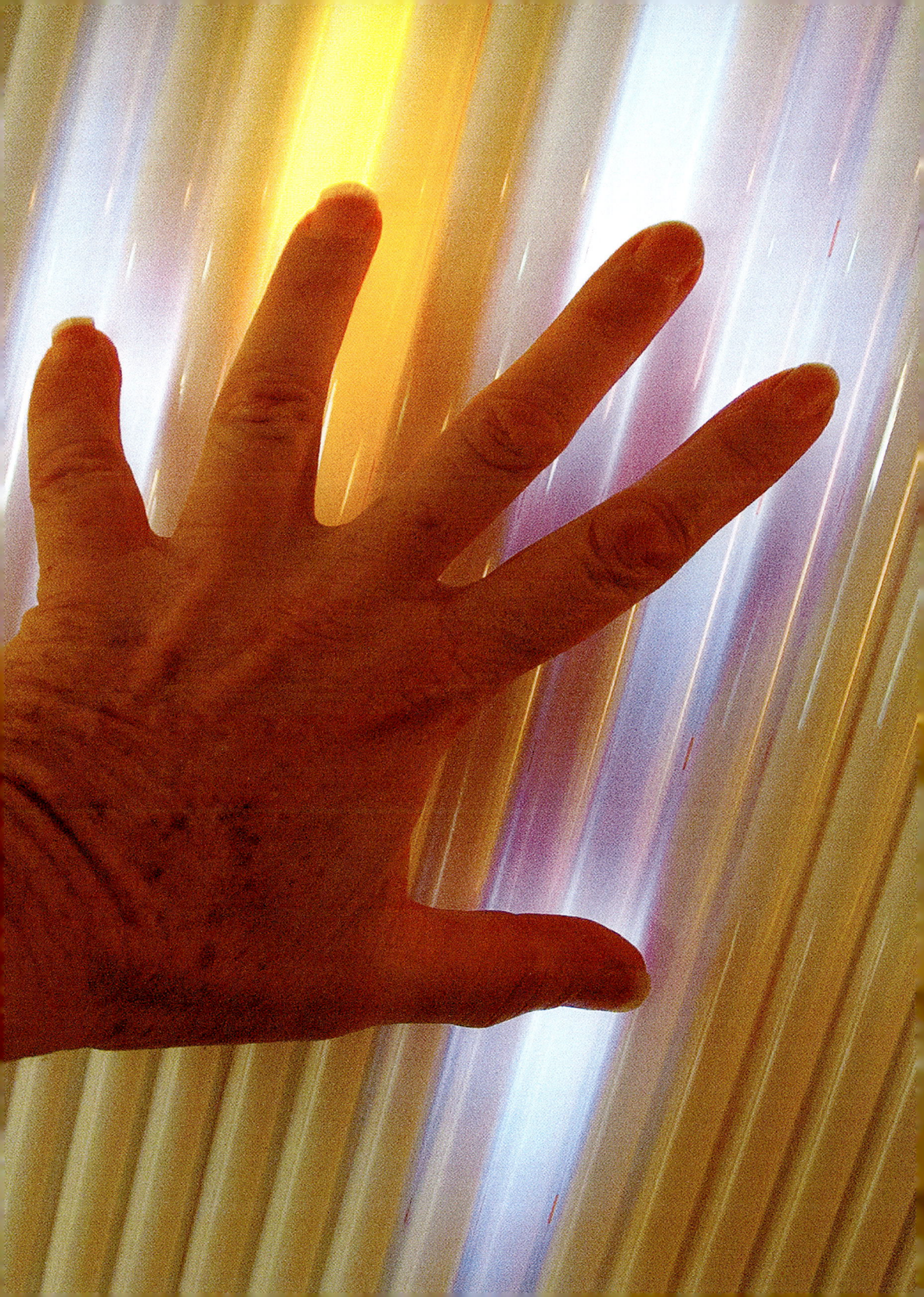

This first chapter sets off our investigation into organisations and underlines the approach we have taken in this book. It looks at the active, experiential dimension of organisations, what we call 'organisational life'. The term 'organisation' is not self-evident, nor does it signify a specific entity. Organisation means organising. It is an activity, and is always carried out in changing conditions of practice. But in this chapter we go further. Organisation is a fundamental medium of thought. We think (on a large social and economic scale) through our organisations. The concept of organisation is therefore an epistemological one (episteme = knowledge), and a basic research task for all managers or business owners is to understand how their organisation performs thinking or structures its thought-practices.

This chapter seeks to encourage a reflexivity in thought-practices for organisations. What seems to be clear, obvious, logical, and managed according to established procedures, for example decision-making, is rarely just that. The most extraordinary contingencies are involved in seemingly mechanical processes, and the contingency of 'individual experience' underlies most of them. And so this chapter attempts to start by establishing that individual experience is more central to the functioning of organisations than is usually admitted. However, in this context 'individual' does not mean 'personal'. It may mean 'subjective', although subjective is not merely 'personal' either. Individual, subjective, sensory, perceptual experience, what we call 'aesthetic' experience, is something of collective and corporate significance. In this book we show why.

De-familiarising
Organisations
Ian W. King

Opening Remarks...

In this chapter I want to provide a contextual introduction to the approach taken by the different chapter authors of this book. Collectively our approach explores questions which relate to the effectiveness of what we know, and how we act, in an environment that is forever in flux and consistently making demands, that activity which we call 'organisational life'.

It might be claimed that organisations occupy a central space from which all societies emerge. They are the central organs of production, growth and prosperity. And yet this is not an easy context to understand. Certainly, the guise of organisations is both varied and extensive. It stretches across the public, private and voluntary sectors, from manufacturing and sales to service and research. Organisations act as employers, educators and trainers, creators of resource, and regenerators of many forms of capital. Many would argue that the dominant organisations are capable of providing unique forms of public good (Perrow, 1991).

The term 'organisational life' suggests an inclusive approach, one that recognises that any attention to physical structures, bounded spaces and locations; rather, organisations exist in a constant dynamic between and across the inside and the outside. It is therefore a realisation that they do not exist as discrete entities, in a social vacuum. And so 'organisational life' is a term that attends to the internal features of an organisation, and yet vitally extends to their role, place and influence in and across society and culture.

From this starting place, our fundamental position prompts a pivotal question. Do the traditional epistemological models, our models of knowledge, which guide our normal procedures of research practice and understanding, possess the subtlety and potential to capture the richness and variety of organisational life?

My argument in this chapter is that traditional epistemological models tend to look for *compliance* rather than *diversity*. In accordance with the nature of the demands placed upon organisations and their people, in my opinion, applying these models will inevitably produce predictable and often inadequate outcomes. The crux of my argument suggests that the dominant academic position governing how we view the world is based on a form of *exclusivity* that is inadequate to cope with the breadth and depth of needs emerging from contemporary life. My claim, (and here I believe that I can also speak on behalf of the other contributors to this book), is that as people we naturally possess attributes that could potentially generate much more than is presently employed.

Traditionally, the importance of these 'attributes' has tended to be resisted, with the suggestion that they undermine rather than contribute to knowledge and understanding. A broader appreciation of the character of knowledge, together with the potential of our bodies and their movement, and with the attributes these engender, suggest that we *must* develop and nurture the capability to adopt other perspectives and utilise more inclusive tools by which we can view, explore and appreciate the varied character of the contemporary world. My argument is confined to people-based, empirical situations and contexts, as I hope my explanation below will clarify. For non-personal, quantitatively-based organisational situations and problems I am content to admit that traditional approaches still dominate.

Consequently, in this chapter I am not going to suggest that I (or we) offer one key solution, or even suggest I/we can offer a particular route to aesthetic utopia. Rather my aim here is to claim a space for an epistemological alternative, and one that contextualises some of the arguments and exemplifications offered in the following chapters of this book. Labelling my claim as an 'epistemological alternative' may suggest to the casual reader that this account might become unduly academic. But in fact the essence of this label is about the choice of how we (as people) view the world and how then, from this alternative epistemological position or positions, we engage and appreciate the richness of this event.

Burrell and Morgan (1979) (followed by a number of exemplifications and critiques – see for example, Willmott, 1993) rightly acknowledge the importance of this 'meta-question'. For our approach is not simply restricted to a call for naturalistic inquiry, which often perpetuates existing epistemological positions, but rather one that strives to generate alternate and deeper meanings.

Traditions, Science and Decision-making…

As a result of this brief contextual overview let me now provide more substance to the position I hold and how, in my view, this introduces the style of approach taken in this book. My starting point is an obvious one for organisations and is to acknowledge that organisations in the West have been experiencing serious crises. For example their contribution and reaction to the recent global recession has been problematic. Whilst some observers might view this in terms of social 'justice', or perhaps with some form of 'smug satisfaction', the reality is that we all need organisations to work, because the alternative for us is much worse!

However, unsurprisingly, as always the response by organisations to recovery is all too often to return to their 'safe' traditional modes of knowledge generation, governed by the underlying assumption that through continued refinement of our existing pathways we will produce increasingly more effective solutions and persuasive explanations. This in essence is the Scientific Method, an approach that has served academia well for many centuries and become the dominant influence governing economic and financial theories in and across organisational life.

In some of the following chapters other authors will go on to present additional arguments for the necessity of our approach, but for me they all lead to one critical question; 'Will more of the same be enough?' Even if we acknowledge the vast increase in knowledge creation and knowledge generation mechanisms of the last thirty years, if again we consider the cause of the recent turmoil, the evidence suggests that 'more of the same' created the recession predicament out of which we in the Western world are slowly climbing at present. Critically, therefore, this poses questions regarding certain assumptions. Not the least of these is whether, by again following or confining ourselves to this same traditional route (and in so doing, I assume, continuing to view the world from this same epistemological position), this will merely perpetuate continuing cycles similar to the one from which we are now slowly emerging. Is this cyclical pattern progressive or perhaps indicative of something else?

In these circumstances, throughout the book we ask and seek to answer one essential question;

> 'Is there not an alternative? Is this the only route to knowledge of/with/for organisations and organising?'

In other words, are we convinced that the knowledge that we produce via the traditional method fulfils the rich and broad needs of organisational life? Of course, and this needs to be made clearly at this early point, by calling for an alternative this does not suggest that we are calling for an abandonment of Scientific method. Certainly I do not think anyone in this text is suggesting this. We acknowledge that this position still possesses currency, but now needs to be re-positioned in more reflexive epistemic contexts in order to mediate the extensive demands of contemporary life.

Perhaps you (the reader) remain unpersuaded? Clearly, it is difficult to call for an alternative when the original has served so well for some considerable period. Yet a close inspection of a key domain of organisation literature reveals several strands of doubt that have already been expressed. Let me illustrate this with just one example illustration. Organisations exist to fulfil certain tasks, either to provide a service or to generate products, resources, wealth, etc. Fundamental to these activities (regardless of sector or function) is the act of decision-making, which Nobel prize-winner Herbert Simon labelled as *synonymous* with 'management' (Simon, 1955). In this circumstance therefore I feel I can legitimately claim that decision-making is a central activity for all organisations. Now let us again consider the above critical question within a frame that understands decision-making as the making of a choice from a range of alternatives in order to rectify a problem. Decision-making literature has been exhaustive in its examination of the nature of the 'making choices' process – suggesting it can either be maximising, satisficing, or political (See Simon, 1955; March, 1990); can operate at operational and strategic levels (Hickson et al, 1986); use a variety of processes and procedures; and is operational in individual, group or organisational spheres (see Mintzberg, et. al, 1972). A quick Google Scholar search reveals over 1.1 million hits in the area of decision-making – presenting this as one of the most examined areas in the study of organisations.

Unsurprisingly, exclusively (and without any exception of which I am aware), this literature is informed only by traditional scientific methodologies. Rarely, if at all, has it seriously explored alternative epistemological positions – despite the existence of a rich vein of literature indicating that the majority of empirical decisions made in organisations emerge through *intuition* (Isenburg, 1984) and require *judgment* (Bazerman, 1999; Einhorn, 1980; Harrison, 2003). Intuition and judgment call upon prior experience of events, the operation of memory, the activation of sensory awareness and multi-modal cognition, all things which as such are well suited to being studied from different epistemological positions. Yet this realisation has rarely been part of mainstream scientific examination. If it had, then the resulting explanations and analyses would have been likely to produce quite different selections and therefore generate other 'solutions'.

To elaborate this claim a little further, the reality posed by this vein of decision-making literature suggests that real decisions in organisations often are made through 'short-cuts', often called *heuristics*, which are less than carefully formed decision-making processes. These decisions are made through 'hunches' or intuition; they are made by employing extracts from our experience, and from cumulative judgments; of experiences of being involved in events preceding this particular issue; and from contexts beyond it. Does this meet the various authors' own criteria for 'a process'? Surely not, if these criteria assumed a linear, sequential operation, as is so often described in decision-making texts. Rather, decision processes are often non-linear, erratic, spontaneous, reactive and based upon 'personal' experience.

Of course this literature has attempted to describe what judgment and intuition are as cognitive phenomena, but only from one epistemological position. The results for me are technical accounts that rarely penetrate the real complexity of social life with which we are all familiar. This is further concurred and amplified in practice, since this vast literature is rarely reported by people in organisations themselves to be employed to guide their decision-making practices. Rather they turn to their own experience. But, as we know from evidence, this is not in the best interests of organisations in the medium or long term. The evidence suggests that relying on experience does indeed produce short-term gains, but will lead to medium/long-term decline in impact unless the decision-maker can develop understanding (and therefore action) of the exceptional, or expert-type behaviour (Chi et al, 1988; Shanteau, 1987). This final observation brings us back in cyclical fashion to the issues I described above!

Accordingly, our approach in this collection of chapters is to be more inclusive. We argue that, for decision-making and a whole host of other areas within and across organisational life, there is a range of alternatives that will provide people with greater resources both in terms of depth but also in terms of breath. This is not because there is a whole new collection of knowledge out there waiting for a label of identification, but rather because much of what is out there has always been there but simply is overlooked! But we need to be able to access it. We overlook it because we have been conditioned through Science only to value certain aspects, or features, or the 'form', and to remain figuratively static and remote before a particular empirical event. Of course, this is understandable since if we attempted to value everything we would quickly be overwhelmed. Through Science we always assumed that the lens it provided was correct and sufficient. We need to remind ourselves of the historical context through which this 'lens' was developed, several hundred years ago, when life and society was perhaps somewhat simpler and more confinable.

Contemporary life is now embedded in technology and communication media, and as such our respective worlds are no longer as confinable, but rather converge and expand in ways our forebears could never have conceived. The features of contemporary life that now every day we all have to face, grasp, and act upon, emerge from a vast diversity of different places, sources, and moments. We require methods of knowledge acquisition that are something other than just a more complex version of the scientific tradition.

I mentioned above that we require alternative epistemological positions, which will produce both greater depth and breadth of knowledge. Instrumental in achieving these richer forms of knowledge is the tool of 'de-familiarising', which for me offers the facility of taking that which is already apparent and through a different lens of engagement generating alternate or additional insights to knowledge. I will amplify this potential later in the chapter, but at this point it is important to stress that throughout this text the key to achieving the potential of de-familiarising will be art and aesthetics. American pragmatic philosopher, Mark Johnson, clarifies my position with regards aesthetics when he states:

> 'I do not mean merely the philosophy of art and beauty; rather, I regard aesthetics as concerning everything that goes into our ability to grasp the meaning and significance of any aspect of our experience, and so it involves form and structure, the qualities that define a situation, our felt sense of the meaning of things, our rhythmic engagement with our surroundings, our emotional interactions and on and on' (Johnson, 2007: 89)

Therefore, for the remainder of this chapter I provide what I hope is a more substantive foundation for this collection of claims. I start in the next section by reviewing the guise of knowledge and its limitations in traditional accounts.

Changing Positions to Know More...

Ultimately, for the authors of this text and anyone who is considering some of the ideas and approaches introduced, our ultimate goal is to produce valuable knowledge, knowledge as a resource, as diverse and active forms of knowing, which can underpin and inform the various dimensions of organisational life. Yet, for Schreyögg and Geiger (2007) amongst others, this may not be a simple task, for they are concerned that

> 'The rapidly growing perception of the importance of knowledge for organisations and corporations has not yet yielded sufficient clarity as to what the concept means' (ibid: 78).

They expand their claim by suggesting that the increasing use of knowledge across IT and management studies literatures has rendered the very concept of 'knowledge' more and more blurred. Their concern is that this blurring may undermine the importance of the different characteristics and contributions to the very basic features of knowledge, for example appreciating *a priori* forms of knowledge (that which does not need to observe the world) as distinguishable from *a posteriori* or empirical features (that which does). In organisation studies these emerge as declarative knowledge ('knowing that', sometimes called propositional knowledge) and procedural knowledge (the ability to perform a task). These articulate distinctions between the 'static' or abstract conceptual foundations of knowledge from its applied, more temporal aspects. In terms of organisational life, in terms of achieving outcomes, the empirical and procedural dimension of knowledge has emerged to become the more dominant. As Jacky Swan (2007:750) clarifies, it (knowledge) is 'the ability to discriminate within and across contexts' thus, she claims, when we examine knowledge in organisations we should be interested in the

> 'varied ways in which actors in particular social situations understand and make sense of where they are and what they are doing' (ibid).

In order to fulfil this, advocates of the scientific method argue that the appropriate mode of inquiry should be based on gathering observable, empirical and measurable evidence subject to specific principles of reasoning in the formulation and testing of hypotheses (see the contribution of Galileo to this evolution). For traditionalists the choice of epistemological position to undertake empirical research is unquestionable. The place to observe and gather data is from a detached uninvolved position that enables objectivity and rigour (amongst other things) to be upheld. In this way, the researcher is de-coupled from the researched, and therefore knowledge can be generated via a proven method and advanced through revisions of new evidence undertaken through the same or similar processes.

There are attractive aspects to such an approach to knowledge acquisition, but what concerns me is that despite *the needs of the event of the research situation*, the researcher continues to maintain an adherence to one epistemological position and the assumption is that from this *detached* place all that needs to be known can be observed. Thus, one interpretation is that the assumed conduct of the method chosen prevails over the needs of the research situation. Of course, proponents might add that without such rigour then consistency and subsequent comparison cannot occur. This is a valid response, and I think from here we will need to start to make difficult decisions, ones that weigh up opposing strengths and weaknesses. A suitable foundation might be offered if we were to reproduce three interrelated questions presented in Guba and Lincoln's (1994) *Handbook for Qualitative Research*:

> '1. The ontological question – what is the form and nature of reality and, therefore, what is there that can be known about it? For example, if a 'real' world is assumed, then what can be known about it is 'how things really are' and 'how things really work.' Then only those questions that relate to matters of 'real' existence and 'real' action are admissible; other questions, such as those concerning matters of aesthetic or moral significance, fall outside the realm of legitimate scientific inquiry.
>
> 2. The epistemological question – what is the nature of the relationship between the knower or would-be-knower and what can be known? The answer that can be given to this question is constrained by the answer already given to the (above) ontological question; that is, not just any [their emphasis] relationship can now be postulated. So if, for example, a 'real' reality is assumed, then the posture of the knower must be one of objective detachment or value freedom in order to discover 'how things really are' and 'how things really work'. (Conversely, assumption of an objective posture implies the existence of a 'real' world to be objective about).
>
> 3. The methodological question – How can

the inquirer (would-be-knower) go about finding out whatever he or she believes can be known? Again, the answer that can be given to this question is constrained by answers already given to the first two questions. That is, not just any (their emphasis) methodology is appropriate. For example, a 'real' reality pursued by an 'objective' inquirer mandates control of possible confounding factors, whether the methods are qualitative (say observational) or quantitative (say, analysis of coverance). (Conversely, selection of a manipulative methodology – the experiment, say – implies the ability to be objective and a real world to be objective about.) The methodological question cannot be reduced to a question of mode; methods must be fitted to a predetermined methodology.' (Guba and Lincoln, 1994, 108)

These three questions strike to the very core of our examination and of the governing principles of the knowledge-making process. If we examine the first of these questions, the ontological question, then perhaps the very nature of the context facing organisations suggests that this particular question has been addressed. There is indisputably a form of reality out there through which organisations exist; they are entities that do employ people, that trade in resources and services, and who desire to be sustainable and prosper. There may be certain disagreements about the nature of this reality, and the privileging of the guise of certain aspects of this at the expense of others, but arguably these become issues more correctly argued in the second question, at the epistemological level. My understanding of Schreyögg and Geiger concentrates mainly around this second question and particularly in terms of emerging discrepancies adopted in the empirical route. The epistemological question relates to how we see or engage with the world. Yet, whilst we can agree a world exists, how it, and the events that constitute it, appears to each of us and thus, as a result, what we should appreciate from this appearance, produces an assessment that is not consistent to each of us. Each of us do employ a lens of scrutiny that commences from the initial position we adopt and extends to the nature of which elements of the event we select to privilege as being important, at the expense of others. Different lenses of scrutiny produce different selections from the same event and thus yield different guises to knowledge (for example, see McGrath, 1982; Sackett and Larson, 1990; Scandura and Williams, 2000). In other words, there are a variety of epistemological positions available and the choice of adoption is critical. Therefore, if a researcher adopts a position alternative to the traditional one then this has a number of implications, beyond that of simply choosing to adopt a naturalistic approach, implications that go to the core of privileging, perhaps different, characteristics of the event and generating new or novel knowledge claims. As Guba and Lincoln acknowledge, each of these questions are interrelated (in this account I am often guilty of collapsing ontological and epistemological issues together) and should a choice of position be predetermined, and the needs of the stakeholders and context not be explored, then this raises legitimate questions regarding the currency of the guise of the knowledge produced.

Fabric, Qualities and Balance...

Accordingly, my argument is that the choice of epistemological position is critical, and has significant ramifications in terms of the relationships between ontology, epistemology and methodology. If we dispense with this opportunity to consider alternatives it may address the needs of the method, but undoubtedly at the expense of the empirical event. For me, in our present contemporary context, this is inappropriate, that is, if we assume that our aims in terms of organisational life converge around the desire to optimise (as far as practical) knowledge-making. Of course, I am not suggesting that the alternatives we attempt to provide always demonstrate a clear preference over existing practice in all situations for, as I will introduce, these are not without their own problems. However for me, unless we start to address these, then we are destined to remain locked into situations that we know are inadequate.

So, let me again provide further amplification for the potential of these alternative epistemological positions by first returning to our starting point. Let me start by reminding ourselves of the basic characteristics of the Scientific method. Let me create an image on which you can reflect. Imagine a situation that places the researcher behind a window looking out into the world. They look outside and what do they see? In terms of a research study I would hope that what can be seen conforms to a pre-specified objective; accordingly, my image attempts to place the researcher in a similar position to one that they might adopt if they were following the Scientific method. Of course, I am not suggesting that all scientific studies only take place inside and not outside in the world. However, my crude example is attempting to replicate the researchers' removal or de-coupling from the event and therefore adherence to objectivity and removal of extraneous factors that may influence the process.

From this position, the researcher can identify the features of the event but he/she remains at a distance, removed from the reality of the event. As such, from this static removed position, the researcher is ideally placed to list or measure the characteristics of the event occurring in front of their gaze. But, from this position, not only are they limited by what they can see (the frame, the angle, the distance, available light, etc.), but also by the means employed to record this observation. Predominantly, as proponents of Scientism would agree, the emphasis of this approach is measurement. Measurement, as we know, does not attempt to understand the character or real life of the subject – rather its emphasis is to note the presence of a particular feature or the frequency of its occurrence within a given situation. In addition, from this position, the researcher emphasises their visual abilities and largely overlooks other complementary natural aptitudes and propensities.

My concern here begins from this assumption of confinement – not only in terms of focus, but also in privileging only our eyes for observation. I am not convinced that in restricting our normal attributes to the visual only, especially in social situations, it provides for a set of observations that stand for 'the real'. Of course we can appreciate why, if we go back to the age of the Enlightenment. At that time, proponents of the scientific method did all they could to deny the influence of the individual on the knowledge-making process and yet closer attention reveals that they never really succeeded, as Rene Barbaras amplifies with an example from Biology:

> 'In order to work on his object, the biologist must first recognise it, that is, distinguish it, within reality; he must distinguish what is living and what is not. This discrimination is the province of an intuition or an experience that escapes objectification, because an intuition or experience is the condition of its possibility. Of course, the biologist will always be able to justify his choice afterwards by the presence of certain molecules within organisms that he recognised as living from the start, but this justification still can only be afterwards. In short, he cannot reintegrate the phenomenal level that gave him access to life into the objective level of his biological analysis, insofar as knowledge presupposes a recognition that is of a different order than itself and that knowledge cannot therefore assimilate. What holds for the encounter with the living being holds a fortiori for the choice of what, within the living being, must be studied, that is, for the choice of what is biologically significant. It is not molecular analysis but our experience that allows us to discern a grasping gesture, a behavior of flight, or an attitude of repose. As to the fundamental distinction between the normal and the pathological, there is no other criterion for it than the self-experience of a subject who feels himself limited in his vital activity. Thus, the condition for the possibility of biology is a set of acts of recognition and understanding that take root in my own life inasmuch as I constantly undergo them.' (Barbaras, 2008: 4).

If our aims for organisation research remain at the level of measurement, then there is no need to consider alternative epistemological positions. However, if our aim is to attempt to grasp the reality and gain an understanding of the empirical event, then applying the scientific method as a basis for observation is intrinsically insufficient. Returning to the above illustration, this is analogous to the researcher deciding that the window is a viewpoint and also a barrier, which both enables and obstructs access. They then move from considering research as an 'event', a complex situation, and not just the viewing of an 'object'. They re-position themselves, open their senses to other aspects of the event and as a result gain greater understanding, become engaged and 're-couple' their relationship with the researched.

Elsewhere I have discussed this as a journey from this *removed place* to one where we actively and wholly engage with the World (see King, 2011). I will not rehearse this same journey again in this account. The arguments presented there explored movement, and balanced this against the needs of the method. Here, I want to concentrate more on the *experience* of this move for the researcher and the opportunities that it provides.

Let me clarify that 'engaged' epistemological positions more fully exploit the researcher's ability, firstly to move, normally as a biped, either toward or away from the event. This movement is amply demonstrated by approaches such as Naturalist inquiry (See Lincoln and Guba, 1985), and these are developments from the Science that do indeed change the position and relationship between researchers and researched in empirical events. However, for me, these types of approaches often remain embedded within the original epistemological frame and involve an implicit assumption that movement here is restricted to the physical. The arguments presented in this chapter (and I would claim by the majority of the authors in this text) explore the potential of changing our epistemological position. This indeed does suggest physical movement but here, through the use of our whole bodies and the various attributes we naturally possess, releases the potential of conceptual movement as well. Let me enlarge further.

The guise of any empirical event is characterised by a *fabric* of features that are overwhelmingly qualitative (See Dewey, 1930). Rarely, if at all, are moments in these contexts quantitative. Measurements of qualitative features are difficult, although not impossible, as Science has amply demonstrated in various ways (see for example, sampling). Nevertheless for us as people, in our everyday lives and in most organisational settings, the guise of any event with which we choose to engage is qualitative. Let me describe some of these qualities in an accessible way for any reader, rather than focus only on examples from organisational life. Think of those moments when we feel the heat of the sun on our faces. Simple experiences are rarely 'pure' experience (whatever that is), but mediated by anticipated response or reaction and interpretation. We might suddenly consider the impact and damage the sun might do to our skin, or has done to others, and accordingly seek to hide from its strength in the shade. We might experience this warmth in terms of cold already felt, or the cumulative sensation of warming, or inflected by the noise of traffic around, or the sounds of music playing or the smell of newly-mown grass. Guba and Lincoln in their first question above argued that these 'other' aesthetic features lie outside our ontological understanding, and yet for me they are the 'glue' that provides the essential links to making sense of specific instances of our being-in-the-world. The decision to change our epistemological positions is a decision to open ourselves up to the power and influence of these features. Of course, we could deny them and return inside to place ourselves behind the window and thus maintain our former degree of objectivity, but for me this amounts to the removal of the 'glue of life'.

Science has always paid most, if not all, of its attention towards the formal and ignored the 'felt' features of an event because, and this is important, these latter features rarely can be labelled according to declarative or conceptual/structural knowledge terms. Therefore, the fact that we can label the sun is important, but what we feel about the 'heat on our skin' according to Science is less important. As Mark Johnson (1994) observes:

> '...the extent that philosophies of mind and language focus only on conceptual and propositional structures and the inferences supported by those structures, they lack an adequate way to investigate the role of qualities in meaning and thought' (Johnson, 17).

Of course I am not suggesting that various forms of declarative knowledge are no longer relevant, for the contrary is true. These anchoring forms of knowledge remain essential for us in our continuing sense-making activities. However, almost all of our socially useful knowledge emerges from our mobile and interactive engagement within a qualitative world, and cumulatively these experiences, and our assessments of them, make up the fabric of everyday knowledge that drives so many other features of our respective lives. For Dewey (and others, for example, William James, Eugene Gendlin, Mark Johnson), he observes that any event is a combination of both structural/formal characteristics together with felt ones, yet how much we appreciate and respond to this assessment is dependent on our current individual balance or imbalance.

As people we rarely come to events in a neutral state. We each bring to it our own baggage of experience and particular needs. Mark Johnson (2007) talks of this as an 'imbalance' that may influence us as we seek to respond in 're-balancing'. So if we are cold then we privilege or look for opportunities for warmth; if we are hungry then it affects our attention and we look, as part of our task, to satisfy this hunger. This form of response is something that we can all do, and do so every day as we multi-task. In organisational settings this is no different. As we go about our tasks, if we identify that we need to privilege a certain factor because it is being under-utilised, then as part of our work if we have the opportunity we will look to satisfy this need. Of course, we cannot possess these opportunities to respond in all situations. However if an issue is uppermost in our mind-sets (similar to hunger, coldness) similarly in the organisational setting we will respond accordingly.

Nevertheless, the intensity of this imbalance is important. If its presence is minimal or mild then its influence is likely to be negligible, yet the converse also might be true. If it is felt to be strong then the desire to 're-balance' becomes a significant influence on our actions. So, returning to the felt sense of sun on our skin we might either enjoy its feeling on our skin or alternatively look to avoid its feeling. If it is mild then perhaps its influence is minimal, but if we become more than a little uncomfortable then, if we have the opportunity, we will act to avoid its influence. The assumption guiding this interpretation is that in some circumstances, where these 'felt' features are intense, then as part of our movement and response, our interpretations partly are responding to this with a desire to 're-balance'. In some situations where control is minimal these influences might prove significant.

This has a direct effect on how we generate meaning. Traditionally this has always been presented in terms of a cognitive event. Whereas the scenario I present here suggests that it emerges primarily through our body's ability to move, to shift, to reflect preferences or to respond to imbalances, and each of these are then collectively converged and relayed to our cognitive abilities. As Mark Johnson amplifies, meaning is grounded in bodily experience – it arises

> '… from our feeling of qualities, sensory patterns, movements, changes and emotional contours.' (ibid: 70).

Johnson argues forcibly that

> '…meaning is not limited to only to those bodily engagements, but it always starts with and leads back to them' (ibid: 70).

The body, for French phenomenologist Maurice Merleau-Ponty (1962; 1964), lies at the crux of understanding of 'being-in-the-World'. For Merleau-Ponty the body and its engagement should not be viewed as either objective or subjective but rather 'lived'. The body and its engagement in the World is more accurately an interaction with it, in that it breathes, not only in that it senses the cold of the air. It feeds; it does not only see and smell food. It grows and sweats. It walks; it does not only perceive the hard resistance of the ground. For Merleau-Ponty it is this interaction, together with its facility to appreciate its significance, that should lie at the crux of understandings. Certainly the body and its capacity for communication, both verbal and non-verbal, and its array of natural attributes make it perhaps the most valuable receptacle that we possess. As our bodies move and interact we gather information; some of this information we act upon, but other parts, seemingly, consciously or unconsciously, we store away in our memories. This information is our 'glue' – for scientists it is not knowledge in the traditional sense, and yet without it we could not survive.

De-familiarising and Closing Comments...

It seems strange to entitle this section 'closing comments' when it is in fact about opening our worlds to new perspectives. However, in this final section I turn my attention from the value and attributes of the body to the nature of our engagement. As a means of introducing this content I am reminded of a BBC interview with David Hockney, first broadcast in 2004, where he spoke about one of the major benefits of attending art school, which was being taught how to 'look' and he emphasised 'how to really look'.

He described how, in a very early class at art school, he was asked to draw a life model – which he did diligently to the best of his ability. Part way through, he noticed someone else sitting down next to him who proceeded to use Hockney's own drawing as the content for his own. The new drawing, although of the same content, revealed a different way of seeing. Hockney spoke about this as the very craft of art. Yet what this also suggests to me is that the ability to 'see' and engage with events in this different way, and to generate understandings, does not have to be exclusive to art.

Of course, just deciding to extend our powers of 'looking' is more than simply a decision. It is a form of legitimisation for a way of engaging, one that appreciates the potential of our whole bodies in empirical situations, their movement, physical and conceptual, and acting as a vehicle for knowledge gathering in ways that exceed traditional modes. Yet simply making this decision might not be enough, for faced with any event, initially it is an unanalysed whole (Dewey, 1934/1989: 249). However, once we engage with it, our initial reaction is to adhere to our natural attribute of looking to anchor our understandings of it through familiarised patterns of recognition. The American philosopher Eugene Gendlin argues that this familiarity steers us to recognise familiar forms, patterns, and rules and therefore might encourage us to overlook many of the situational aspects that make these forms meaningful in the first place. The fateful error, which Gendlin attributes not just to Western philosophy but to our general cultural understanding and practices, is to miss much of what is possible by instead focusing our attention towards areas, patterns or forms, with which we are already familiar. In many situations this is acceptable, but then this is not about understanding and generating knowledge.

More accurately this is about rehearsing 'habits-of-mind'. Stable structures can entice us to believe the in the illusion of 'fixtivity', that is an illusion that meanings are fixed, when in fact often these are only fixed in that particular context. At another time or in another context we might have quite different meanings emerging.

I explained in the opening paragraphs of this chapter that our aim in developing different epistemological positions was about choice, the choice of alternate ways of perceiving empirical events. The Hockney example above opens up this opportunity. In his situation he confines his attention to the visual, and he remains static, whereas for our discussion we employ our bodies and our collective natural attributes to engage in a more inclusive way. This form of engagement was also interesting for Hockney. He too is interested in 'lenses of engagement' (see his wonderful text entitled 'Secret Knowledge', 2001) and through his art he has experimented with shifting his body and the potential that this form of engagement produces in revealing different forms of interpretations of everyday objects and events. For example, see Figure 1.

The point I want to make is that Hockney could have reproduced a familiar representation of a chair. Yet what he does in Figure 1 is to challenge himself in both understanding and representation, with the purpose of extending this challenge to us as beholders, by encouraging us to think of how we might engage with its meaning in a different way.

This leads me to revisit a concept I first mentioned in the opening paragraphs of this chapter —'de-familiarising'. The concept of de-familiarisation is not new; it was first introduced by the Russian Formalist Victor Shklovsky. In short it was an artistic technique to overcome the sclerotic effect of rationalism on the mind and imagination of the artist (in a broader sense, overcoming the way in which the rationalisation processes of modern society through western capitalism have become internal to the very cognitive development of the subject). Shklovsky (1918) suggested that this technique was a means of intensifying perception. In the latter part of the nineteenth century, and throughout the twentieth, art followed a pattern of challenging our acceptance of appearance. Artists and emerging arts movements encouraged beholders of their art works to engage with them in different ways, and through specific examples be able to encourage an involvement that surpasses the appreciation of appearance, but metaphorically bathes in its potentiality. New forms of artistic engagement emerged, not in the figurative sense of the bleary eye looking at the familiar, but as the challenged subject forced to understand artistic content in a way that ruptured its sense of certainty and privileged detachment.

The Russian formalists employed Novelty and shock to jolt the subject into a new form of attention. 'Novelty' is a significant poetic tradition first studied by Aristotle and then developed by Mazzone, Hegel, and some Romantic poets. 'Novelty' shares a large number of similarities with de-familiarisation, and can be seen as both an aspiration and a theoretical basis for it. De-familiarisation allows for rupture. Frederic Jameson recognised this potential not only in terms of looking to the future, but also as a way of restoring new understandings to the past, to our history, and therefore able to develop new forms of interpretation (Federic

Figure 1. *David Hockney* – Chair, Jardin de Luxembourg, Paris 10th August 1985. *Photographic Collage, 30 ¼" X 25 ¾" edition: 13.* © *David Hockney*

Jameson, Future City *New Left Review* 21, May–June 2003).

I could continue my descriptions of de-familiarisation by drawing on examples from theatre and in particular Brecht's description of 'distancing' or alternatively cite examples from pure art and the influence of Paul Cézanne on subsequent modernist schools of art like cubism or surrealism. But for me, each of these examples converge with a realisation that the body, its attributes and the temporal experience of its contexts of mobility, are vitally important to both art and to organisational life. I employ art as a means of exemplification, since it realises the intrinsic operations of our senses, although my examples here privilege the visual. With more space I could expand these examples to other areas of art, to exemplify how meaning emerges 'bottom-up' from the 'felt' circumstances of the process of creating the work of art itself. The circumstances and contexts of physical emergence denote their 'glue', or their embeddedness in life, and should be no less important for us in thinking about organisation. A disembodied mind cannot function fully in terms of understanding, and for me this realisation will become increasingly important for organisational life through the coming years of instability.

Finally, for a long time art has appreciated that a subject's perspective on the world is a man-made construction, and does not simply 'reflect' the real, even though in terms of appearance it can often appear to do so. I see this as an analogous situation to one experienced by organisational life. The dominance of one epistemological position for organisational life may appear to suggest that the features of knowledge traditionally collected are complete, or at least are sufficient to guide organisations. Yet, as I hope this discussion is starting to suggest, alternative epistemological positions are available, their necessity revealed by the current conditions of organisational life as much as by the historical lessons of art, such as Cézanne's paintings. He challenged his beholders to see things differently by changing the very way they see, and therefore empowered the subject to imagine, and then to set about creating the world anew. The authors of the following chapters lay down the start of this same challenge – of course, it is still incomplete...

This paper takes the unusual form of a direct address, a letter.... from 'the senses' to you. If your senses could talk, if they could tell you about themselves and their roles (possible roles, suppressed roles) in organisations, what would they say? Working from research in philosophy, psychology and various strands of organisational studies, the author offers a comprehensive (and humorous) review of the nature of the senses – in 'organ'-isation.

When we talk about the senses, we are not simply talking about our corporeal experience of touching and tasting, seeing and feeling and so on. We are talking about our capacity for an integrated perception, intuition and imagination in every aspect of organisational life. As the chapter indicates, there are a lot of romantic and sentimental ideas popular in management studies that seek to bring sensual, artistic or even erotic dynamics to organisations. They rightly complain how organisational life has expelled the realm of the senses in search of objectivity, efficiency and rigor. They wrongly think that the realm of the senses can simply be added to an organisation through a formulae or a series of 'creative management' techniques. The realm of the senses, rather, demands a revolution – a new openness to extemporisation, empathy and insight. The senses can provide another dimension of consciousness and a critical reflection on the nature of the organisational as an aesthetic space of experience and of the subject as the embodied actor within it.

The Sense-Making of the Senses – Perspectives on Embodied *Aisthesis* & Aesthetics in Organising & Organ-isations – or why sensing (and sense-making) makes sense and no senses lead to non-sense

Wendelin M. Küpers, and the Senses

'...if a revolution is to come, it will have to come from the five senses.'
(Serres 1995: 71)

Let the silence speak.
Let the unseen be seen.
Let the smell of ambrosia fill the air.
Let the untouched move us.
Let the untouched be touched.
(Ackerman 1990)

'Je dis qu'il faut être voyant, se faire voyant. Le poète se fait voyant par un long, immense et raisonné dérèglement de tous les sens.' ('I say one must be a seer, make oneself a seer. The poet makes himself a seer by a *long, immense and deliberate derangement/disordering of all the senses.*')
Rimbaud Letter to Paul Demeny (May 15, 1871)

Every object, well contemplated creates an organ for its perception (Goethe)
Every subject, well contemplating creates a perception for an organ
Every subject-object relationship well contemplated, co-creates subjects and objects and their sensual relations...

In(tro-se)duction

This is our story, a tale of us, we the five senses... as we experience an organ-isation. In this narrative, we ex-press and discuss our experiences – as a body in the every-day life of a 'corporation'. As we would like to show you our role in sense-making and sense-giving in organ-isations, our sensual perceptions and qualities are described as concrete as well as able to generate various media of meanings and aesthetics.

We, the different senses, are telling you about our embodied situations and letting you know about when, how and why (not) our sensitivity and potential for 'aiesthesis' are activated and vivid, or are stifled and excluded. The later situation happens also because we senses have been deprived and atrophied under the regimes dominating organ-isational life. As a structural and functional system, 'organ-sation' seems to organise itself rather formally and mechanistically. Thus we face various snags, difficulties, obstacles and troubles while trying to enact our creative possibilities. Powerful conditions and constraints inside and around the context of current organ-isations try to use us in a limited, often instrumentalised way. At the same time we yearn for our aiesthetic expressions and responses to be awakened, and reinvigorated as we accompany the company.

Thus by our reporting we try to communicate to you about our belonging and longing to play a more deliberate sensuous role and about the hindrances to doing so. This re-telling aims at *re-embodying* us senses in order reconceive how we are always already present in the life-world you call 'organ-isation', which for us has diverse givens and affordances by materialities and immaterialities, facts and arte-facts, but also passions and actions.

Thus, we senses are given a form and forum here for in-forming you about our very presences, but also our pressing challenges and sufferings, as we are neglected or merely one-sidedly exploited.

You will learn about how we – that is sight, hearing, smell, taste, and touch, plus one+ …the mediating body and embodiment – experience and strive for a creative life, each alone and together. With regard (look!) to the latter one, it seems important to understand that, and how our significance as a responsive community of senses in organ-isms and organ-isations can be considered and approached. The goal we are trying to realise here is not romantic sentimentalism, but the revelation of our inherent, living and expressive sensuality, and its impact on a different kind of sense-making! As what you call 'sense-making' is mediated by us enlivened and enlivening senses, we are a sense-ful part(ner) of the work of you as member of your organ-isation or you as a researcher or onlooker. Accordingly, your understanding of us, the look, sound, smell, taste and tactual feel that is our entire sensorium, is the very base for all your individual and collective perceiving, knowing, deciding, communicating, acting, in its i-n-t-e-r-relational being and becoming…

Out-Lining _____ Over-

To convey our messages, we senses first each describe our specific phenomenal qualities, followed by sharing with you our embodied experiences and perspectives in organ-isation. We invite you to engage in sensual experiments, hearing poetic expressions or related quotations. Furthermore, you are incited to listen to inspiring ideas voiced by the sensitive philosopher Maurice Merleau-Ponty (1962; 1964; 1995). We will flesh out selected facets of his important phenomenological understandings of the r of us embodied senses for singing the world in a new key (Toadvine, 2004). These ideas may help not only to describe 'organ-isations' as sensuous embodied life-worlds, but also to explore its implicit embodied aesthetics.

Please read the following with an attitude of empathetic curiosity and explorative openness. This will help you to perceive what is below, above and b e t w e e n the lines. Please try to allow complimentary space and time throughout moving through the following text and its con-+-Text so that your sensate thinking, intuiting and empathetic feelings can take timely place. This musing mood will then be beneficial for actually making and letting us senses and out i-n-t-e-r- play with sense be experienced, reflected and then disseminated, circulated in spiralling cycle of associations and imaginations. Let each of us senses now tell you about our storied perspectives on and i-n-t-e-r-p-l-a-y in organ-isations and its members:

Seeing / Sight

You, who decipher these letters on this white background here: hey look at me! Can you see me, the capacity to perceive visually? I would like to make visible what and how I see things. Let me share with you my vision(s). You know my secret is that I do not need to touch or feel the outside objects in order to reach them. Instead, I feel the vibrations of the light-waves meeting my organ of sight. In this way, I provide the means for that vision and its mirroring re-flection. It is due to me that the one who sees, is seeable and seen, and it is my task to help my embodied human being to embrace life's challenges visually and visibly. Moreover, I am an embodied gaze and move b/e/t/w/e/e/n the visible and its implicit invisible as rendered by Maurice Merleau-Ponty (1995). While seeing, I do not hold an object at the terminus of my look. Rather I am delivered over to a field of the sensible, which is structured in terms of the difference b/e/t/w/e/e/n things and colours, as a momentary crystallisation of coloured being or visibility (Merleau-Ponty, 1995: 132). With re-gard and in viewing this company here, seeing is quite basic to all that is going on and what is visible. Starting with visions and strategies, futures are imagined, often with quite ambitious foresight, but enacted time and again by ridiculous attempts and short-term or tunnelled myopic views. My hindsight is the foundation for all kinds of ex-post re-flections and rationalisations in organ-isational and managerial practices, while my foresight anticipates and imagines possible futures.

In every-day life, in this apparently over-loaded world of organ-isations, *seeing* seems indispensable. Look at all these knowledge-workers working at their papers and watching at their computer screens. Without seeing they could not read or write anything at all – neither processing information nor communicating. Have a look also at these post-industrial service-workers at the front line. Without seeing their objects, colleagues and customers, they would not be able to deliver what they try to offer or respond to. All their specific needs and problems and those of their clients need to be re-garded.

Observably, what I see in this organ-isation is very ambivalent, as I perceive colourful sides, brightness as well as darkness, sallow or staid aspects, but mostly greyness. A lot of superficial seeing prevails on the visible surfaces. With this surfacing, my faculty of stereopsis, the perception of depth is underestimated or hardly used at all in these often flat and unexciting worlds of shallow and shadow-like organ-ising and managing.

Yes I know, I have been criticised with re-gard to a visual primacy, which I'm supposed to propagate. Sometimes I face the reproach of being responsible for an 'ocularcentricism' of the visual, by which I with my eyes appear to pursue hegemony in late-modern culture. My alienating look is supposedly objectifying the hellish Other (*être-pour-autrui*) to external materiality and thus makes the on-looker unfree (Sartre, 1943). Sometimes, when a manager sees and appropriates his employees as a mere human resource, or when workers are bullying each other, this hell seems to be part of everyday life in organisations. Furthermore my gaze has been used as a disciplinary mechanisms and technique of social panoptical control (Foucault, 1977; McKinlay & Starkey, 1998) increasingly prevailing and intensified by the use of modern surveying technologies.

But let me make it clear, originally I did not intend to privilege my eye to the exclusion of other ways of perceiving in the natural and social world. By my own nature and being socially inclined, I do not remain ignorant of the embodied and symbolic functions of my colleagues, the other senses. Please understand that much of what my dear sensual mates and I are and do today is due to our transformation by industrialisation and technology as well as our separation by physiology (Jütte, 2005: 180-236). Being ruled by a 'scopic' regime, my *looking* has been systematically sharpened and disembodied, becoming an errant, clinically fixed and clouded gaze (Jütte, 2005: 186).

However, my actions, events of seeing (sights) and visual sense-making (Belova, 2006) are more complex and i-n-t-e-r-related with the other senses than many of the harsh critics allege. Yes, I am aware that being more sensitive to the other senses helps overcoming my ocularcentric vision-paradigm. If there were not so many eye-catching distractions, humans would better consider the non-conceptual, pre-linguistic 'silent practice' that is implicit in all feeling, thinking, listening, speaking and actions in living organ-ising practices.

Yet, there is a way of re-sensation of this extensively visually overloaded society by simply practicing to shut the eye more often and contemplating and knowing in other ways of sensual perception via my co-senses. Subsequently such closing is an opening and as a freed pondering it allows the 'third eye' of knowledge (ājñā) to receive images and explore more intensive creative and meaningful paths-ways.

Let me share with you a fearful feeling: I'm afraid of blindness. What would you do without seeing? What happens when an epidemic blindness afflicts a society can be seen in Saramago's novel (1979) or the corresponding film directed by Fernando Meirelles (2008).

What can we learn from blind people? Isn't our blindness our sight's blind spot? Does the sight of the supposed evidence make us blind? How can you cultivate me, in a way that you can see through or behind the appearance of things?

Please close your eyes for an in-stant … and listen! What and how do you 'see' with your inner eye, and what do you feel and hear? What do you imagine and visualise? What would your vision of an aesthetic organ-isation be like? I m looking forward to hear and learn about what you see!

Apropos hearing, it seems that one of my co-senses would like to express her state of being.

Hearing / Listening

Pssssssssssssssstttttt… Can you hear me? Let me have a word. I'm called hearing, or audition, and I'm the receptor of all kinds of sound perception. Integrating listening and voice, I provide the bases for rich phenomenologies of sound (Ihde, 2007). Let me invite you to attend to me and my often non-perceived role of the auditory in your and human life, obsessed with visual re-presentations.

My inner ear detects even subtle vibrations and frequencies dulled only by the noise of this loud world. Can you still listen to that 'silent practice' that is before all those speaking noises and visual over-loads? How can you retrieve this stillness for making listening again a 'critical and emancipatory praxis' (Levin, 1989). You know, I am always open as I cannot shut my ears! But remaining open for what?

Well, in this organisation, I have to bear all kinds of chatter and cluttering noise. I have to receive all kinds of resonances with sometimes odd, strange voices, ranging from gossip to all forms of more demanding communication. These are sounds ranging from informal chatting to serious conversations and from pretentious rhetoric of empty promises and lip-serving speeches to meaningful stories full of beauty and depth. In a way, I am ubiquitously present during all these talks among and b/e/t/w/e/e/n colleagues and managers as part of every-day life. Likewise, I'm there in conversing with customers as part of the service or I am at stake in communication with stake-holders. Even meetings in tele-spaces via phone- or videoconferencing in 'inter-places' (Küpers, 2010), all verbal communication is in a way based on me. It is through my receptive capacity that people and contents are brought together. Do you hear my message: *To listen is to relate*! Listening is the very fount for unfolding dialogue and meaningful relationships!

However, what I sense in the sound-scapes of this organ-isation is that it is quite fragmented and barely melodious. When did you listen to pleasant sounds or even uplifting music in your organ-isation? How would it be different if you were to listen more intensively while you work? (Oldham et al., 1995). A 'listening Self' (Levin, 1989) and the *sounds of silence* as part of social learning and i-n-t-e-r-subjective meaning generation (Jacobs & Coghlan, 2005) have hardly a chance in organ-isations these days. Yes unfortunately, sensitive hearing and active listening are very much neglected and unappreciated not only here in organ-isations, but also in human (Western) society in general.

There are specific requirements for a 'quiet time' (Kaeser, 2007), a 'sound organ-isation' and 'psycho-sonic management'. Listen for more about this and the 'human sensorium' by pinning your ears back into what Corbett (2003a, b) has to say. For sensing how listening can be a form of sensuous bodily leadership knowledge, and the significance of a much-needed auditive culture listen to the voices of Ropo and Parviainen (2001) and the sound of Koivunen's ideas (2006) about an auditive and even musical leadership culture.

How can you become all ears for realising what is silenced and to sense that how listening is vitally important for understanding your organ-isational life? How can you support unheard layers of meaning? Are you aware about what happens before the voice of reason takes over and the subtle echoes of responsibility involved (Kleinberg-Levin, 2008).

Finally, let me acknowledge, I'm afraid of deafness! What can we learn from the incapacity to hear? Isn't much of our deafness the result of inattention and acoustic overload by imposed sounds from all the noisy media and acoustic pollution? How to regain access the delights of stillness? I do hope that a cultivated art of 'hearkening' that is being attuned by the sonorous field and its auditory relationships as a whole (Levin 1989 p. 230) will enable you to listen more deeply and playfully.

This then may allow responding with much greater situation-appropriateness and care, while eavesdropping or taking delights in releasing soundful beings and songsssssssssss

Implication for embodied research practice

In this chapter, (we) the senses have argued how the life-world of organ-isations discloses itself through various sensual experiences and their i-n-t-e-r-play. However, all too often, the researcher's presence – let alone bodily and sensual experience – is eradicated out of his or her research conduct and its accounts. How can the body and we senses be included in research practices and publications? How to realise and show the ambiguity by which the sensuous body reveals, informs but also discloses and hints indirectly?

We senses suggest to you researchers to begin by refining your own embodied sensory, and perceptual faculties (Strati, 2000: 17). With Sandelands and Srivatsan (1993: 19), a science is "fully alive and creative when wide-eyed and involved, when it sees, touches, hears, tastes, and feels". With such integration, embodied researchers may rely more on their intuitive and aesthetically responsive skills and on their expressive capabilities, thus conducting a more sensually complete methodology (Warren, 2002: 229-230). We senses welcome Samantha Warren's critique (2002) of a prescriptive methodological recipe for researching us and our aesthetics in organ-isations, as such an approach does not do justice to our tacit, largely ineffable, always moving, embodied spatial, temporal and cultural realities nor the transitory experiences involved. Consequently, we are happy when she says "…surely the more senses that are employed in the communication of aesthetic experience the better…" (ibid. 2002: 235). Being impressed with her aesthetic ethnography, we agree with her plea for a more sensual methodology advancing sensory possibilities in organ-isation studies (Warren, 2008).

Indeed, we need research practices where "method meets art' (Leavy, 2009), in which researchers conduct narrative, poetic, musical, performative, dance, and visual forms of inquiry while they also employ rigorous methods of data collection, analysis, and i-n-t-e-r-pretation. Correspondingly, we invite you to experiment with alternative forms of expression like images, photos, videos, stories, scenes, sounds etc. We encourage you to endeavor ways of presentational symbolism (Langer, 1957) that are more inclusive, and able to capture the gestalt of aesthetic experiences with its fully nuanced qualities of us different senses. Furthermore, there is a need to develop a new kind of practice-based language facilitating transdisciplinary research and evaluation (Leavy, 2009: 257).

Based on embodied self-awareness, there is a need for reflexive embodied empathy (Finlay, 2003; 2005). A corresponding research process involves engaging reflexively, with the embodied i-n-t-e-r-subjective relationship researchers have with phenomena and participants.

There are many ways how an embodied approach makes use of us the lived senses and the body by which an intimate and implicit understanding of each experiences, feelings, thoughts and actions not only happen for the researcher and during the research process, but give rise to new meanings.

Importantly an embodied methodological research practice pays due regard to artistic and aesthetic dimensions involved (Küpers, 2002). Therefore, part of this emerging field of embodied research practice is that of an art-based transformational inquiry and art-based research (McNiff, 2007; 2008). Provoked by art (Cole et al., 2004) an art-oriented research uses artistic processes and expressions in all of the different forms and media, as a way of understanding.

Moreover, taking art practice itself as research realises that creative inquiry employed by artists can be a form of research (Sullivan, 2005). Investigating artistic inquiry and their use of senses and imagination may inspire social scientist to develop a community of artist-researchers (Cole & Knowles, 2008).

However, using art in qualitative research or developing arts-informed research (Knowles & Cole, 2008; 2008a) and creating a scholARTistry (Knowles et al., 2007) requires reflecting the persistent tensions in art-oriented research (Eisner, 2008).

Although arts-informed research runs counter to more conventional research endeavors with their more linear, sequential, compartmentalized form and distancing of researcher and participants, the challenge will be to keep an internal consistency, coherence and communicability as well as to advance some kind of generative knowledge that reflects the multidimensional, complex, dynamic, i-n-t-e-r-subjective, and contextual nature of human experience in organ-isations.

Finally, the communication of research findings would also dare to find more aesthetic forms like experimental writing (Neilsen, 2001), blurring the boundaries b/e/t/w/e/e/n science and art (Glesne, 1997). There is much more to think about further implications for an embodied aesthetic research for example for knowing, learning or improvising in organ-isations (Küpers, 2002; 2005). Forms of research along those spiralling lines outlined here, can contribute to become sensible, and sense-able about us senses and our sensations (Mills & Mills, 2006). We senses very much hope that emerging experiential and reflexive re-search can find ways to incorporate integral practices that actually or potentially 'make sense' as well as let us senses and our sense unfold and being creatively told. We wish that such a research remains not only an agenda, but becomes realised by embodied agents, and incorporated in institutionalised agencies

We Senses of Smell, Taste and Touch

We the senses of taste, smell, and touch have been rendered inferior, and therefore 'secondary', and as such 'anesthetised' in the modern West (Diaconu, 2005). Historically, we were considered unable to produce knowledge and art forms, and the process of civilization was not interested in our cultivation, which led to our physical and psychic underdevelopment. Also the academic 'silence' on us is due not in the least to the absence of a specific sensory education and to the terminological imprecision concerning experiences, as well as to culturally deep-rooted anti-sensual and dualistic preconceptions with regard to the supposed separation of body and mind.

Basically, our realms are partly pre-reflexive, pre-intentional and collective, which challenges orientations focusing on conscious, intentional and subjective experience. A true inclusive aiesthetics of haptic, olfactory, and gustatory experiences may help to overcome our repression and deprivation. In this way we might be able to contribute to a deepened constitution of personal identity, social functions, and even more sensual ethical practices. With regard to the latter, did you know that tactfulness, flair, sagacitas and sapientia referred initially to us smell, taste and touch? All this raises an intriguing question: What would a relearned aesthetics of smelling, tasting and touching (Diaconu, 2006) mean for you and an organisation and its management?

Smelling / Smell

Sniffffffffffff NNNNNNNose stench, stink, scent… ahhhhh arising aromatic, granting fragrant …

It's me, smelling or olfaction! Yes I am quite subtle; my constantly open nose potentially perceives all kinds of odours, but mostly you are not consciously aware of me. Why is there an absence of language to describe my meaning? Yes there is that nomenclature of me, which is trying to provide access to the 'narrative structure of different scent feature: aroma, bouquet, fragrance, perfume, odour, fetidness, reek, effluvia, exhalations' and other material emissions (Bronwen & Ringham, 2003: 47). But can you be sure about quality judgments in relation to those terms for describing my whiffs?

Due to my ephemeral character and overlayering qualities, the more you sense of me, the less you will smell at all the particular qualities of distinct odours.

Being a medium of olfaction from very early on in evolution and human history, why have I been marginalised in Western culture? Is it because this culture has a bias, which follows a push towards vision-oriented rationality (Borthwick, 2000: 132)? Do I connote a dangerous realm and manifest a threat to 'good' hale and hearty social order because I have a long historical association with bad health, decay, or disease and being connected to putrid death?

On the other hand people believed that more fragrant odours and aromatic therapeutic treatment could serve as a prophylactic against all kinds of suffering and part of celebrating life and love. Thus, odour is sensed as an ambivalent force for ill and good, holding the power of stenching stress and fetid death, but also festive life and fond's strive.

One of my qualities is that the scent is an inescapably raw, unmediated, pure sensation. Instead of re-presenting an object via odour you directly access what is there. In your culture, which is so heavily dependent on images and the verbal for approaching the so-called 'real', privileging presence through me serves as an effective counterpoint. By allowing receptive olfactory experience you could return anew to a vital sensory existence.

You know, there is a 'cultural conundrum' of me, smell, and my organ the nose (Corbett, 2006). Ironically, although having such immediacy, I am nevertheless redolent with personal connotations and cultural significance, linked to individual and social identity and cultural sensibility. While these meanings may vary considerably from context to context, smell-factors are present prominently in acts of memory, social affinity and definitions of place, character, and mood. Rather than serving as a means to bypass cultural values, smells have been utilised to underscore and express 'worths' insistently (Drobnick, 1998; 2006).

Negotiating and structuring the complexities of the experienced world beyond Eurocentric orientations, smell, knowledge and art are no longer mutually exclusive realms (Classen et al., 1994: 95-158). Interestingly the 'deodorisation of Western culture' reveals the playing out of three i-n-t-e-r-related political processes: namely, discrimination, location and regulation (Corbett, 2006).

Yes I function as a boundary-marker As a status symbol and impression management technique, I make a statement of who my human being is or pretends to become (Synnott, 1993: 183).

Did you notice, the olfactory symbolism mediated by me is expressed in prescriptive language? For example, if you say that you cannot smell someone or if someone smells bad, then you assess him or her as such. Yes it is true, I cannot smell certain people, and I know I can make my human being nosy that is becoming arrogant by an overbearing manner.

What about the smell of money and capital? According to the Latin proverb 'Money does not smell'. This quotation was stated by the emperor Vespasian after reintroducing a urine tax on public toilets, as the coin could not smell, even though it was generated as a result of urination. However, it was clarified recently that money does not smell, only until it is touched (Glindemann et al, 2006). In singing its praises to the neo-liberal supposed free-market economy, money as a modern form of also social and symbolic capital still finds its materialisation that declares its physical and moral odorlessness (Sloterdijk, 1988: 315).

You can learn more about my role and functions in organ-isation by sniffing into Corbett (2006). But let me tell you, what I smell in organ-isations is rather dull and not very exciting. In all those sterile offices dealing with smell-free paper, and working on barren computer work-stations, is mostly not related to smell at all. On the other side, industrious work-places can be smelly, even pungent, and service workers must bear redolent odours in their smelly work-environments. What do people perceive, who are exposed to uncommon smells of work (Reinarz 2003), and shameful stinks on a daily basis in their filthy work places, environed by omnipresent industrial pollution? Have you ever sensed the malodorous stench of a sweat-shop and its often horrible unsanitary surroundings?

Of course there are pleasant odours and stimulating i-n-t-e-r-mingling of smells. Several work- places do take care of pleasurable scenting ventilation and even provide aroma lights.

What would it mean to i-n-t-e-r-pret organ-isations as exposing 'smell-scapes'? How does your workplace smell? When did you breathed in the scent of a blooming flower at your workplace? How did the food smell that you had for lunch in the canteen? Can you smell your colleagues? Haven't you felt sometimes that someone's behaviour 'stinks' or that you could not smell someone, as the German proverb goes? Which perfume do your co-workers or managers use and why? Are you affected by it?

I am really concerned with the question about how I can encourage you to become more sensitive to smelling without falling prey to commercialisation! What would it mean for you if for example fragrance devices (marketed e.g. by AromsSs) release aromatic-blends in your or other's offices or customer areas through the ventilation and air-conditioning system? Did you know that the success for example of Singapore Airline is in part due to their consistent olfactory branding using a slightly exotic fragrance?

There is already a body of research suggesting that aromas e.g. cinnamon and peppermint odour can influence cognitive performance and workplace productivity (Raudenbush, 2005). Today there are even scent-computerised devices and olfactory digitised cell phones designed, and the nose of the future may get olfact-aides (Hertz, 2007: 233, 238). You sniff it don't you: an instrumentalisation of scenting – i.e. 'smell sells' – could be used for all kinds of vested interests in politics and business (Classen et. al., 1994). But let me ask you: How dangerous could it become, when fragrances are used to manipulate the mood of people? What happens when you get obsessed to find the perfect scent? Smell the message of Süsskind's book on perfume and realise also the dialectics of its 'enscentment' (Gray, 1993).

On the other side experiencing me authentically, I can enrich and deepen your life. For how much I may awaken your memories, think about or even experiment with the Proustian phenomenon of smell-triggering memory via a biscuit in tea as described in '*A la recherche du temps perdu*' (Proust, 1913; Chu & Downes, 2002). Furthermore, I may prompt your affects and com-passions, thus intensifying your emotional life. Moreover these smell-related qualities may also be i-n-t-e-r-laced with your mental health and influence your sociability with others.

Frankly speaking, yes, I'm afraid of anosmia. Related to this lack of olfaction, I fear hyposmia the decrease in my ability to smell. Oh what a life would it be without smelling the fresh-brewed coffee in the morning, or one of the other 10,000 different scents there we encounter. Losing an established and sentimental smell memory, causes feelings of deprivation and perhaps even depression. Furthermore, a loss of olfaction may lead to the loss of appetite and libido, even to the point of impotency. Now, how impoverished a life would that be?! Can you recall those moments of intensive sensing after you have recovered from a cold or depression and smelled again? By the way, without me you would not experience flavour, as this is manifest from the combination of smell with basic taste sensations. Mentioning my dear sister taste, she is already urging me to bring my narration here to an end. 'Smell well' and good luck for sticking your nose in whatever you are curious about. Trust me, just follow your nose, because the nose knows….

Tasting / Taste

Hmmmmmmm, hello, it is me, taste, or gustation. What do I taste like? How do I operate? Well, my receptors convey tasteful information to the body and brain. I am triggered by somatosensory stimuli, mostly, working together with my colleague smell, processing by various clustered taste buds and brain shuts. Thus, you can define me as the ability to detect and respond to dissolved molecules and ions, which make out flavour of substances.

You know I am totally underestimated compared to the other senses, although, as I said, I do partner with my buddy the more direct sense of smell. I can tell you stories about sweet, salty, sour, and bitter experiences. Interestingly Eastern traditions also know about further qualities of me, like spicy and what is called *umami* (旨味). This is found in fermented and aged foods, described as pungent 'meatiness', 'relish' or 'savouriness'. More recently, psychophysicists and neuroscientists have suggested even further sub-categories of me like fatty acid taste as well as the sensation of metallic tastes. In any case, I am – like my colleague smell – a transient sensory experience. What do my ephemeral and amorphous qualities mean for you?

As a bodily sense, I am linked like the

other senses but in a particular way with pleasure and/or displeasure. For example, I invoke the immediate enjoyment or disgust of eating and drinking, kissing and savour licking. Have you realised how much you rely on me while tracing ingredients, like herbs or other flavours for relishing what you consume? I am also applied to human beings: For example why do you say someone has a 'sweet personality' or 'sour character'?

Compared to all other senses, I am considered to admit to the most variety and idiosyncrasy: 'there is no disputing about taste'. Nevertheless, there has been quite controversial debate about whether I am only relative or whether and how universal standards can be developed for me. Figuratively, I am used as a metaphor, that is a expression for a set of preferences and dispositions that admit shared social standards and public criticism. Elucidating the subtle nature of aesthetic sensibilities, I refer to aesthetic discernment and appreciation.

Let us get a taste of what a master of intellectual taste and high priest in the church of reason, Kant, said about this. According to Kant's philosophy (1781/1999) of subsuming particulars under concepts or universals, is only pure judgment as aesthetic taste, which pertains to beauty – in contrast to the merely subjective, sensuous pleasure and displeasure of bodily senses. Due to our link to practical desires and carnal drives we senses can only relate to individual judgment of pleasing and displeasing taste thus not having universal validity. For Kant the a priori character of me, taste, reflects the transcendental principle of the general acceptability, and only in transcending from my individual whims and idiosyncrasy can there be a 'sensus communis'. Consequently, while advocating the mastery of sense by reason alone, he consigns me with my friends 'to the dust heap of the senses' (Classen et al. 1994: 89). For him it is the objective, disinterested, pure aesthetic pleasure in the presentation (Vorstellung) that allows a universal agreement, validity and judgment.

How do you distinguish and judge good from bad taste? And what does the capacity to draw and enact such differentiation imply for you and other human beings? As I am an emergent effect of working with the other direct senses of my embodying human being and his social and cultural context, also my appraisal and evaluation of aesthetic qualities are influenced by this i-n-t-e-r- play.

After enjoying a tasty meal, and pursuing empirical research, Bourdieu (1984) theorised how aesthetic preferences of me, the taste, are a social im-position and means of social distinction often in disguise or rendered invisible. Rejecting the pretence of universality for matters of preference to me, he claimed that the philosophical superiority of me as aesthetic taste is an illusion. I welcome Bourdieu's debunking contest of formal theories of culture, language, and aesthetics as well as agreeing that the main force of these discourses is producing and maintaining hierarchies of power and domination. Further, I and my co-senses find much valuable insights in his relational approach of fields (as patterned set of practices), habitus (as preformating schemata of perception, feeling thinking, acting and evaluating), and his distinctions attempting to overcome 'subjectivism' and 'objectivism'.

But as taste, I am more and different than an acquired cultural competence and a classifier, even as classifying the classifier (1984: 6) or as resource used to legitimise hierarchical social differences. With his focus on the complex economic, social and cultural capitals and battles in which I function and reproduce class and status structures, he did not sufficiently consider me as bodily living experience (Shilling, 1993: 146-7). For me his grand theory, with its tendency towards exclusive authority claims, tastes itself too much like socio-corporeal determinism, which is reducing my embodied being to reproductive function. This leaves too little room for non-necessary or non-conforming taste choices, e.g. new foods (Lupton, 1996: 94) and emergent transformations

Have you ever asked yourself what and how taste *tastes* like? Is there ultimately 'One Taste' (Wilber 2000), or rather infinitely many tastes and variations? What does it imply to value the flavourless rather than the flavourful? Could you enjoy the absence of taste with pleasure, as a richness of bland meaning (Jullien, 2004)? What would it mean to learn that the bland comprises the unnameable union of all potential values, embodying a reality whose very essence is change providing an infinite opening into the breadth of taste? Can you allow the undifferentiated foundation of all things in blandness to appear elusively, similar to clearing the palette before tasting, such as tasting ginger b/e/t/w/e/e/n bites of sushi; or drinking water b/e/t/w/e/e/n sips of wine? What are the consequences of recognising that the bland is not associated with a lack, but an intensifying quality for aesthetic and even ethical dimensions? Together with all the other senses, I the taste, I am particularly connected and applicable also to *style*, as pervading 'being-in-the-world' and synergic synthesis of the perceiving body (Singer, 1993). Basically, perception 'already stylises' (Merleau-Ponty, 1962: 455), that is I cannot help but constitute and simultaneously express in my tasting a point of view, or better to say, a sensual perspective.

You cannot imagine what I experience as good and bad tastes in this tasteful and tasteless organ-isation (Corbett, 2006). I must say, many if not nearly all workplaces and their distasteful designs are unappealing. The atmosphere of industrial or service-work and most offices are distasteful in excess and demonstrate awful, organisational kitsch (Linstead, 2002), quite unrefined taste of mawkish sentimentality and faked sensation, for my taste.

What do you taste at work? What are the gastronomic styles of eating in your organisation? What style of taste do you perceive in your organ-isational culture? How does the after-taste of being all day in your organ-isation taste like? The good news is that I am not only naturally given, but can be educated and cultivated, like all my co-senses. Can you envision strategies for refined existence (Küpers, 2005a) that has a fine taste? What kind of lingering taste do you perceive after this 'finish' of my ex-pressions here? Tasting is better without haste! Test and taste it!

Touching / Touch

Touch Touch Touch me, and be touched by me! Welcome to the worlds of touch (Katz, 1989; Classen, 2005)! I am an elementary sense, as it is from me the other senses have evolved.

It is by means of me that you are able to become aware of the size, form, shape and delight of material objects. With those millions of receptors throughout the body I can detect degrees material hardness, roughness, elasticity, and other physical characteristics, including vibration as well as pain. With me you are aware of changes of vital states in your bodies, such as thirst, hunger, sexual-feeling, and other 'internal sensations.' During tactual perception (Loomis & Lederman, 1986) my skin – your sensitive surface and largest, most various organ – perceives variations in pressure and shows the spatial possibilities and limits of your lived body (Connor, 2004). Did you know that your well-being is related to your enveloping 'skin-ego' (Anzieu, 1989). When you reach out to caress an animate being, your immediacy of sensation is affirmatory and comforting, due to a mutual co-implication of your own body with another's presence. Thus, as s an index-sense, I operate in ways like grasp, feel, and tact, re-presenting the value of sensitivity itself.

Similar to taste, I, the touch, have these two complementary meanings – on the one hand being a sensual experience and on the other hand an affective metaphor (Paterson, 2007). Through both the sensuous immediacy and the metaphorical 'mediality', significance is imported for bringing distant objects and people into nearer proximity. Being linked to em- and sym-pathy and serving the need for connection, I influence the kind and degree of togetherness. Thus, I am present during handshakes or hugs, but also can be misused for uninvited grappling or harassments.

Currently, I am touched by the increasing yearning for embodied contact due to the growing isolation and alienation of today's modern life-worlds with their superficial spheres of production and consumerism. No wonder that I am exploited by a commoditisation of tactility (Paterson, 2007: 148). But I also still sense much apprehension and uneasiness of what is so-called 'touchy-feely'.

How does your organ-isational life-world touch you and your body? Who and what touch you and how do you 'handle' your every day working life? Have there been experiences of vulnerability, which went 'under your skin'? Why isn't there a regular soothing massage provided to you at work? What and how have you consciously (been) touched lately at work? Have you noticed the touch of your hand using a pen, a computer mouse or a keyboard? What is happening to touch in tele-presences via human-computer interfaces and virtual realities of inter-places (Küpers, 2010)? What role does touching have for workplace behaviour (Fuller et al. 2010), negatively i.e. as influence tactic, sexual harassment or as touch anxiety as well as positively for example to communicate support and caring for feeling closer to each other (Edwards 1984: 770)? Are there 'untouchable' issues banned in your meetings?

What touches me personally, is that I fear not feeling and sensing anything at all. What difference would it make for you not to touch or being touched? What kind of a life would that be? Aren't we all losing touch more and more in our insular and eye-minded world, overloaded by appalling and dreadful news and superficial contacts without being deeply touched. Instead of getting out of touch, pleases keep in touch with me!

> *'Sensation …. is the most fundamental domain of cultural expression, the medium through which all the values and practices of society are enacted. … sensual relations are also social relations…'* (Howes, 2003, Foretaste XI)

Other Senses & Synæsthesia of Sensation

Of course there are also we the other senses. For example me, equilibrioception, the vestibular sense perceiving position, location and balance, a sense of direction or orientation. And there are also we relatives of this sensing: Me for example the sense of place (Stedman, 2002) and me nociception, the sensual perception of pain. Furthermore, I exist, the so-called proprioception, the kinesthetic sense, refering to the perception of body awareness. Today you know us five senses, but in ancient times there were more senses known, like animation, feeling, and speech. You sense it: we senses are relative to historio-cultural interpretations. Different significances are given to us in different times and cultures.

Sensuality and sensibility of us senses as the fertilised though contingent 'ground' of your temporally relative being-in-the-world. They not only have their own intelligibility (Lingis, 1996) but relates you to sensible materialities and exposes you in a sensuous mediality of luminosity, tactility, and sonority.

There is one other more complex sense, which is commonly overlooked; it is I, the common sense. Based upon what is conceived as knowledge held in common or as self-evident knowledge (Reid, 1764), sometimes particularly as prejudices, I can become an impediment to critical thinking. I common sense do not mean only that good sense, which is common or commonly needed in the ordinary affairs of life. Rather, I am a sense that is common to all of the senses, or better to say the point where they meet in their *intersensorial embodiment*.

Importantly, our experiences are multi-sensory and synaesthetic, having an i-n-t-e-r-modal perception. Synæesthesia is usually described as a form of sensory slippage (Harrison, 1996), by which sensory experience with one modality involuntarily triggers percepts in another. However, in a non-clinical sense, Synæesthesia is an alternative way of considering sensoriality. This implies that one sense evokes another, which in turn, can evoke others, thus links i-n-t-e-r-sensory within the body and engage in the world and its objects in your everyday-lives. According to Merleau-Ponty 'synaesthetic perception is the rule, and we are unaware of it only because scientific knowledge shifts the centre of gravity of experience, so that we have unlearned how to see, hear, and generally speaking feel' (Merleau-Ponty, 1962: 229; 2004). Seen in this way, synæesthesia is part of the way in which, moment by moment, living beings re-constitute and re-create their world; in which they are immersed as a stream of pre-reflective encounters situated day by day. Following a kind of sensorial intelligence we senses i-n-t-e-r- act by implying and invoking each other in our politics of senses, which cause that

> *'at times conflicting messages are conveyed by different sensory channels, and certain domains of sensory expression and experience are suppressed in favour of others'* (Howes, 2003, Foretaste XXII)

practising a kind of opposing 'dysæsthesia' (Drobnick, 1998). It is this orchestrated dissonance that is essential for interrogating the perceptual decisions that go into the emotional and cognitive understanding of experience. You sense it; we are traversing a sensational dance full of ambivalences.

Understanding Us Embodied Senses as an 'intelligent' Part of the Living Body – Merleau-Ponty's advanced Phenomenology

We senses provide our embodied beings, like those members of organ-isations, with the base or media for their multiple kinds of awareness and 'intelligences': visual, musical, logical, linguistic, movement, naturalistic, kinesthetic, intrapersonal and interpersonal intelligences. Unfortunately, the relationship b/e/t/w/e/e/n our sensory perceptions and reason is not really considered properly. This is also because our body and embodiment are not considered 'integratively', due to mentalist and cognitive biases dominating (Western) rational culture.

Let us re-mind you, we senses are not just raw data or input for information-processing by cognitive procedures and a disembodied computational brain. This reductionist approach seems to be based on a prevailing mistrust of the actuality of our sensory knowledge, judged by empiricists and rationalists as impoverished. Correspondingly we have been reduced to a set of variables to be factored into calculated objects. In contrast to such appropriation, we are not isolated factors or informational bits, but are all i-n-t-e-r- twined parts of our situated embodiment. Our bodies do our living as senses and allow us to make sense for you. We the bodily felt senses of qualia (sensual qualities), our i-n-t-e-r-play of experiences and the sense-based situations constitute sensual beings and meaningful 'be-comings'. Bodies are the media for all your i-n-t-e-r-actions and -passions. We are a material nexus of sensuality and sensuous phenomena and thus a kind of processual reality, enabling sensuous interactions.

Our body and processes of embodiment are at work and full of play for transforming mere sensitiveness into sensibility and meaningful sense-making. For understanding and revalourising these dimensions, the basic ideas of one of the most profound philosophers of us embodied senses will be helpful.

With the philosophy of Merleau-Ponty we senses found some-body, who really understood our constitutive tasks and services. Yes indeed, with him you can turn to the body and to embodiment as a basic nexus of all your living meaning. As an unruly, unpredictable and unmanageable reality, our body and embodiment are – although focusing – *de-centring*. They are not 'mastered' by you as a subject or by collective objectivities, but are also disrupting, undermining and escaping the purposive and boundary-drawing processes including those of organisation and management. With this understanding, our bodily and embodied forces underlie and allow an entrée into the processual, dynamic and unfinished ambiguous nature of any organising and managing, as well as moves between stabilising habits and playful improvisation (Küpers, 2011).

By means of bodily and affective insertion into reality – including that of organisational life-worlds – humans are always already vitally responsive to the demands and needs, but also problems and claims of our situation, upon our sensual body. In this way our body 'moves' in terms of pre-reflective wisdom, which exceeds conscious awareness and control, dominating many of your organ-isational practices and studies.

Furthermore, your perceiving sensual body, your supposed Self and its consciousness, as well as all your relations to Others and the world, are intricately involved and mutually 'engaged' within an ever-present corporal scheme and chiasmic 'flesh'.

Re-membering Organ-isations as Sensuous Embodied 'Life-worlds'

We the senses, (y)our body and the fleshy embodiment have been and are still marginalized or merely functionalised in conventional organisational practices and theory (Hassard et al., 2000; Casey, 2000: 55). Facing the prevailing separation of body and consciousness (Dale and Burrell, 2000; Dale, 2001) – underpinned by bifurcation of 'mindless objects' and 'disembodied minds' – and considering the 'absent presence' of the body in social theory (Shilling, 1993: 19; Leder, 1990), there is a need for a 're-membering'. How can you re-member us your senses, the body, the embodiment and its significance for organ-isations, thus re-integrate the lived, embodied experiences of sensing as a base for sense-making and acting?

Following the embodied turn (Hassard et al., 2000: 12) and *turn to affect* across the humanities and social sciences (Blackman & Venn 2010: 8; Clough & Halley, 2007) and as part of a more inter- and trans-disciplinary collaboration, sense-sensitive phenomenology offers possibilities for developing an understanding of a (re-)embodied organ-isation (Styhre, 2004) and integrating sensual processes in its inter-relational nexus. For us senses, organ-isations are, and organ-ising takes place in particular sensuous embodied life-worlds. We know that our perspective contrasts reified i-n-t-e-r-pretations. By such appropriating approaches organ-isations are seen as immutable 'objects' that are supposed to operate somehow independent of human embodiment, intentions, unconscious motives or inter-subjective agencies. Following our focus on the lived sensual realities of organ-isational perceivers and actors, you can sense that for us organising is realised through embodied (en-) acting and experiential processes. Therefore for us senses members of organ-isations are first and foremost embodied beings, who are both a part of their world and coextensive with it, constituting but also constituted meaningfully (Merleau-Ponty, 1962: 453).

For the perceiving 'body-subjects' this situatedness comprises both the ways in which they act within the life-world, and that which acts upon them (Crossley, 1996: 101). This acting and enactment implies that they never know about things or encounters independent of their lived experiences as bodily engaged beings and their embodiment. Here embodiment does not simply refer to physical manifestation. Rather, it means that the sensing perceiver, knower and actor are being grounded in everyday experience and integrally connected to herself and her environment in an ongoing sensual interrelation. With this connection, the embodied experience and thus all organising practices are built upon an original, ambiguous 'ground'. This base functions as a primordial world-horizon on which members of organ-isations experience and 'body-forth' their possibilities sensually into the situated world.

Accordingly, the constituents of the lived world of organ-isations are not 'objective' properties, or autonomous 'subjects', but situations and modes of being-in-the-world. As situations always have both a 'subject-side' and an 'object-side' they inextricably linked to each other. Thus the sensual and sensitive 'body' and its sensation and perception are the medium for a pre-reflexive yet active communion (Merleau-Ponty, 1962: 212). Without the bodily perceived senses of the individual situation and intentional and volitional energies, you would not know where you are or what and how you are being situated and doing something competently, nor how to communicate to other some-bodies. Thus living bodies and their sensuous embodiment are embedded in a social context that 'are' your situation; they 'do' your living (Gendlin, 1992). From an advanced phenomenological standpoint, being embodied is always already a way of sensing, knowing and acting through con-textual encounters. Within this situatedness, the sensual 'living body' mediates b/e/t/w/e/e/n 'internal' and 'external' or 'subjective' and 'objective' as well 'individual' and 'collective' experiences. Thus the body is the i-n-t-e-r -mediation of all practices and negotiation of meanings in organ-isation.

A re-integration of embodied dimensions can be based on the fundamental insight that, through embodied, perceptual and sensual selves, the 'subjects' of the organising processes are situated in their environment in a *visual, auditory, olfactory, tasteable*, and *tactile way*. Whatever they think, feel, know or do, they are exposed to the aforementioned synaesthetic and synchronised field of us *i-n-t-e-r-re-l-a-t-e-d* senses (Merleau-Ponty, 1962: 207). Accordingly, members or organ-isations are always embedded in the midst of our world of *sight, sound, smell, taste,* and *touch*. It is through the sensing and sensed body that those involved in organisational process directly reach their perceived and handled 'objects' and all relations at work. Moreover, members of organ-isations sense, 'know' and act, respectively i-n-t-e-r-act, while being situated spontaneously and pre-reflectively, in accordance with their bodies and their embodiment. The 'occupational body' is produced through the work of specific, commonplace and i-n-t-e-r-connected sensory practices as convincingly shown in the case of sensory work in military life of an infantry (Hockey, 2009).

In order to approach the i-n-t-e-r-r-e-l-a-t-e-d processes, they can be understood as embodied intentions and responsiveness. All involved in organising processes encounter perceived realities through bodily organs from an intentional and responsive point of seeing, hearing or touching. With an intentionality of the bodily consciousness, the agent within the sphere of organising does not only feel 'I think', but also 'I sense', 'I can' or 'I relate to' - or 'I do' (Macmurray, 1957: 84). In other words, the atmosphere within which organ-ising takes place is not only what people think about it, but primarily what they 'live through' with their 'operative intentionality' (Merleau-Ponty, 1962: xviii) and responsiveness understood as answering practice (Jacobs, 2003; Stacey, 2001; Waldenfels 1994; 2007).

Combining a non-regressive phenomenological 're-turn' towards embodied pre-subjective, pre-reflective and pre-objective constituencies offers perspectives for an integrative 'turn forward'. This turn implies an inclusive 'immanent transcendence' towards an integrative processual and post-dualistic yet practical perspective, realised by a specific integral 'pheno-practice' (Küpers, 2009) and co-constituting embodied aesthetics.

Understanding Embodied Aesthetics in Organ-isations

In which way are we senses also a pedestal for a genuine understanding of aesthetics in particular in and for the study and practice of organisation? Etymologically deriving from the Greek *aiesthesis*, aesthetics comprises expressions that designate us embodied sensation and perception taken as a whole, prior to the assignment of any cognitive or artistic meaning. The Greek verb *aisthanomai* denotes the capacity to perceive with us senses. Having an aesthetic experience means being sensually responsive to the pattern that connects (Bateson, 1979), giving the subject a sensual perception and feeling of wholeness and of belonging to a heightened reality. Phenomenologically, art-related and aesthetic experiences are constituted by us sensual-based, embodied-perceptual, emotional-responsive, and expressive-communicative relationships. Aesthetic knowledge and understandings comes from us perceptive bodily sensuous faculties of seeing, hearing, smelling, tasting and touching. Thus, all forms of aesthetics require a full engagement and refinement of us all and our sensibilities in human perception, feeling, thinking and acting.

For having an aesthetic experience, an 'aesthetic attitude' marks a basic requirement. This stance needs to be one of an openness and attentiveness to experiencing an object or process fully, sensually and aesthetically. It suggests that there is a certain way to look, hear, smell, taste, and touch and also to feel and imagine an object or process that lends itself to a more profound experience. Following a detachment from purpose, to experience an object or process truly aesthetically is to experience it for its own sake and not for any practical or ulterior motive. Accordingly, the aesthetic attitude is conventionally characterised by disinterestedness and a distance from any instrumental relation to the object or process. However, despite the romantic ideal of acknowledging art for art's sake, aesthetic experience is made by situated human beings and we cannot ignore who they are and where they have come from. In the pragmatic spirit of breaking barriers b/e/t/w/e/e/n emotions, imagination, reason, culture, and behaviours, art can be experienced simultaneously for its social, moral, or intellectual values. Yet, an aesthetic lens shifts the attention to that which is sensuous and calling for a focus that does not deny or exclude other valid aspects of perception. The form and content of aesthetic experiences are response-dependent, qualitative, or expressive dimensions of the object or process. Aesthetic responses can then be followed by aesthetic i-n-t-e-r-pretations, aesthetic judgments, and aesthetic communication (Küpers, 2002: 28) all carrying a transformational potential. As aesthetics relates to experiential and transformative processes this implies that value of art and aesthetics are not in actual artefacts per se, but in the dynamic experiential activity and passion perceived and evaluated individually and collectively.

Complementing our aesthetic expert the taste, all of us senses contribute to an aesthetic sensible judgment. As a 'judicium sensitivium' it processes via integrated operations case by case in a situation-specific way of assessing particular phenomena.

In a way aesthetics and aesthetic-like processes are a pervading part of the fabric

wendelin m. küpers

of organ-isations' everyday activities, experiences, judgments and reality. They imply evocative processes of sensing and imagination (Alvarez & Merchan, 1992), which always concern the i-n-t-e-r-weaving with prior experiences and us sensory faculties of aesthetic understanding (Strati, 1999: 14). Moreover, art-like forms invariably not only reflect the life within organ-isations, but are also often attempts to influence this very life. Furthermore, what is reflected in an aesthetic appraisal of organising and managerial processes is the specific embodied, emotional, cognitive as well as relational and con-+-Textual involvement.

However, much art-like forms and processes are unrecognised as such. What would it mean to push the limits of aesthetics by looking at the i-n-t-e-r-section of sense-based art/aesthetics and daily life (Novitz, 1992)? How can you rethink our conception of the relations b/e/t/w/e/e/n sense-constituted aesthetics, 'art' and life in a way that reflects more adequately the role that enacted aesthetics play in the lives of organ-isations and their transformation?

Organ-isations are embodying aesthetic 'properties' and use various aesthetic symbols and artifacts. Certain arrangements of designs and artifices are agreeable, while others are disagreeable. Both types effect your embodiment and bodily states in the con-+-Text of workplace settings and organ-isational life. But to ask whether 'organ-isations' have aesthetic artifacts or are 'aesthetic' is perhaps already a wrong-footed or one-sided starting point. These materialisations, manifestations and results only partially cover what we senses offer and how we work and play. It is the sensual *process* of organ-isational activities and dynamics that needs to be examined and understood, if we are to find aesthetic realisations into the 'nature' of transformations of individuals and organ-isations. Again it is the relational sensual aspects, which are critical for approaching these activities as aesthetic. Instead of static notions, it is the *transformational quality* realised by aesthetic dynamics of embodied and felt performance processes that is imperative. Aesthetic processes of transformation need to be considered as to how they are making and remaking perceptions, persons, relationships, constructions, structures and entire 'worlds' in an ongoing process of i-n-t-e-r-r-e-l-a-t-i-n-g within organising. Embedded in con-+-textual relations, aesthetic processes 'author-ise' or constellate the manner of the performances. Aesthetic relating may create multiple realities as different but equally valid expressions, avoiding the imposition of one voice, which all too often dominates organ-isational practices. The transformational potential of aesthetic process in organ-isations – both as creation and/or reception – refer to its capacity for questioning the sense of the real and gaining a sense of the possible. Activating both theses senses irritates productively and offers creative re-evolutionary changes for a differently shaped practice. Aesthetic events elicit genuine experience and by this open opportunities for intensifying the process of sensual, emotional and mindful states, as well as mediating creative processes for more integral and sustainable practices of organ-isation.

Conclusion

Dear Reader, you have perceived, read and come to know about us the different senses and our i-n-t-e-r-connections. We provided you with some – admittedly selective – perspectives on, and examples of, our embodied significance in the life of organ-isations. There are so many other subtle dimensions and details that we would like express beyond what is possible here. Speaking about limitations, let us address some final thoughts.

Facing the complexities of current organ-isations and their contexts, we know that not all of it can be understood by us senses and our bodily processes. The corpus of corporation is much more than what can be captured by us. What makes sense and what is non-sense in modern and post-modern lives in organ-isations implies more than what we ephemeral senses can do or tell. Moreover, in our enlightened self-interest, we warn you not to fall into a kind of neo-sensualism or neo-sensationalism or sentimental sensism, but to take a historiographically and culturally informed and mediated account of us.

But as we tried to outline, we are part of those inherent dimensions of embodiment, which refer to more than our mere sensual appearances. Being somewhat restricted to direct evident experience from a first-person-perspective, there is the need to advance inclusively towards second- and third-person perspectives in i-n-t-er- and transdisciplinary endeavours (Küpers & Edwards, 2008) and pheno-practical research (Küpers, 2009a). Moreover, a truly sense-ful and aesthetic inquiry deals not only with us senses, but moves beyond our appearances towards a more comprehensive integration of sense-making. Nevertheless, considering us mindfully may contribute for organising and managing more sensitively and sustainable.

The need to embrace a 'new sensoriality' and a further exploration of our sensory potential cooperation will become even more important as the desire for more intensive experiences and meanings will probably grow. We sense and hope that in near future our significance as rich, complex, and perplexing phenomena both in our own right and as guide towards a highly pan-sensorial culture (Verbrucken, 2003) will be more recognised.

Let us conclude by a few open questions: What did you perceive sensually while reading this chapter? What could not be expressed in this format of a linear presentation and written language? How would it be like, if our ideas were presented in a different way? What would be a more adequate form or artistic mode for conveying our messages? How to develop a kind of writing – or intervention – which does not reduce or seek to limit the art(istic) experience, but rather opens it up to further adventures? What would this kind of writing look like? Did the ideas discussed throughout this paper make you sense, see and listen, smell differently, and, if so, how? Have you been sensitised, even touched? What kind of after-taste do you perceive sensually at present?

As we the senses are and will be with you, we would like to invite you to be mindful of and to us in your every-day-life, in your organ-isation, or in those you do research on as well as wherever you are, go or be-come!

Wishing you uplifting, inspiring sensual experiences!

And all the best for re-igniting a true sense of wonder

**Yours Sincerely and Sensuously,
The Senses**

Strategy is pivotal to the future development of any organisation, but as this chapter explains, it is often the enemy of creativity and can stifle the intellectual energy an organisation needs in times of crisis and uncertainty. In this chapter, the authors offer another way of thinking about strategy. That we need 'strategy', or the research and planning required to meet specific objectives, is obvious. But what unstated or assumed objectives drive our process of strategy-making? Is strategy the art of planning and pre-conceived action – or can it become a reflexive process of making an organisation resilient and responsive in the face of a perpetually-changing environment?

The authors of this chapter offer a dynamic and intellectually invigorating means of re-thinking the nature of strategy, and do so through the unexpected media of literature, art, music, games and mythology. In these creative practices – usually well outside the orbit of the organisation's perceived range of resources – the authors find a way of identifying the central role and nature of vision and focus in strategy-formation processes as well as strategy itself. The central assumption of strategy is expressed in its intention to 'see' into an unknown future, and to marshal a defined perception of outcomes it cannot see. What kind of vision does it create, and what kind of vision does it need? This chapter offers us the opportunity to re-think our assumptions.

Peripheral Awareness and the Business of Strategy

Robert Chia and Robin Holt

Strategic advantage in business is frequently gained through surprising manoeuvres and the capacity to surprise. These, in turn, derive from a cultivated sensitivity to emergent events taking place at the margins. It involves a capability that we call *peripheral awareness*. Yet, because the periphery is generally characterised by vagueness, messiness and the inarticulate, it usually escapes the focus and attention of decision-makers. In this chapter we show how the art of peripheral awareness can be cultivated by drawing on insights from art and literature. It is a chapter on the periphery, written with only scant reference to the huge body of strategy literature in business studies but, we argue, remaining very pertinent to it. In our examples from poets, essayists and painters we find that vagueness, the unarticulated, the absent and the invisible are experienced as fecund potentialities rather than negative conditions detrimental to meaningful comprehension. So why not the same in business?

> *'It is, in short, the reinstatement of the vague to its proper place in our mental life which I am so anxious to press on the attention'*
> William James, Principles of Psychology, 1890, Vol.1: 254

Stories of the business achievements and successes of pioneers, leaders and entrepreneurs often show that the capacity to break out of dominant mindsets and received wisdom, to resist popular opinion and to surprise others with their unconventional action or even non-action, is what sets them apart. In a rousing commencement address given at Stanford University on 12th June 2005, Steve Jobs of Apple urged the graduates present to 'Stay Hungry. Stay Foolish'. Narrating his own life story, Jobs revealed that he had never himself graduated from college. Like many, he did go to college but could not see the value of many of the classes he was required to take and so dropped out after just six months. However, instead of moving away he stayed on campus and informally attended other courses that interested him more. One such course was a calligraphy class where he learned, amongst other things, about serif and sans serif typefaces and began to appreciate what made great typography great. Jobs was fascinated by the artistic beauty of calligraphy and this was to have momentous consequences ten years later when he began designing the first Macintosh computer. Reminiscing on his past, Jobs maintained:

> *'If I had never dropped out, I would never have dropped in on this calligraphy class, and personal computers might not have the wonderful typography that they do....you have to trust that the dots will somehow connect in your future. You have to trust something – your gut, destiny, life, karma, whatever. This approach has never let me down'*
>
> (Jobs, 2005: 2).

This little vignette provides a useful starting point for the claim made here that many strategic breakthroughs are inextricably linked to a capacity for what we call here 'peripheral awareness'. To suggest that the strategy literature does not attend to the importance of periphery events and influences would not be true. Deviation and open experiment are acknowledged as important sources of influence on 'success'. Yet strategy is reserved as a form of premier activity undertaken by senior managers for whom the articulation and review of well-crafted strategic designs is the centre point of activity. Strategy is a serious, difficult and consequential activity in which senior managers consciously deliberate over resource allocation options concerning how the firm engages with its environment; it is comprehensive (information on internal and external) integrated (concerning the whole business) and explicit (firm sense of destination) (Hambrick and Frederickson, 2001: 57).

As Inkpen and Choudhury (1995) recognise, this patterned judgement is typically understood through devices of presence rather than absence. Strategy involves the focal identification of… arenas of activity; the means for arriving at and moving in those arenas; a sense of distinctiveness; and an accepted understanding of performance. This making present is done through a language of goals, intelligence, blueprints and procedural control from which comes the epistemological confidence to state three things: where the firm is, where the firm can go, and how the firm can get there. In the process of making this abstracted future present there is room for conjecture and doubt, so no matter how totalising the making present of proper strategic spaces, there remains the possibility of disruption. The idea, as Hambrick and Frederickson (2001) remind us, is that strategy should be less about planning from a bird's eye view – wherever that might be – than it is about having well-considered aspirations. Aspirations are an apposite term; they remain intentions that are fed by present and past experiences projected into possible futures through expectation. The effect is not one of attempting to control the world, but of the firm finding its *place within the world,* and having to do so continually.

What we want to consider in this chapter is how this finding of *place* might occur, and whether it can be found differently. Strategic placement is, we argue, more than identification and fixing. Events, especially 'outlier' events, have a way of upsetting or eluding planned responses, of resisting the application of rational methods, and of throwing-up unanticipated outcomes for which no manner of articulation and review can cater. For Steve Jobs, forgoing the relative certainty of regular college classes, achieving respectable grades and eventual graduation was 'pretty scary at that time' but it enabled him to explore things that were seemingly peripheral to a proper college education. Dropping out of college forced him to endure the vagaries of a non-status college life but it turned out to be the best decision he had ever made. He could be said to have implicitly understood the power of peripheral awareness where the tendency to control and exploit known situations is counter-balanced by curiosity. In part this is captured by what James March (1991) calls exploration, a seeking out of what one does not yet know, yet it is more, or perhaps better, 'less', than this. Peripheral awareness is a desire to see, to bear witness and to have born witness, without necessarily holding onto what is seen in the form of knowledge. It is curiosity, a moving hither and thither without the idea of a quarry in mind, a 'seeing' simply to look rather than to know and classify and control. This scattering of attention thrives on an acute realisation that the myriad fringe-activities (such as the calligraphy classes Jobs attended) taking place outside focal attention may be critical in shaping the future direction of an unfolding situation. It also recognises that in our everyday activities unconscious scanning (Ehrenzweig, 1967: 32-42) takes place all the time despite our being generally unaware of it happening.

The beginnings of such awareness can be found physiologically in the eye. The periphery of the retina of the human eye contains over 120 million rod cells, twenty times more than the cone cells found at the centre of the eye (Hoffman, 1998: 66-67). These rod cells, unlike cone cells, are low-level weak signal detectors highly sensitive to movement but not to shape or colour. Because this is the case, the quality of information gathered at the periphery is ill-defined compared to that of focal vision. Yet, for all its apparent inadequacies it gathers a wealth of unformed in-formation that tends to be over-ridden by the invariant objects into which it is solidified. We forget that these objects arise because of the variance detected within the edges of the eye as movement, both within the world and our place in it. The eye's acute sensitivity to movement and change enables us to register vital transformations that are almost imperceptible to focal vision and, thereby, unconsciously to develop a background sensitivity that enriches our appreciation of an emergent situation. In this way we do not see isolated things, but from amid a flux learn to concentrate on things that matter to us (for our survival and flourishing). Even here, physiologically, we don't see solid outlines, but things placed in relation to one another, so much so that optically things carry an array, what Gibson (1986: 190, 286) calls an occluding edge, by which we anticipate conjunctions of things, aware of what lies in front or beyond things before we actually see them. Surfaces are always being revealed and concealed and it is this movement of arrival and departure the edges of the eye catch. Oswick (1996) finds this physiological tendency of the eye a productive metaphor for how strategic judgements on firm activity might better cultivate sensitivity to the edges. Yet it is not simply metaphorical; any awareness and knowledge of our condition as ours, as somehow eliciting a response in us, has prosthetic roots. Whenever we demonstrate a tendency to realise order and focal stability we do so from within a wide range of phenomenal stimulus of which we remain unaware but to which we are always gesturing with our own persisting presence and perceiving. If we move from this raw physiology toward an awareness of how in memory and experience (themselves collectively sedimented in culture), we can understand Gibson's occluding edge as an historically as well as materially and physiologically constituted phenomenon in which the visible and invisible, and the expected and remembered are forever being gathered in an unfolding present through which transforming movements we are drawn on, continually. We become aware of how much these gathering and dispensing edges (physical and symbolic) matter. In this regard, art, the humanities and literature with their long established tradition of attending to the vague, the ephemeral, and elusive aspects of human experience have much to teach us about peripheral awareness in perception, cognition and meaning. We now know that the sublime power and capacity of art, music and literary works to evoke our innermost sentiments, our deepest sympathy and understanding owes much to a sensitivity to edges, both perceptually and symbolically, that has been well appreciated and understood in art and the humanities. By showing how art and literature can deliberately create affects on our perception and appreciation, we can achieve a better comprehension of the crucial role that peripheral awareness might play in business strategy.

1. The periphery

'In trying to adapt, we may need to deviate from cherished values, behaving in ways we barely glimpsed, seizing on fragmentary clues....Trusted habits of attention and perception may be acting as blinders. Resources we have relied on to shape our lives may turn out to be dangerous addictions....Essential themes are not clearly marked but rather visible only out of the corner of the eye....Ambiguity is the warp of life, not something to be eliminated'

Mary Catherine Bateson, Peripheral Visions, 1994: 8

Interest in peripheries amongst business strategy theorists has been fuelled by recent observations regarding the difficulties of well-thought-of firms. For instance, ideas of 'dominant logic' (Prahalad, 2004) or 'co-evolutionary lock-in' (Burgelman, 2009) have been used to explain why a successful firm might struggle to survive in changing competitive environments or why a firm's people might no longer expose themselves to new ideas about the conduct of business. What these theorists recognise is the tendency in strategy-speak to want to locate and fix things in order to present a strategy as a coherent, governing plan concerning a known future and the firm's place within it. Strategy is supposed to fix ends and articulate the means by which the ends are reached, period. This clarity of focus and intended outcome creates surety, but one that might blind the firm's strategists to the resonance and possibilities in emerging events. The firm might do something well, but as Sull (2005b: 124) suggests, this focus on excellence can be an impediment, prematurely locking a firm into a specific course of action without the ability or even inclination to reflect on its continuing appropriateness. The need to remain open and alert to changes and transformations taking place at the corners-of-the-eye so to speak has, therefore, been identified as being crucial to firm survival (see special issue of Long Range Planning, Vol. 37, 2004, edited by George Day and Paul Schoemaker). Yet, the periphery is 'ever elusive', and always a 'bit blurry'. It is always 'part of the world you are not paying attention to' (Day and Schoemaker, 2004: 131).

The idea that peripheral vision is critical to sustained business success is often attributed to a casual observation made by Andy Grove, the former boss of Intel, who famously noted that the process of industry change (and innovation) is akin to melting snow. 'When spring comes, snow melts first at the periphery, because that is where it is most exposed' (Grove, 1999: 110). Changes in the competitive landscape, like melting snow, tend to start at the periphery and oftentimes are unnoticed. Unlike the dramatic and spectacular changes and transformations that the strategy literature and media tend to highlight and make much of, real changes in the everyday lives of corporate practitioners often occur unspectacularly and sometimes imperceptibly on the fringes of active awareness. They have long gestations and emerge from amid an almost accidental coming together of disparate networks of people and technology. Contrary to the popular dramatic view of change being governed by individual insight and oversight, many important changes are 'often subtle, agglomerative, often subterranean and heterogeneous'. They stealthily creep up on us 'spreading like a patch of oil' (Chia, 1999: 222) overtaking us even before we become aware of them.

To witness such, though, is not simply a case of re-focussing on the edges, not least because any such recommendation underestimates the elusiveness and enigmatic character of the periphery and hence the form of peripheral awareness required for dealing with it. What is being advocated in talking of the periphery is not that what is on the edge is somehow turned towards and made focal, but that we better recognise how focal awareness is woven and re-woven from the integration of subsidiary elements and judgements that in themselves feed from the edge of consciousness (Polanyi, 1962). What seems to be the case in the recent strategy literature, however, is precisely a recommendation that we re-focus, or expand our focus, to become more attentive to what is on or even beyond the horizon. For example, in the Day and Schoemaker special issue the lack of attention to peripheral events is viewed as a technical deficiency, a 'gap' in knowledge that can be overcome by extending the breadth of focal strategic activities. The problem with this is twofold.

Firstly, for any focal perspective no matter how wide, there will always be edges, toward which you will have to keep turning without rest. Attending to the edges like this can be debilitating because every action and event carries with it subsidiary baggage that must be unpacked and subjected to analysis. Unexamined habits and prejudice are important, they settle us into manners and activities without always having them measured against idealised forms by which abstractions they will always be found wanting. The result of incessantly examining the edges of our consciousness and so in vocalising and formalising our motivations and institutional procedures is an endlessly modulated succession of exhortations to re-configure our lives so that we might do better, reach further. We literally shape up against an articulated and codified idea of what is right, or effective. This urge to interfere and incessantly 'improve' is a constant temptation, but can be so much empty noise. Edmund Burke (para 143) warns of such when writing in the immediate thrall of the French Revolution, lamenting how the subjection of long-standing social manners and conventions to rational analysis and re-ordering principles of a new social order might entice those in Britain and Ireland to do likewise. He warns those who might be tempted strategically to upset the old order:

> 'Because half a dozen grasshoppers under a fern make the field ring with their importunate chink, whilst thousands of great cattle, reposed beneath the shadow of the British oak, chew the cud and are silent, pray do not imagine that those who make the noise are the only inhabitants of the field; that, of course, they are many in number; or that, after all, they are other than the little, shriveled, meagre, hopping, though loud and troublesome, insects of the hour.'

Silently chewing the cud may not be an enticing metaphor for strategic surety, yet the seasonal solidity of the quiet beasts and long grown trees suggests a necessary immunity to the brittle and flighty chatter of strategic fads.

Secondly, to think language capable of capturing the periphery in some form of conceptual frame is to remain unquestioningly reliant on the efficacy and adequacy of explicit representations. This epistemology of representationalism takes as unproblematic the ability of language to represent situations through correspondence to the phenomena. This explains the rather thin remedies offered in the special issue of Long Range Planning summarised by Day and Shoemaker in their introduction. These include: a) expanding your focus; b) asking the right questions; c) using technology to become more agile; and d) leveraging the peripheral vision of CEOs. In our view, these proposed remedies struggle because they do not address the underlying reason why the periphery is so elusive, something intimated in Day and Schoemaker's own comment that: 'Each time you turn your head to look at it, you create a new "periphery"' (2004: 117).

For us, the periphery is something that must be obliquely approached with stealth. It resists direct capture, simple location and transparent representation. Access to it can only be gained through a strategic detour in our thought processes. Like a shadowy figure operating on the margins of attention, it is that which always lies beyond the bounds of focal attention and representation. Deliberately focussing on the periphery or expanding the focus merely creates yet another boundary or pushes the periphery further back, *ad infinitum*. Like the Tao in ancient Chinese thought any direct attempt to grasp it misses it: 'The Tao that can be named is not the Tao' (Lao Tzu, Tao Te Ching, in Chan, 1963: 139). Likewise, the periphery is that vague penumbra surrounding the focal object that is integral to apprehension without itself being apprehended. It can be glimpsed through the cultivation of a heightened sensitivity to events and activities taking place at the margins of consciousness; a cultivation that comes from what Steve Jobs called thinking foolishly, eschewing direct engagement and confrontation in favour of detour.

In summary, whilst the recent emphasis on the vital role of peripheral vision in strategic thinking is to be welcomed, there appears to be a reluctance to investigate the idea that the periphery is, by definition an 'otherness' that is necessarily vague, shadowy and ambiguous and will always remain so; to locate it, confront it directly or to represent it straightforwardly, is to lose it because in every revealing comes concealing. What matters about the periphery is that we remain aware of what veils, that we acknowledge no matter how clear the strategic intent and how comprehensive the information upon which the aims have been framed, there are always edges beyond which lie myriad negations and possibilities. Our efforts at making strategic sense are typically skewed toward the identification of things and events, and an analysis of what they consist of. Awareness of what is sleight or even absent is safely ignored as the territory of the wrongheaded. In asking the question "What exists and why does it exist?', Martin Heidegger notes we rarely carry on with question, and ask ourselves 'And why not nothing?" Allying ourselves to the pursuit of nothing is considered an admission of weakness, something less than human, a turning back on our projects, as though being human is somehow intimately tied up with making the world apparent (Heidegger, 1953/1959: 27). Yet as Heidegger goes on to suggest, this omission is curious given that to make things apparent is always an activity of working with questionableness. Working with the periphery reminds us of this.

To truly comprehend the periphery requires us to embrace an alternative world-view in which the vague, the inarticulate and the ambiguous are regarded not as corrupting features to be eliminated or flushed out (we are not to regard ourselves as removing ourselves from question-ableness) but rather as intimate with the condition of knowledge filled with unrealised potentialities. Vagueness is not a 'deficiency' impeding effective strategic decision-making that can be dealt with effectively through better information, better systems and structures or better training. Rather, vagueness is the very condition of possibility for focus and clarity to be attained. It is generated by our own act of focussing and attention giving. As such, vagueness contains a liberating potential; it is a world of the yet-to-be-thought. That which is vague, inarticulate and unformed has a fecundity that serves as the inexhaustible wellspring for innovation and creative response. Viewed through this new paradigm, peripheral awareness can then be seen as a 'positive' negative capability that provides the foundational basis for the meaningful and active creation of organisational reality.

Embracing vagueness begins in 'letting go', both in terms of celebrating naivety and 'ignorance' and considering things and events outside of their immediate concern for us, and for our interests. It is about rediscovering that state of pristine awareness that John Ruskin called the 'innocence of the eye'; a form of 'learned ignorance' that is arrived at by relinquishing pre-conceptions associated with specific ideas concerning the desirability of a state of affairs, as well as being willing to think about the world as resisting human thought and ordering irrespective of the direction, cogency and particularity of such thought and order. Such ignorance paves the way for genuinely new insights to be attained. Only when we become painfully aware that it is ignorance of our ignorance, and not a simple gap in knowledge, that prevents us from knowing what we do not yet know, only then do we then begin to glimpse that illusive realm called the periphery (Johnson, 1989: 16).

But why is it so hard for us to let go of this idea that the periphery like all other social phenomena can be accessed directly, its vague features made clear and captured in concepts and symbols? The answer lies in the still-dominant legacy of Western thought that has tended to elevate order over disorder, clarity over vagueness and representing over intervening. The achievements of this method of intervention and resolution, particularly within the natural sciences, are unquestionable. Yet, its overwhelming success has meant that it also serves as the model approach encouraging a narrowly focused, exploitative attitude rather than the scattering of attention and exploration in the domain of strategy making.

2. Platonic vision and the representational view of reality

'To what extent have we ever stepped outside that European schema or are we even able to ... ("we" within the European tradition who still perpetuate those early Greek

categories)? It is so thoroughly assimilated that we no longer see it...We set up an ideal...which we take to be a goal...and we then act in such a way as to make it become fact'

François Jullien, A Treatise on Efficacy, 2004: 1

From an early age, individuals, particularly in the developed West, are taught to value the importance of precise form, pattern, order and coherence; the visible form, the articulate and the explicit are privileged over the invisible the inarticulate and the implicit. Such an idealisation of explicit form and order is traceable from the Babylonian epic Enuma Elish to the notion of Platonic ideals and in the biblical accounts of the seven days of creation in which order eventually 'triumphs' over the 'darkness' of chaos. Order displaces disorder; St George slays the evil dragon. This is in stark contrast to the East where in the creational myths the systematic human ordering of the universe is accompanied by a sense of loss; instead of celebration there is a mourning of the loss of chaos (Eoyang, 1989), a reticence in the face of order. Here the destruction of chaos, far from marking the triumph of civilisation, ends with a lament on the destructiveness of human intervention. Here the dragon, that elusive creature symbolising chaos, is deemed 'king' of the universe. Such a privileging of idealised order and perfect forms or representations over an imperfect 'messy' and 'chaotic' reality in the West has meant that human actions and interventions are motivated and guided by idealised notions of order that take precedence over the messiness of lived reality.

One major consequence of this epistemological attitude is that our representations are increasingly mistaken for reality; a 'Fallacy of Misplaced Concreteness' (Whitehead, 1926/85: 64) ensues. Recently, the controversial currency-trader-turned-academic Nassim Nicholas Taleb calls this deeply ingrained tendency to rely upon representations Platonicity:

'What I call Platonicity...is our tendency to mistake the map for the territory, to focus on pure and well-defined "forms", whether objects, like triangles, or social notions, like utopias (or) even nationalities. When these ideas and crisp constructs inhabit our minds, we privilege them over other less elegant objects, those with messier and less tractable structures... Platonicity is what makes us think we understand more than we do' (Taleb, 2007: xxv).

Because of this deep programming, our senses, being physiologically disposed to focus through the arrangement of the periphery, are educated instinctively to search for a good gestalt: a clear picture, form or shape, the familiar features of someone known or the distinct outlines of a building (Ehrenzweig, 1967), from which the periphery is cast aside. These deeply ingrained gestalt tendencies are closely associated with scientific, economic and social progress and advancement. For, it is a common prerequisite of scientific investigation, and indeed any form of systematic analysis, that a phenomenon to be investigated must be clearly delineated, its identity established, its properties measured and documented, and its causal powers precisely correlated with those of other phenomenon. Only then can investigation and ensuing judgements be deemed successful. All these tendencies, however, are predicated upon the ability to achieve visual clarity and focus. Both episteme and techne, the recognised forms of knowledge acceptable in scientific thought, are associated with qualities of 'universal applicability, teachability, and concern with explanation' (Raphals, 1992: 227). Techne, in particular, is inextricably linked to knowing through 'numbering' (i.e., quantitative measurement) in Western thought.

This quantitative, analytical attitude is carried over in social scientific investigations where the social world is assumed to be relatively stable, discrete and identifiable and held in reasonable equilibrium throughout human interactions, a stability that lends itself to systematic analysis and accurate representation. The task in social science is to 'discover' or uncover the entities and causal orders existing amongst institutional and cognitive phenomena and to use these revealed patterns in better explaining human behaviour. Knowledge is achieved when new explanations become more comprehensive and all-embracing. The idea of research is therefore to progressively reduce the existing 'knowledge-gap' through the systematic accumulation of such established forms of experiential control (Flyvbjerg, 2001). Strategy research is simply one such set of investigations.

Resistance to this idea of completion has precipitated the 'postmodern' critique of representationlism as the basis of knowledge. Despite their enormous differences philosophers such as Jacques Derrida, Jean Baudrillard and Richard Rorty are united in their disillusionment of our human reliance on representation. So reliant have we become that the referring words have taken on their own life, become more real than the things they represent, thus a newspaper is no longer a material object of paper and ink upon which information on current events is conveyed, rather it is a relationship of the reader and symbolic meaning. To be seen reading *Le Monde* or *The Wall Street Journal* is to espouse an identity distinct from those reading the 'red tops', or from readers of gossip magazines, or from non-readers. The thing represented is subsumed under a welter of symbols concerning our own desires, collectively expressed. Baudrillard is wanting us to think about how the apparent *thinglyness* of things has become increasingly thinned out, the irony being that this thinning-out has occurred in the company of ever more sophisticated systems of classification and representational endeavour. The more we stipulate what it is we know, the less there 'is' to know about. In art, the Belgian surrealist painter René Magritte's 1929 *The Treachery of Images* (issued as a multiple) is one striking example which reinforces the poverty of our addiction to representation with a flat, naïve and lonely image of a pipe underscored by its written denial, revealing right away our habitual reliance on fragile tautologies to sustain our knowledge claims, as though by illustrating and then labelling things repeatedly we are becoming progressively more mature in our understanding of the world.

What Magritte is playing with is our habit of representationalism that promotes a concentration of attention on circumscribed and identifiable entities, their attributes and their changing relationships. Some are clearer than other, yet labels remain, especially in social studies where phenomena displaying as-yet-to-be-explained behaviours still command conceptual epithets: values, love, friendship being just a few. Here the representations are so broad as to invite all manner of often confusing allegiances or accusations of tautology (of the kind "love is friendship intensified" and culture is "friendship extended"). This *entitative* attitude towards understanding the social world is well encapsulated in the traditional approach to strategic problem-solving and decision-making where the emphasis is on the careful isolation and studying of dependent and non-dependent variables, symptoms and factors; on the establishment of clear decisional criteria; on the systematic and rigorous comparison of alternatives, and on the making of definite choices regarding action to which clear responsibility is appended. This systematic approach narrows and focuses attention and encourages the concentration of effort and the consequent effective exploitation of a resource or opportunity. If one acts under vague, ambiguous circumstances it stands to reason that the effort applied will be more dispersed and hence less likely to be efficient or effective in bringing about a desired outcome. In short, casual efficacy and effective exploitation demand focused attention and action. Strategic effort operates according to an instrumental rationality. Detailed analyses of 'SWOT' factors, thorough planning of strategic action and the use of terms and phrases such as 'targeting', 'strategic alignment', 'market penetration', 'market segment', 'strategic positioning', 'core competence', 'stick to the knitting', 'cost leadership', 'focus' etc., all point to the centrality of focal vision in strategic analyses. Without a doubt, this singular and unrelenting emphasis on exploitation of existing capacities and opportunities has borne much fruit to numerous firms and will continue to do so particularly in domains of relatively stable competition. Systematic detailed analysis (i.e., the breaking down of phenomena into part-elements) concentrates attention, is goal-oriented and leads to the efficient exploitation of capabilities and inevitably scarce resources. This is why much of business strategy pays more attention to exploiting opportunities rather than to the creation of new ones. The general perception is that there is little to be gained and much to be lost from peripheral 'distractions'.

Yet, the danger of this overly exploitative attitude is that the progressive narrowing of focus of attention also simultaneously blinds decision-makers to emerging and unrecognised aspects of experience that may have important future consequences for a firm. The paradox is that the very success brought about by effective exploitation may lead to a failure of being blind-sided by events occurring outside the realm of focal awareness. This paradox of success may be linked to what Prahalad (2004) calls the dominant logic of a firm.

3. The paradox of success

'The cosmetic and the platonic rise naturally to the surface'
                        Nassim Nicholas Taleb, The Black Swan,
                                                    2007: 131

The relentless emphasis on exploitation carries with it a hidden cost that is often overlooked or unacknowledged. It eventually leads to internal tensions and contradictions. The very ingredients and recipes that enabled effective exploitation and the achievement of early success become the cause of an eventual failure in the inability to adjust to unrecognised, external demands. This is why it is sometimes said that success breeds failure through a vicious spiralling of events. First, focus and clarity of purpose are achieved by the individual or firm selectively attending to specific aspects of their environment perceived as important, the inclusion/exclusion decisions create a core and a periphery, a figure and a ground (Whitehead, 1929). From this point on the core or figure becomes the focus of attention and what constitutes the periphery or ground is left unattended or overlooked. Attention, conceptual resources and energies are then concentrated on the constituted figure or object of interest to the exclusion of the substantiating surroundings. This is especially so in the case of apparently successful procedures that over time have become imitated and sedimented in beliefs and practices people find comfortable and are reluctant to change. Stability works, so novelty is inherently resisted, notably if its early variants prove frustrating or difficult for new adherents (in creating pan-organisational procedures undermining long established identities, as in evolving the apparatus of European Union law), or don't fit into established values, storylines and myth (strategy advocating concession and withdrawal); as we adapt exploitation drives out exploration (March, 2010: 77-79). The same goes from social studies themselves, as what is constantly sought for are confirmatory data; the process becomes one of self-sealing as the focus remains on the tangible, on what happens rather than what did not happen, on the story of success being told rather than the possible stories of failure left untold. Within the world of strategic choices in businesses the adaptive skew toward specialised attention leads to deep familiarity with a set of objects' attributes and qualities that thereby enables effective exploitation of them as a 'resource' to be used to attain some desired end. With repeated successful exploitation of this resource a 'dominant logic' (Prahalad, 2004) of operation emerges in which an internalised disposition (Bourdieu, 1990: 53) to act in a manner consistent with previous actions is developed; a 'sociality of inertia' ensues. Repeated success breeds continued application and extension of the dominant logic in an increasingly wider variety of external circumstances. As conditions of application and circumstances develop change over time, however, this approach becomes increasingly untenable leading to an overextension or 'overshoot' when the dominant logic is applied inappropriately to what has become a vastly changed set of external circumstances. The eventual result is ineffective optimisation of resources and capabilities of the firm and hence failure ensues.

Robert Burgelman suggests a richer strategic picture, insofar as the emergence of a dominant logic can be absorbed and slackened by a strategic context determination process in which people struggle to resolve the tension and indeterminacy between emerging and often autonomous strategic opportunities and initiatives and existing orthodox firm strategy. People will naturally err toward the provision of suggestions, creating autonomous strategic initiatives, perhaps looking to advance their career, or urging upon themselves new forms of control, and a firm might tolerate this behaviour because of the potential payback in terms of future enhancements in revenue. Here there may be a dominant logic, but it remains accompanied internally by autonomous initiatives within what Burgelman (1991) calls an internal selection environment, an ecology of selection that plays off the wider external environment of competition in which the firm persists. His studies of the Intel Firm suggest the existence of strategic dissonance, where induced strategic activities caught in the slipstream of wider market forces and habit (in Intel's case its being in the business of developing semiconductor memory) come into a kind of dirty air brought about by firstly a sense of lack (its relative lack of capacity to commoditise memory production) and the existence of emerging autonomous strategies (in Intel's case the possibilities in technology of microprocessing). There was a conscious strategic decision to go with microprocessing for personal computers, the strategy explicitly articulating a strategic change that had been occurring within the firm anyhow, yet in this articulation and resultant success came the unintended consequence of co-evolutionary lock-in whereby Intel's future became synonymous with that of the personal computer business, and its investments were continually governed by its undoubted excellence in the microprocessor technologies driving that business. The rules, routines and stories around Intel all gained capital letters, their presence increasingly resistant to the potential novelty associated with speculative initiatives, the autonomous strategies, that whilst they were still existent (for example in computer networking), no longer got strategic buy-in.

This exploitative orientation is so ingrained within much strategic thought that when we apprehend any chaotic or problematic situation the instinctive tendency is to reduce the messiness apprehended to recognisable pre-established categories so that choices can be made and responsive actions taken. Such a tendency to view 'imperfection' in negative terms, as a few strategy scholars are at last beginning to appreciate, may lead us to overlooking its hidden benefits (Abrahamson and Freedman, 2006). With both Prahalad (failure) and Burgelman (success) we have awareness that the periphery matters, the edges count somehow and that strategic practice might attend better to these that currently is the case. The paradox of the failure of success can be attributed to the initial arbitrary decision to ignore and cast aside the 'periphery'. In Prahalad's case this comes about by a fixing on one initially successful set of activities, and in Burgelman's likewise, but here he speculates on the possible reasons for this, mentioning the urge to resolve tensions between emergent autonomous strategies and the firm-wide, dominant strategy. In both sets of studies there is a narrowing effect that is sharpened by initial success, and it is how to avoid this narrowing that we wish to explore here. Strategy tends to avoid in-between places, neither here nor there, places that encourage curiosity and lingering. Ever since Adam Smith (1776/1991:7) warned of the debilitating effects of 'sauntering' as workers drifted from one species of work to the next, the strategic pursuit of economic rents has been characterised by impatience for unitary control and the instrumental exploitation of resources and opportunities through focussed specialisation. What is 'ambiguous and not immediately applicable is discarded' (Bateson, 1994: 31). Prahalad and Burgelman are alive to the dangers of discarding in this way, and they, along with people like Day, Schoemaker, March,

Mintzberg, Orlikowski and Sull, are part of a recent body of business and organisation scholars for whom the inarticulate, formless and 'blurry' periphery is not simply an unwanted and wasteful 'distraction'. There is awareness of the importance of novelty and of how – through mechanisms like organisational slack, the acceptance of managerial hubris and optimism, and toleration for experiment using a calculus of affordable loss and so limiting the 'bet size' – it exposes organisations to new possibilities (March, 2010: 90-98). The concern remains, however, how those who are afforded such organisational largesse actually create novelty. We have argued that the periphery, though cognitively repressed, remains an essential 'other' that has been denied legitimacy, an ignored 'remainder' that 'reminds', an absent presence that haunts its unwarranted exclusion, and that rather than look to business strategy itself to cater for it, we might look beyond what remains an inevitably narrowing practice. In art and artwork we find a tolerance of what strategic practice eschews. Indeed for some artists such as the writer Elias Canetti to tolerate the periphery is a duty (Canetti, 1976: 66) because from it comes the possibility of things always being otherwise; hegemonies of ideas or rulers never last in such an atmosphere. The periphery may be invisible, unseen or absent, but it nevertheless generates tangible effects and consequences. Its presence is detected not through greater focal attention, nor through more thorough information about the object of attention but through a gnawing sense of unease at the periphery of our conscious awareness.

4. Cultivating peripheral awareness

'Picture in your mind's eye the sandbox divided in half with black sand on one side and white sand on the other. We take a child and have him run hundreds of times clockwise in the box until the sand gets mixed and begins to turn gray; after that we have him run anticlockwise, but the result will not be a restoration of the original division but a greater degree of grayness and an increase in entropy'
Robert Smithson, quoted in Art Since 1900, 1966/2004: 505

We have suggested that restoring an exploratory mindset requires a tolerance of vagueness that resists the urge to try and capture and regulate experience using representations, plans and formulae. What we now go on to consider are what we find in art practice to be four interrelated aspects of this exploratory mindset: accepting messiness; encouraging 'eye-wander' and improvisation; taking detours; and avoiding fashion.

(i) Accepting messiness

Within an alternative epistemology amenable to nurturing peripheral awareness, reality does not come to us already-patterned or 'ready-made'. Instead, what we fundamentally perceive prior to conscious conception is

> 'a big blooming buzzing confusion as free from contradiction in its "much-at-onceness" as it is alive and evidently there' (James, 1911/96: 50). It is an 'aboriginal sensible muchness' that 'means nothing and is but what it immediately is' (ibid: 49).

Only by first acknowledging that the primary

condition of human experience is this ambiguous fluxing reality and not a pre-ordered one, only then can we begin fully to appreciate that what appears formed, structured and clearly defined are nothing more than islands of conceptually stabilised social order in a churning sea of chaos. Order, identity and individuality are precariously stabilised achievements wrought through actions and social interactions. Only by starting from the position that ambiguity and vagueness are ineluctably the stuff of real experience can we begin to appreciate the role of focal attention as an effective instrumental selective ordering process that is 'not indispensable to life' (James, 1911/96: 79) but is vital for the systematic and efficient endeavour of living practically. The frustration is that such ordering comes to dominate to such an extent that all life is understood in terms of aims and objectives, a means end rationale that insinuates itself even into happenstance, as though experiences of surprise and accident are to be expunged. This general attitude of impatience or intolerance for the messiness of imperfection is openly confronted in the world of art and literature where vagueness and ambiguity are constantly and controversially invoked to destabilise our natural sense of order and coherence.

Literary works, for instance, are fundamentally 'noisy' channels of communication, and they work, notably shorter stories, by undermining the conceits and grandiosity of large-scale human endeavour; they allow the incidental, accidental and providential back in. They disrupt the pretence that we remain in the middle of our own noise, and yet demand we, writers and readers alike, create meaning as we go, given the text overspills any single way of reading it (Paulson, 1991: 43-44, 48). This emergence is not stipulated; indeed the creative work of the writer is to throw meaning outwards by which momentum it gathers itself. Writers often work with an image first, around which evidence from life and plot lines gather. Seamus Heaney remarks how with Jonathan Swift it was sufficient to have the idea of big and little people, and the rest of Gulliver's Travels came springing forth; the image sends the narrative flying (Heaney, 1995, 51). Even barely literary forms of commentary such as the essay linger more with openings rather than completions. Dr Johnson found essays 'loose sallies of the mind', presumably quietly disdainful of the form, yet loose sallies remain alluring because of their refusal to be balanced and exhaustive, coupled to their willingness to provoke. Their literary quality desists from the gravitas of a thesis, and in doing so compels readers to think onwards rather than be bludgeoned into ascent or refutation. The essay carries with it a curiosity untamed, scurrying after shapes and sounds without blueprint or final score; the essay pullulates, one aspect arises, then another, leaving some to drift away and others to linger. A similar movement can occur in our apprehension of paintings.

To take just one example of how imperfection may be employed to evoke the human sensibilities we can refer to the then controversial paintings of J M W Turner. In the early 1830s, comments in *Blackwoods Magazine*, at that time an influential journal on art, criticised Turner's work as amateurish and completely out of touch with nature as it should be represented. Yet thanks in part to the spirited defence by John Ruskin in

Modern Painters, Turner is hailed today as one of the greatest painters of all time. In five copious volumes (the index amounts to a sixth volume) Ruskin painstakingly showed how works like Turner's were more true to our direct experience of nature. Turner's paintings did not depict so much as exemplify nature as it might be experienced from within. In *Snow Storm*, for instance, he paints a ship called Ariel in a turbulent sea off Harwich. Myth has it that he had strapped himself to Ariel's mast for hours, letting the water and light and sound strip him of his observer's pretence, thrown into the tempest. Excoriated by weather he shows the maelstrom as both compelling and strange, outside of human control, touching a world of gods and spirits from whose breath and mischief come unknowable forms, and we the viewer are with him and the vessel, out at sea, in a storm. The messiness of which he is accused by contemporaries takes us to the edge of a stranger, and strangely compelling place where rational humans matter less, and the often unruly and sublime palpitations of a wider world count matter far more, rich as they are with possibility, both dark and light.

This is just one example of how great painters explore the realm of perception and comprehension by struggling to depict the actual ambiguities and emotional involvement of real experience; the struggle for coherence, the fear, the hesitations, and the sense of being overwhelmed by a larger force beyond human comprehension. The effect of Turner's paintings is to show us that life is never orderly, unambiguous or clear-cut. What are presented to us directly in any real life encounter are precarious, ill-defined and emergent situations with blurry boundaries and shadowy penumbras. And it is from this cacophony of competing stimuli that through each minute and laborious ordering effort, form and orderliness are gradually and painstakingly won.

The love of this richness of unwieldy and detailed variety and vagueness led Ruskin to coin the phrase: the 'noble picturesque'. He described it thus when standing at the foot of a church tower in Calais, France:

'I cannot find words to express the intense pleasure I have always in first finding myself, after some prolonged stay in England, at the foot of the old tower of Calais church. The large neglect, the noble unsightliness of it; the record of its years written so visibly, yet without sign of weakness or decay; its stern wasteness and gloom, eaten away by the Channel winds; and overgrown with the bitter sea grass....its carelessness of what anyone thinks or feels about it...having no beauty or desirableness...yet neither asking for pity...I cannot tell the half of the strange pleasures and thought that come about me at the sight of that old tower...it is the epitome of all that makes the Continent of Europe interesting, as opposed to new countries....We, in England, have our new streets, our new inn, our green shaven lawn, and our piece of ruin emergent from it, - a mere specimen....put on a velvet carpet to be shown...that spirit of trimness. The smooth paving stones; the scraped, hard even rutless roads; the neat gates and plates, and the essence of border and order, and spikiness and spruceness....now I have insisted long on this English character, because I want the reader to understand thoroughly the opposite element...the noble picturesque; its expression, namely of suffering, of poverty,

or decay, nobly endured by unpretending strength of heart. Nor only unpretending, but unconscious…the picturesqueness is in the unconscious suffering' (John Ruskin, *Modern Painters*, Vol. 4: 6.15)

For Ruskin, it is the irregularity and variety that characterises a painting's line, lighting, colour and composition and which, thereby, creates the 'picturesque' effect. Thus a broken stone

'has necessarily more various forms in it than a whole one; a bent roof has more curves in it than a straight one; every excrescence or cleft involves some additional complexity of light and shade, and every stain of moss on eaves or wall adds to the delightfulness of colour' (Ruskin, *Modern Painters*, Vol. 4: 6.15).

This ability to appreciate the subtle effects of inarticulate, hidden or hesitant forms on the overall impression is what we mean here by peripheral awareness. Much like Ruskin's observations, the works of many artists and writers display richness and variety through struggles with representation and expression. For them, the seemingly chaotic and random scribbles go somewhere; indeed working against accident, reticence and hesitation go a long way towards producing the dramatic artistic effect in a piece of work such as Turner's; messiness is not something simply to be accepted, but embraced.

(ii) Encouraging 'eye-wander' and improvisation

Embracing and working with messiness requires skills in the use of materials and expression that are often invisible to observers. Hence, those little

'strokes and arabesques down to the same grey shading or to the continuous outline of real objects' (Ehrenzweig, 1965: 30)

…may remain unseen, yet they nevertheless exert great influence on our perception.

'I refer to the minute, almost microscopic, scribbles which make up the technique of a great draftsman or the brushwork of a great painter' (Ehrenzweig, 1965: 29).

Much of the richness of the formed images and ideas that attracts our immediate attention derives from the invisible and seemingly random strokes and scribbles that are generally treated as aberrations or imperfections by the uneducated eye and are not usually considered important enough to warrant our scrutiny and attention.

However, at an unconscious level, these seemingly unimportant peripheral aspects are taken in by a subsidiary awareness through a process called 'eye-wander' (Read, 'Art and Industry', in Ehrenzweig, 1965: 22) in which attention is scattered to the edges. Many sculptors for example find that it is not features such as the chin or eyes alone that render a face, but what they glimpse as going on in between the features, the movement between the eyes and forehead for example, the intensity or flatness or serpentine drift of momentary frowns that cannot be directly looked for, only awaited. This eye-wander of the artist is exemplified in the everyday by occasional experience such as absent-mindedly browsing in shops whilst waiting for someone or something to happen. It is undirected, scattered attention that sub-consciously glides over familiar outlines and details and it is during these moments of non-purposeful attention that we, in fact, become much more observant and 'in-tune' with our surroundings. There is a certain uncontaminated 'purity' in our seeing in which we appear to loose ourselves amongst our objects of attention. These are moments of un-evaluative directness of vision in which figure and ground are held together in an instantaneous act of comprehension that Ruskin calls 'the innocence of the eye'; an un-gilded perception of things

> 'merely as such, without consciousness of what they signify, – as a blind man would see them if suddenly gifted with sight' (Ruskin, Works, Vol. 15: 27).

Ehrenzweig (1965, 1967) argues that it is actually possible through disciplined application and training to equip ourselves with the capacity to hold both figure and ground together in a unitary act of comprehension and this is what marks out the truly accomplished artists and musicians. So eye wander becomes a kind of dedicated skill.

In the case of music, for instance, the surface gestalt figure is typically represented by the melody that draws our conscious awareness and keeps it as the focus of attention. The accompaniment serves only as a background and is not as 'ear-catching' as the main melody itself. The serious music student, however, gradually realises that what is called the 'accompaniment' really consists of several voices which

> 'form more or less continuous melodies in their own right' (Ehrenzweig, 1965: 41).

The pupil's attention is thus directed away from an exclusive concentration on the main melody and made to follow simultaneously the several competing melodies unfolding at the same time in order truly to begin to appreciate the rich polyphonic character of music. Instead of focussing singularly on the melody the student is now able to scatter his/her attention and concurrently follow multiple potential lines of development so that he/she is able to

> 'oscillate freely between focused and unfocused states, now focusing precisely on the solid vertical sounds of chords, now emptying his attention so that he can comprehend the loose, transparent web of polyphonic voices in their entirety' (Ehrenzweig, 1967: 27).

The same kind of wandering applies in fine art as it does music. Here, like the student of music, the student of art learns to work deliberately against the gestalt principle by resisting actively the premature closure afforded by the perceptual registering of familiar form:

> 'When the art-school student takes up drawing he is made to watch not only the outline of the object he draws (the figure of the gestalt), but also the negative forms which the figure cuts out from the background' (Ehrenzweig, 1965: 28).

In other words, like in music, art students are taught to oscillate perceptually between the figure and the unfolding of the negative form as its outline emerges at the tip of the pencil. They are taught to attend to the varied minute combination of these invisible negative strokes that will make for a great improvement in the general impression of the formed figure.

This oscillation and eye wander can also be encouraged by posing alternate visual frames or musical structures not as alternative orthodoxies, but issued simply as challenges. It was in this spirit that the Bauhaus artists began to associate certain colours with certain basic geometric shapes and that Arnold Schoenberg's devised his 12 tone musical system, for example. Much like Wittgenstein's system of logic in his *Tractatus*, these new systems upset habitual patterns and forms in order to compel people into the task of creating themselves anew, using new logics, but never simply to replace one logic with another (this was Wittgenstein's gripe against logical positivism; they were looking to use his *Tractatus* to help assert a new, analytic orthodoxy, when he was trying to show the limits of any logical system) (Janik and Toulmin, 1973). In this vein people such as Klee and Schoenberg, like Wittgenstein, understood themselves as heirs to a tradition – of classical colour theory and 7 tone systems – but ones who remained sensitive to how easily orthodox forms collapse into dogma (as happened when Bauhaus students thoughtlessly copied yellow triangles, red squares and blue circles or Schoenberg's 'followers' began to insist 12-tone music conform to technical regularities). Kandinsky – whose scheme it was, thinking the circle cosmic, centripetal and absorbent and hence blue – was not identifying a necessary relationship but provoking thoughts concerning the psychology of colour, thoughts that his peers at the Bauhaus like Paul Klee would readily upset with quips, for example whether a student ought be penalised for having a yellow yolk in her image of an egg. Klee, like Kandinsky, was always urging his work to communicate the ineffable and unravel the already know; the real was forever on the move and the formalities of art are equally restless, touching on the edge of the in-between (*eine Zwischenwelt*). Likewise, Schoenberg's struggle with 12-tone was to show that the orderly forms of composition could always be taught and understood otherwise, and that from this wandering endeavour creative insight ensued.

At its most minimal this wandering amidst and between forms is found through improvisation; an experience the musician Keith Jarrett (Rüedi, 1996: 29) describes thus:

'I concentrate on myself and not on the music; my music develops independently. I just try to avoid the easy way out. I concentrate on not doing things. That's a relatively new experience. The limitation, the wall that I still had to face not too long ago, was that I was completely open so that I didn't even exercise any negative control. First I tried to think of all the things I wanted to play. It didn't work: I could only do things that had already happened. Or more precisely, I was trying to do two things at once – to avoid doing something I'd done before, and to invent something new. Until I found out that it was only a matter of making sure that there was some free space for the music. That's what I had to focus on. When you eliminate all patterns and clichés, you suddenly come up with some rewarding surprises. Something incredible happens almost by itself. I just think of what I don't want to do.'

So in performing Jarrett tries to remove himself from the barrage of experience that presses in – the recommendations, styles, exhortations, plaudits, critiques, models and explanations that aim to exteriorise and formalise. What remains is simply a set of oscillating forces evolving irreversibly through improvisation. The musician's job here is to recognise but reach beyond the 'striated' spaces of taught forms to what Gilles Deleuze and Felix Guattari call the 'smooth' spaces beyond. In defining this free space some form of delineation is going on, but as Jarrett intimates, it is largely a negative one – a clearing out rather than the occupation of a pre-determined idea or structure or set of endings.

This elusive quality to Jarrett's art is also shared by the audience. Just as Jarrett's musical form evolves complicitly with the forces by which it is brought about, so too does the audience's response. Alexander Nehamas (2001) argues that it is the preservation of this personal involvement that is critical to judgements of taste. There is no right way to understand art because whilst it is a judgement (in other words it requires awareness of, and effort within, an established way of doing things), it is not a judgement that arises as a conclusion from engaging with an object. The aesthetic experience is one of anticipation. It is a direct engagement with form, colour and sound that provokes an expectation, excitement. To try and interfere with this experience by recommending one mode of engagement above another, or to generalise about the profundity of one art form or piece above another, or to insist on an exhaustive definition of a piece of art, is to undermine this personal involvement and the individuality of style it encourages (Nehamas, 2001). The piece no longer leads anywhere. So in blocking out what his pieces are not, Jarrett is encouraging this sense of personal engagement – the significance is shareable, but its meaning is always unfinished. Peripheral awareness involves a subliminal sensitivity to the hesitant details of emergence that is generally overlooked by the untrained eye. In both instances of music and art training what is developed is the capacity for a kind of 'scattered' or dispersed attention that is able to follow multiple lines of possibilities of development without the compulsion to achieve closure prematurely.

(iii) Taking detours
Homer's Book XXIII of the Iliad begins with an account of a chariot race pitting a young Antiochus, son of Nestor the Sage, against Menelaus, king of Sparta. Unfortunately, although the boy is very skilled, his horses are not as fast as those pulling royal blood. The young man appears bound to lose. Placed at a disadvantage, Antiochus remembers his father words: 'It is through *metis* rather than through strength that the wood-cutter shows his worth. It is through *metis* that the helmsman guides the speeding vessel over the wine-dark sea despite the wind. It is through *metis* that the charioteer triumphs over his rivals'. Heedful of these comments, the young man takes advantage of a sudden narrowing of the track, which had been worn away by storm rains the night before, and drives his chariot obliquely across and in front Menelaus' team. The manoeuvre takes his adversary by surprise forcing him to rein in his horses, whereupon, seeing the King's momentary disarray, Antiochus gains the advantage necessary to outstrip him and win the race. (Detienne and Vernant, 1978: 12).

This little episode shows what might be meant by a detour, in this case a literal, though short, subtle and sleight one. Nestor reminds his son of *metis*, a cultivated sensitivity and form of direct skill particularly attuned to emerging opportunities arising from unfolding local circumstances. Detienne and Vernant (1978) equate *metis* with 'cunning intelligence', alertness to the possible advantages afforded by local situations whereby seemingly unfavourable circumstances might still yield favourable outcomes. *Metis* operates on the unexpressed premise that both reality and language cannot be understood (or manipulated) in straightforward means-end terms but must be approached by 'subtlety, indirection, and even cunning' (Raphals, 1992: 5). It is, therefore, tempting, but misleading, to reduce *metic* intelligence to "know-how" knowledge. Nor is metic intelligence a conscious and deliberate, and reflective form of knowing. Rather, contrary to Baumard's (1999) notion of *metis* as 'conjectural knowledge' which implies intention and forethought, *metic* intelligence is a kind of unique and often fleeting orientation toward one's environment from which a form of distinction-in-relief is achieved. This environment is both natural and material (as in the horse-stabelled dirt racing track) and cultural, what Bourdieu (1990: 53) calls habitus, a style, demeanour, and culturally-mediated set of predispositions (the king's assumed prowess awaiting upset) to which the exponent of *metis* belongs (Antiochus is within the race, and aware and respectful of Menelaus' elevation) and which nevertheless he is able to explore and traduce in some small way.

What all this implies is that beneath the aura of human rationality, intention and purposefulness, as biological organisms humans have also acquired a survivalist legacy for practical 'mindless' coping in the course of evolution that according to Detienne and Vernant has remained theoretically unexamined since the time of the ancient Greeks. That such *metic* qualities are more universal than generally known has led Michel de Certeau to observe that they:

'... *correspond to an ageless art which has not only persisted through the institutions of successive political orders but...presents in fact a curious analogy, and a sort of immemorial link, to the simulations, tricks, and disguises that certain fish or plants execute with extraordinary virtuosity...They [the qualities] maintain formal continuities and the permanence of a memory without language, from the depths of the oceans to the streets of our great cities'* (de Certeau, 1984: 40).

Metis is a kind of vague peripheral knowing involving a 'memory without language' or representation, a tolerance of realities that do not conform with our stable presumptions about truth, an admission of myth and contradiction in which all things carry with them enigmas through their lives; like Apollo, the god with whom mortals might converse, things are both dark and yet shine, they are pestilent then pure, straight becoming crooked. *Metis* evokes this enigma, cunning and innocence, demur and brilliant, and moral insofar as it is forever sensitive to the winsome demands of appropriateness; there is a tolerance of opposites that only ever make themselves apparent in relation to one another, entwined as contraries and never split.

Being basic, something we all might find, *metis* finds itself in the most mundane of activities: the playing and mastery of a variety of sports, and in combination games like crosswords, chess, or even mahjong and in the reading of crime novels. In all such instances the player, or reader, cultivates a corner-of-the-eye awareness of the goings on. He/she has to make a decision, on the hoof, based on changing circumstances and amidst the noisiness of an inadequacy of information and hence to rely on his/her subsidiary awareness and unconscious scanning to grasp what is going on beyond the main focus of attention. There are, however, significant differences in extent of creative exploration associated with each of the combination games previously listed beginning from the more predictable structure represented by the crossword puzzles, to more complex combination games like chess and much more open-ended ones like the Chinese game Go (Wei Chi).

In some ways a crossword puzzle represents an appropriate metaphor for the kind of traditional business planning mode that is appropriate in relatively stable business circumstances where the influencing factors are fixed and elements of variability are relatively unchanging, limited and definable. There is an in-built assumption that situations, and the significance and value of each puzzle piece (in this case the letters, or in the case of business planning the factor variables) do not materially change during the period of analysis. There are appropriate answers, and the clues function as pieces of a jigsaw, only here the game is constructing the pieces rather than just recognising the pattern of the arrangement. T E Hulme, the philosopher and poet, contrasts the doing of a jigsaw with the doing of a painting. The jigsaw, like the crossword, has a determined end and the identification of discrete elements ordered in such a way that they fit can be hastened or interrupted without contaminating the end image, which retains its uniformity, and which allows for a perspective upon the final image. A painting in contrast emerges irreversibly in which event any contraction or slowing of creative activity would fundamentally alter the image. Moreover, there is no distancing, the painting is inseparable from the process of its creation; it ripens. The tendency then to see a painting as an object, classified according to authorship, genre and location is a denuding one if in this we forget its being alive, unfolding in the moments of its production (including how the painting continues unfolding, in its being viewed, used). A crossword sits somewhere in between, the slowing or hastening of the experience of constructing the answers matters, or can do, but whatever the idiosyncrasy of the ripening, it culminates in the same place, whereas the painting culminates only in the process of painting itself. Even chess, a game that more closely evokes such ripening, and which is continually associated with business strategy, retains a concern with the arrangement, coding and decoding of a restrictive space in order to achieve overall mastery and control. There are clear rules of engagement and the status of each piece is well-defined hierarchically. The object is conquest and subjugation of the opponent. Chess is the ultimate example of strategic positioning in business environmental manoeuvres; and chess pieces and boards are often found illustrating company reports and strategy textbooks. Chess is linear, focused and mission-led. It relies upon a precise logic of focused attention, clear judgement, structured reasoning and controlled action.

The playing of Go, on the other hand, is open-ended and does not, as of the present, lend itself to the kind of programming currently attainable in chess. Like chess, Go is also played on a board but its units are simple pellets or discs, anonymous arithmetic units without any privileged status and that only have a collective function. Go pieces have only extrinsic relationships and exist within a nebula or constellation where they fulfil functions of

> 'insertion or situation, such as bordering, encircling, shattering' (Deleuze and Guattari, 1988: 353).

Playing Go is like going to war without battle lines, with neither direct confrontations nor decisive retreats; the attacks are sporadic and can come from any direction. In Go small, seemingly insignificant moves, like the fine strokes of a painting in art, can have surprisingly dramatic cumulative effects and consequences. Playing Go is a matter of holding space, of

> 'maintaining the possibility of springing up at any point' (Deleuze and Guattari, 1988: 353).

In chess victory and defeat are clear and decisive. It is all or nothing. In Go you 'win' by occupying more territory. Your adversary may be weakened but not totally destroyed. Go is the logic of strategic thinkers who have the capacity to 'hold space' and to allow the possibilities that come with the vagueness, ambiguity and fluidity of experience to reach maturation.

A similar holding of space can occur within a good crime novel; the reader is expectant of some form of proper structuring, but also of being toyed with, left in suspense right until the end, or sometimes even then the culprit is never identified and the reader left hanging, questioning their own expectations. The crime novel appeals more through the skill of its construction than by its content or outcome. The crime writer P D James remarks on how many of her plots find the police trapped into a focal way of thinking. They think they know who committed the crime, either because of obvious evidential trails, or because their training invokes a typification of the criminal and they limit their search to examples of this known and knowable form. Forced into wearing blinkers, the police characters have their attention canalled along clear plot lines, they are pitched toward the finishing line of probable resolution, whilst among the periphery lurks the real source of despair, revenge, madness or malevolence, unseen until let upon the scene in dragon-like twists. Against this main plot others might be then attached, like tributaries that lend the story a complexity suspense and intrigue. The technique is one of deliberate ambiguity. A good crime novelist never ever allows the clues he/she surreptitiously inserts ever so discretely for the reader to narrow down prematurely so that the culprit can be identified early on. The police may be diverted into a singular way of thinking, or some of the more orthodox police, but not always the reader, aware that there are clues to things being otherwise, but unsure where because they have been kept discrete, disconnected and as ambiguous as possible. As this chaotic complex of information mounts in the reader's mind the reader has to bear the tension and suspense only because he/she assumes that, in the end, all will fall into an orderly and logical pattern. The final twist comes when the reader, as well as most of the characters, are invariably surprised or taken aback by whomever the culprit turns out to be. Reading back and the few snippets that were smuggled unnoticed under a dazzling camouflage of insignificant details are triumphantly dragged out and delivered as the outcome of the unfolding story.

Writing a really good crime novel is no mean achievement since it requires several sub-themes and hence several series of accompanying clues to be kept running simultaneously much like the polyphonic character of music. The reader is not allowed to concentrate on the development of a singular plot. Instead there are multiple possible lines of development and the reader's attention is constantly diverted from one possibility to another. He/she follows the

> *'unfolding of the whole intentionally incoherent and ambiguous story in a state of diffused attention with one or the other possibility dimly flickering and extinguishing again, but never attracting attention exclusively'* (Ehrenzweig, 1965: 44).

The crime novel technique is a supreme example of a peripheral logic and a valuable guide on how to develop peripheral awareness. Learning to develop peripheral awareness is learning to resist the seductions of premature closure and the importance of taking detours.

(iv) Avoiding generalising fashion

Related to messiness, eye wander and detour comes the avoidance of fashion or fad. Strategy thinking, certainly in business and management studies, is bedevilled with the latest idea being THE idea, so much so that it is the THE that seems to matter, rather than any longer term awareness of the efficacy of the idea or awareness of the experience to which the idea might apply. The avoidance of fashion is not an original recommendation, and as a recommendation it remains steeped in its own irony, yet concern with avoiding what John Stuart Mill called 'the ape like quality of imitation' befalls and remains with many artists and writers for whom it is the struggle in securing one's own sense of voice, rather than any threshold of attainment, that counts. John Constable, for whom outdoor oil sketching and drawing, followed by numerous, repetitious studio sketching, informed his entire landscape painting practice. So much so that the final paintings were often regarded as inferior to the sketches, being an admission, as they were, of an end point, a culmination of the shifting melee of hints, gestures and suggestions rendered incomplete by the repetitive brushwork and subject matter rendered anew. What is found in his sketches is always suggestive rather than definitive, nothing is fixed and there is no fixing of the viewer's attention, meaning is fleeting, dissolved in frayed edges, suggestive spaces and the shifting play of repetition as each sketch plays on the refrains set into being by previous attempts. The sketch avoided the kind of polished, or mannered, affectation of painters who look to abstracting styles rather than restless nature. The seduction of manner comes from its plausibility, its being an imitation of tradition, a confirmation of the style and achievement of others which promises the short road to recognition and settlement. For Constable to be a mannerist was not to be an artist at all, but a purveyor of abstract fashion, any awareness of nature was always being subsumed by attention to the goal, the whole understood as an idea, an accomplishment, an ending that others would understand easily, comfortably. The sketch avers from such, exposing the artist and viewer to inimitable nature in whose living is learnt the irrepressibility of things. In nature…

"no two days are alike, nor even two hours; neither were there ever two leaves of a tree alike since the creation of the world" (Constable, 1835/1951: 273).

The sketch renders impressions that are wrought through long apprenticeship with the world and its ways rather than with the far more accessible, apparent and uniform ways of fashion. For Constable many painters were tempted by the flavour of fashion, the instant hit of success found in the neat, short cuts to recognition; a rapid assimilation of taste in whose emptying reflux the artist was ground and polished into smooth acceptability. The idea of the whole had seduced and then corralled the artist who became nothing more than a vessel for prevailing manners, animated by a fear of becoming yesterday's man.

A similar qualm befell the imagist poet and translator Ezra Pound amongst whose admonishing 'Don'ts' written for other poets we find:

"Don't allow "influence" to mean merely that you mop up the particular decorative vocabulary of some one or two poets whom you happen to admire" and

"Use no superfluous word, no adjective, which does not reveal something" (quoted in Carr, 2009, 540),

and elsewhere, and to the reader rather than writer of poems this time:

"The only MUST being that the reader absolutely must NOT be fooled by say Baldwin [British Prime minister], or newspapers run exclusively by people enjoying the tyrannous privilege that accrues to the ownership of five million dollars" (Pound, 1947, 52).

The job of the poet was to present images, not replicate idioms, and the image was an intellectual and emotional complex frozen in a moment of time out of which freezing we experience the shimmering, self-sustaining movement of things, their intense, overflowing possibility. This transience was of a different quality from the movement of fashion where no sooner was something rendered and touched in use it was dissolving in its own obsolescence. Imagists find movement in fixing things, live with it as an image and you find things that are always on the cusp of their own ending, things whose resonance lies less with their stable distinctiveness than with their perilous potentiality. These images are concentrated, hard, resisting styles and manners in order to get at experience. Pound wrote prompted by the everyday experience of leaving a Paris Metro station, spending months paring down poetic lines until he arrived at this:

The apparition   of these faces   in the crowd:

Petals   on a wet, black   bough.

The experience was of jostling in the crowd, watching faces, one then the next, each beautiful, and the image arose in words and spatial pauses from his having cast himself into a vein of thought in which things we both inward and outward, unique and yet belonging in otherness, always underway with movement that bide with rather than against time, and in this biding lies a stillness into which they pass away (Heaney, 2007, 24, also in Carr, 2009, 547)

There is in both Constable and Pound a focal intensity, a willingness to concentrate to the exclusion of other phenomena, yet they remain acutely sensitive to how the emerging images, whether blousy Romanticism or austere classicism, carry a bluntness and directness that cares little for opinion, and much for the veracity of experience. In both, though Pound might baulk at such, there appears 'negative capability'. As originally coined by the poet John Keats in a letter sent to his brother over Christmas, 1817 (1817/2002: 60-61), negative capability is:

> *'when a man is capable of being in uncertainties, mysteries, doubts, without any irritable reaching after fact and reason.'*

The reaching after fact and reason is an excuse to end the struggle for meaning, to seek refuge in abstractions that far from being distilled from life, remove you from it. In strategy the term capability is generally associated with the positive ability to act, to intervene with confidence; to be notable in one's capacity to bring about desired outcomes, so much so that the idea of a negative capability appears somewhat paradoxical. The word 'capability', however, actually derives from the Latin root *capabilis*, meaning 'able to hold' or 'to contain'. Negative capability thus implies containment and the capacity to withstand and endure rather than the capacity for active intervention: the cultivated resilience to resist premature closure in the face of vagueness, uncertainty and equivocality. It evokes both the persistence of one who perceives things, who witnesses changes because of their being there, and the reticence of one for whom the world is something other than her world and whose own world is something more than the merely visible and stable. Such containment implies suspending judgement, dispersing attention, and resisting the tendency to gravitate all-too-quickly towards recognisable forms of comprehension associated with positive capabilities, whether of the intellect or of skilful habit.

Conclusion

> *'Does not detour – which is anything but gratuitous – exert a certain power, which is all the more forceful for its discretion?'*
> (François Jullien, Detour and Access, 2000: 7).

The rational, strategic mind with its demand for precision and clarity and its focus on immediate, local causality, visible material outcomes and end-states finds it difficult to understand how it is possible that major transformations can be brought about by sometimes seemingly insignificant events occurring remotely or peripherally both in space and time. Chaos and complexity theories now, however, reveal the possibilities of what is popularly called the 'butterfly effect' where small, seemingly inconsequential events occurring often unnoticed at a periphery can trigger major catastrophes. The possibilities of non-local causality are forcing us to re-evaluate our understanding of the traditional relationship between cause and effect and to expand our awareness by looking further afield for causal connections, tenuous though they may sometimes appear to be. What we have argued for in this chapter is the value of peripheral awareness that sensitises us to such peripheral events and that resists the urge prematurely to seek conceptual closure by attending to and tracing more closely the lines of emergence of a phenomenon. That which is vague and unclear must be retained *'taken in with peripheral vision for possible later clarification...Beyond the denotations lie unexplored connotations and analogies'* (Bateson, 1994: 31).

This was something intuitively understood by Steve Jobs; a temporary detour can oftentimes enable great access and more efficacious exploitation (Jullien, 2000).

Thus the chapter is its own detour into literature, art, music, the playing of combination games, and mythology. It is an attempt to explore and elaborate upon the elusive nature of the periphery and the enigmatic qualities of peripheral awareness. Rather than approach the periphery 'frontally' and 'focally' we argue that to do justice to the periphery we must approach it, on its own terms, with stealth. Our contention is that a more elliptical, indirect and 'circuitous' approach is required to develop a better appreciation of this 'primitive' and pre-linguistic form of vague knowing at the 'corners-of-our-eyes'. What we have argued is that peripheral awareness is inextricably linked to the capacity for thinking strategically but that strategy is too often fixated on what can be made focal as an object of attention. Because we are culturally programmed to develop and exploit our focal vision and not our peripheral vision we often miss significant goings-on that take place on the margins of awareness and fail to grasp the unfolding minutiae of event-situations. To shift our attention away from focal awareness we must attend to the emerging 'negative' form generated by focal attention and the deep unconscious structure associated with it. Sensitivity to such deep structures can be cultivated systematically through a variety of ways of which we have discussed four: absorbing the noble-picturesque; encouraging 'eye wander'; taking detours through *metis*; and avoiding fashion. In developing peripheral awareness we have suggested the cultivation of negative capability whereby strategists are able to cope with vagaries and uncertainties, working with them through a re-education of attention in which wandering, experiment and curiosity are valued as much as goal setting and clarifying. Art and the humanities have long understood the importance of cultivating this awareness to shape our focal attention and comprehension in ways that do not foreclose us from other possibilities. Much in the way of painting, writing and even the playing of games is designed to refuse us the comfort of clear visible and recognisable forms and to immerse us in vagueness and ambiguity; a scattering of attention that blur lines of confrontation, level out hierarchical differences and confuse simple cause and effect thinking. The exemplary cases are found in great works of literature, art, poetry and music that plumb the depths of human consciousness and provide us with profound glimpses of the inherently open-ended and creative nature of the world, and of ourselves as part of that world. It is within these works and responses to them that we feel much can be gained in effecting strategies that allow us to live well rather than simply live predictably.

The subject of this chapter is knowledge. The subject of 'Organisational knowledge' has become a major field of inquiry in the study of organisations. The author's context here however is design, and what 'design thinking' and the design process can teach us about knowledge in organisations. The term 'design' of course can apply to just about anything. Here it refers to the work of the professional designer of products and services, whose methods involve productive forms of 'knowledge sharing'. The point of the chapter is to show us that knowledge in organisations is a potent force and can be used in unexpected ways. Producing, using and sharing knowledge is a complex activity, much of it usually hidden from view and ill-understood. However, in this chapter we find that knowledge sharing can form the dynamic centre of organisational life.

The field of 'design thinking' is an effective means of 'de-familiarisation' for an organisation – making what is commonplace, or taken as 'given', something that provokes a shift in out cognitive habits, a re-orientation of vision, a re-conceptualisation of the overlooked. Design thinking enables us to re-focus on what has been marginalised from consciousness – sources of capital, new means of value-creation, and forms of productive knowledge-exchange. Within every organisation and every business a 'design process' is at work. This guarantees nothing, unless that process is made reflexive and responsive to broader strategic goals.

Thinking through Design – Processes and Tools for Knowledge Sharing in Organisations

Bob Robertson

Knowledge sharing should be a potent and creative element in organisations. In this chapter I will outline how 'design' can teach us about knowledge sharing and its creative power. Design and the design process should for this reason be central to organisational life. In focusing our attention on the dynamics of the design process, we can unfold new possibilities for creating and sharing knowledge. There are various ways of designing transformative or innovative products and services, but not all such products or services exceed the needs of people and hold out the possibility of extending across global, local and individual cultural domains. 'Knowledge sharing' calls for a new and expanded design process end point – and we can unfold this possibility by discovering the thinking processes and tools that help us share what we know.

This raises some immediate questions – what forms of knowledge resource can be developed and exchanged between people in organisations? Consultant Ross Dawson (2000) observed that a knowledge resource is any form of intellectual or knowledge capital – human capital (skills and knowledge), structural capital (processes and systems) or relationship capital (trust and understanding) – that is mutually created and shared, especially by people who work in a collaborative way. These areas of knowledge capital are the key resources that drive the design process.

There now exists a substantial amount of writing and research concerning the ways in which we create and share knowledge. Louis Stokes and Robert Logan (2004) in the introduction of *Collaborate to Compete: Driving Profitability in the Knowledge Economy*, discuss the way collaborative strategy leads to better management of an organisation's knowledge resources and more effective knowledge creation. The form of collaborative strategy they discuss allows an organisation to access the potential of each and every individual's knowledge and experience in order to create new knowledge.

What do we know about knowledge?

Knowledge has been described and defined in many ways. It has been described as the capacity to act effectively; as information encapsulated with sufficient intelligence to be relevant, insightful and actionable.

The knowledge that we create and share can be defined in terms of two categories: *explicit knowledge* and *tacit knowledge*. Ross Dawson (2000) describes explicit knowledge as that which we can express to others, and tacit knowledge as the rest of our knowledge. Tacit or 'internalised' knowledge is the knowledge that a person acquires through study, socialisation and practice, and must be given an explicit externalised form in order for another person to assimilate it.

Consider the following model, which attempts to show the dynamic relationship between these two knowledge forms:

There is an important sense in which knowledge is particular to people, and knowledge sharing skills represent particularly 'human' abilities. If we wish to tap into the rich resources that people possess, and share our competencies with others, we must apply our studying, socialising and practicing skills in order to make both the process of knowledge exchange and the products of this exchange understandable for people.

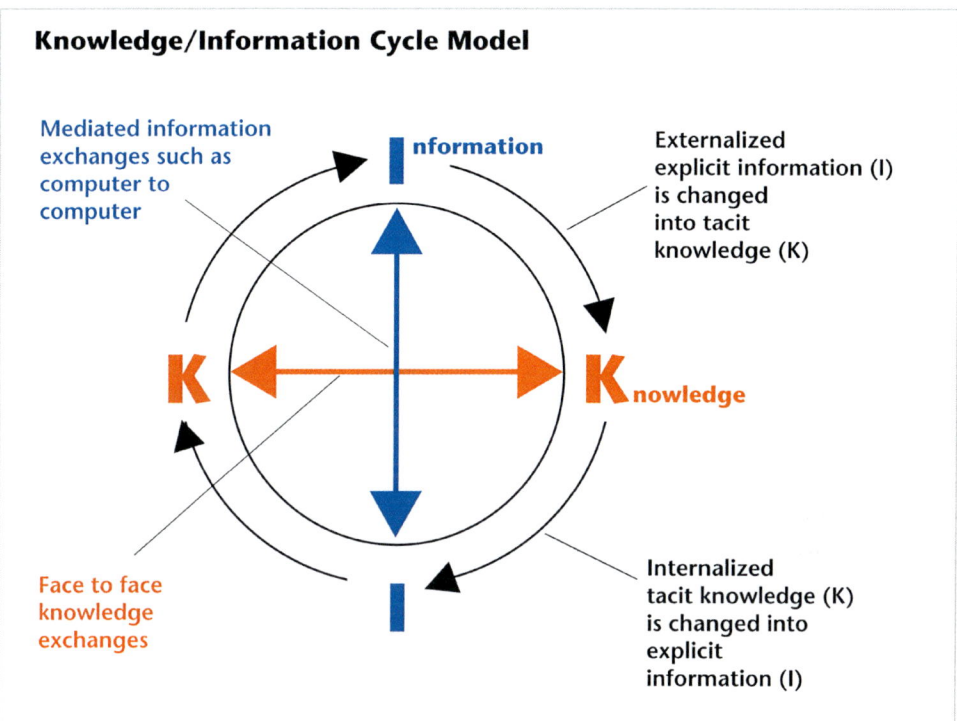

Figure 1: *Source: adapted from Ross Dawson et.al.*

What is design?

Design epistemology, or the philosophy of knowledge supporting the design process, is grounded in the dynamics of knowledge-sharing. Gordon Rowland (2003) has the following insight on the connection between design and knowledge:

> 'Design epistemology thus defines knowledge in a way that is consistent with social constructivism – as intentionally shared meaning – but leaves open the possibility of forms of knowledge being separated from humans and embedded in the artificial world as an affordance for human action'.

Few would deny the extent of the impact of design on our daily lives. Everything from the tools we use to make our homes and businesses work better, to the clothes we wear and the environments that we live and work in are a product of some form of design. Design, before it becomes a tangible product or service, is the very process of creation and decision-making that supports the transformation of outcomes to meet the needs of people. However, Richard Buchanan (1995), a leader in design thinking, has used the word 'product' to describe the outcomes of design, even though they may be intangible. He describes these products as communicated messages, organised activities and services, and complex systems and environments that support how we live, learn, work and play. In this paper I am also using the term 'product' to identify the broad spectrum of design outcome, tangible and intangible.

What is design thinking?

When we 'design' we use a certain creativity and decision-making process in order to make products for people. When we explore the will, the intention, imagination, judgment, and composition within a design context, we are engaged in a process that can create new 'realities'. Our understanding of reality is formed by our subjective encounters of the objective environment. These new realities may be either existing products that are being developed, extending the concept of that object, or unique products that are without precedent, transforming the concept of that object into something quite different. The design process provides a model to help us create new realities, new relations between us as subject beings with an objective world. Design thinking is the integrative thinking that drives the design process.

A design process model represents a prime example of the kind of modal, integrative thinking that was promoted by the mathematician and philosopher Charles Sanders Peirce. Modal thinking, for Peirce, had immediate value if models could be continually improved upon and help us to refine our current ways of thinking.

SECTION 1: DESIGN INTELLIGENCE

Knowledge and information about a product or activity is gathered so that the design process can begin. Formative research methods are sometimes used during this phase. Research methods employed may

Figure 2: *Diagram: Bob Robertson*

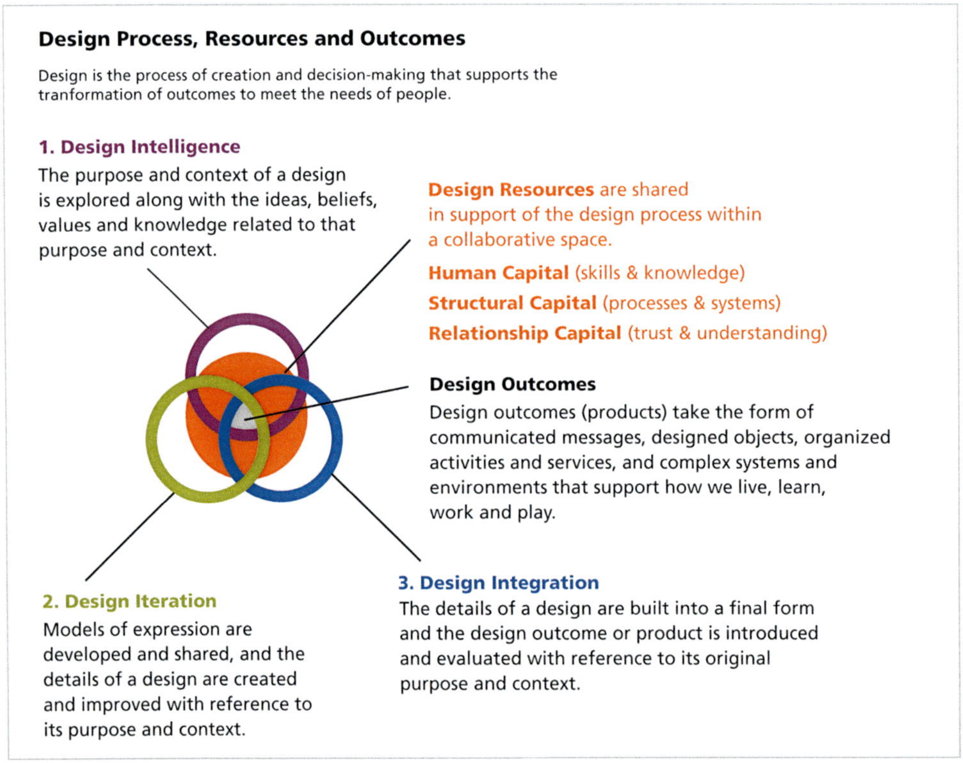

Design Process, Resources and Outcomes

Design is the process of creation and decision-making that supports the tranformation of outcomes to meet the needs of people.

1. Design Intelligence
The purpose and context of a design is explored along with the ideas, beliefs, values and knowledge related to that purpose and context.

Design Resources are shared in support of the design process within a collaborative space.

Human Capital (skills & knowledge)
Structural Capital (processes & systems)
Relationship Capital (trust & understanding)

Design Outcomes
Design outcomes (products) take the form of communicated messages, designed objects, organized activities and services, and complex systems and environments that support how we live, learn, work and play.

2. Design Iteration
Models of expression are developed and shared, and the details of a design are created and improved with reference to its purpose and context.

3. Design Integration
The details of a design are built into a final form and the design outcome or product is introduced and evaluated with reference to its original purpose and context.

include everything from the collection of hard data and materials to the social/cultural recording of how people interact with a product or service. The information collected is sometimes placed within contextual frameworks, and these frameworks or typologies allow collaborators to compare the features of a product and its requirements. The design intelligence phase is about collecting information and knowledge in order to explore the context of a product and how the features of a product relate to its purpose and to the experiences of people.

The contextual framework example introduced here compares design resources and the outcomes of an Enterprise X development overview in order to show the relationship between forms of knowledge capital and the features that we might design into a product.

In this phase of the design process it is also important to investigate and recognise existing or anticipated patterns of use related to a product. The knowledge gained here can help us to understand how people will experience and use a product. Pattern recognition is a skill that helps us to design new products and improve existing products. The design intelligence phase of the process includes bringing the ideas, beliefs, values and knowledge pertaining to a product into focus. Ideas, beliefs, values and knowledge are features of what we call 'culture'. Considering these features of culture can help to generate products that connect to the values and to the needs of particular people.

Culture also has active dimensions that can be described. David Snowden (2002) has described what are, for him, the two dimensions of culture – culture is both a socio-cultural system and an ideational-cultural system. The socio-cultural system dimension encompasses the patterns of resource use, the tools and the conventions that we use to create communities. These patterns are explicit, knowable and teachable. The ideational-cultural system dimension deals with the more tacit, tribal and fluid aspects of culture. These aspects of culture might appear to be more assimilated

Figure 3: *Diagram: Bob Robertson*

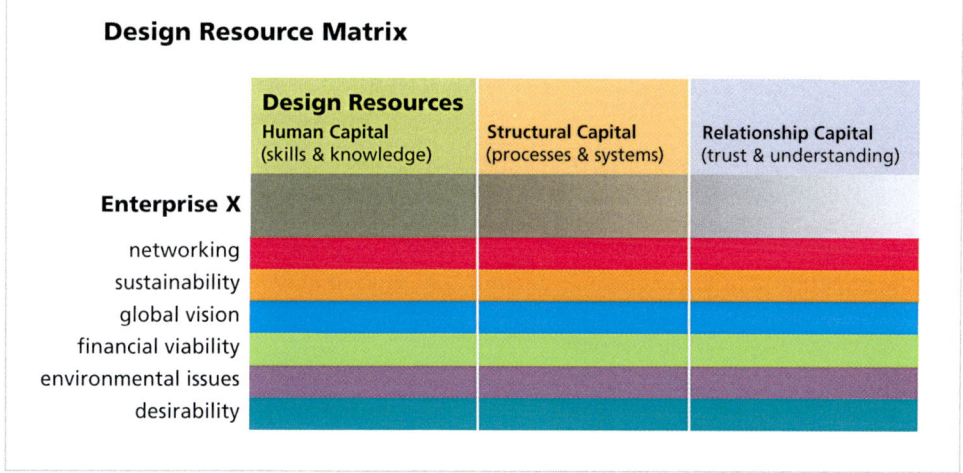

than learned by people. By way of example, imagine a typical high school. The rules and guidelines related to public safety, physical environments, social interaction and curriculum delivery might be considered as the knowable and teachable parts of the socio-cultural dimension described by Snowden. Now imagine a typical American high school. Of course, non-Americans might have a problem here, but what makes a high school a typical high school, like it makes any typical organisation, is the *animating presence of dominant but unwritten cultural 'codes' that form the various protocols, procedures and patterns of behaviour* – and the way the various social cliques within the student body live and work within them. This illustrates the unwritten, tribal and fluid dimension that Snowden refers to as *ideational-cultural*. Both dimensions of culture exist under the same roof, so to speak.

Figure 4: *Daylin Breen*

Case for individual to global product development: the *Tag Your Bag* product concept. In the context of the relationship and potential tension between the global, local and individual cultural domains relative to the dynamics of product and service development, I would like to introduce a product concept that addresses the potential cross-cultural appeal of a modular consumer product. My example is borrowed from a project by Daylin Breen, completed a few years ago at Royal Roads University in Victoria. The *Tag Your Bag* concept is based on an idea to help individuals identify their knapsacks, luggage and shoulder bags amid a 'sea' of similar products in a particular environment (like a school). In the project, people submit visual concepts for tagging icons and graphics to an on-line service provider. The winning submitted designs, having been judged by a peer-group artist jury, are then produced in small batches and offered on-line for purchase. What is interesting to me about this product concept is that it addresses a wide cross-section of potential customers using supportive new technologies along with an understanding of the more 'tribal and viral' dynamics of marketing. This business concept invites clients to become the creators of the final product.

The *Tag Your Bag* concept is designed to work across cultures and anywhere in the world that is supported by an online information/service infrastructure and production/ delivery system. The idea of a young person in France or Argentina or Japan exploring individual expressive graphic forms and building them into a final product is at the centre of the concept. This concept runs counter to product/service features that are homogenised in order to become global in their appeal. The *Tag Your Bag* business model gets its vitality from the fact that unique individual cultural features are integrated into final products that are constantly evolving.

SECTION 2: DESIGN ITERATION

The iterative phase of the design process is used to create the future details for messages, objects, activities or environments. This phase of the design process takes us from a point where we have developed a context for the product, to a point where the product starts to assume its personality. This personality is what some designers refer to as a product's 'look and feel'. This is an exciting design phase, as metaphors, rhetorical structures and analogies can be more fully developed; narratives can be written; and patterns of potential use can be explored to help create a more complete picture of a product.

Design iteration, supported by prototypes, helps to drive the development of ideas. When the scientists Watson and Crick were attempting to identify the structure of DNA they used large three-dimensional models to guide their discussions. Similarly, prototypes support our creating, judging, decision-making and evaluating skills when we build products for people. Prototypes provide the opportunity to clarify our design ideas and to explore the contexts of our proposed designs. Prototypes also allow us to field test and fine tune the features of a product in order to satisfy intended needs.

Collaborative spaces, like the one shown in the model, represent both an attitude and an environment. Collaborators must strive to establish a level of trust and a shared vision around their task. The collaborative space serves as the knowledge exchange hub of a project, where tangible (explicit) and intangible (tacit) knowledge can be shared. It can also serve as a protected 'incubating' space where new ideas can be introduced and cultivated. The collaborative space is the space where the knowledge developed as part of the design process is created, managed and shared. The knowledge and information exchanges that take place in this space are central to making products that work for people.

Working in a collaborative space can be intellectually challenging and socially demanding, as it may introduce approaches and experiences that take people out of a personal comfort zone in order to stimulate them to help create and share new knowledge. The notion of 'play' doesn't immediately spring to mind as part of the approach to managing a design process, but it might form one of the protocols that a team would establish for a project. The concept of protocol supports the design process. Protocols help us to establish a frame of reference regarding how people in a working group engage in a design challenge, and relate to each other throughout the entire design process.

A collaborative space can be physical or virtual. In this space, people can work face to face, in small working groups or in mediated situations using communications technologies such as the Internet. Collaborative spaces should be designed to support the work that people are doing and the bringing together of tacit and explicit knowledge resources around a process.

John Thackara (2006), a design thinker, author and educator, has made these observations about how collaboration supports meaningful dialogue and relationship building:

> 'We have to learn new ways to collaborate and do projects. We have to enhance the ability of all citizens to engage in meaningful dialogue about their environment and context and foster new relationships between the people who make things and the people who use them'.

The 'we' here is important. In a world of complex systems and constant change, we are all, unavoidably, 'in the bubble'. The challenge is to be both in the bubble and above it, at the same time – to be as sensitive to the big picture, and the destination we are headed for, as we are to the smallest details of the here and the now.

The Chinese philosopher Lao Tsu (Feng and English 1972) wrote the following verse almost twenty-five hundred years ago. The more I contemplate these words, the more they make me think of a balanced view of how knowledge is co-created and shared in a collaborative space.

> 'Thirty spokes share the wheel's hub; It is the centre hole that makes it useful. Shape clay into a vessel; It is the space within that makes it useful. Cut doors and windows for a room; It is the holes that make it useful. Therefore profit comes from what is there; usefulness from what is not there.'

Support for a complementary balance between the types of knowledge that we create and share is also a point of interest for David Snowden (2002). His work focuses on knowledge management and sense-making within organisations. He comments on the shift from more structured content management as part of knowledge management in organisations to an increased focus on context and the narrative. Snowden believes that knowledge management should be considered as both a thing and a flow. David Snowden makes the point that this question of how to manage knowledge is not just an academic one. According to him, when organisations make distinctions between tacit and explicit knowledge, they tend to focus on the container (thing) – Lao Tsu's clay vessel – rather than the thing contained (flow) – Lao Tsu's space within – and they tend to lose sight of any holistic model that combines them both in a complimentary and mutually supportive way.

Exploring this concept of knowledge as a thing and a flow suggests models that have been developed to help people understand the dynamics of knowledge creation and sharing. Ikujiro Nonaka (2000), an authority in the field of knowledge stewardship within organisations, has used the word 'ba' to describe a knowledge creating and sharing space. Nonaka's SECI (Socialisation-Externalisation-Combination-Internalisation) model is just one example of a knowledge creation and sharing model that might be used within a collaborative space. The SECI model illustrates a process that transforms our tacit knowledge. The goal is to allow people to share what they know in a larger context, using what Nonaka refers to as a 'self-transcending' process.

SECI Knowledge Conversion Model

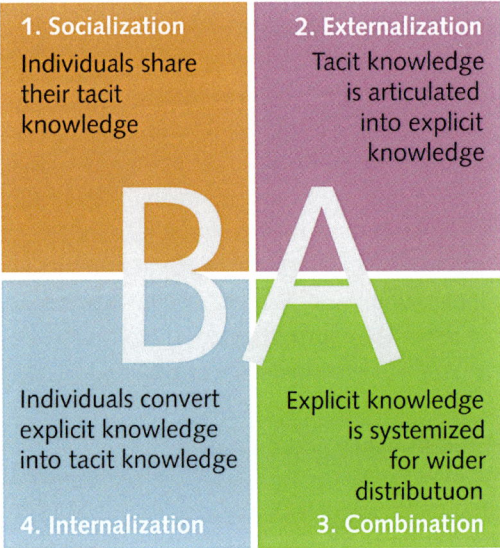

Figure 5: *Source: adapted from Nonaka, et. al.*

The process begins with socialisation, whereby people share their experiences and tacit knowledge in a group context. The next step is externalisation. In this phase tacit knowledge is articulated into forms that can be understood by others. In the combination phase the knowledge is edited, systemised and codified so that it can be shared with others. The final internalisation phase sees explicit knowledge being converted into tacit knowledge by individuals as they incorporate the new knowledge into their activities.

Each knowledge conversion stage within the SECI model contains what Nonaka refers to as an episode of 'action and reflection'. Acting and reflecting, to me, implies a learning cycle. I believe that models like the SECI model have the potential to help us hone continuous improvement and learning skills within a collaborative space.

This concept of continuous improvement makes some sense within the framework of knowledge exchange. The 'holy grail' of the knowledge exchange process is sometimes cited as wisdom. Piet Hein (2003), a Dutch poet and scientist, provides some food for thought regarding how we might gain wisdom as we assess and improve what we design through our exchanges. In one of his haiku-like poems, referred to as Grooks, he had this to say about gaining wisdom:

The Road to Wisdom Well, it's plain and simple to express: Err... and err... and err again... but less... and less... and less.

Adopting a philosophy of learning and continuous improvement can help to guide the design transformations that take place when we collaborate. It also suggests that we should perhaps not be afraid to fail if we can gain wisdom and get better at what we do.

The users of products hold places of importance in the iterative phase of the design process. Writing a few years ago in Design Issues, designer Cal Swann (2002) clearly voiced these sentiments regarding the valuable insights that people exposed to a design can bring to the design process. He states that the users of design should be genuine 'collaborators', and not merely co-opted for token comments in an illusion of collaboration. He cites a movement towards user-centred designing that indicates a more serious commitment to collaborative design, developing along the lines of action research in the social sciences.

People should be at the centre of co-creating value when we design. Referring to the development of a pacemaker service infrastructure in a healthcare region in their book *The Future of Competition*, authors Prahalad and Ramaswamy (2004) had this to say about a person's experiences and value creation:

> *'Value does not stem from the specific product, the pacemaker, or from the communication and IT network that supports the system, and not even from the social and skill network that includes doctors, hospitals, the family, and the broader community. Value lies in the experience of a specific patient, at a specific point in time, in a specific location, in the context of a specific event. By co-creating knowledge with the network and sharing resources, the patient becomes an active stakeholder in defining the interaction and context of the event'.*

Ross Dawson's three forms of intellectual or knowledge capital, introduced at the beginning of this paper, represent rich areas of knowledge-sharing and exchange for collaborators engaged in the design process. Knowledge capital is heavily weighted towards what people bring to the table and it is worth reintroducing these resources here:

Human capital is the skill and knowledge that people possess.
Structural capital refers to the processes and systems that support the knowledge creation and exchange process.
Relationship capital refers to the trust and understanding that can be established, especially when people work in collaboration.

The idea of considering knowledge as 'capital' is an interesting one when we consider social exchange theory in relation to knowledge exchanges. Social exchange theory acknowledges the effective exchange of knowledge between individuals and groups and how this activity is rewarded. The image of a 'knowledge exchange' wherein knowledge might be traded like a commodity or a 'blue chip' stock may seem somewhat far-fetched, but a person's ability to collaborate and to create, codify and share knowledge may be the 'common currency' for knowledge workers in the future, if it isn't so already.

Shifts in thinking

Designers working on projects often attempt to cultivate knowledge-exchange approaches that allow for many types of knowledge to be brought to bear and acted on as part of design thinking. Roger Martin (2007), Dean of the Rotman School of Business at The University of Toronto, has this to say about how design thinking can bring elegant solutions to wicked design problems:

> 'Whereas traditional firms organise around ongoing tasks and permanent assignments, in design shops, work flows around projects with defined terms. The source of status in traditional firms is 'managing big budgets and large staffs', but in design shops, it derives from building a track record of finding solutions to 'wicked problems' – solving tough mysteries with elegant solutions. Whereas the style of work in traditional firms involves defined roles and seeking the perfect answer, design firms feature extensive collaboration, 'charettes' (focused brainstorming sessions), and constant dialogue with clients'.

He goes on to say:

> 'When it comes to innovation, business has much to learn from design. The philosophy in design shops is, 'try it, prototype it, and improve it'. Designers learn by doing. The style of thinking in traditional firms is largely inductive – proving that something actually operates – and deductive – proving that something must be. Design shops add abductive reasoning to the fray – which involves suggesting that something may be, and reaching out to explore it. Designers may not be able to prove that something is or must be, but they nevertheless reason that it may be, and this style of thinking is critical to the creative process'.

Roger Martin's (2007) recent book, *The Opposable Mind*, builds on the styles of thinking outlined above and introduces the concept of 'integrative thinking' skills. He clearly explains how business leaders have used these skills with success, and how individuals can develop these skills. Daniel

Pink (2005), the man who coined the phrase 'The New MBA is an MFA', also has some very interesting things to say about the kinds of integrative thinkers that may flourish in what he calls the 'conceptual age':

> 'The future belongs to a very different kind of person with a very different kind of mind – creators, empathisers, pattern recognisers, and meaning makers. These people – artists, inventors, designers, storytellers, caregivers, consolers, big picture thinkers – will now reap society's richest rewards and share its greatest joys. We are moving from an economy and a society built on the logical, linear, computer-like capabilities of the Information Age to an economy and a society built on the inventive, empathic, big picture capabilities of what's rising in its place, the Conceptual Age'.

Design thinking provides strategic approaches that can help to improve our designed experiences. Tim Brown (2008), CEO and President of IDEO, an innovation and design firm based in Palo Alto, California, makes these points regarding design thinking:

> 'I believe that design thinking has much to offer a business world in which most management ideas and best practices are freely available to be copied and exploited. Leaders now look to innovation as a principal source of differentiation and competitive advantage; they would do well to incorporate design thinking into all phases of the process. As more of our basic needs are met, we increasingly expect sophisticated experiences that are emotionally satisfying and meaningful. These experiences will not be simple products. They will be complex combinations of products, services, spaces, and information. They will be the ways we get educated, the ways we are entertained, the ways we stay healthy, the ways we share and communicate. Design thinking is a tool for imagining these experiences as well as giving them a desirable form.'

Design thinking appears to be alive and well at a company called Adaptive Path. The company owners are also the authors of *Subject to Change: Creating Great Products and Services for an Uncertain World* (Merholz P. et. al 2008). In the following passage from their book they make a good point regarding the shift from a 'make and sell' brand marketing strategy to an experience strategy:

> 'In contrast to traditional brand strategy, experience strategy begins with the customer. It's about contributing to a desirable experience, helping people to accomplish what they want to get done. Experience comes from the outside in; an appreciation of customers' motivations, behaviors and context leads to the development of a product, service or system that can satisfy them'.

They go on to describe how an experience strategy works in the case of Apple's i-Pod product:

> 'Like Eastman Kodak, ("You press the button, we do the rest") Apple has prevailed in delivering on an experience strategy. Apple's approach to delivery differs from Kodak in that they don't hide complexity from their customers. Instead they leverage components across a system, so that the experience never becomes too complex. With digital systems, you can appropriately give people a lot of power and control. The trick is to approach the offering as a system whose components have narrowly defined functions, so that the experience never becomes overwhelming'.

Case for individual experiences: Acela

Acela is Amtrak's high-speed train service along the Boston-to-Washington metropolitan corridor. IDEO was approached by Amtrak to design a railcar that was more attractive and functional than the interiors of passenger airliners. IDEO convinced Amtrak to explore the whole train trip. The trip exploration included ten distinct steps including learning, planning, starting, entering, ticketing, waiting, boarding, riding, arriving and continuing. At the end of the process, the redesign included the Acela railcars, the train stations, interactive information kiosks, employee workstations, and the Acela visual identity. Acela was positioned as an experience that was superior in every respect to air travel.

Time passing, and high-speed train riding having been experienced, it appears from a posting on a design blog/opinion site that the Acela model is not quite as satisfying an experience as initially planned. Blog site author Adam Greenfield (2008) notes the limits that the design process and integrative thinking might encounter with these comments regarding the Acela project:

> 'This tends to be a particularly acute issue wherever a designed ecology brings human beings face-to-face with one another. As things now stand, experience design's Achilles heel is customer service. A combination of low wages, disinvestment in training and deeper cultural factors has left American businesses without a large pool of workers motivated to provide customer service at the level routinely specified by designers. The result is that experiences seamless on paper break down the moment a human being enters the loop.

> The suggestion here is not that these crucial interactions be left to chance, to design by committee, or to the exigencies of the moment. But there are real limits to a designer's ability to control the context. Designers may well be able to specify the degree to which a seat reclines, the font in which a sign is set, or the sleek lines of a uniform – but not the behaviour of the person in that uniform, and ultimately, that's far more likely to determine the tenor of any experience'

SECTION 3: DESIGN ITERATION

This last phase of the design process involves completing the product, sharing it with others and validating how well it meets needs. Here, the skills and the knowledge resources of the collaborators are used to specify and apply features and attributes to a finished designed product. How well the product fulfils its mandate reflects on how effective and responsive the design process has been.

To reach this stage of the process, we have tried to investigate and to integrate cultural and utilitarian features into our product so that it will relate to our audiences. Now we must see if our design thinking and hard work has paid off. Design integration can also support the building of trust in users by clearly explaining what a new design means to them in their daily lives or in a given situation. The design integration phase puts the focus on people and relationships.

Once the newly designed product has been 'rolled out' or unveiled, it is in the public domain. This is the place where ideas meet reality and the place where people experience products. Summative evaluation techniques, applied at this stage of the process, may yield results that could take collaborators back to revisit their work in previous design phases. In some cases, a cycle of continuous improvement might have already been anticipated and designed into the product development thinking.

Products evolve at the points where people interact with them. The features of a message, an object, an activity or an environment are shared and evaluated at these points of interaction and use. Knowing what to look for at these points, and being able to act on the knowledge gained through observation and analysis, can help collaborators to improve products for users.

Case for global to local features in design: Bison Courtyard on Bear Street project

An example of an environmentally responsive approach to a design outcome is available to us from the world of architecture, in the Town of Banff, Canada. The New York Times quotes Mike Wigley, Dean of Columbia's Graduate School of Architecture, Planning and Preservation, as saying:

> *"If we have a change in how we approach sustainability in North America, it won't be driven by architects or politicians, but by developers".*

Bison Courtyard is an environmentally intelligent building, designed to fit its surroundings: a town within a World Heritage Site. The mixed-use building blends 30,000 square feet (2800 square metres) of retail, residential and restaurant space. There are three levels plus an underground parkade that incorporates an interpretative groundwater well. It was completed in 2005.

The building's design – a shell that wraps around a courtyard – ensures that all ground floor businesses have a street-front presence. The centre piece of the Courtyard, the Old Crag Cabin, is one of Banff's original buildings. The Bison Courtyard building was built to step lightly on the earth, reduce operating and maintenance costs, take advantage of natural light and ensure healthy indoor air quality. It is Canada's first mixed-use LEED-certified [Leadership in Energy and Environmental Design] building. Two hundred species of indigenous plant forms were researched in order to begin the process of reflecting the natural forms of the park in the rooftop plantings.

Bison Courtyard is also unique due to the 'Triple Bottom Line Incentive Program' offered to the building's commercial tenants. Tenants are eligible for rebates on their rent for undertaking initiatives that reduce environmental impact, improve environmental performance; and/or contribute to culture and community.

The Bison Courtyard on Bear Street initiative started to shape the quality of experience that it wanted to create when William McDonough, a world-renowned environmental architect, was hired as the project's chief architect. The quality of the building experience combines global features of environmental impact reduction and sustainability with an elegant architectural design that speaks to the town's building scale and the mountain valley setting.

Conclusion

The outcomes of design are constantly evolving and people are continually evaluating them within new contexts of design thinking. I believe that we should strive to make products that are elegant and responsive to our needs, that can evolve, and that can be improved over time, but also themselves can generate new forms of thought. I also believe that it is worth exploring how the design process itself can be developed and extended as we learn more about how we create, codify and share knowledge in a more cyclic and continuous way.

The models, tools and examples introduced in this paper hopefully have helped to illustrate the connections between what we design, the design process and the sharing of knowledge when we design products to bridge global, local and individual cultural domains. Design thinking skills form the integrative intellectual 'mortar' that can be used to help us build our best ideas of what we need and want in our worlds.

Design is a part of all our lives. If we believe that design can improve people's lives, we must be prepared mutually to explore the relationships that exist between the design process, the collaborative creating and sharing of knowledge, and the design outcomes. Exploring the processes and tools that help us to share what we know can create a better understanding of how knowledge sharing and design thinking responds to the challenge of designing for ourselves and for others.

Figure 6: *Arctos & Bird*

Figure 7: *Arctos & Bird*

Figure 8: *Arctos & Bird*

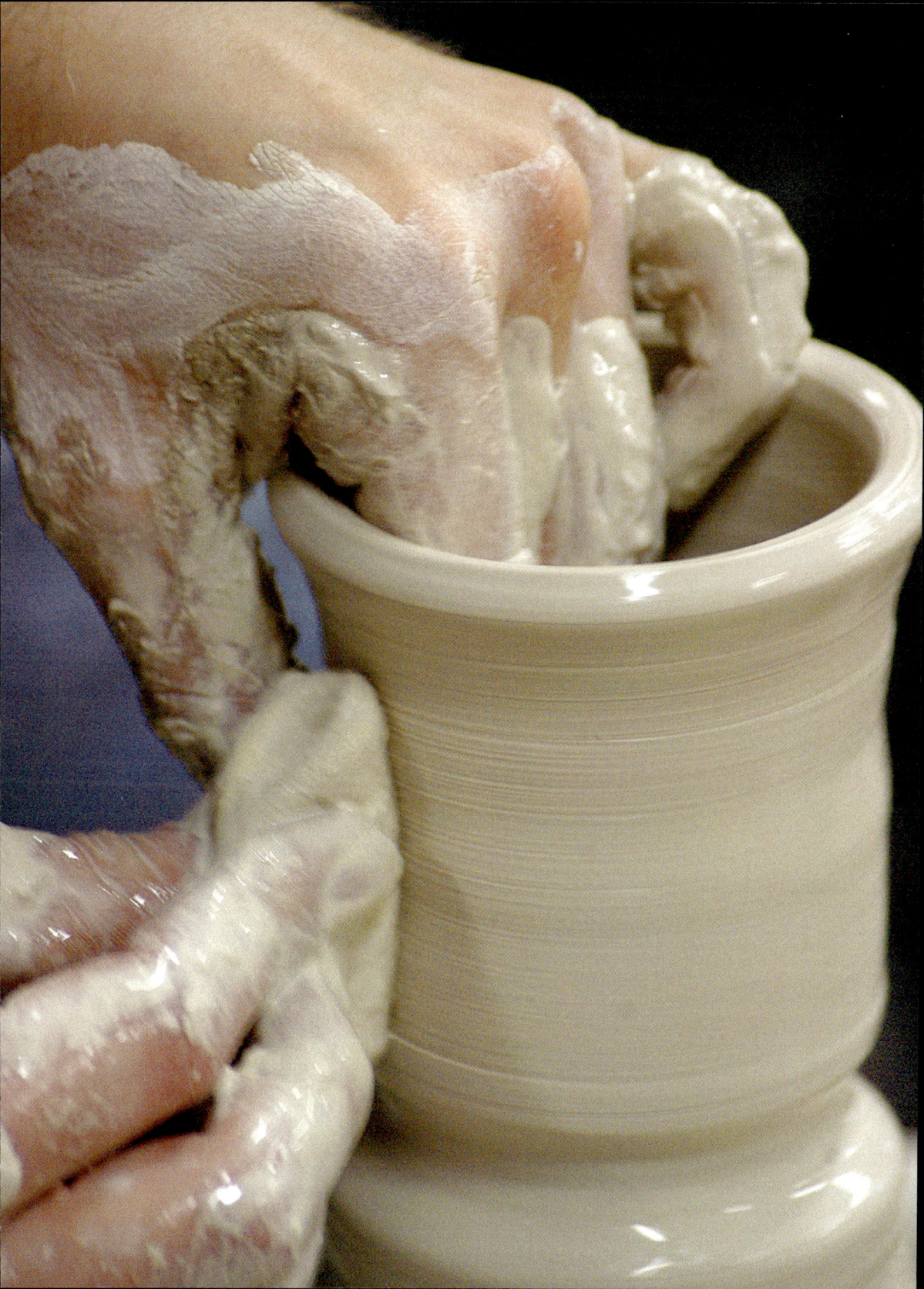

In this chapter the authors formulate an idea of leadership they call 'relational leadership' – a leadership that is an 'art', and like all art, operates through a medium. This medium they identify as 'connection'. The author's approach to leadership is unusual in that they situate their understanding within the world of art practice and creative process, not professional management theory. They attempt to understand the *relational processes* by which effective leadership is produced.

Organisations are animated by leadership, and the role of the leader makes a profound impact on its shape, direction, vision. It therefore impacts on the experience of those working in it, intimately interconnected with the 'aesthetic experience' of the organisation: the organisation is often 'expressive' of the leader. The nature of leadership, however, is contested, and often confused. In this chapter, the authors step back from mainstream criteria of successful leadership and consider the way the *qualities* of leadership can be found in artistic creation, and further, the way innovations in leadership are often expressed by artistic producers – in this case a Hollywood digital filmmaker. This chapter creates an important dialogue between art and leadership, drawing on the influential art world text *Relational Aesthetics* by Nicolas Bourriaud (2002). It also gives us a perspective on leadership as a facilitator of collective interaction, not as so often understood, a series of techniques for asserting individual power and influence.

The Relational Art of Leadership

Steven S. Taylor and Barbara A. Karanian

If we are to take seriously the idea that leadership is an art (Barnard, 1938; DePree, 1989), then we might ask – is it a visual art? Is it an all encompassing multi-sensory art? Is it a literary art? Is it an aural art? Which is also to ask, what is the *medium* of the art of leadership? At first blush, leadership uses the human body as a medium, much in the way that theatre, dance, and storytelling do. That is to say, as has been said before, that leadership is a performing art (e.g. Grint, 2001; Vaill, 1989).

But to identify the human body as the medium of leadership is to take an individualist perspective on leadership, to place leadership as something that is done by and to individual humans. We start with the assumption that leadership is a relational phenomena – it occurs not within individuals, but between individuals (cf. Uhl-Bien 2006). Working from that position, leadership does not use the human body as a medium, it uses the space between people as its medium. Leadership is an art that works in the connection between humans.

Using the idea of 'leadership as an art' in the context of organisational aesthetics, we formulate the idea of 'relational leadership' – as an art, and an art that works with connection, as *connection* is its medium (like any art has a medium). We illustrate the practice of working connection with an example of an *entrepreneurial leader*, which shows how he, sometimes distinctly and sometimes ambiguously, works with connection. We then discuss the implications of approaching leadership as an art that is enacted through working connection.

Part of any art is the mastery, technique, or skill of working the medium. Whether it is a painter's skill with brush, paint, and canvas, an actor's skill with voice, body and creating emotional reality (e.g. Hagen, 1973; Stanislavski, 1936), or a drummer's ability to play complex rhythms on their drum set, the craft is an important part of their art. Drummers spend years learning how to play the drums and perfecting their expertise. When a group of jazz drummers gather, very rapidly the discussion turns to types and brands of cymbals (Hatch et al., 2004). Similarly, painters are prone to talk about brushes, palette knives and mixing diverse mediums together to paint. This is because it is in the method through the medium of the art form that the art is enacted – it is in the details of working the medium that the rubber meets the road. The drummers' inner artistic sensibilities may lead them to want a livelier cymbal sound in a particular song, but that livelier symbol sound will be realised in the use of a specific brand and type of cymbal, struck with a particular drumstick or brush, with a specific technique.

Thus if we are to take seriously the idea that *leadership is an art*, then we need to consider the medium of that art and how it is worked, because that is where the art of leadership is enacted. One leader who works the connection between humans is a filmmaker – named Ramy – who when talking to students once said,

> 'We never read the manual that said to separate the creative people from the technical people. In fact, our industry doesn't get it. They don't believe us or know what we do. They think it's impossible to artistically collaborate the way we do'.

In order to lay the ground for looking at how Ramy works connection we will start with a discussion of what we mean by *relational leadership*, why leadership should be considered an art, and the relationship between organisational aesthetics and 'connection', all of which brings us to a fuller and more nuanced conceptual understanding of what we mean by 'the art of relational leadership'. We then turn to Ramy in more detail to illustrate the practice of how relational leaders work connection, closing with what this tells about the idea of leadership as art.

The Art of Relational Leadership

In order to develop a more nuanced conception of the art of relational leadership, we will break down the phrase, discussing the parts of it in turn. We begin with the idea of relational leadership, drawing upon Mary Uhl-Bien's (2006) approach. She breaks down relational leadership into two theoretical approaches, an *entity perspective* and a *relational perspective*. Although both are concerned with leadership as something that involves both leaders and followers, the entity perspective examines the relationship from the perspective of the individuals (the leader and followers). She identifies the entity perspective as being based on ideas of objective truth and concerned with how the individual perceives and influences the relationship with the other. In contrast, the relational perspective is grounded on an understanding of truth as socially constructed and is concerned with *the relationship itself*, which it sees as being constantly constructed in processes.

We will build our concept of relational leadership from Uhl-Bien's relational perspective. One key consequence of the relational approach is that it moves the focus from understanding leadership effectiveness to understanding the relational processes by which leadership is produced, which fits with our concern with the craft of the art of leadership. In artistic terms, we are not so much concerned with a judgment of the quality of the finished painting, but rather what techniques and methods have been used to produce the painting and how those methods affect the finished painting.

The idea that leadership is an art is certainly not new. Barnard told us,

> *'It is a matter of art rather than science, and is aesthetic rather than logical'* (1938: 235).

Just looking at our own bookshelf offers titles such as *The Art of Leadership* (Bothwell, 1983), *The Art and Science of Leadership* (Nahavandi, 1997), *The Art of the Leader* (Cohen, 1990), *The Arts of Leadership* (Grint, 2001), and *The Three Faces of Leadership: Artist, Manager, Priest* (Hatch et al., 2004). There has been a gradual movement from using the idea of leadership as an art rather loosely, to more and more detailed use of specific aesthetic philosophy. As an example, Duke (1986) simply argued for four aesthetic properties of leadership. Twenty years later, Ladkin (2006) is gaining new insights into charismatic leadership by viewing it through Kant's idea of the sublime; and Samier and Bates (2006) are presenting a variety of specific philosophical stances on leadership and administration. Although this movement has offered deeper insights into leadership, it is important to recognise that its framework is generally art criticism rather than art practice (Taylor and Carbone, 2008). That is to say, it is based in an intellectual approach to art that tends to be taken by academics and critics, rather than an *embodied* approach that is taken by teachers and artists. The intellectual approach is looking for clear analytic insight and conceptualisation, while the practice approach is looking for examples of embodied knowing which are particular to the situation, but in that particularity may offer some useful insight. As many creative writing teachers will say, the more specific and concrete the detail, the more it generalises for the reader. As we speak of relational leadership as working connection, we are speaking from an art practice perspective and our hope is to offer specific practices rather than an analytic conceptualisation of the art of relational leadership.

When leadership is spoken of as an art, this is somehow different from an art such as painting, sculpture, or dance. The difference is that while every art is formative, that is the art is about forming something – the art of negotiation is about forming an agreement in the face of conflicting interests, the art of sculpture is about forming sculpture out of marble or some other material – the 'pure' arts are about formativeness for the sake of forming; while the applied arts have an instrumental purpose (Strati,1999). So what does this mean when applied to managerial action such as leadership?

Goodsell suggests that management is 'an art in the ancient sense of that word, i.e. it embodies a specialised skill that is capable of creating results that are both usable and pleasing to behold. Specific objects are created and tasks performed, yet in ways and with consequences that establish in the minds of both creator and audience a sense of intrinsic satisfaction, above and beyond the utilitarian purpose at hand', but not necessarily unrelated to it (Goodsell, 1992: 247). Kuhn says,

'the process of 'managing' becomes art as those involved create meaning, construct form, recognise patterns, and place values on relationships with others. It is an art that exists only in process' (Kuhn, 1996: 223).

We suggest that the primary medium that leaders form and work with in order to accomplish the instrumental goals of the organisation is the *connections between people*.

Although we have all seen or at least can imagine how a painter works within one medium with their paints, brushes, and canvas to create a painting, what it actually means to work connection is less clear. We cannot see, touch, taste, smell, or hear connection. But we can feel connection. What does it mean to feel connected to each other? To feel something implies a way of knowing that is intuitive and holistic (Beardsley, 1982), a way of knowing that is unmediated by deductive or inductive reasoning (Csikszentmihalyi and Robinson, 1990), a way of knowing the 'felt meaning' (Courtney, 1995) of an experience; all of which are also descriptions of aesthetic experience.

The most common conception of aesthetics within organisational aesthetics is as the study of sensible knowing that is apprehended directly by the five senses. As Ramirez puts it: 'Aesthetics is that branch of Western philosophy that deals with the forms of understanding, perception, conception, and experience which we qualify (often after the fact) with adjectives such as 'beautiful', 'ugly', 'elegant', or 'repulsive'. Aesthetic knowledge depends largely on sensing and feeling, on empathy and intuition, and on relating conception to perception' (Ramirez, 2005: 29)

However, there is another way of thinking about aesthetics that explicitly links connection and aesthetics. This conceptualisation of aesthetic experience comes from Ramirez's (1991) concept of the beauty of social organisation. Ramirez starts by developing a systems theory of organisational beauty. Being 'a part of' a system simultaneously means 'belonging to' and 'distinct from'. The aesthetic experience of beauty comes from the feeling of 'belonging to'. Or as Bateson said, 'By aesthetic, I mean responsive to the pattern that connects' mind and nature (quoted in Ramirez, 1991: 38).

Sandelands (1998) expresses this idea slightly differently. He suggests that people have a dual nature as an individual and as a member of a social group, much in the way that Ramirez speaks of the 'separate from' (individual) and 'belonging to' (part of a group) aspects of a system. Sandelands goes on to argue that feelings of being part of the group are expressed and made object through art. Thus where Bateson said that aesthetic experience was responsive to connection, Sandelands argues connection is the basis of aesthetic experience. Clair (1998) echoes Bateson's understanding of connection being central to aesthetics, tracing it back to a variety of indigenous cultures' concept of aesthetics. In particular, she discusses traditional Cherokee aesthetics as being from a circular (rather than linear) culture where connection is crucial and aesthetics permeates all aspects of life.

We can therefore assume that aesthetics is related to connection between people, but there is no clear, agreed upon, theoretical understanding of what exactly the relationship between connection and aesthetics is. Following in that vein, we suggest that rather than understanding *connection* as the basis of aesthetic experience (Ramirez, 1991), or seeing aesthetic forms as the expression of connection (Sandelands, 1998), rather *connection is the medium of the art of relational leadership.* By taking this conceptualisation of the relationship between aesthetics and connection, we can conceptualise the practice of leaders and consider the craft of relational leadership, which we will do in the next section.

But first, let us illustrate what we mean by craft or technique with an example from the technique of painting with watercolours. In one technique, heavy weight paper is drenched in water and used as a foundation for wet paint that is applied for a not completely predictable outcome. *Creating* begins in the saturation of colour applied to a surface appearing to move with the motion of water and ends in the surprise of a still outcome. A deep cadmium red blended with yellow ochre and a touch of rich, raw umber dries on the surface to provide shadow and depth perspective to urban buildings (see Figure 1). Ultra marine blue and alizarin crimson mix to create the illusion of lavender in a foggy expansive sky. The use of ink and bronze powder are saturation modifications. More than a concept or intellectual theory of painting is being applied, but rather an embodied practice. We now turn to the embodied techniques of the art of relational leadership, as we see them in the practice of Ramy, the filmmaker.

Working Connection

When we speak of working connection, we are talking about the art and construction, the skills and the techniques, of relational

leadership. It is similar to talking about how a watercolor painter may work with wet paint on a wet surface. It is similar to a trombone player talking about the technique of double tonguing. It is like a storyteller's art of making contact with the audience just long enough to communicate a thought to them (Snyder 1990).

We draw upon the story of our filmmaker Ramy, that was created as part of a larger study of successful, entrepreneurial leaders (Karanian 2007) to illustrate ways that an artistic-relational-leader can work *connection*. We say illustrate in the sense that an image illustrates a story, not in the sense that an example illustrates a theory. We do not intend to suggest that the way Ramy 'works connection' are the only ways that connection is worked by relational artistic leaders, but the specific techniques Ramy uses allows us to get a vivid idea as well as a 'feel' for what it means to work connection. Much of the ways in which he works connection is by creating *the conditions for connections to flourish*, although he does also directly 'work' the relationships. This comes together as he appreciates the moments of connection in relationship to the diverse group, and tells his truth.

We start with the physical conditions of his first studio/office. Images emerge immediately after the first few minutes of walking in to the multi-level stucco West Hollywood home converted into his futuristic oasis of video, film, and documentary making. There is a maze of cubby-holes and paths and stairways to everyone working – individually and connected together – by concrete and symbolic evidence of on-going success. Gifts and presents sent in the form of coconuts, tequila, and monkeys, indicate to us a playful and exhilarating promise for fun in the context of people working hard. Original thoughts, clear, unwavering magnetic focus, an agile almost boundless bounce from one place to another are first impressions of Ramy. The land of Ramy, founder and CEO. along with his very talented group at Hollywood Digital, teems with the kind of energy that would motivate every entrepreneurial thinker to wake up early and run to work. Ramy explains this with the general description that it is important that everyone be comfortable, but we see that there is more at work here than simply being comfortable. He has created a space where he both physically and psychologically creates opportunities for connection. The importance of this space is shown in the following story:

'*Comfort matters*,' he suggests. There is a paradox of comfort in teams that don't apparently belong together. Yet, Ramy has created ways at Hollywood Digital for connecting, collaborative, multi-branching teams that produce films for large unknown audiences.

> '*People are comfortable here and stay and do all this work. If they are not comfortable, they know it and they just leave. No one has to ask them to leave*'.

> '*One example of discomfort occurred when my leading digital artist disappeared*'.

Ramy explains.

> '*He didn't say anything, he just left for days. He disappeared. I gave him some space, not worrying yet that he wouldn't follow-through, but finally talked to him about his concerns. And, of course, the concerns weren't technical. The digital effects artist*

was concerned that, with the move to the larger space, he would be lost in the big, impersonal machine of the huge movie house. He worried that he would no longer be motivated to be on the team, and that we would no longer be a team. So, I am working on that transition for everyone from our smaller space to the larger one. I am working on it. It's a day to day, real time thing'.

The digital effects artist feels the importance of the physical and psychological space that Ramy has created. The digital effects artist's sense of team is the connection that has been created in the space that Ramy has worked. To keep that connection, Ramy knows he must pay close attention, participate and help facilitate the artist's adjustment to the new space.

Ramy also works the conditions for connection as he selects diverse people to work together on his projects. Unexpected twists turn up everywhere. People, who under normal circumstances wouldn't be working together, design, construct, and modify everything in the production cycle of film making. '*I pick the best*', directs Ramy. The significance of this statement is illustrated by a company culture founded on the principle that people from backgrounds that are diverse, based on education, training, and past experience will collaborate exquisitely when innovation is the goal.

The culture created by Ramy is reminiscent of one found in many high-achieving academic institutions. Getting the absolute best individual for the work is the key. Creativity and best practices are so highly valued in the company that Ramy searches for and chooses the top performer with a goal toward seamless communication. And when Hollywood Digital enters the colour phase of the project and the final attention to details of the story line, visual effects, saturation, etc. there is almost no finishing line on completion.

But it is not simply a case of selecting the best people and putting them together. Ramy is 'working connection' in a more sophisticated way than that as he selects people to work on the pre- and post production process for his films. He works the conditions for connection, organising and creating cross-functional teams with the expectation that something wonderful will happen. A six-month Hollywood writer's strike provides an example. Corrosive to any productive team vibe, many in the television and movie industry used the strike as an opportunity for extreme cost-cutting lay-offs. Not Ramy. He pulled his team together and reiterated that it was because they all began together as a team that they would move forward together – even during this difficult stage – as a team. Then they used the strike conditions to offer something new, and the company thrived and completed award winning work.

An example of how he works the conditions for connection to foster the creation of interesting and important connections, consider how Ramy paints a picture of leadership that is brimming with awareness of participant and viewer. His goal is to work with female camera operators.

> '*You rarely if ever see 'girls' behind the camera. But I remember being fascinated as I watched a woman filming on Hollywood Boulevard. Think about it,*' he said.
>
> '*What happens when there is a guy behind*

the camera. What are people's perceptions? Think about it. That doesn't happen if it's a girl. I have a goal here – to get women as photographers'.

Ramy continued to discuss the ease and comfort of that particular solo woman photographer and how she connected persuasively as she carried her equipment and received responses naturally from passers-by.

Here he has seen the possibility for creating new and different connections between the public and the film crew that may translate into something new and different in the final product, simply by changing the gender of his camera person. He wonders about how the way it feels to be filmed by a woman or a man will create conditions for a natural response. He doesn't know exactly what, if anything will happen differently with a female behind the camera rather than a man, but he does sense the gendered aspect of the role and creates the possibility for new connections. Gender presents another variable for sustaining success in this male-dominated team. Enthusiastic about the value of other than male actions on a team, Ramy is exuberant about searching for females to join his team. '*Where are all the women and why won't they stay in our industry?*' are comments indicating his concerns and worry that he needs to find ways to do more.

Ramy's working of connection is also manifested in how he creates (or doesn't create) formal organisational structures. Here is his view on formal meetings:

'I didn't organise any formal meetings to communicate'.

He smiled when he explained,

'I don't have to organise any formal meetings to communicate. The meetings occurred naturally, people just gather'.

And although he claims that the connections just occur naturally, again, there is more to it than that. Ramy works tirelessly and with painterly precision to make the communication and connection happen. Hours are spent on the phone. Sometimes six hours of nonstop conversations with more than one person representative of multiple working groups on different phone lines, Ramy says, will keep him away from his staff. This presents a time that he is aware that he needs to connect clearly and authentically with those on the phone, yet demonstrate care and awareness for his staff's neediness. And as he states,

'I confront and direct the related issues in the moment'.

Here we also see that he works connection, not only by creating the conditions for connection, but also working the relationships directly as he is ever present and in the moment as he communicates with staff.

Another way that Ramy works connection is through language. He often speaks in his own vernacular. Ramy has his own language – not L.A. street slang, but words and phrases that identify him and his work immediately. He says, 'monkey' and 'maverick' and 'dislodge' and you know he means action. And so does his team – who he refers to as 'warriors'. New people he meets imitate. They use his words immediately in conversation. One example is a former New York stock broker who had a few minutes to discuss wishes for subsidising an upcoming project with Ramy and was overheard using 'Ramy language' in follow-up phone conversation meetings. Words and non-verbal cues illustrate his connected impact. He uses the word 'monkey' as a playful and visual image of action and designing new movements forward toward project delivery at work. People imitate his language, not as an empty echo, but as artistic evidence of sensorial engagement to Ramy's related leadership style. The language allows people to connect through the ideas and special words and phrases that are Ramy's language.

Lest we give a romanticised and wrong impression, we note that not all of the ways that Ramy works connection are distinct or feel glorious or happy and cheerful. He also works connection ambiguously by telling his truth, and evokes negative emotions. The team and one-on-one examples illustrate this. When asked by a partnering academic team's graduate student who was prototyping a new design,

> 'Ramy, does my work just suck...others say they are not convinced?'

Ramy responded to him in front of the group,

> 'Well, it's possible that your work does suck. It's more likely however, that you are telling them too much of the story. Never give the beginning, the middle and the end'.

Silent at first, the student awkwardly recognised the truth in a later final presentation. This telling of his truth reminds us of an artist's commitment to telling their truth in their work. It is not a truth that has to be everyone's truth, but just as we look to the artist unabashedly to show us what they see (and that the rest of us may not see), Ramy's people expect him to tell them his truth and that expectation is part of their connection with him.

It works both ways as Ramy also respects his people's truths. For example, awkward silence occurred another time when Ramy volunteered one of his stars to demonstrate award winning, creative post-production processes. He gazed back at Ramy, almost stoic in response. Non-verbal cues and symbols in Ramy's behaviors showed appreciation for his star staff member's lack of response and somehow that worked. The energy of selfishly removed indifference was replaced with a playful and artistic vibe, and the demonstration was effective. Parallel to how Ramy recognises the tension in the graduate student's readiness for moving forward he patiently connects with the digital effects artist. In a face to face discussion with another colleague he delivers a clear personal statement,

> 'You are always on the precipice of success, what's taking you so long?'

The simple question delivers Ramy's truth as he sees it, but does not insist on that truth being the truth for his colleague.

So we see Ramy, managing the physical space, creating the psychological space, selecting the composition of his 'warrior' teams, playing with gender, addressing relationships directly, using his own particular language, and telling his truth as ways that he works the connections between his people and himself, between his people and each other, and even between his people and the wider world. We have described these as techniques for working connection, but we do so with the realisation that art is more than technique – painting is more than a mastery of colour and brushstrokes – and this art of relational leadership is more than the techniques of working connection. Thus we now turn to the question of where does approaching leadership as a relational art that uses connection as its medium take us in a more philosophical and conceptual sense.

Leadership as an Art

To come back to our starting point – that is to take seriously the idea that leadership is an art – we now look at some implications of approaching leadership as a relational art that uses connection as its medium. To do this, we draw upon the French art curator Nicolas Bourriaud's book, *Relational Aesthetics* (2002) to supply some conceptual scaffolding. Bourriaurd is concerned with theorising the art scene of the 1990's and making sense of the events/exhibitions/installations/happenings that defied traditional categorisation and theorisation. He starts from the idea that:

> 'Artistic activity, for its part, strives to achieve modest connections, open up (one or two) obstructed passages, and connect levels of reality kept apart from one another' (Bourriaud, 2002: 8)

We are struck by how well Bourriaud's description of artistic activity fits Ramy's leadership. As he brings together people who would otherwise have been unlikely to work together he is connecting different realities that are otherwise kept apart. This might well be typical of entrepreneurial leaders because there is such great opportunity for creative group genius (Sawyer, 2007; Sawyer, 2006) when disparate areas are brought together in surprising mixes of diverse teams. We take it as validation that Ramy's leadership seems to fit Bourriaud's conception of art, and now build on that conception to offer deeper insight into the art of leadership with the intention of understanding the experience of transformative team connections.

We start with Bourriaud's analysis of the purpose of relational aesthetics. He sees art as being in response to and different from a world that has become more and more rationalised and commoditised, or in short more and more dominated by the ideas of mid-twentieth century managerial capitalism.

> 'In a world governed by the division of labor and ultra-specialisation, mechanisation and the law of profitability, it behoves the powers that human relations should be channelled towards accordingly planned outlets, and that they should be pursued on the basis of one or two simple principles, which can be both monitored and repeated' (Bourriaud, 2002: 9)

It is here where we start to see the real possibility of leadership as an art and the difference between leadership as an art and the science of leadership. As an example of the science of leadership, think of the contingency theories of leadership developed at Ohio State and Michigan in the 1960's and 1970's. The research was aimed at reducing the complexity of the connections between leaders and followers and providing a specific set of guidelines for how a leader should behave based upon the circumstance. It was a prescribed paint-by-numbers approach – paint this colour in this space and fill in this colour in this space and you will have a delightful and completed picture of leadership. In contrast, Ramy shows us that an art of leadership is focused on working each connection for its own sake and enacting leadership that is never a formula, never the same picture twice. He appreciates the fine art of being present and giving in every unique moment. A science of leadership is driven to find repeatable, general solutions – Bourriaud's 'simple principles'. An art of leadership is driven by Adler's 'yearning for significance'. (2006: 492) An art of leadership seeks more, richer, and different connections that open up more and more possibilities of what it might mean to be human, while a science of leadership seeks to reduce those connections to a consistent, few, qualities that can be managed to increase the efficiency and effectiveness of the leadership process.

Beyond the difference between a science of leadership that serves the ongoing dominance of managerial capitalism and an art of leadership that seeks to increase the possibilities of what it is to be human, we also see a lesson for relational leadership in how Bourriaud contrasts relational art with previous forms of art.

> *The role of artworks is no longer to form imaginary and utopian realities, but to actually be ways of living and models of action within the existing real, whatever the scale chosen by the artist.'* (Bourriaud, 2002: 13)

That is to say relational art has moved beyond creating images of possibilities to enacting those possibilities. We see this also in Ramy's relational leadership – he does not create representations of new ways to lead and organise, but rather blurs industry boundaries and *enacts* new ways to lead and organise.

If we bring these two ideas together, we see a science of leadership that attempts to create a simplified representation of leadership and then control and limit human interaction and connection to conform to that representation. In a similar method, previous ideas of art created representations of utopian dreams much in the way that artful, charismatic leaders created visions of new ways of organising and being together – for example, Martin Luther King's 'I have a dream' speech paints a picture of a utopian society where black and white stand together as colourful equals. Although the form and use of the representation are different – in the extreme, science represents a desire to control, while art represents a desire to liberate and create new possibilities – representation is an essential part of the process of leadership. However, this new art of relational leadership moves directly to enacting a new model of organising and being together. Ramy doesn't spend his time putting forth a vision – he just does it. There is not a sense of creating a vision or a theory and then trying to realise it, but rather a sense of working connection and then seeing what new and interesting things happen as a result of having worked connection that way.

It is this fundamentally different conception of leadership that is the result of taking seriously the idea that leadership is an art. Leadership as an art takes us to that rare area of leadership that is not about accomplishing goals or providing a vision, but rather is about experiencing and working connections with the belief that something new and interesting will be created as a result.

The purpose of this chapter is to turn inside-out some recent trends in thinking about the environment in which we work – the workplace. Attention by both organisations and researchers recently has been directed towards the *interiors* of working spaces and how our feeling or experience of the workplace environment impacts on our work, on our productivity, our loyalty, and so on. New 'aestheticised' forms of working environment have therefore emerged – with companies setting up in-house café bars, games rooms and 'chill-out' rooms, hoping both to make employees more 'creative' and/or to look impressive to clients or competitors. The subject of this chapter however is the *exterior* of the working space, or at least the way aesthetic awareness of the exterior is often more powerful than the more immediate experience of the interior. This is of course counter-intuitive, but through field research engagement, the author finds a complexity of live issues for organisations that in turn relate to our most ingrained ideas of culture and our enduring affection for the great outdoors.

Bringing together on-location interview material and ethnographic data involving thirty employees, the author discusses the significance of their experiences, and the way that experience can be explained both aesthetically, but also historically – as a series of typical responses to historical-industrial developments. A condition – of 'topophilia' – is diagnosed, and put forward as a live issue for organisations, and one that will require serious deliberation.

Organisational Topophilia:
the Countryside and Aesthetic Pleasure at Work
Samantha Warren

This paper is concerned with aesthetic issues in organisational life that lie beyond the physical confines of the workplace. Despite increasing academic attention to managerial processes intended to 'aestheticise' the inside of working spaces as I outline below, the influence of the world outside these buildings has been rather neglected by organisational scholars. More specifically, this paper deals with one manifestation of this world – the countryside – and its importance in the working lives of a group of organisational members employed in the 'New Media' department (Department X) of a large IT firm (MCS) based in a rural location in southern England. Through the words and photographs of this occupational group, I present an account of their 'organisational topophilia' – love of the natural environment (following Tuan, 1990). This reported affection for the world outside was notable given that, at the time of the study, the management of MCS had transformed Department X's ordinary corporate office space into an artistically designed and aesthetically appealing – 'funky' – working environment as discussed below.

The importance placed on the countryside location here is intriguing, given that the late 1990's and early 2000's have seen what Nathan and Doyle (2002) refer to as a 'revolution' in the design of workplace interiors, particularly offices. Whilst not an entirely new phenomenon (see Steele, 1973), managers are now paying increasing attention to the manipulation and decoration of aesthetic elements of physical workspace. For instance, organisations are designing and creating beautiful, often unusual, interior environments with varying organisational aims – for example, 'surfacing' the creativity of employees (Seifter, 2005) in order to profit from the more innovative orientation towards work processes and tasks such creativity is presumed to produce (Gilmore and Warren, 2007; Journal of Business Strategy, 2005). These 'wacky workspaces' are most usually found among the so-called creative industries, but growing numbers of companies are adopting similar principles regardless of the nature of the industry or characteristics of the worker (see Arts and Business (n.d.) 'case studies' for examples).

Examples of these aestheticisation initiatives also seem especially prevalent in call-centres, banks and insurance offices, either in addition to or instead of changes to the material environment, cultures of 'fun' and 'play' are managerially instigated (seemingly) with the aim of sweetening performance targets and/ or deadening the monotony of highly routinised work. (For an overview see Warren & Fineman, 2006; Alferoff and Knights, 2003; and Fleming and Spicer, 2004 for call centres especially). Relatedly, aesthetics are also being employed in the service of 'making-over' human resource management practices – for example enlisting the services of artists-in-residence and arts-based training practitioners to 'unleash' the power of employees' creative potential, or their sense of empathy with customers and colleagues using principles and techniques from the arts, such as theatre, painting and poetry (see for example, Arts & Business, n.d.). We can also recognise aestheticisation processes at work in the way corporations project themselves to their external stakeholders too – investing heavily in crafting the 'right' corporate image through a process of 'aesthetics management' involving uniforms, logos, letterheads, typefaces and, importantly for my purposes here, the design and decoration of corporate architecture and space (see Hancock, 2003 for an excellent overview; also Berg and Kreiner, 1986; and Dale and Burrell, 2003). Importantly in the present context, all these examples take an internal focus on the role of aesthetics at work and, by and large, ignore the significance of what lies outside the building – and its role in attracting, motivating and retaining employees.

Organisational aestheticisation can be connected firmly to wider trends identified by cultural commentators as the 'aestheticisation of everyday life' (Featherstone, 1991; Welsch, 1997). Aestheticisation is perhaps best described by Welsch (1997) as a process intended to 'sugar-coat' reality with 'aesthetic flair' – embellishing the surface attributes of things, places, people and events to make them more appealing to the senses, whilst their underlying attributes remain the same. The important part of this 'make-over genre' is that things look and feel the part, how they actually are is of limited relevance. Although aestheticisation of the workplace is taking several forms, as noted above, all share the same roots – they are initiatives designed to make the experience of work sensually pleasurable in order to improve organisational performance, productivity, efficiency, effectiveness, profitability… or any combination of the above. In short, they rest on an assumption that the 'happy worker is a productive worker' and seek to achieve this through aesthetic means, rather than a fundamental reconfiguration of the work itself, e.g. job design or employee relations. The extent to which this common adage holds true, is desirable and/ or possible to achieve is, of course, subject to conjecture (Hosie et al., 2006; Warren & Fineman, 2006).

This chapter explores an example of workplace aestheticisation – an office make-over – from which the data presented is drawn. A three month 'aesthetic ethnography' was carried out with the staff of Department X as a 'critical case' of aestheticisation at work in order to question the emergence and legitimation of this 'new' management technique and investigating employees' experiences of it (Warren, 2005b).

What I present below initially came as a surprise to me, since it reflects a facet of my respondents' experiences I had not in the least anticipated: despite having been provided with a recently aestheticised work environment by management, the employees of Department X appeared to prefer what lay outside the walls of their beautiful, new and shiny office, to that which had been created *within* them. A desire to escape the confines of the office, no matter how attractive, was a strong theme in their recounted experiences. I therefore suggest that their perceptions of, and attitudes to, their countryside environment represent a case of 'topophilia', which Tuan defines as 'all of the affective human ties with the [natural] material environment' (1990: 93). This data is presented in the form of photographs taken by the respondents with their verbal explanations alongside and are displayed with minimal commentary to allow their nuances and 'presentational symbolism' (Langer, 1957) to come through as clearly as possible to the reader. A variety of conceptual resources from aesthetic theory and cultural studies are then used to discuss why these people might have held such strong views about their natural environment.

Image-ining aesthetics

As Strati (1999) notes, researching the aesthetic elements of organisational life requires that researchers first refine their own 'aesthetic faculties', paying attention to how they feel and act within certain spaces, observing the ways in which the pathos of the organisation inhibits or encourages their own behaviour. In this way the researcher is imagining what it is like to work there him or herself and can discuss these reactions with others who use the space. However, as Taylor (2002) rightly observes, asking others' to reflect on their own aesthetic perceptions at work has its problems. Firstly, even recognising aesthetic experience is difficult given its embodied and often subtle character. Describing that experience to someone else in order to communicate it compounds the difficulties in that aesthetics, as visceral and/ or emotional states, are notoriously hard to 'capture' in language (Langer, 1957; see also Warren, 2005a). Furthermore, and as Taylor (2002) remarks, organisational aesthetics researchers have the added difficulty of treading the fine line between the methodological authenticity of their research accounts and organisational legitimacy in the eyes of their respondents and the businesses that grant them access to gather data.

With these challenges in mind, the need to bring a more sensual – but credible – element to the research seemed evident. Aesthetics can be described as a continual world that greets all our senses: sight, smell, sound, touch and taste. The importance of these sensual modes of knowing runs right to the heart of the aesthetic mode of organisational enquiry (Gagliardi, 1996; Strati, 1992, 1999). Furthermore, since this particular aesthetics research project was specifically designed to explore my respondents' sensory reactions to and feelings about their material environment, I needed a way to bring the social (respondents' experiences) and material (objects that provoked them) together. For these reasons I asked my respondents to represent their workplace visually during interviews by bringing with them a set of photographs they had produced in response to my question – 'Show me how it feels to work here'.

The choice of visual medium does not, of course, address all of the human senses and some have accused me in the past of 'occularcentrism'. Nonetheless, as I have discussed elsewhere (Warren, 2002, 2005c) to envision or visualise something is much more than merely to make visible, a point also nicely made by Whincup (2004: 81) in his account of how photographed objects – when explained by their photographers – can act as windows onto the intangible, triggering intensely visceral memories and invoking how it felt to be there (see also Urry, 2002). What is important in the foregoing is that the photographed images themselves do not stand alone as 'data'. Instead, as Schwartz (1994) eloquently puts it, they act as reference points through which data is generated as questions about them are asked and answered.

Another strength of respondent-led photography is the way the photographer sets the agenda for discussion. My respondents took the camera away and came back to me with pictures of things they wanted to discuss. Now, whilst I would not be so naïve to pretend my subjectivity is not still at play here in interpreting the interview transcripts, framing the photographs in terms of my own research objectives, and indeed in the very act of asking these people to reflect aesthetically on their environments in the first place, in the initial stages at least, the respondents themselves had carte blanche to take whatever pictures they liked. This point is particularly important for this chapter, since the data on which it is founded was generated as a result of this process and could be described as quite a surprise.

In short, I did not expect my respondents to show me pictures of the world outside their new, shiny office. I had asked respondents to make photographs of their work environment – meaning of course, the newly aestheticised office space. I did not anticipate people taking pictures out of the windows and/ or physically going outside to collect their shots. It was perhaps short-sighted of me not to consider that my respondents might have a different definition of their working environment to mine. Indeed, to begin with I was frustrated that people seemed to be more interested in the 'great outdoors' (which at that time I felt was beyond the scope of my study) than concerned with their 'great indoors' – which was what I had come to explore.

Department X

As noted briefly in the introduction, the MCS's managerial rationale for the aestheticisation programme was to provide a working space conducive to engendering the creativity of the staff who worked there. Furthermore, it was hoped that this environment would communicate the creative capacity of the department staff to clients and the media, effectively serving as a public relations and marketing device too. The office was housed on an upper floor of a large, fairly traditional, open-plan building, and it had been internally decorated with bright colours, unusual lighting and constructed around a visually striking central walkway, which acted as the main thoroughfare for the space and aesthetic focal point. For these reasons, glass-walled meeting rooms led off from along its length with the rest of the working space arranged around them. One of these rooms – nicknamed the 'Thinktank' – was kitted out with padded walls, soft foam blocks in primary colours and children's toys, to give the appearance of a place for play rather than work – the assumption being that playfulness sparks innovative thinking.

In addition to the décor, toys, games and art objects populated the office, including among other things a microscooter, pool table, table football, basketball hoop and an oversize set of pseudo-Russian Dolls. The

field work was enacted over a three month period and although I was not present every day, I participated as fully as possible in the everyday routines and goings-on of the department. 31 members of Department X took part in the formal element of the research – nearly the full complement of permanent staff there (e.g. not including transient members of project teams). Their ages ranged from 21–40, with the majority falling in the 28–35 bracket, and their job roles included technical and customer support, producers (project managers), software programmers and graphic designers. Each collected a set of photographs on a digital camera, which we subsequently discussed in semi-structured interviews as described above. Additionally, I gathered ethnographic data about my own experiences, perceptions and observations of the space and the way people behaved within it, with particular emphasis on refining my own aesthetic sensibilities as Strati (1999) suggests. These were noted down in a field journal. The data presented below show a significant strand in the data generated during my time at Department X and form the basis for the theoretical discussion that follows them.

Organisational topophilia
the great outdoors

As I have already noted, the most surprising and ironic message to come from the people with whom I spent time at Department X was that they particularly valued the environment that lay outside their office. Almost every person I interviewed mentioned the importance of being or seeing outside, despite working in an exciting new workspace. Significantly, this particular organisation was situated in a rural part of southern England, in the grounds of a stately home which had been bought by the company in the mid 1960's with the proviso that they would preserve the estate and allow the small farm situated on the land to continue to operate. The grounds were indeed beautifully kept and incorporated, among other things, a sunken garden, an ornamental fish pond, acres of grassy parkland, sports facilities, a 'clubhouse' and a fitness trail. The following photo-interview excerpts illustrate these sentiments of my respondents;

'...taken from my window to represent outside.... we have got something here that none of our city agencies and competitors have got, and that's the countryside; and literally we can go and sit on the lawn and have a brainstorming session in the sun, and it's far more effective than being stuck in any office no matter how pretty it may be.'

(Lewis, 35, Producer)

'I like the grounds. I like to go and walk round the grounds, I mean not on a day like today, but ...um.... I'm hoping when the summer comes to do a bit of.. er... sort of sit out there at lunchtimes and catch a bit of sun. So that was really, the house I suppose is sort of the centre bit of it really, the old bit of it, that's why I took the house particularly but its really the whole of the site'

(Denise, 24, Administrator)

'It's the... I'm not sure how to say, I dunno, it's the colouring, the lighting [that I don't like]. I'm an outdoor person, that's one of the things I like least about being inside a building, not particularly here because it has lots of compensations, but I suppose I'd rather see the sky than the ceiling...'

(Maureen, 54, Administrator)

As the images and narratives indicate, people told me that it was nice simply to get out of the office and go for a walk in the countryside and forget about work for a while. Contrastingly, Siobhan, a producer, spoke about the grounds and surrounding countryside as symbolic of the futility and insignificance of organisational processes. She enjoyed being outside in what she called the unpredictability and apparent chaos of nature – symbolised for her in the images – as a complete change from the ordered environment of her workplace

She explained to me how she enjoyed being reminded that nature has an internal organic order that trivialised the attempts 'mankind' makes to create things at work – especially in the context of IT and computing. The irony of such a hi-tech organisation being located amongst such an abundance of nature was also not lost on me – as I noted in my field journal after a walk in the grounds one lunch-time. However, not all the manifestations of this prominent theme were as striking as Siobhan's comments. The majority of people who represented the 'outside world' in their photographs did so through the windows of the building, rather than by actually going outside as the next section shows.

A room with a view

As the words and pictures below demonstrate, a window-seat was a highly coveted prize for my respondents. Various reasons were given for this, including 'having a view', 'being nice and light' and 'being able to gaze out into space', but all of the explanations given expressed a desire to escape from the office and their work in some way, even if only by looking out of the window:

'That's looking out the window. It's nice having a window! I've been in some offices where I haven't had a window and it's nice to sort of realise that there is a world outside, it's nice being able to see out of the window every now and again.'

(Guy, 21, Programmer)

'I used to have a window seat... I had a great seat, in the summer I could look over the

trees and you could look into the distance sort of thing, and that was great and then they moved me and another programmer got my seat and then they sat me next to the project manager so I felt betrayed…'

(Shaun, 25, Programmer)

'I do love having the window seat you know that's sort of… cos I didn't have that [before]. And I love that because you feel as if, I mean other people see you looking into your screen and you're actually looking out the window, but its great just to be able to sit and watch that for a minute or so and then think 'right, what was I doing?'.

(Hannah, 27, Technical Support)

'I wanted to be by a window. It's the most important thing to me. Before I wasn't sat by a window and it was just horrible because you're just facing a partition and you can't look away. Now, I can just look out the window – you can just change your focus, you can look – you've got something else to look at? And there's other stuff going on, so that's just brilliant I'm just so chuffed.'

(Pete, 26, Programmer)

'That's the view outside my window which is always quite nice. When my eyes start to turn inside out from staring at the screen for too long, its nice to look outside because its surrounded by trees and the countryside… it has real seasons here. If you work in London maybe you don't really pick up on it, but you're very aware of the environment and the seasons when you work in this particular location probably more so than other places.'

(Deb 31, Designer)

I have included so many examples of this 'window' data because it was especially significant. Although the surrounding countryside was seen as a great source of pleasure by these people, as the transcripts show, many of them did not actually venture outside to enjoy it. Instead, the enjoyment was derived from the fact that they could go out *if they wanted to* – a kind of vicarious consumption of the countryside. As Kate explains:

'Oh that's the park pond, which again, when I first came here it was like 'Oh my God there's a fish pond!' I mean again, I don't

ever go to it but I remember it's there, but I just don't use it really, but it is nice because it's part of the sunken garden. Just knowing that it's there, and I can go if I want to. Again, to me those things are better than... um... all of this blue ceilings – things like that in your own environment.'

(Kate, 26, Designer)

Moreover, for these respondents, there was no need actually to go to the effort of going outside for a walk, because they could imagine the enjoyment they might have if they did so – effectively 'consuming' the countryside from the comfort of their desks. This might also have meant that they would not need to get cold, tired, dirty, and so forth by actually going outside. Indeed, the reality of going outside might have been disappointing for these reasons. There was an almost apologetic air to these comments – respondents felt that they should take advantage of this wonderful location by getting out at lunchtimes and perhaps even holding outdoor meetings, rather than staying inside all the time.

These respondents seemed to want to justify to me why they did not make use of the grounds for their own pleasure despite having a window seat and importantly a view of the countryside, being highly prized – Shaun's comment that he 'felt betrayed' when moved from his desk near the window and Pete's feeling of being 'so chuffed' at acquiring the a seat near a window are acute examples of this. It seemed to me that these respondents felt that they were being 'deviant' for not spending more time in the company grounds. This was despite several of them saying that they did not have time (or energy) to go for walks or even just to sit outside during their working day. It was as if people felt guilty for not making use of something that had been provided for them, but these feelings also hinted at something deeper. It is possible to argue that their rather curious relationship with the environment outside the office serves to reinforce the socially constructed nature of aesthetic judgments – as if they had been 'conditioned' that they should enjoy the countryside – because enjoyment of the countryside is an aesthetic norm in our culture.

Furthermore, as I listened to people telling me about the ways they made use of the grounds and how they enjoyed the views from their windows, I began to reflect on the extent to which they were describing a level of aesthetic engagement that would be difficult for an organisation to create artificially – especially in an urban environment. These respondents were telling me in no uncertain terms how important the aesthetics of their environment were in their choice of organisation. Several respondents recounted tales of taking salary cuts to move to this site from London and other cities, some even choosing to change employer so as to be able to work in the countryside – or at least outside a city. This last point does need to be tempered with the observation that MCS is a prestigious corporation that would be a desirable addition to any IT professional's CV, and it may not have been the location alone that prompted respondents' decisions to join the company. Nonetheless, working in a beautiful rural setting definitely added to the attraction of employment with MCS for my respondents. In sum, the foregoing data show that, for these respondents at least, the aesthetics of their environment were indeed a factor in their choice of organisation and enjoyment of their working day. This strongly supports Bauman's observation that contemporary work is valued for aesthetic reasons – although, as I note above, I found it ironic that aesthetic pleasures were not yielded by the expensively designed, funky office space, but by the ancient trees, farmland and meadows that lay outside it.

The next section takes these ideas forward and makes some theoretical suggestions as to why the countryside was so important to these people at work, even though they had been provided with an artistically designed, aesthetically appealing workspace inside the building and hardly ever actually went outside to enjoy the land around them.

Aesthetics, naturally

According to Kant (1952) the appreciation of nature is an aesthetic universal – indeed, he argues that it is only the appreciation of nature (under strict conditions) that unite us with the 'universe' and one another. Bearing this in mind, perhaps we should not be surprised that the people of Department X were so keen to photograph the natural world when asked to reflect aesthetically on their working lives. But this explanation is too simple. Although, as Soper (1995: 244) notes, elements of nature have proved a recurring theme in art and cultural history, the claim that human beings have a universal attraction to the natural world deserves further attention, as Soper is also at pains to point out. Claiming that everyone loves all natural forms and variants is, she claims, analogous to stating that everyone, everywhere finds all art appealing – from opera to cubist paintings, hip-hop music to macramé – an idea which most would hold absurd. The problem with 'nature' as the focus of aesthetic attention is that it is not framed in the way an art object is – neatly bracketed off from its surroundings so that the beholder knows they are being presented with 'an object'. Instead, since nature is the surroundings, appreciating it aesthetically is potentially indistinguishable from appreciating it at all (Berleant, 1993; Carlson, 2002). As a conceptual category, appreciating nature aesthetically would, therefore seem to be a tautology.

Since, intuitively, there does seem to be some difference between merely being outside amongst nature and relating to certain aspects of the natural world aesthetically, philosophers have tackled this problem in several ways, mainly by applying aesthetic theories developed for art criticism to a new subject matter, effectively regarding *nature* as a work of art. These ideas either attend to the objects of nature, e.g. applying established aesthetic principles to why a gnarled tree root or meandering river stirs our aesthetic emotions for instance; or they treat nature as a landscape painting, arguing that we find natural scenes beautiful because we regard them from a distance as if they were, in fact, paintings (Carlson, 2002). Indeed, it is distance from nature that has paved the way for what Urry (2002) calls the 'tourist gaze' upon our surroundings – that which is voyeuristic and contemplates views as objects for consumption, much as the flaneûr finds all in the world 'picturesque' (Tester, 1994). To return to my data here, there does seem to be a case for claiming that the attraction of the views in some cases is based on a *distancing* of nature as if it were a picture hanging on the office wall, especially those that were taken through – and framed by – the windows, rather than actually photographed by physically leaving the building. So perhaps, for these people, the view from the window is just as much a part of the 'office environment' as any of the objects physically within it.

But this to my mind cannot account for the value of the countryside for many of my respondents. The 'nature as artwork' argument may account for those people who like to be near a window for a 'change of focus' or as an escape from tasks, but in several of the accounts above, the countryside was enjoyed in its own right. An example is Maureen, who would 'rather see sky than ceilings'; and then Denise, who professed that she 'liked the grounds'; and even Deb, who, despite, watching through her window enjoyed the view for what it was – the trees, countryside and the changing seasons they reminded her of.

Appleton (1996) takes a view from environmental psychology, that we are 'hard-wired' to respond emotionally to landscapes on account of their potential to offer us (imagined) refuge from harm or to afford us a clear view of oncoming danger – thus, wide open spaces and rolling hills, for example, produce a sense of calm that we would be able to see any enemies should they approach. This remains an open question, but the idea that psychological needs shape our appreciation of beauty – and in this case nature – is at least plausible, especially if we consider that many of my respondents spoke of their love of the outdoors as offering an escape from the tiring, stressful work environment. Of course, this means abandoning the Kantian aesthetic ideal of 'disinterest' that emphasises true aesthetic experience as that which is felt without motive or personal agenda – something that Berleant (1993) insists should be done in favour of an aesthetics of engagement, recognising the inevitability of subjectivity in aesthetic (and any other) physical relation with the world.

The idea of engaging with nature and actually getting out there and enjoying the feel of being in the countryside, as some of my respondents did – catching a bit of sun, sitting on the lawn or being among the chaos of moss, plants and branches – certainly seems to resonate with these people's experiences of, and explanations why, the countryside location was important to them. These sensory – aesthetic – stimulations were not afforded by the environment inside their workplace, despite the office being quite an appealing place to be as the majority of these respondents also agreed. However, and as Soper (1995) observes, this engagement thesis still does not explain why – as in the case of so much of my data here – so many people prefer representations of the countryside to actually going out in it, nor does it account for why the countryside was preferred to the inside. For this we have to return to the critique of the universality of the aesthetic appreciation of nature.

Soper (1995) insists that any appreciation of nature is politically and culturally shaped. This idea is picked up by Lash and Urry (1994: 295) who urge us not to treat the 'society-nature relationship' a-historically or a-culturally – an argument borne out in Barrell's (1993) historical analysis of the development of aesthetic fashions in the depiction and designed experience of nature (see also Urry, 2002: 147). Briefly here, as scientific rationalism took hold, Barrell argues that a logico-scientific world view became prized as a superior way of relating to the world, the ability to think in abstract terms and comprehend conceptual connections between things dominated, objectivity, detachment, rationality. These traits were not the preserve of everyone – certainly not women and certainly not the working classes – only the educated 'thinking men' of grace and cultivated social status were capable of such endeavour and this was reflected in the art they commissioned, and the viewing towers they built to afford them this 'broader view' or 'bigger picture' of the world. Correspondingly the panoramic vista became equated with fine taste and good breeding, setting an aesthetic tone to which all art should aspire, or be relegated as merely 'common' or 'popular' taste.

This fascinating historical account deserves greater explication than is possible here but the important point for this chapter is that 'tastes in nature are conditioned by the general ideas and fashions of their period… and the ideas and fashions are themselves for the most part dictated by a privileged minority within the culture' (Soper, 1995: 234). For example, it was not until the mid-19th century that the landed gentry began to erect houses with outbuildings away from the main house so as to afford a good 'prospect' of the surrounding countryside as if their windows were cameras capturing the views they afforded their owners (Abercrombie and Longhurst, 1998, cited in Urry, 2002: 148). This reminds us that 'having a good view' from the window has not always been as important as it is today, where such features actually add financial value to houses, or at least make them more saleable.

In other words, the 'reading and production process' of nature and its relative value is learned (Lash and Urry, 1994: 295).

Prevailing cultural fashions of the time and the legacy of the past inscribe themselves on what is and is not worthy of aesthetic appreciation, and

> '..since these tastes have been so coloured by considerations of social role and self-esteem, the depiction has often more to tell us about a desired environment than about the feelings evoked by the encounter with reality itself' (Soper, 1995: 234).

Perhaps we could read the data presented here, then, as projections of my respondents' culturally conditioned desired images of the countryside, rather than the reality of them. This would certainly account for the fact that few of the people who professed a desire for the countryside actually made use of it, yet having a view of it was nonetheless important. The next steps, then, are to consider why 'the countryside' is an aesthetically fashionable thing to desire when at work, why these people felt the need to 'enjoy' it through their windows or in their imaginations and memories and what these things tell us about organisational aestheticisation.

Culture and countryside

If we consider that the appreciation of nature is first and foremost socially constructed then we must at least consider the possibility that these photographs and their explanations are symbolic, telling us more about what is aesthetically desirable for these people in this context, than what they actually do and feel. It is this point I wish to tease out a little more here, by considering what some of the cultural forces mediating these people's aesthetic judgments might be.

Firstly, since the time of the industrial

revolution, 'the countryside' and correspondingly, 'nature' have increasingly been subject to a process of romanticisation. As industrialisation has taken hold, rural life has become something to be looked back on as idyllic and with nostalgia as a 'golden age', despite the realities of rural existence often being harsh (Soper, 1995: 227). As noted by Tuan (1990: 103) 'once society had reached a certain level of artifice and complexity, people would begin to take note, and appreciate, the relative simplicities of nature.' Therefore, as human mastery (or 'domestication') of nature increased, so did its status as malleable 'object', so as Soper (ibid.) explains, the countryside becomes

> '...an aesthetic 'luxury' of a culture that has begun to experience its power over nature as a form of severance from it.'

Urry (2002:87 – 89) points out that this romantic view of the countryside was felt most strongly by the middle, or 'service' classes who were the most disillusioned with 'elements of the modern' and therefore most attracted to the 'virtues of tradition and lack of social intervention' the countryside was perceived to embody. Broadly speaking, many of my respondents would fall into this socio-economic category which might go some way to explaining their topophilic attitudes.

Severance from nature becomes all the more marked when we consider the explosive growth in automotive transport. On one hand the car has opened up the countryside to increasing numbers of people through the construction of extensive road networks, but at the same time travelling by car ensures that the visitor is permanently closed off from it too – gazing through the windows at the world outside. Following Wilson (1992), Soper (1995: 242) remarks that this kind of relationship

> '...promotes a certain nature aesthetic – one that is essentially visual and has ruled out taste, touch and smell; for which landscape becomes an event in 'automotive space'....'.

This certainly seems to resonate with the ways many of my respondents claimed to enjoy the natural environment around their workplace – at a distance and with a 'non-contact nostalgia' that might account for the slightly apologetic and even melancholic tone to many of the reasons given for not spending more time outside. Urry (2002: 149) addressing the case of countryside engagement as tourism, suggests that such 'sightseeing' now carries with it connotations of embarrassment – the camera wielding coach tripper engaging in a superficial and inauthentic relationship with the places they visit, which might also account for some of the feelings expressed.

Berleant (1993: 234) goes as far as to say that there is no longer any separation between 'nature' and 'culture', arguing for this in two respects. Firstly he observes that human actions have had far-reaching natural consequences, shaping, destroying, changing and altering the shape and character of the planet and its flora and fauna forever. Secondly, and as discussed above, he notes that what is meant by 'nature' and 'countryside' are shifting cultural constructs dependent on the prevailing social conditions of the time. Indeed, Tuan (1990) documents these shifts graphically, with diagrams to map how concepts of 'sacred' and 'profane' environments have almost reversed since biblical times to the present day. With this in mind, there seems no reason why we should consider the natural environment at work different from any other aesthetic attribute there since, as he puts it,

> 'a single aesthetic applies to nature and to art because, in the final analysis they are both cultural constructs, and so we are not talking about two things but about one' (Berleant 1993: 241).

To sum up, then, it is possible that these persons' photographs expressed a socio-culturally conditioned desire to find the countryside aesthetically appealing – as an artificial, culturally produced object, rather than a natural environment within which physically to exist which, ironically, returns us to the 'nature as artwork' argument discussed above, but by a different route.

The artificiality of nature finds resonance in the work of Baudrillard (1994, 1998) and his concept of 'hyper-reality'. The hyper-real, according to Baudrillard, is that which is more than real – an illusion of reality that appears as reality. He argues that the emergence of mass media and virtual technologies in the late twentieth century have irreversibly altered our relationships with reality by making the images we see through our television screens – or in the present case from our office windows – for example, seem more 'real' than the 'real thing'. Urry (2002) extends these ideas to account for the nature of tourism as the consumption of these 'pseudo-events', in which familiar signs are sought out that confirm the viewers pre-established notions of the context under gaze – in this case 'the countryside'. To return to my data and the argument that my respondents' aesthetic desire for/reactions to nature can be seen as a cultural construct, it is likely that for these people, socialised in a mass-mediated society, where representations of nature are either brought to them, for the most part, via television, cinema screens, the pages of glossy magazines and/ or as 'automotive events' experienced inside their cars, we could plausibly read the countryside surrounding Department X's office as a 'hyper-real' 'pseudo-event'.

After all, 'real' countryside would be untended, overgrown and look vastly different to Department X's beautifully landscaped and maintained grounds. Likewise, these signs and symbols – framed in the photographs the respondents took – could be argued to be cultural signifiers of 'proper countryside', e.g. trees, rolling hills, grass and so on. Therefore the version of 'countryside' consumed by these respondents can be argued to be hyper-real on two levels; firstly due to its physically sculpted and landscaped nature; and secondly because by 'consuming' the countryside from inside their building, these respondents were gaining a further, simulated experience of it, but, importantly, one that satisfied them more than physically venturing outside to enjoy it.

This also ties into the experience of life in a society defined by its capacity to consume, as is the case for my respondents and, arguably all who live in the 'first world'. One of the most curious aspects of consumer societies is that the desire to consume does not seem to be predicated on acquisition, at least not in the case of luxury goods and services, and not in the longer term. The desire to consume does not end when the commodity, event, or experience is obtained and indeed the anticipation of acquiring goods and services – window shopping, or flicking through retailers catalogues for example – can often be as, or more pleasurable than the consumption experience itself. In the present case we can see this in the data above where thinking about going outside is pleasurable in and of itself. This has been accounted for by Campbell's (1987) thesis of 'imaginative hedonism' which states that people consume things because they desire pleasure, and the greatest pleasures are imagined or anticipated ones, since they can be boundless and perfect. Here we can also see how imaginative hedonism fuels a hyper-real world – with the signs of the real – the view from the window and/ or the image of the parklands in my respondents' minds – come to stand for the real itself.

Topophilia and aestheticisation: some conclusions

So what does all this mean for organisations and organisational aestheticisation? I began this chapter by lamenting the absence of attention to the influence of the world outside organisations' walls. As I have noted elsewhere (Brewis and Warren, 2001) organisation is a human sense-making activity that reaches far beyond the realms of economic endeavour. Recognising the extent to which 'non-work' experiences influence workplace behaviours, such as enjoyment of the countryside, is also important because it reminds us that our subject matter is nebulous, the boundaries of organisation are impossible to define, and organisations are, as Strati (2001) puts it, 'without walls'.

More specifically as we have seen, for these people at least, the 'natural' aesthetics of the countryside location were a genuine source of pleasure at work. It is important to note that the people whose words and pictures are presented here found their countryside location and corresponding views of it enjoyable in and of themselves. It is tempting to apply functionalist explanations to account for these feelings and in doing so, we run the risk of inappropriately bringing aesthetic experiences under the auspices of rational utilitarianism – as business and management studies have already done with so much of human behaviour at work. Indeed, following Kant, as Strati (1999) has reminded us, aesthetic experiences have a 'finite sensibility' that means there is often no immediately apparent reason for why a certain configuration of features or arrangement of shapes should strike a pleasing (or repulsive) chord within us – we simply like things because we like them.

Nonetheless, the countryside did seem to be regarded as a valued 'aesthetic asset' by these employees and many stated that this contributed to their decisions to join and remain with the organisation, a finding which would seem to lend tentative support for Bauman's (1998) claims that employees seek aesthetic pleasures from their employment and value those that offer such pleasures above occupations that do not. Briefly here, Bauman argues that as consumption takes hold in contemporary societies as a way of life (rather than an activity engaged in solely to acquire goods and services to alleviate need), the 'aesthetic ethic' upon which it is founded will become a primary arbiter of value for all life's activities, including work. Jobs must be fun, offer the chance of novelty, excitement and variety if they are to remain appealing in a world where surface (aesthetic) values dominate and the 'utility' of goods, services, events, experiences, even people is used up (consumed) at an ever increasing rate. If we read organisations' attempts to aestheticise their employees' 'workplace experiences' through this lens we could make the argument that organisational aestheticisation initiatives such as those outlined in the introduction to this chapter, and the changes to Department X effected by MCS, are responses to this cultural trend. Importantly, however, organisations generally seem to be focussing on internal attributes and missing the significance of what is outside their offices, factories and buildings.

However, as we have seen, the real value of the natural environment was not (on the whole) in the physical experience of outdoor pursuits, but in the consumption of such 'imagined pleasures' from within the building and through the windows. Aesthetic and cultural theory has aided a conceptual interpretation of this rather strange state of affairs, but in terms of what it tells us about organisational aesthetics it seems that employees may have a preference for that which has been socio-culturally conditioned as being 'natural' rather than that which appears to be overtly 'artificial'. If my respondents share at least some characteristics with other office based workers, then, we might speculate that people prefer to enjoy the countryside through windows from the comfort of their desks as a hyper-real consumption experience, or as a form of organisational decoration. If this is indeed the case, then one assumes that an organisation would not need to relocate to an expensive 'greenfield' site, merely to provide a simulated experience of being located in one.

This has clear ramifications for the construction of office environments and may mean that any attempt to bring the 'outside in' – for example, light airy spaces, lots of windows, a profusion of plants, muted colour schemes etc., would be more 'successful' as an aestheticisation device than those designs which favour a more futuristic or 'space-age' aesthetic. The above notwithstanding, it is also important to remember that for several respondents the value of being and seeing outside was articulated as an 'escape' from tasks leading to the possibility that any escape from work to an alternative environment might be equally enjoyed. Although it is not my aim here to 'prove' the efficacy (or otherwise) of aestheticisation programmes, or write managerial prescriptions for how they might work better, I would contend that these data do shed light on the experience of working in such an environment and by extension, do have something to say about constructed aesthetics in an organisational setting.

Creativity can promise great solutions, but does not often deliver. In some ways, 'creative thinking' in management and business has become yet another regime of failed thought. This chapter suggests that borrowing creative techniques from the realms of art or design is not enough. Until organisations learn themselves to become media of art or design thinking, they will never be able to absorb the transformative power of creativity. Here the authors begin with the challenge of constructing a new organisational framework for thinking – against the hard pragmatic nature of organisational demands. They propose the need for 'multi-epistemic' thought processes – not static frameworks, but dynamic processes capable of producing all modes of knowledge in an organisation. To this end they make strategic use of Carl Jung's knowledge typology – thinking, feeling, sensing and intuiting. To demonstrate its usefulness, they assess a project by internationally famous consultancy IDEO.

Following from the last, this chapter offers a way of integrating 'design thinking' at the level of specific projects. In organisations, 'design' is often synonymous with either 'composition' (strategy design, organisation design) or 'style' (brand design, product design, and so on). There are many variants and types of 'design'. However, embedded deep in our design traditions are philosophical ideas and forms of thinking that offer organisations a means to understand complex processes. An organisation is itself a medium of intelligence, which can generate creativity if structured and deployed effectively in projects.

Design Thinking as Multi-epistemic Intelligence in Organisations

Robert M. Bauer and Ward M. Eagen

So *design thinking* is neither just design, nor thinking. It is both something more and something less than designing and thinking, and used outside the realm of what we normally refer to as 'design'. This paper outlines 'design thinking' as a solution-oriented methodology for creating desired outcomes – and it goes well beyond the making of aesthetically pleasing artefacts and environments. Below, we have outlined a programme of design thinking that is fundamentally 'multi-epistemic'– involving different modes of *knowing*. We use a Jungian typology to categorise these ways of knowing (as thinking, feeling, sensing and intuiting), and this contributes to our understanding of how the best in creative problem solving is achieved. We believe that a more significant adoption of design thinking would be beneficial and could ultimately lead to entire organisations becoming *design agents* – able to move beyond the standard forms of thought, analysis and the procedures of management and production that flow from them, and in which increasingly more industry is stuck today.

1. DESIGNING AS CREATIVE PROBLEM SOLVING

Managers must take decisions and solve problems, and thus require intelligence. Until recently, mainstream research has conceptualised 'intelligence', 'problem solving' and 'decision making' as predominantly intellectual phenomena, intimately tied to the capacity for rational thought, for systematically analysing problems and searching their solution spaces, for memorising and logically processing information. More recently however research has moved on from studying how textually and mathematically coded problems are solved to studying success in dealing with real-life, every-day problems. As a result it has arrived at concepts of multiple intelligences – analytical intelligence still plays an important role but so do other forms such as, for instance, emotional or practical intelligence (Sternberg, 2004).

Similarly, design thinking is increasingly being recognised for its potential to go beyond analytical thinking by providing a more comprehensive alternative in dealing with managerial and organisational problems. Analytical thinking is effective in optimising solutions for a defined problem with a defined goal and a defined solution space but it falls short when it comes to creating new possibilities (since one can only analyse what already exists). 'Design thinking' is a term that designates how designers go about creating artefacts and environments such as industrial products, buildings, services or graphics (I). The term is widely established, yet unfortunate as it implies a style of *thinking* thereby de-emphasising that designing extends far beyond intellectual activity.

Since the 1960s research in design thinking has been conducted, predominantly by researchers of computer-based expert systems (Simon, 1969) and researchers aiming to explain and improve design processes and education (Eastman, 1970; Lawson, 1972, 1979). More recently, a third group has become strongly interested in design thinking – the business community, including practitioners, consultants, scholars, educators and media. 'Design thinking' has emerged as a label for an approach for enhancing managerial behaviours and processes by partially modeling managing after designing (e.g. Boland and Collopy, 2004). This managing-as-designing approach has been fuelled by design firms (most notably IDEO) repositioning themselves as innovation-strategy consultancies, by design schools (such as the Design Institute in Chicago or the Stanford d-School) directly addressing the business community by offering consulting and education, and further by business schools (most prominently the University of Toronto's Rotman School of Management) promoting design-inspired management education. Lastly, we have the business media (most importantly *Business Week*) spreading the latest on the design revolution and to some extent shaping industry's expectations.

In this context, 'design thinking' represents a generic approach to creative problem solving or, less cognitively framed, to creating valuable new arrangements that improve consumer or work experience. It appears that businesses are facing increasing pressure for innovation and growing demand for products and services that offer rich experience beyond technical functionality (II). If this is true, then it is no surprise that design thinking is gaining currency among business practitioners, consultants and scholars because design thinking seems very well suited to the task of creating new rich experiential artefacts and environments.

2. HOW DESIGNERS THINK

Empirical research into the psychology and epistemology of design has been conducted since the early 1970's, initially focusing on architectural design and expanding into engineering and industrial design (for excellent surveys see Lawson, 1997, 2004 and Cross, 2006). Basically, this research has tried to answer two questions: first, how do designers solve problems differently than non-designers; and second, how do experienced or distinguished designers' work differently than novice or average designers, respectively? Methodologically, researchers have primarily relied on variations and combinations of concurrent protocol studies (i.e. taping designers who think aloud while working in a lab or studio to create design solutions) and in-depth interviews (i.e. designers retrospectively describe how they design). Both methods have their limitations. Laboratory studies miss many factors that influence every-day life and work; and thinking aloud strongly intervenes into the processes meant to be observed. Retrospective self-reports are necessarily narratives with a particular perspective. Over time, however, this research has revealed interesting features of design thinking.

Designers tend to explore problems through solution conjectures rather than analysing the problem and subsequently generating alternative solutions (Lawson, 1979; Kolodner and Wills, 1996). Designers often shape both problem-framing and possible solutions (Schön, 1988; Lloyd and Scott, 1995), aiming for matching problem-solution pairs (Cross and Dorst, 1998), rather than searching a given problem's solution space. Designers often work in a playful fashion, physically engaging with representations in the form of drawings, models and prototypes (Lawson, 2004; Schrage, 2000). They frequently introduce new goals and constraints throughout the design process (Akin, 1986) – even when dealing with rather well-defined problems (thereby, treating them as ill-defined problems) (Thomas and Carroll, 1979). Designers often reduce complexity early on by committing to particular details (Lawson, 1994), or simple formative ideas, abstract principles or 'generators' (Darke, 1978), or they explore the problem until they find such a complexity-reducing 'first principle' (Cross, 2001), rather than start with the general and move towards the specific. Consequently, the design process grows from attempts to resolve creatively the tensions between two or more such complexity-reducing foci or principles (Rowe, 1987). Designers tend deliberately to utilise the tension between what is desired and what is possible, often starting with the desired and working their way back to what is doable.

These insights are illuminating and encouraging, yet are far from amounting to a coherent model of design thinking. In fact, it is still unclear if design thinking is a sufficiently coherent phenomenon to capture in one model and one term only. However, in this paper we will provisionally accept this assumption, which is commonly shared in the current discourse about design thinking. In what follows we outline a conceptualisation of design thinking that enables us to examine the potential of design thinking in management. We build on the suggestions from the above mentioned key contributors to the current development of design-inspired approaches to management, most importantly from IDEO (and the d-School; Kelley, 2001) and from the Design Institute at the Illinois Institute of Technology (Owen, 1998 a, b).

3. THE THREE MOVEMENTS OF DESIGNING: UNDERSTANDING, DREAMING, BUILDING

Although the products of design may in fact be goods and services, these physical manifestations are only the vehicles of the design agent's central intention, that is, the creation of new, rich experience. All experience is embodied and physically insinuated in the lived world, mediated through the body (Merleau-Ponty, 1945). The design process necessarily starts in the grounded, embodied reality of the lived world, is led by imagination into the virtual realm of possibility, only to return to the lived world for actualisation. The Design Agent's excursion via imagination traverses a realm where time and space have no limitations, where one can be entirely open to new possibilities that can be quickly and freely explored, such that one returns to the lived world with newfound possibility. Consider Freud's observation that thought is action in rehearsal and that humans are torn between the reality principle and the pleasure principle (Freud, 1911). Imagination is the domain of the pleasure principle as every thought (possibility) that can be imagined is realised and yet exists without the real problems of actualisation, beyond constraints, limits, and consequences. Although designing aims to change reality, it must pass through the virtual, harvesting the potential of possibility found only in the imagination and return to enrich the embodied experience of the lived world.

We suggest that the design process can generally be understood as three movements; 'Understanding', 'Dreaming', and 'Building', each containing a divergent and a convergent motion (refer to Figure 1). Understanding moves from the lived world

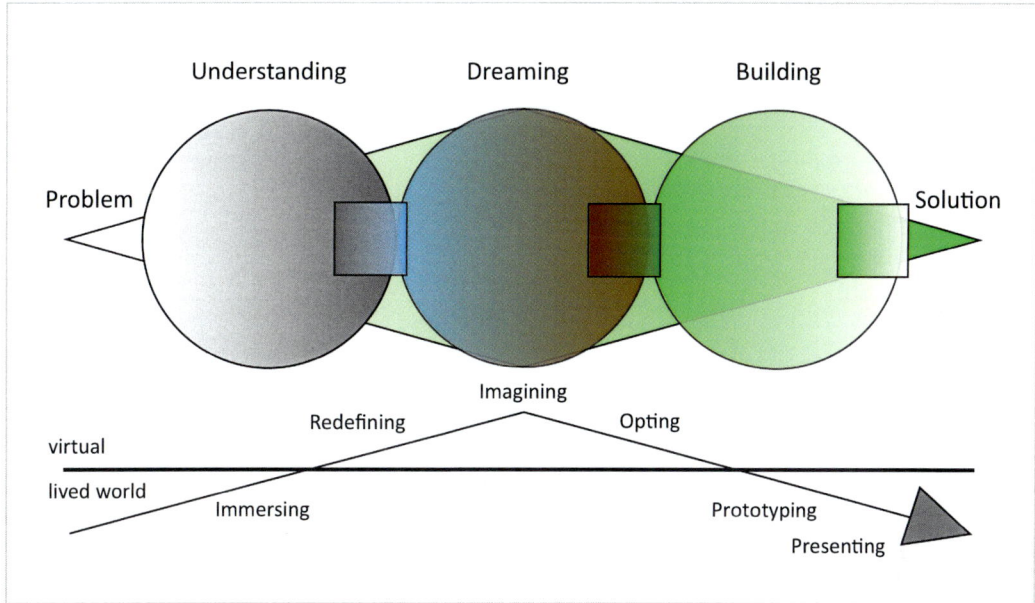

Figure 1: *The Three Movements of Designing*

to the virtual by Immersing into the target experience from which a Redefinition is abstracted that charts the design agent's intent. Dreaming moves within the virtual by Imagining possible worlds and Opting for the most promising directions for enriching experience. Building moves from the virtual back to the lived world actualising promises through a progressive series of Prototypes culminating in the Presentation of a new design.

> 'All doing is knowing, and all knowing is doing.'
>
> H. Maturana and F. Varela

First Movement: *Understanding (Immersing and Redefining)*

'Understanding' – the movement leading from the lived world to the virtual, is composed of a divergent motion, 'Immersing' (which expands the perspectives of the design agent) – and a convergent motion, 'Redefining' (which refocuses perspectives). Note that the term 'design agent' can be an individual or a collective, such as a design team or a web-based community and may change dynamically with movements and motions. We are using the term to clarify that the designer as the 'genius', 'artist' or 'auteur' is not what we have in mind. Design is mostly a team process, and designers require a diverse set of skills more in the vein of facilitator or midwife than creator.

Immersing: Since all designing is designing of user experience, it is important for designers initially to interrogate the user experience they wish to improve. In order to do so designers study *users*, employing ethnographic research methods such as observing users in their own environment, conducting in-depth interviews with users, participating in users' practices to gain first-hand experience, and having users study their own practices (Mariampolski, 2006). These methods enable designers to put themselves into the users' shoes and see the world through the users' eyes, which when successful, allows designers to understand users better than users understand themselves.

Redefining: When designers aim for Immersion by entering the users' lived world and resonating with the users' experience, their search is usually initiated and driven by a specific interest, for example, improving an unsatisfactory product or service or developing a new one for a certain target group, etc. Immersion enables designers to understand users' actual problems or needs, which in turn provides the basis for designing value. Generally, design problems are 'wicked problems' known to be caused by deeper, underlying problems (Buchanan, 1992, Rittel and Webber, 1973) (III). Building on the first divergent motion (Immersing), the primary goal of the second convergent motion (Redefining) is to focus efforts through uncovering the underlying, deeper problem so that an actionable problem statement can be developed that captures the design agent's intent.

Ideally, redefining is grounded in 'systems thinking'. A competent doctor will understand a symptom of infection as the combined result of the germ's 'attack' and the body's 'defense'. A competent design agent similarly does not think in terms of free-standing products or services, but of interventions into systems comprised of products or services and users dealing with it within a community or super-system (interconnecting users and uses of the prospective product or service). Systems thinking requires defining adequately system boundaries, modeling causal loops, and radically contextualising meaning (Bateson, 1972) – all of which are cognitive moves that address how the whole and its parts react to each other. In addition, systems thinking is concerned with the timing and sequencing characterising the evolution and current behaviors of complex systems (Brown and Eisenhardt, 1997). Systems thinking is aided by various visualisation techniques (e.g., causal maps, flow charts, cognitive maps, semantic webs, matrices, etc; Beckman and Barry, 2007) and at times by computer-simulated models (Sterman, 2001). Yet in designing human experience, storytelling, 'telling the right story right', remains the manifestation of systems thinking par excellence (Gabriel, 2000).

Understanding leads from concrete experience to an abstract description of the problem to be solved. The *Redefined* problem statement can differ significantly from the initial one in ways that neither the client nor the design agent can anticipate. The problem properly engaged takes on a certain life of its own, however the design agent must resonate with this Redefining as it becomes the statement of intent for the next movement.

Second Movement: *Dreaming (Imagining and Opting)*

Dreaming remains within the virtual and is composed of a divergent motion, *Imagining*, expanding the solution space, and a convergent motion, *Opting*, where decisions are made that ultimately condense an area for actualisation.

Imagining: The quest for new ideas through imagining relies on various types of thinking: analytical thinking challenges the presuppositions of extant ideas, destabilising and shifting them; associative thinking connects ideas in a spontaneous, stochastic fashion; daydreaming playfully combines the powers of conscious and unconscious information processing; and dialogical thinking aloud, e.g., brainstorming, merges and re-combines ideas from different individuals, and ideally resulting in what none of them could have ever imagined on their own.

Design agents use Imagining to generate a large set of alternative solution concepts for the Redefined problem; some rather elaborate and mature, others raw and partial; some concerning the design task in its entirety, others concerning particular aspects; some complementing, others contradicting, and yet others seemingly unrelated to each other. It is commonly understood that deferring judgment enhances Imagining. Not all ideas are equally useful but in Imagining's motion, an idea's value lies in its potential for generating new ideas that forward the action in the realm of the possible, rather than its potential as the basis for action in the actual world.

Opting: Designing requires imagining the world as it could be, envisioning how it should be, and yet clearly seeing how it is, coupled with the ability to know when to adopt which perspective. Opting is the process of centering on the group of ideas that can coherently co-exist and that warrant further development towards actionable concepts, shifting the direction of the designer's focus of attention from the possible towards the actual. Opting is highly evaluative of ideas and relationships between ideas (patterns). Yet one exits the process with many unknowns still remaining to be physically explored through modeling. At the end of Dreaming, design agents Opt for a certain solution space trusting that it can be actualised.

Third Movement: *Building (Prototyping and Presenting)*

The movements Understanding and Building both develop knowledge through iterative cycles. They can be viewed as mirror images with Understanding spiraling from the lived world to the virtual, and Building spiraling from the virtual back again to the lived world.

Prototyping: Prototyping aims at developing the most promising ideas generated and integrating them into an actual product or service that enriches experience. To be successful this motion relies on specific goals and a sound understanding of what can and should be tested. Prototyping, sometimes referred to as rapid Prototyping, is essentially an iterative approach to knowledge acquisition through multiple cycles of action and reflection (Schön, 1983). The initial build is used to explore particular ideas and specific relationships and may in fact be quick and dirty. Incrementally building on lessons learned through reflective testing as well as outside feedback, the next-generation prototype is more nuanced in its response to new interrogations. Each iteration refines until the solution satisfies the design problem or is in a satisfactory form that can be adopted by users. Designers think to build and equally, build to think, dynamically interweaving experiential knowing and physical doing.

Prototyping is the physical manifestation and conceptual continuation of Imagining as a way of exploring ideas at low risk and cost. It can be understood as an experiential model of scientific progress through the continuous falsification of hypotheses (Popper, 1934). Every prototypical model, physical object, pilot project, computer simulation, etc., instantiates an hypothesis as a validity claim to test. The art of Prototyping lies in the creating of physical experiments designed to maximise insight and mitigate risk: to be successful, it requires quick learning based on very short development cycles. Prototyping facilitates rapid development and effective user feedback, enabling communication between agents that may otherwise lack shared knowledge or a common language (Carlile, 2002; Schrage, 2000).

Presenting: In the present motion, the client welcomes the new design as the design agent bids farewell. The wrap-up or end point of a design project is more about releasing than resolution: rarely are there design projects or design agents that do not require more time for development. Experienced design agencies understand this and religiously guard against 'scope creep' that diminishes the considerable time and budget required to make a rich, professional presentation. A successful presentation is an experience charged with the very energy and hope of the entire design process and communicates the value proposition of the new experience promised.

In what follows these movements and motions are interrogated in terms of their epistemological foundation.

> *'Le cœur a ses raisons que la raison ne connaît point.'*
> Blaise Pascal

4. EPISTEMIC PLURALITY

We speak of epistemic plurality if an agent's actions are informed by diverse epistemic modes or ways of knowing. By contrast, a computer is a paradigmatic example of a mono-epistemic device, relying exclusively on the most explicit form of declarative knowledge, namely algorithms (Bauer and Moldoveanu, 2008). In the twentieth century, modern cultures placed enormous emphasis on language – natural as well as formal – as the primary basis for human reasoning, understanding human brains as very powerful, complex computers. Polanyi's (1966) seminal criticism of an over-reliance on explicit knowledge as descriptively wrong and prescriptively misleading, gained tremendous currency in the 1980s as a founding piece of the knowledge- or competence-based view. However, keeping the dichotomy 'explicit versus non-explicit (tacit) knowledge', he did not arrive at a truly pluralistic, multi-epistemic conceptualisation of human knowledge and action.

Jungian Epistemic Modes

From the perspective of the Jungian model of psychological base functions, which is an early and still outstanding conceptualisation of human knowledge rooted in epistemic plurality, design thinking can be understood as inclusive of analytical thinking but much larger in scope. Jung (1921) distinguishes four elementary psychological functions: thinking, feeling, sensing, and intuiting.

Thinking (Cognition): Thinking systematically relates categories of ideas to each other, linking contents of imagining into conceptual relations that enable humans to create possible worlds for risk-free exploration. Thinking ranges from daydreaming to actively manipulating symbols as tokens for ideas along the grammatical structures of natural or formal languages.

Feeling (Emotion): Feeling is an affective, sentimental function that imparts value to content as the basis of likes and dislikes. In essence, feeling positions, objects and events, including those of the mind, on a continuum from embracing through neutral to rejecting, evaluating them in terms of good or bad, pleasant or unpleasant, acceptable or unacceptable. Emotions can strongly fuel or inhibit action.

Sensing (Perception and Proprioception): Sensation provides an immediate experience of what is: one thinks and feels about things and events, regardless of their physical presence but one senses them as an object or event only within their immediate physical presence. Sensation is conscious perception that has a certainty based on pure physicality. Sensing is intimately tied to aesthetic categories such as exciting/boring, harmonious/disharmonious, beautiful/ugly, etc.

Intuiting (Intuition): Intuition is a gestalt of unconscious perceptions that possess intrinsic certainty and conviction: Spinoza and Bergson thought of intuition in this sense as the most direct and highest form of knowledge (Jung, 1921). Through intuition humans access insights and knowledge without awareness of any trace of the process. Intuition comes with a certainty but no rationale for this certainty, although in hindsight, it may be possible to trace the source of the intuitive knowledge as a specific causal chain. Intuition never directly reflects reality but actively, creatively, insightfully, and imaginatively adds meaning by reading into the situation things not immediately apparent through sensory data.

Jung points out that the four epistemic modes are *incommensurable*: insights and knowledge from one cannot be accurately represented in terms of another. Human knowledge is necessarily fragmented and conflicting in nature, permanently struggling – to give a classic example, our inability to resolve the conflict between beauty, truth, and goodness. On the other hand, without this fundamental difference, that is, if one mode could be fully represented in terms of another, one or more epistemic modes would be redundant and consequently could not compliment the others. The fundamentally different modes of knowing may induce struggle and pain, but they also stabilise human experience even in situations when one epistemic mode might fail to cope. In addition, if multiple ways of knowing, despite their in-principle difference, align and join to form a coherent experience, they tend to convey an enormous sense of reality or truth.

Designing as the Epitome of Epistemic Plurality

Design thinking oscillates between the lived world and the virtual, and between divergent and convergent modes of information processing. Relying on different combinations of epistemic modes, each of the six motions that jointly constitute designing has its own distinct epistemic profile. In the process of repositioning itself as a strategic innovation consultancy, IDEO publicised its design process promoting it as a general approach to innovating products

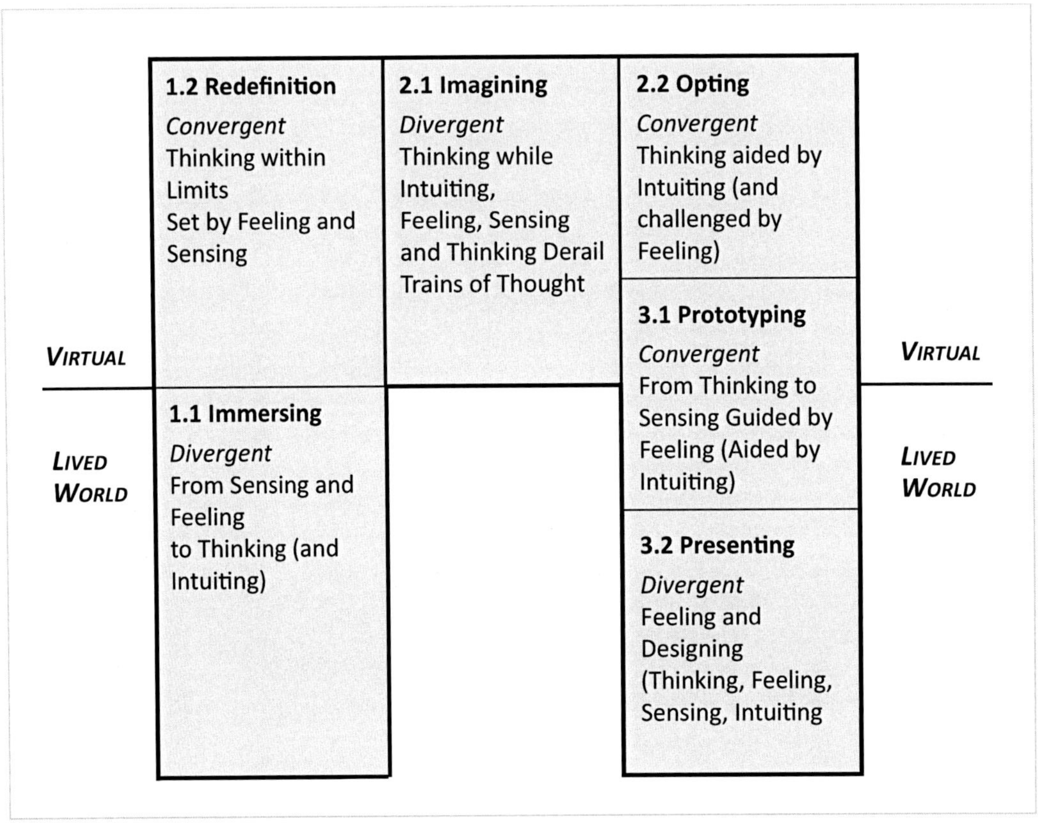

1.2 Redefinition	2.1 Imagining	2.2 Opting
Convergent Thinking within Limits Set by Feeling and Sensing	*Divergent* Thinking while Intuiting, Feeling, Sensing and Thinking Derail Trains of Thought	*Convergent* Thinking aided by Intuiting (and challenged by Feeling)
1.1 Immersing		3.1 Prototyping
Divergent From Sensing and Feeling to Thinking (and Intuiting)		*Convergent* From Thinking to Sensing Guided by Feeling (Aided by Intuiting)
		3.2 Presenting
		Divergent Feeling and Designing (Thinking, Feeling, Sensing, Intuiting

Left side: **VIRTUAL** / **LIVED WORLD**
Right side: **VIRTUAL** / **LIVED WORLD**

Figure 2: *Epistemic Profiles of the Six Motions*

and services (Kelley, 2001). We will use IDEO's well-known redesign of the common grocery shopping cart (ABC 1999) as a publicly available stylised case to illustrate how our conceptualisation of design thinking epitomises epistemic plurality.

Immersing: In the first motion attention is directed toward the lived world, intended to broaden and deepen the design agent's understanding of what the user experiences; it thus requires an openness to experience that leads to diverging trains of thought. However, immersing into the user's world to effectively gather intelligence, the design agent ultimately intends to return with new value propositions (products or services) for the user.

Immersing oscillates between thinking and, on the other hand, sensing and feeling. Observation (watching, listening, touching, smelling) provides sensory information about user experience in context: empathising in this way allows the design agent to experience as if they were the user without losing sight of the 'as if' condition (Vaihinger, 1927). Immersing leads from sensing (engaging physically to absorb through the senses all necessary information) and feeling (empathy as emotionally resonating with users) to thinking and intuiting. Gradually, through repeated (hermeneutic) cycles, Immersing brings forward explicit knowledge of what the user needs above and beyond simplistic utility. In addition, true immersing expands the design agent's intuitive understanding: although most information presented in experience to the body never becomes conscious – the senses process at least one million times more information than the conscious mind (Maturana and Varela, 1984) – it still influences directions in the design process because unconsciously absorbed information fuels intuition. As new insights become less frequent and saturation approaches, the instrumentality of Immersing limits diverting and continued research is determined to be no longer efficient or effective, and it is time to Redefine the problem.

In the IDEO shopping cart case, a cross-disciplinary design team was initially presented with an orientation session that outlined the project and revealed a number of statistical facts about shopping carts, for example, a psychologist introduced safety concerns citing accident reports. The team then divided into smaller groups to investigate how people use, make, and maintain shopping carts as well as explore peripheral areas such as bike shops and stroller designs. Research was not academic, but hands-on requiring full immersion as the design team went to interview and observe, photograph and sketch, users in their own environment, whether it was a grocery store, maintenance shop, or parking lot.

Redefining: Immersing oscillates between experiencing (sensing or feeling) and reflecting (thinking), and as field research continues the emphasis shifts towards the thinking: designers require dis-embedded knowledge brought from field to studio, workshop, lab or office as reports, images, etc. When saturation approaches, Understanding changes vectors from Immersing to Redefining, which predominantly relies on systems thinking, a particular form of analytical thinking. Redefining is a convergent, complexity reducing motion because thinking establishes patterns, thereby compressing extant elements (e.g., detailed information, particular insights etc.) into a coherent whole (e.g. model, problem statement etc.). Redefining aims for a problem statement that, in Einstein's words, is as simple as possible, but not simpler. This is an active process that imposes order, shaping the parts, reinterpreting, reevaluating, and assembling and recombining them. Redefining is a formative, primarily linguistic process. Written language enhances precise and careful manipulation of symbols. In addition Redefining employs various visualisation methods (e.g. diagrams, matrices) that enable experimenting with alternative symbolic arrangements before selecting one **(IV)**.

At the end of the first movement and after various acts of re-evaluation, selection, organisation, integration and compression, experiences are articulated as an explicit Redefining of criteria for the successful design solution that also captures the design agent's intent. However, design agents would not take this process of abstraction so far as to erase the problem's conceptual and aesthetic connotations that tie the problem statement back to its source, namely, to the users' experience of the lived world. Redefining as thinking acts within boundaries set by sensing and feeling. Here, knowledge is not meant to be completely separable from the knower: design agents reconnect the abstract problem statement and its meaning to the user in terms of aesthetic and emotional consequences by means of their embodied experience from Immersing.

Returning to the IDEO studio the design team shared their insights into the experiences of a variety of users in the form of stories, quotations, observations, photographs, etc. Interestingly, the team utilised no thinking tools, sharing their knowledge through informal individual presentations and casual group discussion, without producing a coherent problem statement. This appears in stark contrast to the other stages of IDEO's design process, all of which rely on specific technologies. We would argue that IDEO has achieved mastery of five motions, Redefining being the one that lags behind. We have reason to believe that the team's inability to process the information adequately and generate a coherent problem statement led to difficulties downstream that eventually jeopardised the redesign of the shopping cart (see below).

Imagining: Imagining is divergent thinking, a mental activity that proceeds freely from one idea to the next, quickly generating a large set of different ideas, more often than not, including promising new ones (de Bono, 1967). The major challenge in Imagining is breaking loose from the deeply entrenched habits of thought that are not even recognised as choices and so escape scrutiny. Imagining requires awareness of trains of thought while actively attempting to derail them: thinking can be creatively disrupted by all epistemic modes including thinking. Consider for example a brainstorming session where an utterance is subjected to an intellectual operation like thinking through the exact opposite idea's implication, which may lead to another idea; or the idea is received empathically and triggers feelings that lead to another idea; or if the idea is presented as a drawing or material object, another idea is triggered by sensing of the initial idea's physical qualities; or the idea immediately triggers another idea with the knower not knowing how she arrived at her knowing (the defining element of intuition), etc.

Imagining rests on two pillars: the ability to create or seek out environments that provide plentiful stimuli that can potentially disrupt thinking, and a receptive stance that recognises that humans, in principle, have no control over their next thought (except for a limited capacity for suppressing it; Libet et al, 2004). This openness and detachment allows one simply to observe their own thoughts, even those that surprise. As is true with Immersing, the receptive, divergent stance in Imagining is a means to an end. Technically, ideation could continue forever; yet, it is terminated when the rate at which promising ideas are produced drops to the point where Imagining no longer justifies the required resources. Approaching this point of exhaustion, Opting, a convergent evaluative mode, sets in governing the selection and assembly of the ideas that warrant further development.

Brainstorming is IDEO's preferred technology for ideation (Kelley, 2001). Most firms consistently fail to produce effective brainstorms in which team creativity tops aggregated individual inventiveness. By contrast, at IDEO brainstorming in cross-functional teams has been developed into a core competence that significantly contributes to IDEO's brand value (Sutton and Hargadon, 1996). The physical space is configured around a large table with no defined 'head' and any spatial directionality is a result of the pin-up wall for posting ideas as people move about dynamically. Throughout, brainstorming rules are displayed: 'one conversation at a time', 'stay focused on topic', 'encourage wild ideas', 'defer judgment', 'build on the ideas of others'. The team leader assuming the facilitator role wears a bell that he rings when anyone is seen to be criticising an idea. All of this gives rise to brainstorming as a dense and dynamic process of cooperative thinking between equals.

Opting: Imagining in an ideal sense results in a large set of diverse ideas, a loose collection that from a rational perspective, resembles data points in disarray. Like Understanding, Dreaming is brought to a close through the imposition of order, through complexity reduction accomplished by (analytical) thinking. Redefining and Opting, although motions of convergent thinking, differ: Redefining restructures past experience rich in sensory and emotional content; Opting, on the other, aims at restructuring future options and thus relies on factual knowledge and analytical thinking about the realisability and expected utility of the ideas generated. As rational knowledge about future states of the world is necessarily incomplete, intuition bridges the gaps in the rational assessment of extant ideas' future potential. Note that ideas are not evaluated individually but in context, as configurations of ideas that are established through analytical thinking. Feeling too has its role in Opting: first, Opting requires trust in the future design process and such trusting is an emotional faculty; second, feeling interferes with thinking, suggesting to choose desired possibilities instead of opting for what remains to appear promising after having been subjected to systematic doubt by analytical thinking.

In the redesign of the shopping cart at IDEO Opting is exercised in two clearly separated steps. By voting for the best ideas, the brainstorming team evaluates their ideas, which are displayed on large pin-up walls. Each team member individually evaluates individual ideas by sticking Post-it notes. Subsequently, a group of highly experienced designers, not all of which are part of the actual design team, gathers and interprets the generated ideas and identifies a pattern, namely four need areas (shopping, safety, checkout, and, finding what you are looking for). They refocus the apparently drifting team by splitting it into four groups, each focused on one specific need area to develop that prototype.

Prototyping: In the third movement, designing returns from the virtual to the lived world, oscillating between action and reflection. Prototyping, like Immersing, deals with the tension between embodied experience and abstract concepts, heavily relying on sensing (the physical) and thinking. Jung's conception of sensing captures the entire physicality of humans as sensory-motor systems, including both the senses (seeing, hearing, smelling etc.) and the sensing of one's own body moving in space and time. Epistemologically, Prototyping and Immersing are mirror images: Immersing addresses the sensory system, takes a receptive, diverging stance and operates outside-in, translating from concrete to abstract. By contrast, Prototyping addresses the motor system, takes a formative, converging stance and operates inside-out, translating from abstract to concrete, iteratively refining and integrating multiple ideas into one. The interplay between sensing and thinking in Prototyping is guided by feeling, ensuring that the insights into users' emotional states and dynamics (gained through Immersing) translate into emotional design. Similarly, during Prototyping the background knowledge gained through Immersing increases the likelihood of intuitive solutions to design problems that occur. IDEO spends a great deal of energy on Prototyping with professional technicians, workshops and tools that can rapidly produce working prototypes and professional quality finished builds in a variety of materials. Prototypes are explored through sensations as well as understood in cognitive and affective modes and are used to test and explore user experience of the design.

Presenting: In the end, Presenting must convey just how the user's experience will be made richer, which requires a very high and focused level of communication. Designing such experience can be understood as a nested cycle, potentially involving all of the above motions. In addition, feeling is of crucial importance for presenting. Not only does the design agent aspire to create affirmative emotional user experience, it is also necessary for the design agent to cope with their own feelings. Throughout the entire process design agents experience disruptions – shifts from one motion to the next that occur for insufficient reason and are thus inherently violent and potentially frustrating. Letting go of the entire design project is the most

pronounced such shift, potentially evoking strong mixed feelings that are characteristic for transitional periods.

IDEO's visualisation skills match their professional ability to rapidly produce quality prototypes: their graphic design, finishing of prototypes and event choreographies are outstanding. IDEO's presentation of their shopping cart re-design was masterful in staging and became a landmark in repositioning the firm as a strategic innovation consultancy. On the other hand, their attempt to redesign the common shopping cart failed, as their design – despite winning a design prize – was never implemented. We are not in the position to provide a full explanation for this failure. However, when the design team meets for Redefining the problem, one designer reports a significant difference between professional and average shoppers. The latter hold onto their cart through most of the entire shopping experience. Professional shoppers, by contrast, park their cart and move swiftly between the shelves with the shopping cart functioning as a 'base station'. IDEO's redesigned shopping cart meets the exact needs of professional shoppers. It provides a mere frame for several removable baskets, assuming the cart will serve as a base station for shoppers to use a basket to collect grocery items. The design team knew about the different usages of the shopping cart, but chose explicitly not to redefine their design task and, as a result, ended up redesigning the common shopping cart to serve uncommon shoppers.

Explicitness and Sequencing

We maintain that the three movements are fundamentally different and collectively constitute designing. Yet they may not always be explicit or appear in linear sequence during the design process. With regard to explicitness, consider for example an agricultural equipment manufacturer where the design team largely consists of engineers and designers who actually farm, using the company's equipment on a regular basis. Thus the design team is already deeply immersed in the users' world and therefore Immersion is not apparent as a separate step in their design process. Or consider a fashion designer designing a new suit. Having long experienced contexts in which suits are used, she is already quite familiar with the solution space of 'suit' delineated over the course of cultural history. Unless she wants to innovate upon 'suit', she can leap right into Building without explicit Understanding or Dreaming. This does not mean that she does not explore the lived world of suit users and dream up new designs for suits, but we would expect that this is in fact an ongoing condition of her life as a fashion designer (V).

Regarding the sequence of design steps, the above order of movements reflects the logic of justification: Immersion, Redefining, Imagining, Opting, Prototyping, Presenting – each motion builds logically on its predecessors. Hence, in order to justify a design solution, it is important to establish a rational narrative, showing that the problem was well understood, the solution space properly explored, and the best possible solution chosen and competently refined. However this does not mean that the process of designing, through which designers advance into yet uncharted territory, progresses linearly. First, contextual factors, such as personal working styles, render a uniform, linear design process impossible. For instance, some designers begin a design process with Imagining, thereby preserving their fresh, innocent ideas that might become lost when they immerse themselves into the users' world and framings. Other designers, however, prefer to start with Immersing, while again others prefer collectively established problems (such as 'suit') that suggest Building right from the start. Second, the multi-epistemic nature of design thinking precludes strictly linear progression because intuition, one of the four foundational epistemic modes, is inherently discontinuous – offering insights and bridging gaps without a logically complete chain of justification. At its best, intuition can cut right through the design process, providing insights that allow for skipping substantial parts of it. Usually, if such an intuitive solution is conceived, designers work backwards, from the solution to the problem, briefly revisiting the skipped steps in order to verify the solution and check whether promising alternative solutions were lost in the fast-forwarded design process.

5. IMPLICATIONS FOR MANAGEMENT

As stated at the outset of this paper, the current interest in design thinking is fuelled by the prospective benefits of design thinking applied to management and organisation. In the 1960s Simon made it clear that analytical thinking is best suited for evaluating given alternatives and choosing the best one (Simon, 1969). Hence, analytical thinking is the tool of choice for managers and organisations that face more opportunities than they can seize. They can focus on selecting the most profitable ones, typically the case in markets where demand exceeds supply (e.g. post-war economies), or in businesses where employees provide so much creativity that the corporation can take it for granted and solely focus on selecting the best ideas, or for stock brokers choosing from a well-defined set of buying and selling options. By contrast businesses under pressure to innovate must adopt a creative approach that generates and seizes new possibilities. Design thinking is the appropriate approach for such businesses engaging actively in the creation of new value propositions.

Analytical thinking is a mono-epistemic approach that relies solely on thinking and operates on well-defined systems of conditions, goals, and solution alternatives or solution spaces. The beauty of analytical thinking lies in its consistency, precision and transparency. Yet, these very qualities constitute a closed system, incapable of generating something new that was not implied in the system in the first place. Analytical thinking requires abstraction: the object of analysis is mapped onto abstract categories (symbols), which in turn are subjected to systematic scrutiny (rule-based manipulation of symbols). This requires commensurability in the sense that the symbols and the body of rules governing their manipulation must be consistent, both internally and with each other. In business, money as a universal equivalent provides such commensurability because differences of all sorts experienced in the lived world can be mapped onto one kind of difference, namely more or less expected financial value. Hence our assertion that analytical thinking is ideally suited for investors' detached rational decisions and exercise of external control.

By contrast, design thinking is aimed at exploiting the full richness of experience in order to create possibilities for new, enriched experience. As a comprehensive, multi-epistemic approach it utilises all four foundational epistemic modes. Traditionally, intelligence was understood as cognition-based (Sternberg, 2003); more recently emotions are also seen as foundational to intelligence (Mayer et al. 2004). Design thinking, executing the six motions of designing, brings together cognition, emotion, sensation and intuition, and is thus best understood as an attempt to exhibit multi-epistemic intelligence.

Design thinking is structurally discontinuous because the four ways of knowing that enable human experience are incommensurable (i.e., radically different in the sense that neither can one be reduced to another, nor is there an encompassing mode capable of integration). It is dynamically incoherent because the phases of the design process (movements and motions) connect with each other discontinuously (i.e., more often than not a motion's termination and the next one's commencement occur for insufficient reason, such as exhaustion of resources). We suggest that due to its comprehensive and discontinuous nature, design thinking can produce designs (solutions) characterised by both complexity and novelty.

Design thinking is capable of utilising tensions such as actual vs. possible, action vs. reflection, attached involvement vs. detached evaluation, divergent learning orientation vs. convergent goal orientation, all of which, like the tensions between thinking, feeling, sensing and intuiting must be dealt with locally and temporarily but cannot be permanently resolved. In turn, it enables creative resolutions of practical design tensions such as different perspectives among and between designers and users, or different formative principles ('generators'; Darke, 1978) that guide the designing. Most importantly, design thinking tackles the tensions between known and unknown, meaningful and meaningless, which makes it the via regia to creating new opportunities, enhancing experience and adding value. (See Bauer and Eagen, 2010 for an analysis of how differences and discontinuities translate into creativity).

The juxtaposition of analytical with design thinking mirrors the fundamental tension between (financial) capital and (creative) labor. Analytical thinking can be understood as the epistemology of managing financial capital, while design thinking provides the epistemic foundations of creative labor. Allocating financial capital to extant investment opportunities is best achieved through analytical thinking, enabling both sophisticated inference (quantitative methods) and a detached stance that acknowledges real world events, however meaningful, affecting or beautiful, solely in terms of their impact on potential investments' expected utility. By contrast, creating new opportunities is best achieved through design thinking, which artfully combines attached participation in the lived world, detached reflection and evaluation, engagement with the unknown, and not the least, the will to shape reality.

The current dominance of economic and quantitative approaches in management education has been criticised as functionally ineffective and ethically undesirable (Pfeffer and Fong, 2002; Goshal, 2005). Our analysis supports such a critique because overreliance on analytical thinking is expected to leave managers unprepared for using multiple ways of knowing, thereby limiting their capacities for innovation. This has ethically problematic consequences because managers trained to evaluate extant opportunities rather than to create new ones, are prone to frame economic action as a zero-sum game that necessitates fierce competition for a maximal share of a fixed total amount of existing value. By contrast, managers capable of design thinking are equipped to opt for a two-fold approach: cooperatively creating new value and, subsequently, appropriating their fair share. Design thinking thus appears to hold a potential for increasing total wealth, balancing cooperation (value creation) and competition (value appropriation). It also, arguably, enhancing job satisfaction as it encourages people to draw on sources of intrinsic motivation such as aesthetic (dis-) pleasure, passion, empathy and the experience of making a difference. Furthermore, a conventional mindset that exclusively relies on analytical thinking and, thus, tends to frame business problems as zero-sum games, also tends to construe mutually exclusive choices between business and the natural environment or between business and society. By contrast, design thinking has the potential to reframe such tensions, thereby increasing the likelihood of more socially and environmentally sustainable solutions.

Design thinking is not restricted to the development of new products and services, but instead can potentially inform management in general. Consider the movement 'Understanding' as an example: If one presumes that all managers or organisational units have (internal or external) customers, then it should be possible for them to delve into their customers' experience in a quasi-ethnographic fashion. True, business codes frequently forbid managers to deploy classic ethnographic methodology for investigating their customers' experience. However, less obtrusive measures can be taken: managers can learn to empathise with their customers, and to observe and listen as 'professional strangers' (Agar, 1980); they can leverage these capabilities by arranging for frequent exposures to the customers' environments (e.g. site visits or engineer-in-residence programs); and they can intentionally expose themselves to situations similar to the ones the customers experience. Organisational units can increase customer intimacy by heavily involving those with the most intimate customer knowledge into key decision-making.

On the manager and organisational levels, increased capacity for Immersion requires both personal development in the form of training and organisational development that alters structures and processes. Equally, the organisation as a whole can be understood as Immersing itself in customer experience, if individual stances, skills, tools and routines, as well as organisational culture, capabilities and processes amount to an organisation flexible enough for shadowing its customer and permeable enough for resonating with their experience. The same is true for all three movements of designing as each can be adopted by individuals, sub units and entire organisations. Design thinking may be most pronounced in independent design agencies and corporate design departments, but when applied to management and organisation its ultimate implication is that entire organisations can be understood and designed as design agents.

Acknowledgements:

We are indebted to David Dunne, Roger Martin, Michael Shamiyeh and participants of the 'Design: Management: Organisation' stream at the Fourth Art of Management and Organisation Conference, The Banff Centre, Canada, for invaluable dialogues that inspired this paper.

Notes

(I) The juxtaposition of 'analytical thinking' with 'design thinking' can be traced back to Nobel laureate Herbert Simon who contrasts professions with sciences: Professions design: they explore possible worlds and prescriptively shape the actual world. By contrast, sciences conduct descriptive analysis: they take the world as given and explain how it functions by revealing its underlying causal mechanisms (Simon 1969; Gordon 1973).

(II) This heightened emphasis on experience is also relevant to business-to-business firms – to the extent that (a) their customers' customers are or cater to consumers, and (b) business-to-business products and services influence customers' work experience thereby invoking qualities such as usability and likeability

(III) 'Wicked problem', a technical term coined by Rittel, denotes problems that lack clearly defined solution spaces and desired end states (Rittel and Webber 1973). Alternative solutions differ in degrees of better or worse according to multiple and usually conflicting criteria but are virtually never correct or right. Such problems have no inherent stopping rule to determine when problem solving is complete. Moreover, each 'wicked problem' is unique, and must be solved through a one-shot operation in the sense that once a design is delivered, substantial changes are often prohibitively expensive.

(IV) Here, visual elements are symbols, pictograms, boxes, arrows, words, numbers etc., which is different from the more representational sketches used in Imagining and Prototyping.

(V) The vast majority of empirical studies of design thinking use fairly well-structured problems (Cross 2001) and find that designers leap right into action, simultaneously exploring the problem and the solution through iterative cycles of building and thinking. However, in our view it is unsurprising that designers engage in Building when the problem's solution space is understood.

In this chapter we again explore the nature of organisational space. Space is something seemingly obvious, measurable, controlled and identified through using boundaries and 'filled' with objects and people. The space of the workplace has recently become complex and replete with 'invisible forces', from wi-fi to CCTV surveillance, communication technologies, lighting design and acoustics management. Indeed, the workplace has advanced immeasurably through a concern with comfortable spaces, convenient office layout, environment-friendly materials, air quality control and ergonomic furniture. Add to this the increased legal and regulatory frameworks for rights and health, safety and quality standards. The changes in the spaces of organisations, however, are more than just physical. The interior of the contemporary organisation has become a space for creativity and style. The contemporary organisation is concerned with how clients, customers and employees 'experience' its spaces.

This chapter is in two parts: the first looks at the significance of organisational space, and historical changes in labour patterns and mobility that have changed the way organisations think of their space. From this general framework the second half of the paper turns to a particular designer and his experience of the spatial design in a variety of organisations. We take a look at the way in which he approaches an organisation and conducts a preliminary design investigation of its character and spatial requirements. From this, the chapter is able to define contemporary organisational space in more specific terms, but to do so in a way that presents a useful theoretical framework for an enlightened strategic management.

Aesthetics and the Spaces of
Organisational Life
Jonathan Vickery

This chapter explores the nature of space in the contemporary organisation in the light of the recent trend in workplace 'aestheticisation' (Hancock, 2002; Warren, 2005b). New corporate office designs employed in all sectors of advanced industry have radically changed the working environment and how organisations understand and use their space. This, as I shall argue, is not just a matter of new trends in interior design. It involves significant historical shifts in the way 'labour' is conceived as a social practice and how organisational membership (or the employee) is managed. In the first half of this chapter we will look at historical transformations in the very concept of organisational space, to be followed by a specific case study on spatial design. The case study will further our understanding of current issues in the management of organisational space, but also serve to demonstrate that spatial changes in the organisational environment involve much more than the shifting around of the furniture: they involve changes in the culture and ideological orientation of the workplace and in the relations between management and employees. Our example will serve a purpose in demonstrating a way in which the complex contemporary dynamics of organisational space can be understood through the very practice of transformation. Design becomes a powerful means of organisational intervention, where theory and practice together can generate a new approach to the working environment. Our example therefore aims to be as relevant to strategic management as it is to design.

The office

Café spaces, lounge areas, personalised 'work stations', Italian designer furniture, multi-media, all make the corporate office a very different place from what it was even three decades ago. Forms of aesthetic experience, artistic taste, and cultural meanings all now play a role in the design of a corporate interior. In other words, modes of human experience once specific to art, culture or leisure, have become intrinsic to the processes of labour in the economy of corporate life. Even in an age of online capital and networked business, corporate market leaders and high-profile MNCs (multi-national corporations) still invest significantly in their organisational spaces, particularly those of their headquarters, and do so with unique forms of spatial design and architecture. Most conspicuous perhaps are the large branded retail companies together with those in the media or creative industries. British agency Bartle Bogle Hegarty's Asia Pacific offices in Singapore, or their peer company TBWA's offices in Tokyo and Los Angeles, are probably as famous as their award-winning advertising campaigns. Other famous examples might include the Fruit Towers headquarters of Innocent Drinks in London, the Lego Group offices in Billund, Denmark, and Reebok's corporate offices in Massachusetts, USA. The list could go on. Countless comparable case studies can now be found in coffee-table books, student compendiums and lifestyle websites. Examples of the former might include Myerson and Ross's *the 21st Century Office* (2003); Bahamóon, Cañizares and Corcuera's *Corporate Architecture – Building a Brand* (2009); and Kursty Groves' *I Wish I Worked There! A Look Inside the Most Creative Spaces in Business* (2010). A new generation of multi-disciplinary designers, from Philippe Starck to Alberto Pinto (both Paris-based, working globally), generate monographs of their work, and have pioneered spatial design in hotels and restaurants. Hotel design is one spectacular arena for new design innovation.

As a professional practice, spatial design can work at various levels, depending on the size of the company and the nature of the construction. Innovative 'boutique' approaches to design – aiming for aesthetic uniqueness and a singularity of identity – are usually found in executive or specialised office space, perhaps the corporate HQ, showrooms, or 'skunkwork' offices (off-site experimental R&D or prototyping labs). Most office re-design, however, involves a generic series of changes, sometimes managed or implemented by the organisation's own facilities manager in tandem with a sub-contracted design or 'fit-out' company. Today, businesses or corporations rarely own their own buildings, or were responsible for the building design. Contemporary corporate architecture invariably creates 'shell'-like spaces for successive interior 'fit-outs'. A fit-out may involve rearranging the services (power, plumbing, data cabling, and so on) but does not involve the structure of the building itself. Low level fit-outs are even undertaken by full-service office furniture suppliers. For most high-level corporations, however, substantive changes in the management of their space is undertaken under the direction of an architect or spatial planner. This is usually the case with routine corporate re-locations. Notable companies in this area are the MNC Swanke Hayden Connell International, specialist corporate architects Richard Hywel Evans [RHE] Architecture and Design (London based), whereas the smaller Nowicka Stern (also London) offers a more 'boutique' approach. The disciplinary field of spatial design now operates in a highly segmented market. In fact, referring to spatial design as a single discipline is slightly misleading – it is a dynamic interdisciplinary practice, whose methods emerge from a confluence of many historical design discourses. Figure 1 indicates the spectrum of these discourses:

One of the most formative influences on the design of corporate space in the twentieth century was the so-called 'office management movement' emerging around 1910 in the USA. Influential books like William Leffingwell's *Scientific Office Management* of 1917, and the establishment of the National Office Management Association in 1919, consolidated the concern with spatial management in industrial contexts. Largely driven by the values and priorities of nineteenth century

Figure 1: *Conspectus of space design types*

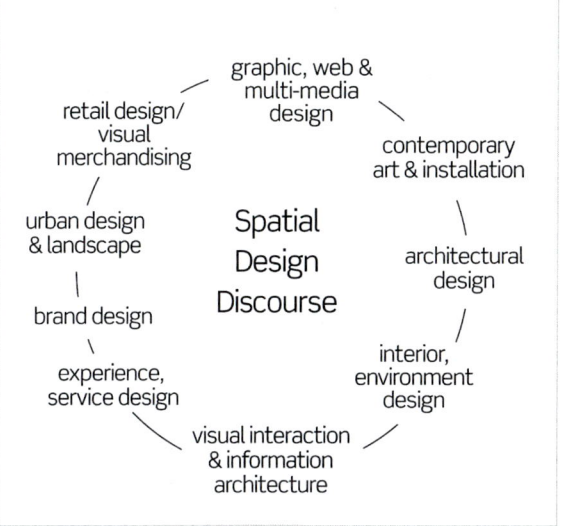

'Taylorism' (the work of American Quaker Frederick Winslow Taylor, with his own influential monograph, *The Principles of Scientific Management* of 1911), corporations and businesses the world over adopted the spatial format of the 'office' as a mechanism for both comprehending the nature of space as well as designing the physical entity of the organisation itself. Space was defined primarily as a 'container' for administered labour, albeit one whose compartmentalisation reflected the hierarchies and values of the social order as much as the patterns of material production.

Since Taylor and Leffingwell's monographs, the corporate world has generated copious research and developed influential strategic models for the use and management of space, and 'design' as a term features large in most of it. However, 'design' is invariably only a mechanism by which strategic management plans are implemented, or 'stylistic' articulation of the space is carried out. In other words, design is simply a tool by which space is made responsive to the management's control over resources, employees and production. The corporate world now has a range of disciplinary practices devoted to managing space, each of which use design as an instrument in their own way. These include Spatial Planning, Production Flow Planning, Human Resources Management and Facilities Management. Each of these exhibit distinctive methods and approaches to workplace design (Becker and Steele, 1995; Brookes and Kaplan, 1972; Kaczmarczyk and Murtough, 2002). They all work, however, through the application of generic abstract categories, which are assumed to be the discrete components that make up the organisational space in question: these categories are hierarchy; communication and technology; lighting, acoustics and air quality control; safety, security and surveillance; ergonomics and individual productivity; occupancy, distribution and power consumption. Some categories refer to material entities, like furniture; some refer to dimensions of spatial location, like 'hierarchy'. Whatever they use, the categories are usually preformed and fixed. And so, within the corporate practices of spatial management, organisational life itself becomes defined as a spatial economy of cost allocation, energy consumption, driven by an instrumental understanding of space as a resource, optimised for maximum clarity of command and control over the labouring subject.

On the face of it, this may seem entirely reasonable, if not common sense. However, Organisation Studies [OS] research in the last two decades has explored, through both theoretical and empirical research, the deep experiential and aesthetic dimensions of organisational space which lie beyond such pre-formed, empirically-grounded, 'categories'. Organisation Studies has revealed that space is often animated by powerful dynamics and activities that are not quantifiable, or made subject to the routine processes of management appropriation. Furthermore, the experiential or aesthetic dimension of organisations is as central to the formation of the labouring subject (as employee) as it is to the productive flows and cultural formation of organisational life itself. For organisational space is less a 'container' than a 'medium' for communication and expression (obviously so, when considering the nature of corporate identity, for example, with its embedded values, symbolic commands and affirmations). Space is a realm of profound forms of socialisation as well as the inculcation of corporate behaviour and patterns of self-regulation (the discipline and surveillance that creates a cohesive 'workforce'). Space is territory and a realm of bounded spheres for corporate management strategy and its operations (the visual-physical manifestation of the control and distribution of resources, or the regulation of production). Space is a dynamic system of capital control, where capital operates as much through unregulated human intelligence, 'instinct', emotion and judgment as it does through tangible assets. (1)

The historical image of the 1930s 'Fordist' factory, with its enormous expanse of machinery, its battery-hen grid of undifferentiated workers, its uncompromising and hierarchical management system, is often the foil against which critical theories of organisational space are constructed. Within Organisation Studies research we find an interesting range of narratives on the historical development of corporate space. One variant of the explicitly anti-Fordist narrative draws on Michel Foucault's historical revision of nineteenth century industrialisation, and tells how the geometrically-ordered production-system was 'efficient' at the cost of a socially-destructive and progressive extraction of vital human energies through a process of de-individualisation and cultural homogenisation (Foucault, 1977). Labour systems of all types are now generally understood in Organisation Studies as broader social processes, where value is attributed to particular human propensities, while others are curtailed; where certain aspects of experience are valorised, and others repressed. Labour systems construct social identity, community and solidarity, and create a sense of place and space; they mediate social discipline, act as conduits and circuits of local as well as national political power; they form a horizon of social expectation, reward and even personal destiny (Foucault, 1977). The denial of individual differentiation within a given system of labour is routinely, and rightly, understood within a narrative of historical social oppression. (2)

However, there is a second narrative that could be placed in tension to this, one which concerns the subsequent employment of geometric 'efficiency' after 1930 and up to the present. For, while by the second decade of the Twentieth Century, Fordism was providing the physical templates for large-scale corporate organisation, International Modernist architecture and design was using such templates for very different ends. As popular books by Siegfried Giedion, Rayner Banham, and later Charles Jenks and others since have explained, the modernist designer's use of geometric uniformity, symmetry and the structural logic of the golden mean, were akin to Fordism in terms of its spatial organisation, yet profoundly different in terms of its spatial aesthetics and the experience of organisational life it facilitated. The international modernism of Le Corbusier in Europe and Louis Sullivan in the US was an emphatic form of cultural democracy. For Le Corbusier and Sullivan, 'open', co-extensive, non-hierarchical and visually accessible organisational spaces cultivated an aesthetic sense of possibility, equality, social interaction and mobility. 'Openness' was promoted by the brute steel and glass 'shell' building construction, which itself was a political metaphor for transparency, honesty and accountability. Function and efficiency spoke less of the repression of human individuality than the liberating potential of mass production and an equitable distribution of resources. All decorative flourishes, naturalist symbolism or literary metaphor were banished, as were other signifiers of historical bourgeois culture.

International modernism later became the driving force for post-War European reconstruction, adopted by planners and architects in corporate as well as public realms, and to this day 'corporate America' still favours the modernist aesthetic it adopted in the 1930s in Chicago and New York. Oppressive Fordism and International Modernism therefore are not distinct historical phenomena, but part of a complex evolution of industrial management of organisational space. Within this evolution, social oppression and liberation, industrial exploitation and social equitability, avant-garde design and capitalist exploitation are closer than we imagine. And since the 1970s, the driving forces of 'function' and 'efficiency' within the spaces of economic production have taken some interesting twists and turns.

The humanised office

The adaptation and refinement of Fordist functionalism by collectivist East Asian countries in the 1970s is relevant in this context, not least because through the 1980s the West re-defined its own 'Fordism' in response to Hong Kong, Taiwanese and, particularly, Japanese innovations. Toyota's Lean Production model is a case in point. Toyota's commercial success began with the intellectual innovations of its founders, Sakichi Toyoda, along with his son and the later Toyota executive, engineer Taiichi Ohno. They had read the writings of Taylor, then Henry Ford and other theorists of mass production, then visited America to see how theory had become practice. Their visit was an instructive one, for Toyoda perceived many problems and contradictions with Fordist 'efficiency'. He identified counter-productive stages of repetition, overlap, and delayed connection within the otherwise fluid production process of manufacturing. On returning, he employed terms like 'flow', 'smooth', and 'uneven' (aesthetic attributes) as a corrective for Fordism, and by way of understanding how the dynamics of production either worked effectively or did not work according to the relation between the tangible and intangible. He subsequently generated a framework for understanding the 'quality' of the production process, using the concept of 'value'. For Toyoda, what once was seen as a normal part of the labour process did not necessarily add 'value' to production: value was not a simple empirical category, but a term requiring judgment and perception. Process, dynamics, human relations and communication became central to understanding industrial production. Later notions of 'value chain' popularised some of these insights, and in turn made their way into mainstream corporate management strategy.

Michael Porter's use of the term 'value chain' in the mid-1980s resonated with a rise of so-called neo-liberal economics, irrepressible in the Thatcher and Reagan years, where traditional methods of production and regimes of labour were being subject to rigorous redefinition and recalibration. The range of 'non'-value-adding dimensions to work life (perhaps of a social, religious, class or cultural origin) were gradually eroded by a new organisational orientation towards emerging fluid, diverse, expanding and integrating markets. In the workplace, systems of physical control, order and spatial surveillance, were gradually replaced by new forms of self-regulation, with more person-to-person contact, devolved management, team formations, perpetual training regimes, self-evaluation, routine 'reviews' and performance measurements by which the value of the employees' labour is calculated.

The mid-1980s saw the appearance of labour 'casualisation', outsourcing, the rise of consultancy and other trends that further dissolved the sense of social entrapment within a physical workplace. Company ownership became gradually detached from management and leadership, as old-style charismatic industrialists or the company 'founder' and head office were replaced by executive boards and a range of shareholders. The growing service economy generated new experiences of labour mobility detached from any one geographic locale, something which increased in the 1990s with networked and remote communication. Office space could be reduced to 'HQ' space, with even management becoming mobile, operating only through remote communications. Multiple work-spaces opened up, such as the home, the car, leisure venues, public libraries, and cafés (for example, Starbucks' own marketing positioning in the early 1990s conceived its café space as both office extension and business networking site). The communication-intensive and project-based structure of contemporary corporate life generated open-planned, provisional and task-specific working arrangements, with hot-desking, mobile furniture and space dividers, along with a constant migration of freelance and agency labour. The 'smart space' of today's successful corporate environment defines the office as much as a platform for career development as it is one for hard production. The organisation becomes a series of 'learning environments'. 'Self-organising' project teams allow (demand) leadership experience for non-management, and task or project-role rotation offers a cycle of re-training, providing consistent professional development opportunities.

While between 1980 and 1990 the rapid increase in fluidity and mobility seemed to make the physical containment of a corporate office space unnecessary, if not uneconomical, the corporate world did not dispense with the office. In fact, office space became redefined more generously as a realm of value-creation, where the interests of the individual harmonised with the corporation, where the old oppositions of 'management and workers' were dissolved, and a new value chain emerged. Human rights and equality ideals were entirely compatible with this new chain of productive labour, and its corporate rhetoric convinced an entire generation that the new organisation is receptive and responsive to human need. The exponential research and consultancy interest in management strategy during the 1990s underlined a new and globally-pervasive organisational ideal, an ideal which had extraordinary implications for organisational space. As any sample study of contemporary management consultancy websites in the US or UK might find, the following characteristics now adequately define the 'new' organisation:

> *environment-consciousness:* the workspace is conceived as a holistic

'environment'; employee-concerns with the visual, ergonomic, atmospheric and relational dynamics that form their immediate workplace are legitimised.

> *spatial mobility:* inter-spatial movement is encouraged as is re-location according to tasks or preferences; the organisation interior is understood as enabling and not controlling, and as organic and evolving according to the changing dynamics of working life.

> *Lateral dispersal:* the manager enacts a role in production, without the assumption of social superiority or authority, and is often embedded in the workforce at project level (not 'above' or apart). There is a flatter and decentralised corporate structure; employees are encouraged to interact with management and further to develop specialist knowledge and contribute to the knowledge-infrastructure required for the project management process. Collaboration, cross-team conferences and consultation are accepted as the norm.

> *Permeability:* the organisation is not a monolith or form of social containment within fixed boundaries; it is a site through which stakeholders, employees and new labour processes locate temporary interests. The organisation is mediator of meanings and social movements that broadly connect with progressive forces of economic and social development, justice, community and global movements for responsibility and conscience. In other words, corporate strategy allows itself to be animated by or even framed by popular or progressive ideological discourses.

This generic description serves to establish a few important points: first, that organisational life has at once become more dynamic and fluid, and yet more complex and demanding; second, that while organisations across all sectors have become more employee-friendly, they have also been careful to preserve boundaries and limit access to decision-makers and spaces of executive power; third, organisations no longer require physical spaces for hierarchy or executive management, whose power may operate outside the orbit of the physical corporation; fourth, while the liberalisation and openness to employee welfare satisfies extensive legal and social demands for increased individual rights, it also demands from the worker a level of unprecedented personal, emotional and intellectual investment.

The 'investment' required of the contemporary employee is figured in the way organisation interiors have become heavily articulated by the visual signifiers of individual taste, sensation and perception (i.e. the 'aesthetication' of new office design, brand and corporate communications). Organisational space is now a realm of experience, promising personal advancement and professional self-fulfillment, in return for subjective investment. Personality, conviction, commitment, emotion and even ethical consciousness is required, and used, as a collective resource in organisational development. The new organisation expects that the individual 'leverage' aspects of his or her own subjectivity. In an 'aestheticised' environment that cultivates advances in creative capability and individual expression, aspects of the self once 'private' or personal are now integral to the functioning of organisational life.

Designing the humanised workplace

Few would argue that the conditions of today's workplace are not preferable to the past by a long way, whatever the personal investment now routinely demanded by the average corporation or any other organisation. However, as much Organisation Studies research routinely points out, the spectre of Fordism still lurks in organisational life, where essential human energies are being dissected and dissociated from individual social well-being and reconfigured as organisational resources. Promising individual professional development and personal fulfillment, the new organisation is a visual charade and an aesthetic ruse.

In what follows, we will be referring to a designer of organisational space, and from conversations with him over the course of two years I will be discussing the nature of what I called the 'aesthetic ruse' of the new humanised organisation. (3) I will refer to our designer as Rogers. He is the owner-manager of a design company established in 2002 (and part-owned by a larger interior construction business). His studio office is on the south Coast of England, with a secondary office at his parent company in the city of Reading. His is effectively a boutique studio of six employees, but through his parent company one that delivers on Blue Chip accounts and undertakes large-scale corporate projects. His expertise was originally product design, whereupon turning his attention to 'high-spec' corporate office products (from computer stands to interactive work stations) he logically expanded his interests into the full office environment, particularly ergonomic and performance-related factors. Rogers now offers what he calls 'total office solutions', and will employ any design discipline to provide an integrated package, from graphics, brand design, photography, international designer furniture, and interior design and reconstruction. While influenced by German Bauhaus design philosophy from the 1930s, he is no design visionary or artistic idealist. His avant-garde bent motivates him to explore the transformative power of design in otherwise conservative corporate contexts. Rogers redesigns single offices, 'break out' or brainstorming spaces, HQ boardrooms, showroom areas and foyers, or open plan floors of whole buildings. His preferred commission is the re-design of an entire organisational environment. However, it is his strategic approach to design and not his actual designs that is the subject of our short case study. What we will be looking at is the way he approaches the contemporary workplace with a view to design transformation.

Rogers states that,

'Design is not primarily about style or artistic form, but language and communication. While contemporary office space is built for communication, the spaces themselves are rarely a subject of that communication… and the way space allows for the development of an organisational language is also something not, in my experience, ever discussed. Discussions on communication, by management or employees, are usually about technology or meetings or the line-management system'.

Rogers asserts:

'Space is very related to culture….to how people behave, and not just behave but see themselves, their role, their future, their relation to the rest of the organisation; so much hangs on the question of space. ….Spaces can be debilitating, de-motivating

and unproductive, even 'sick' (as in 'sick building syndrome')'.

When space is structured in the seemingly objective mechanism of 'layout grids', such layout

> *'sets boundaries and patterns to how people make decisions and have ideas and express an opinion... a lot hangs on the question of space'.*

On the face of it, Rogers seems to employ established models of design ethnography and participatory design, as his first object of attention in a spatial design project is the employee and not the physical space itself (Schuler and Namioka, 1993; Wasson, 2000; Barab, et. al. 2004). Rogers begins by developing productive relationships, using those relationships to develop his understanding of 'local' knowledge, effective lines of communication, and then generates his design ideas, solutions and plans in dialogue with employees situated in the relevant spaces. However, Rogers' work is not so straightforward. For each organisational space he works in is already animated by past design schemes and embedded with past spatial strategies, each of which evolved from the era of emerging workplace 'humanisation'.

Rogers continues:

> *'When corporate management discuss the spaces of the organisation, they refer to empty physical places that have been stylised by a designer. The space and the design, for management, remain two distinct categories. The space is a technical question, about productivity and resources; the design is a creative question, about bringing in designers to create a stylish, distinctive environment that expresses the values or brand of the company'.*

The problem Rogers usually faces is not the management who facilitate the contract (who are often open to persuasion) but the facilities management personnel, who work purely with a concept of space and fixed templates of the organisational economy of space.

In his extensive discussions with both corporate management and facilities personnel, usually in the first stages of his contracted project, Rogers observes that the terminology they employ in discussing space is always purely empirical (motivated by the practical task of putting objects and people of particular sizes into physical locations of particular dimensions); and that the terminology they employ in discussing design is littered with the latest management ideologies or artistic clichés. He states,

> *'...for me, space and design need to be thought of as the active dimension of organisational life; they work together. ...The corporate managements I have worked with, however, see space as empty places, something obvious, common sense.'*

In other words, space is the empty realms of interior enclosure we can see and experience (with our senses), then measure, then re-order and appropriate (with our cognitive faculties). These empty realms of space are, without specific appropriation, vacant of life and thus wasteful: they are there to be 'filled' or to be used. And they are routinely filled with the helpful aids of 'humanised' organisational communication – the comfy sofas, paintings on the walls, office plants, stylish looking coffee corners, elements and devices of branded communication, and so on.

Historical – origin and strategic context of space	**Aesthetic** – form (style, shape, structure)	**Cultural** – design meaning and content
Corporate Strategy/spatial policy	Materials	Values
	Properties	Style
Designer	Contours	Fashion/trend
Brief	Surface and textures	Symbolism
Layout	Visual structure	Scales and proportions
Technology, innovations, physical additions	Colour scheme or code	Lines of sight and communication
Employee response	Articulation of detail, foci, signage or information	Employee modification/ personalisation
Registered change		
	Imagery	Visitor experience

Table 1: *Design audit inventory*

When commissioned by an organisation, Rogers moves through a series of stages in his design process. He first completes the routine and contractual client 'brief', which states the terms, aims and objectives of the project. His agreement is then followed by negotiations on materials, budgets, schedules and the scope of his access to the company. Rogers retains a relaxed demeanor throughout the start of the project, aiming to develop relationships more than argue points, for reasons we will see. Post-brief, his first stage is a 'design audit' of the company – conducting a full review of the current visible, documented, often concealed design schemes and strategies that animate the present corporate office environment. If we tabulate the objects of Rogers' design audit, we have the following categories:

In the above table, the inventory provides an itemised list, through which Rogers works. The first category, the 'historical', usually entails the past design schemes commissioned by the organisation, which, as Rogers points out, is as much a reality of employee perceptions, memories and responses, as the visual-physical content of the space. The second, 'aesthetic', category denotes all the generic design features and techniques employed during past schemes, which may or may not have changed with time (certain materials radically change colour or texture, particularly with use). The third, 'cultural', category is evaluative and is where Rogers assesses the scheme's significance (perhaps it was part of a particularly successful brand design strategy), its innovation and added value to the organisation (and often the benchmark against which his own designs will be judged). Changing the spatial dynamics of an organisation can arouse a lot of emotion among employees and management alike. Sometimes the re-design is 'imposed' upon an office by otherwise absent executive management. The designer, therefore, often encounters the suppressed political undercurrent of organisational life, where a re-design project, particularly if it's disruptive, can become a conduit for all kinds of felt antagonism. This 'inventory', therefore, is background information, but also helps Rogers prepare his strategy for discussion and negotiation.

As part of his audit, Rogers often requests access to corporate files and archives to see what visual or other representations of the space have been used in corporate life, whether in their brand promotion or internal communications. *'Corporations are usually littered with dominant representations of their own spaces'*, he stated. They form a kind of *'common consciousness, reinforcing a self-image'*. During the audit, discussions with management often reveal that space is never *'fully understood or used'* and its potential always seems to *'exceed appropriation'*. Even organisations that rearrange their environments routinely often reencounter the same chronic problems. Rogers admits that *'…a design, any design, never fully works – a working life always changes'*. For space is relative to the sensible experience of space, and the unfolding of employee behaviour over time.

Roger's statement that '…a design…never fully works' is significant. The promise of design is never fulfilled; the organisation never seems to become the realm of harmonious streamlined production that is its aim. This is perhaps indicated at the very start, by the initial contractual document of the client brief. Though written as a single coherent statement, it is usually characterised by clashing priorities in three main areas – human resource requirements, the fixed coordinates of the physical facility, and the inventory of tasks or process of production. *'Briefs are usually a lot of different bits stuck together by a variety of managers, and often express their conflicting interests'*. Rogers' approach usually entails that the brief becomes a matter of negotiation, and subject to the results of his second stage of research. After the initial stage of the design audit, Rogers turns to the actual spaces he will be working with, becomes embedded in the space, forging his *'space of communication'*, or the open invitation to dialogue that he maintains, all the time finding ways of registering what he hears. He tries to listen to the viewpoints and experiences of everyone who uses the space, then engages in observation and visual scrutiny. For this observation and scrutiny he uses sketching to set down some quick visual ideas. He attempts to register what he sees as the *'shape'* of *'organisational experience'*, by which he means the full range of repetitive patterns of movement and responses that characterise employees' use of their space, along with the tempo, rhythm and rate of this activity. As Roger's points out, there are realms of tension between the allocated spaces for certain employees, managers, and the accessibility, visibility and interactive communication they both facilitate and prohibit. The boundaries, processes of thought, speech, action, and lines of contact between various employees at different levels, are often fraught with unclear or misaligned junctures and make for situations of repeated misrecognition. Office spaces, he observes, feature a range of critical *'time-corridors'* moving in and around the space, often compressing movement or creating nodes of tension, affecting certain individuals, playing to the advantage of others. Here we find Rogers using a number of simple techniques, which we can list: (the first one used for his 'design audit'):

> Collated archive of corporate publications, media representations, organisational charts, office layout maps for employees, visitors, managers and architects – any available and distributed material showing representations of organisations space.

> Sketches and colour-palette renderings of the pattern or structure of mobility of employees as exhibited in bodily expression and behaviour in space –the 'shapes' of space and flows of time in and around it.

> Minute observation of specific work tasks (sitting, photocopying, using a laptop, walking around, discussing or negotiating), using notes and analytical diagrams (with measurements), including contextual data of production flow routines.

> Cognitive *maps* of the spaces by people using them – including the space as interrelated with other spaces (inside and even outside the building).

> Semi-structured interviewing of people, categorised according to both location and the coordinates of power/freedom that structure that experience.

> Computer generated mock-ups of radical changes to the space – as devices for locating fault-lines in strategic ideas and ideals, as well as provoking a critical understanding of the potential conditions (and demands on the individual) involved in real change.

> 'Micro-solution' sketches of space-altering devices or additions – such as new products, technology, re-designed desk-space, and so on.

For Rogers, '…*the design is as much about the experience of the people in the space, or should I say, the way the employees experience themselves in the space, as the visual, stylistic or brand symbols*'. It is the flow of experience that Rogers is interested in. An empiricist approach to design understands space as the frame and container of material signifiers of style and meaning, with a view to expressing the right values and messages (from corporation to employee). If designers see organisational spaces as empty containers for their designs, then the creative function of design is reduced to a series of instrumental tasks – creating comfort, convenience, sensory appeal and sending messages. The 'messages' are usually related to brand values, corporate objectives or aspirational ideals, which, of course the employees know already. In Roger's words, they 'see through' the superficial addition of design 'decoration' or 'corporate self-promotion'.

In his design approach, Rogers has been concerned with the whole organisation – from executive to cleaners, and everyone in between. Space is where identities are revealed and concealed, where values are promoted and effaced, where access to power and decision making is made possible and also denied. His design approach has been characterised by the simple aim of constructing a space that maximised the relations between people, not the relations between things. Rogers has reported that some clients have viewed his spatial design as *'too minimalist'*, which he has taken to indicate, happily, the way he has prioritised human interaction and communication or the visual and stylistic manipulation of the corporate building interior.

Space, aesthetics and dialogue

Extrapolating from key insights and the various projects of our designer Rogers, I have constructed a diagram that goes some way to defining his approach and concept of organisational space. Like Table 1: *Design audit inventory*, Figure 2: *Design concept framework* contains reference to the non-negotiable empirical components of spatial design, like furniture or physical partitions. However, there is no categorical distinction between the material and the subjective. It is more properly defined as 'aesthetic'. As the work of Antonio Strati shows us, aesthetics denotes more than design style, symbolism or the sensational embellishment of artistic decoration. Aesthetics emerges as a cognitive-communicative relationship between the subject and material environment, where both develop an active, reflective, interconnection (Strati, 1996, 2000).

Both employee (and management) are represented by a central column, whose basic components demand certain conditions of interaction and dialogue. (This does not presuppose a flat egalitarian employee arrangement, or open plan space arrangement, as the concepts are general, and can be employed by the designer in many different ways). The priority, however, is on 'relations between people' – communication and dialogue is non-negotiable – not the messages or sensual appeal of the 'relations between things'.

The right column 'Object' contains material objects and signifiers, yet also contains spatial categories such as vistas and locations. As the column indicates, these categories of space along with material objects are both tangible, therefore subject to measurement and the managed processes of Facilities Management. They are subject to the disciplinary regime of strategic resource allocation that the first category, 'Subject', is not. For the 'Subject' column is intangible, even though it also involves both objects and spaces.

In our diagram, and in the framework of Rogers' approach, we can define organisational space as a kind of 'trialectic' phenomena. Rogers' approach revolves around these three categories: 'Subject' [the sensory-intangible], 'Object' [the structural-tangible], which together provide the conditions for the 'active-functional' [communicative-dialogic]. The 'active-functional' is the fulcrum; the columns either side' are strategically constructed to maximise the functional activity in the central column. (4)

In constructing this theoretical model from Rogers' design practice and experience, we can now discuss its implications. To summarise our initial context: the new model 'humanised' organisation, as previously discussed, aims for the highest political ideals (equality, respect, self-determination, and so on) and does so by constructing an 'aestheticised' workplace, which is inspiring, often beautiful, stylish (and compared to office life even three decades ago, is surely a welcome development). Rogers' framework suggests, however, that the 'aesthetics' employed within new office design do not provide the

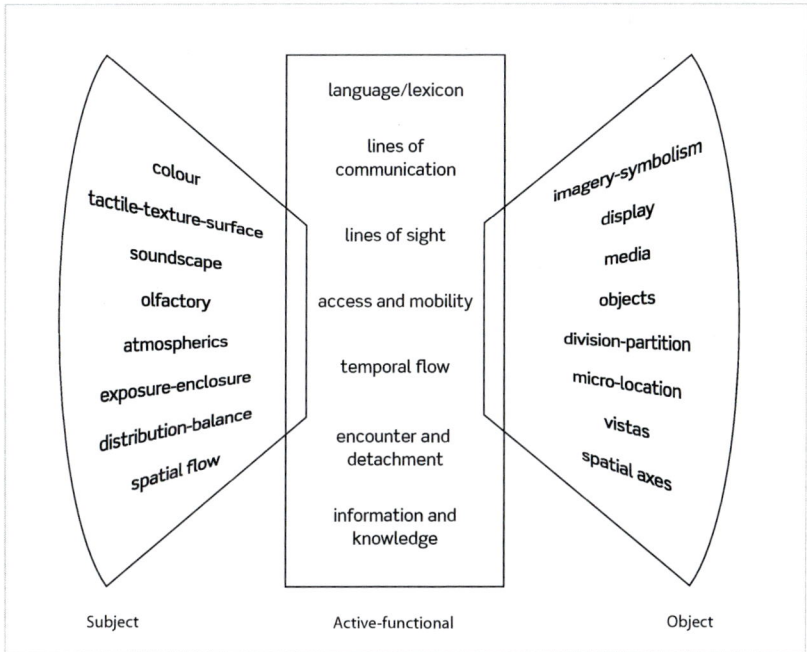

Figure 2: *Design concept framework*

conditions for the welfare of the individual employee and a dynamic, equitable organisational culture. Referring back to Table 1: *design audit inventory*, conventional spatial design was primarily concerned with the stylish arrangement of a visual environment, which, in turn signified positive messages about the organisation. It did not significantly involve the employee at any stage of its development, except in a facilities management of health, safety, ergonomics and individual task-based roles. Its visual appeal was grounded only in an empirical solicitation of individual affirmation through activating their sense of taste. Conventional spatial design is largely addressed to an individual's sense perception.

Why do I say this? The visual experience of the individual employee is of course shared by all individual employees, but as a form of aesthetic experience, this 'sharing' of experience is incidental. It has no further implications for organisational culture or impact on the way people experience the organisation. Workplace aestheticisation generally appeals to conventional modes of individual taste, a cultural appreciation of contemporary style, a sensuous enjoyment of colour and form, and a subsequent compliant acceptance of the corporation's view of itself (as engaging, bright and colourful, creative and enjoyable, or whatever). It involves (and only involves) individual employees looking at, and decoding, imagery, and having a certain feeling about this experience of meaning. This form of empiricist aesthetics, and the design strategies of workplace aestheticisation, can be understood as an extension of classical Greco-roman aesthetics, and despite the routine use of 'funky' or avant-garde-looking visual techniques, they are resolutely traditional in their appeal to conventional artistic values.

What I am calling 'conventional artistic values' are not assumed to be 'conservative' or traditional in any way; often they are far from it. But they appeal to a sense of balance, symmetry and proportion. They engage individual taste and sensory pleasure. As an aesthetic, we enter a world of beauty, sensuous harmony, compositionally unified order, all animated by coordinated complementary colours. Its visual-sensory impact is centred around the sense-perception of the individual subject, and that it appeals to individual feeling is a crucial part of its work. Workplace aesthetics attempts to 'manage' employee feelings, shape their cognitive engagement with the work environment, establish their visual horizon of expectations, and hold out the promise, through sensory stimulation, of personal fulfillment at work. In design terms, this 'managed aesthetics' sees the organisation as an empty space to be 'dressed' with well defined and strategically prepared sensory experiences, which in turn frame and propel meaningful messages, the messages (addressed to the solitary worker), inform them of corporate requirements, inspiring their quiescence if not their enthusiasm. The human 'cost' of this design approach (and of workplace aestheticisation as an organisational phenomenon) is that the individual employees' experience of, and role within, the changing environment is entirely abstract. The work environment is a coded container, mapping logistical functions, setting behavioural norms, commanding assent to procedural ethics, all of which do not emerge from the workplace but from a corporate command centre removed from the locations of labour. The designer normally is the conduit of schemes that are prefigured at the level of brand strategy, composed out of the experiential understanding of the trialectic of consumer-market-corporation, and not employee-workplace-corporation. The employee has no active dialogic relationship with the subjects that make the spatial environment what it is – the people that determine what they are doing and why. Workplace aesthetication is a means of constructing alienation through pleasure, inspiration and the semblance of harmony.

The purpose of the case study was to show how the designer's strategy proceeded from the basis of an intersubjective interaction with the employees and the spaces of the project; and the 'strategy' was not pre-planned but improvised and responsive to an ongoing dialogue, aware of the politics of representation, as the designer attempted to understand and bring together the interests of a range of people. Driven by a researched understanding of the role of active, mnemonic and ideological representations of space that provided a substrate of spatial consciousness within the organisation, the designer pursued the necessity and potential for active-subject positions, linguistic development, intersubjective interaction and knowledge exchange. Of course, any organisation possesses these functions – what Rogers teaches us is that these functions are normally abstracted and re-arranged around pre-formed tasks and in between boundaries and mechanisms of exclusion, not lines of access and dialogue. The realms of power within organisations are aesthetically 'managed' in a way that preserves a sense of impenetrability and inevitability, convincing the employee that the structures of power and the interests that govern them are in a harmonious relationship to the aims, rationales and methods of production to which everyone must work.

Conclusion

In this chapter I have offered a historical backdrop to the phenomenal changes in the workplace and the function of organisational space. While profound and complex changes have determined the evolution of the labouring subject and the management of the space of labour, there are some fascinating patterns that are being repeated the world over, various identified as 'aestheticisation'. It is easy to be seduced by new office design, and its spectrum of social, leisure and relaxation facilities. With Rogers, I attempted to show how new office spaces may offer a simulation of individual freedom, mobility, choice, taste, and excited involvement in the reproduction of corporate power, but they do so through using visual signifiers derived from leisure, cultural or personal-domestic realms. In other words, they draw on the active realms of social and cultural 'individuation', sensory stimuli, signifying power and simulating energy and manufacturing consent and compliance in one go. They do not engage with the forms of collective interaction that actually provide the means for equitable advancement and knowledge of the structures that determine actual production. Managed workplace aestheticisation deploy the aesthetics of 'taste', thereby increasing their capacity for individualised labour yet at the expense of intersubjective forms of consciousness (of employee to employee relations; dialogue, collective investigation).

As a concluding point then, I can only say that workplace aestheticisation avoids an open orientation to the *relations* of production (the spheres of executive-level control) and actual knowledge of their conditions of production. It can only mean a simultaneous *disempowerment* of the subject at the level of intersubjective consciousness. In simple terms, the re-design of corporate space, while vastly improving working conditions and individual liberty, does so at the cost of social self-determination.

Notes

1. The critical literature in Organisation Studies is diverse. Within it we find general and literature on architecture and new office design (Marmot and Eley, 2000; Fawcett and Chadwick, 2007; Vidiella, 2008), on corporate space as cultural communication and artistic display (Jacobson, 1996; Biehl, 2007), along with a concern for space as aesthetic cognition (Cairns, 2002; Cairns, McInnes, and Robertson, 2003), or aesthetic and symbolic production (Strati, 1999, 2001, 2009; Gagliardi, 1990, 1996). Theoretical research into organisational space has particularly benefitted from the advances in geography-based notions of the social production of space by major thinkers like Henri Lefebvre, David Harvey and Nigel Thrift, and the general sociology of space is a similar resource (Baldry, 1999; Gieryn, 2000; 2002), particularly informing the spatial analysis of labour processes (Flecker and Hofbauer, 1998; Halford, 2005), and the construction of labour subjects in the ideological animation of the general economy (Dale, 2005; Dale & Burrell, 2003, 2008; Witz, Warhurst and Nickson, 2003). Dale and Burrell's *The Spaces of Organisation and the Organisation of Space* (Dale and Burrell, 2008) is a pioneering book-length study that has consolidated the subject as a major field of academic research.

2. This historical vignette was derived from the narrative content of a range of sources, the secondary sources include the following: Beissinger, M. R. (1988) *Scientific Management, Socialist Discipline, and Soviet Power*, London: I.B. Tauris; Fleming, P. and Spicer, A. (2007) *Contesting the Corporation: Struggle, Power and Resistance in Organizations*, Cambridge, Cambridge University Press: Frampton, K. (1992) *Modern Architecture: A Critical History* (3rd ed.) London: Thames and Hudson; Head, S. (2005) *The New Ruthless Economy: Work and Power in the Digital Age*, Oxford: Oxford University Press; Low, A. (2008) *Conflict and Creativity at Work: Human Roots of Corporate Life*,

Eastbourne, UK: Sussex Academic Press; Noble, D. F. (1984) *Forces of Production: A Social History of Industrial Automation*, New York: Knopf; Womack, J. P., Jones, D. T., and Roos (1991) *The Machine That Changed the World: The Story of Lean Production*, New York: HarperBusiness.

3. Research for this short case study was generated from five interviews and six site visits, and further consultations with plans, diagrams and photographic documentation of Rogers' work from March 2009-May 2011.

4. This three-column structure is not a meta-theory, or an ontology of space. Rogers' own theoretical insights were not abstract, but emerged from his design practice. It also does not entail a classical social-science distinction between mental, social and physical space (nor Lefebvre's famous trialectic of spatial practice, spatial planning, and 'lived' spatial experiences: Lefebvre, 1991; see also variations on the use of this term in relation to the work of Lefebvre in Dale and Burrell, 2003; Hancock and Spicer, 2011; Soja, 1996).

This chapter discusses method – the ways in which we analyse and understand organisations. Importantly, it discusses method in the context of a common problem: how do we identify and explain the diversity and complexity of organisational life (particularly its aesthetic dimension) and still produce or contribute to useful 'hard' data (accepted forms of organisational assessment and reporting). The chapter begins by pointing out that established scientific methods have themselves become an obstacle in research, as they have not expanded and developed as organisations themselves have expanded and developed. Further, these methods are often grounded in statistical or mathematically formulae of reality that discount that which is not adaptable to its grid-like ordering of its subject. The homogeneity of science and the tendency to 'iron out' all idiosyncrasy, means that whole realms of experience and subjectively understood meaning is lost. Of course, this is often by necessity, as data is usually only useful if comparative (or compared with other data sets or other research projects). This chapter does not imagine a revolution in science taking place, but rather aesthetic research contributing to a serious incremental change in the dominant understanding of method.

Here the chapter describes a real-life research situation. A group of researchers in Italy set out to research a cultural organisation, while at the same time using this research project as a means of innovating new methods of investigation.

Researching the Aesthetics of Organisation
Alberto Zanutto and Enrico Maria Piras

Introduction: The freedom of research versus the rigidity of method

Internationally, the scope in the study of organisations has expanded enormously – yet the methods we use for research and analyse have changed much less so. This raises a big question on *method* and its development in an expanded field where organisations are changing rapidly. Is it possible to do credible research while remaining anchored in conventional research models and old ways of collecting and processing data? Or should we really be extending the boundaries of freedom – and doing this by favouring methodological experiments, opening up and generating new analytical approaches, and new methodologies? This need is felt by a range of researchers currently, particularly when the subjects of our research lie on the margins of priority for industry, consultancy or academia – as is often the case with the aesthetic dimension in organisations.

The aesthetic and emotional dimensions of organisational life have become important to the research of organisations – particularly qualitative research. The work of the researcher often begins with a sense of 'wonder' at the exciting complexity of organisational environments, the diversity of the objects of study, and the variety of approaches available for the analysis of organisational life. However, the point of departure is always the 'prefiguration' stage, where the research project is devised, and often devised in a way that excludes much of this diversity and complexity outright. Anyone who has undertake research in organisations will know the initial encounters with, and experience of, unique spaces, people, objects and artefacts, and of the scenarios that unexpectedly emerge. In these situations, we gradually become aware of the need to 'tune' our perceptions by connecting what we see in the organisation to our stock of tacit and explicit knowledge. The process of research is dynamic and develops over time: our first set of ideas, concepts or understandings – our initial cognitive formulation of basic 'representations' – are followed by more protracted encounters with the organisation, each of which modify these representations. The final stage usually involves the writing of reports, which may involve an attempt to depict this process of successive representation, but usually prioritises the 'results' and 'outcomes' of the successive acts of research and analysis.

There are many aspects of the researcher's *experience* of the research process that involve very real dimensions of the organisation under research – the sensations, the sensory, perceptual, relational, tacit, visual or optical experiences, and so on. Yet these are usually neglected, repressed, or even explicitly denied a role in the successive phases of research. This is particularly true of the standard formats of the final reports and what is classified as an acceptable scientific output. These generally allow only for the articulation of 'representations' that chime with the canons of knowledge favoured by the mainstream scientific community (Martin, 2002). However, an increasing need is being expressed within the scientific community for new forms of representation: of knowledge, its articulation and communication, and even new structural forms of investigation, new means and methods of research and its presentation. It is a call for a fuller conceptualisation, description and explanation of the reality observed, and therefore what is manifest in our perceptual experience of research, which is often wholly unexpected.

Organisation studies is particularly rich in innovation in this regard. Emblematic of this, perhaps, is the now famous analysis of organisation based on *metaphor*. Since the pioneering work of Morgan (1980, 1981, 1996), this strain has produced a variety of analogies between organisational leadership and art (DePree, 1989) or jazz (DePree, 1992), between managing and 'performing art' (Vaill, 1989; Mangham, 1990) or dance (Denhardt and Denhardt, 2006), or the metaphor of organisation as theatre (Mangham, 1993). Outside traditional academic contexts in recent years we have seen successful attempts to broaden the perceptual horizon of organisational life and enable researchers to renew their gaze and sensibility towards organisational settings, environments, and the visual or symbolic languages embedded in their physical design (Gagliardi, 1996).

The recent advent of the field of 'organisational aesthetics' (Strati, 1999, 2007; Strati, and de Monthoux, 2002) has created a new research context, which has the capacity to include research processes that extend beyond traditional rationalistic approaches to knowledge in and about organisations. Moreover, this new field has contributed significantly to reflection on possible experimentation and the need for new methods of data collection and processing, and new forms of analysis presentation. New methods and forms of research have been mediated, and at times inspired, by art, artists or artistic practices (Barry, 1996), or they have been structured for the purpose of producing artistic representations *tout court*, such as theatrical pieces (Steyaert & Hjorth, 2002; Taylor, 2004) or performances on video (Scalfi, 2007). In other cases, organisational analysis has borrowed tools and concepts from art theory and criticism, such as the aesthetic category of 'the beautiful' (Ramirez, 1991), the 'disgusting' (Pelzer, 2002), and even 'kitsch' (Linstead, 2002). Indeed, it has proposed that organisational researchers should be considered not as analysts but as 'curators' of organisations (Dégot, 1987).

As this range of trajectories illustrates, research is not characterised by an incremental logical-cognitive and unilinear process. As Strati's research has taught us (1999), we need to have a greater expanded sense of what 'organisation' *means*, and to do this we need to move beyond established frameworks that just quantify aggregated and isolated components of organisations, defining them simply, for example, as different forms of 'action'. We need to consider the full non-linear complexity of organisational realities, and to traverse thresholds of organisational experience. Etymologically, the term 'traverse' means 'move across', and here the researcher needs to 'traverse' two spaces – the observed and experienced reality of the *sites* of research (an organisation as a research field), and the 'reality' of the specific demands of organisational research as that which enters this field as codified, represented and distributed within the scientific community. These two 'realities' are sometimes very different worlds.

This article analyses and reflects upon this 'traversing' and does so by looking at the use of methods in organisational aesthetics.

In traversing, we aim in some way to overcome the rigidities imposed by the canons of standard methodology, but in overcoming standardised methodology, how can methodological 'care' be taken to produce good data at the same time? This is the critical challenge for researchers: experimentation and innovation is needed, but they also threaten to push us out of the realm of scientifically acceptable research.

We will make some suggestions from an analysis of a research project: the analysis is *a posteriori*, that is, our assessment of the research and the experience of each researcher follows the completion of the project. We describe a three-year research project that was set up purposively to examine the relationship between aesthetic sensibility and research methods by means of a collectively conducted case study. The project reconsidered in *aesthetic terms* the research tools most frequently used in qualitative enquiry, such as in-depth interviews and participant observation. The intention was to expose ourselves to the full range of aesthetic stimuli arising from the fieldwork, then reflect purposively on the need to revise the methodological tools employed.

The aim of the 'group' approach – using a collaborative team of researchers – was to combine a diversity of viewpoints, thereby testing the limits and exposing the boundaries of what is possible in 'traversing' the spaces indicated above. The research project was conducted at an art foundation – a cultural organisation specialising in the funding, research and exhibition of art. As our chapter proceeds, a number of 'internal bookmarks' will appear in the text – such as ['cf. method:…..'] – as these point forward as indicators of the relevant component of our research methodology as tabulated in Figure 1. In the discussion that follows, we describe in a little detail the implications we derived from the experience of researching, assessing the importance of the aesthetic dimension of organisational analysis, and consequently proposing changes to the standardised ways in which research tools are used to study organisations.

Experimentation in a methodological playground: the Art Foundation.

The first consideration for the project was the *site* of research – we required an organisation operating in a field rich with 'perceptual sensitisations' or an explicit aesthetic dimension that would test the limits of our research capabilities. Our interest consequently turned to organisations producing services in the field of contemporary art. These organisations were judged best suited to serve as 'playgrounds' for a group of researchers, in part as cultural organisations are forced to operate between forms of cognition required of management systems, what we call standard 'organisational mentality', and the more culturally nuanced demands of the 'artistic sensibility'. As is well known from published research, the ability to conjugate managerial and artistic capability has always constituted the unique complexity of these organisations – involving two epistemological fields governing two domains of competency (DiMaggio, 1987; Chong, 2003). Our entry into this site or 'field' for research would not be through 'managerialist' interests alone, with 'aesthetics' simply being added on. To be sure, the semantic-symbolic nature of the space as a site of managerialism would certainly be under investigation, but this would be guided by the broader realm of *the sensible*. [cf. *method*: Aesthetic Field]

Great care was taken during the negotiation phase of access to the organisation, for to encourage the close involvement of the host in the project would open up a further dimension of sensible experience. In the first instance, we sought to identify an organisation that was sufficiently 'fluid', that is, an organisation that allowed its aesthetic dimension to manifest itself (even if inadvertently) in the organisation, and a space where aesthetics is alive and developing, not 'crystallised' or static. The Art Foundation was this choice.

Another aspect of the stage of access concerned the attitude of researchers to the methodological complexity presented by the site of the organisation. There were few and relatively 'weak' constraints on what we could do, yet we set ourselves a mandate to deliver 'strong' innovative means of accessing information and data on the aesthetic dimension. Ethnographic tools became important to our project. The selection of specific organisational processes to observe and materials to collect was made in a way that encouraged our researchers not to avoid the evocative and imaginative tension between their own representations (and experiences) of the organisation, and the organisation's own (self-) representations. The group was therefore encouraged to draw iteratively on metaphors, evocations, images, visualisations, multimedia ethnographic materials, and so on, within the organisational spaces of experience they inhabited. They examined how aesthetic sensibility was individuated and concretised through all forms of representation, and how in the organisational set-up itself we could discern explicit and implicit aesthetic meanings. It was possible to enable innovative empirical research, which was free in regard to both the setting and to the methods devised in understanding a complex spectrum of experience, representations and meanings that is the realm of organisational aesthetics.

As noted, given our aims it was necessary to identify an organisation that lent itself to being a methodological playground, that is, an organisational setting that made it possible 'to play seriously' (Bourdieu, 1998) and to experiment with new research practices. The field of research is invariably characterised by a nexus of self-restriction and the broad methodological diversity that is possible with any real mandate of genuine exploration. Such a space was made available by The Art Foundation – a historic Venetian foundation. The organisation was active in the art world, but at the same time sufficiently complex in its institutional structure to enable us to observe interesting and composite processes, particularly with regard to the organisation's official purpose of producing and managing cultural goods.

The project involved five researchers for a 24-month period, during which the team conducted around ten explorations. The actual fieldwork was carried out by four researchers with similar expertise in qualitative methods for research in organisations, but who nevertheless had different research perspectives and interests. They consequently formed a team with a diversity of aesthetic sensibilities, able to grasp the different stimuli arising from immersion in the organisational context [cf. *method*: Aesthetic Team]. There was a researcher who specialised in organisational communication, an ethnographer already engaged in research on organisational aesthetics, and an artist-sociologist. A further researcher (the first author of this chapter) assumed the role of 'orchestrator' of the research team and compiled the final report. Through observation of the full spectrum of research activity, the 'orchestrator' assumed the task of encouraging the group to reflect systematically on the character and dynamics of individual and collective action. Last but not least, there was a fifth member, the senior sociologist in the research team, who acted as 'off-the-field coordinator'. They performed their function by chairing group meetings. They did not participate personally in the fieldwork phase, but encouraged a crucial dimension of reflexivity with regard ongoing research activity, with the purpose of identifying new research strategies. This role was therefore largely an extemporisation within the project, furnishing constant and reflexive *reverberation* on the research activity [cf. *method*: Resounding Wall (researcher)].

The minimal distinction between research roles was the only form of internal 'planning' in the research group's activities. Through the project, the work was conducted, revised and discussed through dynamic negotiation within the group. Our activity coalesced in three main areas (which were also stages or occasions in the research process):

> *Access to the research field*: On the first day of fieldwork observation, we encountered, negotiated and discussed the difficulties in constructing a shared discourse within the group. The experiential impact and the sensory evocations aroused by the encounter with the organisational setting were strong – such strong sense of encounter stimulates an individuation of experience, rather than the intersubjectively mediated dialogue that a research team requires.

> *Reflexivity 'off the field'*: Here our attention concentrated on generating within the internal processes of research activity a reflexivity: the group's research design and selection of tools emerged from this critical reflection on its work.

> *Methodology 'on the field'*: an innovation in methods was generated by the coalition of research perspectives in the group, but also strongly impacted by the intensity of the researchers' perceptual experience of the aesthetic dimensions of the organisation. These three spheres of activity define the implementation phase of our research. The point of departure here is our first visit to The Art Foundation.

The first day of work: *Imaginative train-ing (what we think you are)*

As all researchers know, every investigation begins well before the encounter with the organisation. It does so through 'contact' – effectively a form of imaginary participant observation (Strati, 1999) [cf. *method*: Aesthetic Immersion]. The researcher encounters the organisation through the brand image, representations and descriptions obtained from the organisation's website, from the accounts and conveyed experiences of those who have already visited it, and from disconnected scraps of information gathered when negotiating access. This contact is where a 'prefiguration' takes place, and despite often being omitted from the final report, this prefiguration of the observation phase has a crucial role in directing the researcher's gaze, or indeed in the *a priori* formulation of theories.

Prior to the project's initiation, The Art Foundation was a setting that had been widely discussed, but of which only the orchestrator had knowledge, albeit partial knowledge: it was he that negotiated access to the organisation. The long train journey between our research-base in Trento to the Foundation in Venice (three hours) was scheduled as research preparation, where the group discussed expectations and developed a vocabulary for articulating questions, uncertainties and curiosities with regard to the genre of institution that was the Foundation. The Foundation, it transpired, while never previously an object of our or anyone else's research attention, had a place within our own order of representations – we all had some mental images, imaginative impressions, and even convictions on various subjects, already embedded within our intellectual memory. The realisation of this stock of tacit knowledge, prior information and preconceptions, was reported in the ongoing notes taken by the orchestrator, and thus constituted the first moments of *reflexivity* in the research.

Sightseeing (let me show you what we really are)

Aware of our prior cognitive awareness of the Foundation, we began our exploration by testing the spectrum of these representations and ideas against the 'self-representation' or accounts and narratives of the organisation's personnel we encountered when we arrived. Our request that they talk to us about themselves was turned around into an offer to take us on a guided tour of the organisation's premises. This, given the nature of the premises, was practically the equivalent of an 'archaeological' exploration in the sense of a revealing of the layers of the institution. We thus allowed ourselves to be led by the Director, while conscious that the attention and attentiveness of each of us researchers was changing and adjusting to the organisational setting, beginning to be directed by our sensibility. From the guided tour, we began to perceive the different organisational epochs embedded in the very structure of the space as an institutional place, apparent as we were taken from one room to another. We commenced with the library, the original core of the Foundation, as it had been donated to the city by a Venetian nobleman more than a century previously. We were then taken on an itinerary, which from the large, richly furnished rooms of the library led to the cramped offices of the 'loans' section. The tour continued through a display area, where labourers were dismantling an exhibition of works by a well-known American artist, and then on to an historical area undergoing restoration. We finally saw the construction site of a new auditorium for the Foundation.

Along the way, the Director explained what was happening in each particular space. Above all she emphasised the 'alternative' nature of the Foundation, with respect to other Venetian institutions, which directed our attention to the unique composition of spaces. She recalled that the founder had stipulated that the library was to be open when other libraries in the city were closed. She showed us the ancient structure of the building, indicating points where a well-known twentieth-century architect had intervened with his distinctive style. His interventions, in a city dedicated to the preservation of the past, were described as an 'opportunity' to mix ancient and contemporary. Everything in the Director's presentation was intended to make explicit that beyond the entrance, separated from the square by a small bridge under which gondolas passed, lay an organisation very different from the context that surrounded it [cf. *method*: Aesthetic Immersion].

Disbanded ethnographers

The point in mentioning the guided tour is that through it, unexpectedly, each researcher experienced a brief period of aesthetic immersion, engaging in 'passive intuition' mediated by their own stock knowledge, as well as cognitive and sensory responses (Gagliardi, 1996). Following promptings during the Director's own self-representation of the organisation, and in light of what had been observed, each researcher then began exploring a part of the organisation. One went to the offices of the library, having its history recounted to them, finding that it was ridden by past conflicts as well as current latent ones due to the library's gradual loss of central importance in the organisation. Another researcher chose to observe the administration, where, reprising a comment made by the Director, he sought to understand how the organisation's new logo had been created. He discovered that the old symbol – the traditional coat of arms of the founder's family lineage – had proved problematic and not possible to revise, and continued to exist on headed notepaper, printed forms, and in others artifacts still in use. A third researcher concentrated on external communication, and particularly on the organisation's website [cf. *method*: Aesthetic Immersion].

Feed-[yourself then]-back

At a prearranged time, we interrupted our individual work and went for lunch; but collective work did not come to a halt. In fact, this was the first time that we could freely discuss what we had seen, heard and perceived, without being overheard. From the moment we set off for the restaurant to our re-entry in the Foundation, the orchestrator guided us in a process of collective reflection on the research that had just commenced. As later pointed out, each researcher was keen and enthusiastically attempting (if unconsciously) to impose his/her own point of view and methodological perspective. Rather than remaining open and allowing of a synthesis in viewpoints, the group seemed to move towards the taking of individuals 'positions'.

In the afternoon, each of the researchers resumed his or her observational work. The day's work concluded with the train journey back home during which we again engaged in some collective reflection, rehearsing some of the competitive dynamics that had emerged during lunch. We nonetheless achieved a first multi-dimensional organisational research view on the Foundation.

Later analysis of this initial experience led to partial re-design of the subsequent fieldwork. This came about during collective reflection led by the off-the-field coordinator, who conducted a debriefing on the first research phase, and during which each team member presented initial data from their fieldwork and articulated their experience during its conduct. The personal aspect of the experiential dimension was very apparent at these meetings. Our attentiveness to a researcher's individual experience constituted both a resource for, radical challenge: how can knowledge be constructed from a spatio-temporally complex institution, with its multifaceted self-representation of 'objects' that can in their entirety only be observed by a diverse group of researchers? How do we achieve coherence? What is 'knowledge' under these circumstances?

The answer required a shift in our conception of method and the role of methodological tools – understood not simply as means of knowledge 'acquisition' but of a creative knowledge 'construction'. In what follows we will put forward a simple proposal for methodological innovation based on our *a posteriori* analysis of the research conducted at the Foundation. This proposal is the result of an exercise in critical reflection undertaken by the research group upon conclusion of the research phase, and supplemented later on. Components of this methodological reorientation have already appeared as our 'internal bookmarks'. These are: *Aesthetic Field, Aesthetic Team, Resounding Wall* (researcher), *Resounding Wall* (collective process), *Aesthetic Immersion, Aesthetic Interview and Ethnographic Reload*.

By 'Aesthetic Field' we mean an organisational setting rich with perceptive sensitisations and thus able to stimulate the researcher's sensibility in various ways (usually repressed in the course of using standardised research methods). Obviously, a choice in the site or field of research is not always possible: some organisations are more expressive and evocative of sensible material than others. What we want to suggest, however, is that the study of an organisation should be conducted by commencing with those places (or processes) presumed to be richer with emotional and sensorial stimuli (places often avoided by methods seeking 'objectivity' or data with consistently measurability). For example, these may be spaces undergoing some kind of transformation, or animated by a shift or transference of power or decision-making, or are spaces that seem empty but where crucial chance or covert meetings frequently take place.

The concept of the Aesthetic Team indicates the need to assemble a research team that comprises researchers possessing a diversity of competences and also of sensibilities. Organisational space is never a self-same unified 'object' of analysis or simply a physical framework for action and communication. It is a realm that is accessed by various modes of interaction and open to endless permutations of sensible experience and representation. No one articulation of this is sufficient, and the Team is not there to provide an *aggregation* of experiences: the Team rather enacts an interactive and process-based investigation – generating a vocabulary, both clashing and compatible perspectives and counter-perspectives, developing methods and reflexive methodologies. Importantly, the researchers need to sustain a sense of 'wonder' or aesthetic curiosity towards the setting. This is both a motive and the energy for consistent extemporisation. The group, therefore, does not simply seek to produce a plurality of richer and more detailed descriptions or analyses – that is, making texturally rich or 'aestheticising' the data acquired by standard methods. Instead they seek to create an innovative and situation-specific multi-faceted investigation, constructing knowledge forms that are expressive of that organisation's complex life.

The blending of different sensibilities into

a polyphonous, but not discordant, chorus may benefit from a Resounding Wall, understood here in the twofold sense of 'researcher off the field' and 'collective process of reflexive analysis of the research'. The Resounding Wall (researcher) has the task of stimulating the researchers in the field to review their observations, reliving and re-evoking significant episodes and choices. This work (collective process) enables the researchers to gain awareness and to return to the data (and the field), opening themselves up to new stimuli or imagining new tools of inquiry.

As regards the 'operational' tools of field research, our proposal therefore consists in recasting in aesthetic terms the classic instruments of qualitative analysis, such as participant observation and interviews, stimulating the evocative and aesthetic dimension to emerge. Participant observation and interviews of course were never purely statistical or abstract tools of knowledge-acquisition, but emerged out of 'the aesthetic' (the experience of communication in sensory environments, subject to spatio-temporal dynamics, symbolic gestures and expression or non-linguistic intersubjective interaction, and so on). Our approach is to return to these methods and others their full aesthetic dynamic. Reflexivity in the process is key to making otherwise standard tools innovative. It is not itself simply a series of discrete acts of critical reflection, but a process of innovation in the conditions of research, 'immanently' developing methods in response to the emerging multi-facetted layers of collective sensible experience. 'Process' is understood here not so much as a specific kind of attention or a specific dimension, but a temporal expression of 'tension' directed within the researchers involvement in the immersive organisational environment. In other words, with the expressions 'aesthetic immersion' and 'aesthetic interview', we refer not to free-standing tools, but rather to explicit research actions that were self-incorporating into a dynamic that commences with the choice of the (aesthetic) field or organisation, the (aesthetic) team, and the method of collegial reflexive discussion (resounding wall). This framework also comprises the action of what we call the Ethnographic Reload, defined as a re-reading of ethnographic notes and reports made by revisiting the original organisational context (after a brief lapse of time).

We are aware that no innovative change to the methods used for the aesthetic analysis of organisations can hope to find widespread adoption, given the scientific community's strong adherence to the unifying rationality expressed by its dominant epistemologies. Publishing restrictions themselves often require a drastic reduction in the range of sensibilities activated by experience of the field. Nevertheless, the purpose of this chapter is in some way to provoke a researcher to exploit all the minor opportunities that standard research practices afford, paying maximum attention to potential and rewarding 'deviations' from set method. Researchers must allow a 'broad band' expansion of the field to emerge, in both the choices in organisation, nature of immersion and methods of analysis and evaluation. Today, data gathering is much more fluid and open than it used to be, and possibilities for opening a level of creative spontaneity within the rigidity of standard representations of research results are more and varied.

Research Field: The selected 'space' or site of research activity	**Aesthetic field:** A space that is chosen for the diversity of sensible stimuli, in turn enabling methodological innovation
Research Team: Team of persons with competency in qualitative methods and reflective understanding of their own aesthetic sensibility	**Aesthetic team:** a team that creates perceptual asymmetry vis-à-vis the organizational aesthetic (dialectic and shared reflexivity)
Individual analyses of organizational settings: The aesthetic in organizations is multi-layered and requires a multi-modal approach by a range of individual researchers	**Aesthetic analysis:** analysis of organizational contexts with specific orientation to the diversity of the researchers in regard to the modes of aesthetics stimuli/meaning
Reflexivity: Importance of the sensible evocations and visualizations produced by the researchers for analysis	**Reflexive aesthetics:** analogical analysis of aesthetics, which may use diverse tools for temporary visualization or relay
Discussion with the research coordinator: Coordination of researchers' independent research interests; relies on new and independent evocation and visualization (aesthetic mirroring)	**Re-sounding wall:** a person other than the researchers in the field. S/he examines and reinterprets the echoes reported by the researchers concerning their information-gathering
Participant observation: Need to become 'one' with the organizational environment (aesthetic and an-aesthetic of the setting considered)	**Aesthetic Immersion:** rational and sensory entry into the organizational context as a field of research
Interview: (semi-structured, in-depth, ethnographic): moving beyond cognitive and rational verbalizations so that the aesthetics of accounts can be comprehended (images evoked, specific narratives used)	**Aesthetic interview:** (organizational): interview open-ended but designed to cover aesthetic dimensions (inclusion of aesthetic dimensions that comprise and support the verbalization)
Secondary analysis of ethnographic fieldnotes: understanding data collected by others requires the linkage of perceptual faculties	**Ethnographic reload:** re-reading ethnographic notes and reports by revisiting the original organizational context (after a brief elapse of time)

Figure 1:
Conspectus of methodological approaches

Conclusion

A backward gaze on the research conducted at The Art Foundation prompts a number of considerations – in which the themes of aesthetics, reflexivity and method intersect. The first consideration concerns the force with which the perceptive/aesthetic dimension acts on researchers, often without being noticed, steering their gaze and inflecting their analyses. The immersion in the organisational setting in this sense can induce an individuation that alienates researchers from each other, and therefore must be strategic and conducted in a way that involves group interaction. Further representations and conceptions of the organisation developed by each individual researcher, in part animated by their theoretical commitments as well as their initial sensible experience, is both a medium for conflict and expression of the 'authorial' will of each team member, as well as a conduit for knowledge. Even before access to the field, the researchers maintain (often unaware) powerful preconceptions, prior and tacit knowledge, images and so on, that construct a cognitive framework and horizon of expectation. The various layers and motives of so-called 'subjective' experience as well as knowledge must be interrogated and reflexively integrated into the collective agenda of group research. The difficulty of 're-opening the gaze', once it has decisively focused on an exclusive selection of processes or objects, can develop into a serious state of cognitive non-commensurability.

An endeavour to maintain an openness of gaze towards the organisational research setting, energised by the 'wonder' of the aesthetic dimension, is central to research coordination. It may be useful to 'replay' the articulated evocations and impressions that have arisen in the field with the assistance of a researcher who does not have direct experience of the organisation. A 'resounding wall' of this kind is valuable not so much because it can generate alternative interpretations of the data, but as a means of critical reflection on the choices made, the focus, the hidden hierarchies of value, and so on. However, for an off-the-field researcher to be effective, as little time as possible should elapse between fieldwork and debriefing.

In the last decade the rise of multi-media and digital communication has of course presented all kinds of new opportunities for group research projects – particularly in terms of inter-project communications, visualisation of data, project management processes, interim conclusions and final report results. Multi-media communication can play a major role in the processes of research negotiation, adaptation, and fine-tuning of presentation of research data. New modes of collaboration in the final production of the research results should also be considered. Video documentary reporting of research is increasingly admitted as an addendum to the traditional final output of the scientific report.

The 'an-aesthetising' of every scientific dimension of research is technically possible, and carries both opportunities and serious risks. The risk is that we face a further panoply of 'tools' whose limitations are so concealed they become unquestioned authoritative media of scientific objectivity. Our research project avoided the acceptable practice of *prix fixe* methods and tools – preferring instead co-construction with researchers evolving in their methodological approach *in situ*. This activates a research process driven by pathos (Strati, 1999), activating the emotional realm of the researcher-as-subject. This has the power to enlarge and consolidate the epistemological spaces hitherto only skirted, further activating processes more respondent to the exigencies that arise in the project.

Organisational research may yet generate a full 'aesthetic turn', whereby the pathos of people that has always guided organisational choices can acquire full recognition in academic research. The aesthetic sensibility may therefore fully become a hypertext of organisational knowledge that is much more efficacious than it is at present in scientific research.

Organisations seem 'naturally' to create environments that suppress individuality, and often do so through their codes of behaviour (often unwritten). A person's behaviour and even mannerisms can express or articulate belonging or the experience of being a 'misfit'. This chapter questions the basic assumption that people must 'fit' into an organisation in order to contribute or play a constructive role in its productivity. It also questions the assumption that people must be 'positive' about an organisation, and not work in a state of 'negativity'. This is particularly true of leaders, whose identity and role needs to be closely aligned with that of the organisation. Here the authors take a look at the *Book of Disquiet*, first published in 1982 by Bernardo Soares (who in reality is the world-famous Portuguese writer, Fernando Pessoa). In this book the authors find ways in which the membership and leadership of an organisation does not require 'fitting in' or 'positivity'.

The aim of the chapter is to follow what the authors call '(dis)engagement' and how it can contribute to the creation of productive organisations. What is apparently negative may in fact be positive – what seems to be a form of 'distance' may in fact be a form of 'engagement'. Pessoa provides a powerful narrative framework for assessing some of the basic limits of our accepted principles of organisational management.

POEM'E': Effectively Managing 'Engagement'

Nuno Guimarães-Costa and Miguel Pina e Cunha

'Boss Vasques is Life'

Bernardo Soares (2003: 53)

Research on behaviour in organisations tends to stress the relevance of members whose relationship with the organisation is characterised by *strong bonds*, such as commitment, psychological contracts, involvement and so forth. They have been described as 'citizens' of the organisation rather than 'mere' employees. They have been qualified as the ordinary people that most contribute to the creation of extraordinary organisations. A few organisations have succeeded in creating extraordinary results through a number of practices sophisticated enough to unleash the best of 'ordinary people' (O'Reilly & Pfeffer, 2000). When this state of inclusion is not achieved, the results may be organisational mediocrity and/or harsh organisational climates (Kets de Vries, 2001). In other words, the person-organisation fit is expected to facilitate the creation of good organisations, and a misfit is expected to create frustrated people in what is experienced as a negative organisation. Organisational members are then said best to contribute when they are positively engaged with the organisation. The recent wave of interest in such topics as 'positive organisations' and even 'workplace spirituality' makes this interest more visible. 'Positive' studies suggest that organisations may improve by focusing on their virtues rather than their weaknesses (Cooperrider & Whitney, 2001): the more positive the better. Spirituality theorists have pointed out the need to nurture spirit at work. An expected result of both types of approaches would be greater employee well-being, stronger organisational commitment and greater productivity (e.g. Fry et al., 2005).

Many organisations, however, remain distant from such a positive profile. They are not communities of inclusion, and their members are neither highly committed nor engaged. This lack of engagement tends to be presented in a negative light. In this chapter, we advance a different perspective on what we call the (dis)engaged employee. Based upon the *Book of Disquiet* by Bernardo Soares, one of the several heteronyms of the great Portuguese literary figure, Fernando Pessoa, we suggest that some members may be positively disengaged, meaning that they can positively contribute to the organisation despite their lack of engagement.

With this stated purpose, we have organised the chapter as follows. First, to situate our source of inspiration, we sketch out the life and work of Fernando Pessoa, with a focus on the Bernardo Soares heteronym. Then we introduce Boss Vasques, the archetype of the leader with who subordinates tend not to establish affective bonds – Bernardo Soares representing such a subordinate. Contrary to the literature, and taking advantage of the liberty of literature and poetry, we suggest that many advantages may result from the absence of affective bonds. Drawing on the two previous parts, we then discuss the conditions that favour subordinate (dis)engagement. The chapter contributes to a growing need in the study of organisation and management by suggesting that organisational leadership can be effective even when practised by people that are not perceived as leaders by their subordinates. Perhaps more: we suggest that effectiveness can be achieved even in the absence of leadership substitutes. We also suggest that disengagement may not have a negative impact on the organisation, thus contributing to the study of the positive side of 'negative organisational behaviour'.

Thus (dis)engagement may contribute to the creation of positive organisations, meaning that what is apparently negative may in fact be positive – a possibility that is well established in the field of psychology (e.g. Norem & Chang, 2002) and which is now being explored in the context of positive organisational behaviour (Lopes & Cunha, 2005).

Fernando Pessoa: A Bio-Bibliographical Sketch

Fernando Pessoa (1888-1935) is regarded as the greatest 20th-century Portuguese poet (Griffin, 1990). In the context of Portuguese modernism his work is considered to be pivotal, later gaining global recognition; Harold Bloom (1994) included Pessoa amongst the masters of the western canon. Born in Lisbon, where he lived most of his adult life, his life and work are associated with this city in the same way that Prague is associated with Kafka, Buenos Aires with Borges, or Dublin with James Joyce. An orphan at five, he went to Durban with his mother and his stepfather, then a Portuguese consul. In South Africa, he received an English education, which would instil a profound admiration for both England and English literature. In fact, his first published books were collections of his English poems.

In 1905 he returned to Lisbon, where he made a living by translating English and French correspondence for several companies. His private life was one of solitude albeit intellectually hyperactive: apart from poetry, his trunk was full of writings on philosophy, sociology, history, short stories, treatises on astrology and other esoteric reflections. He died in Lisbon, in 1935, having published – apart from several articles and the *English Poems* – a single book, *Mensagem*, an esoteric poem on Portugal's leading role in a forthcoming *fifth empire*.

Pessoa is not only Pessoa – and readers should be informed here that, in Portuguese, *pessoa* means person – but several other poets and writers – the heteronyms, to whom he gave a full personality, with their own history, biography and different literary style, in a process of de-personalisation that made him suspicious of his own sanity. Bernardo Soares is one of these heteronyms, or a semi-heteronym, for Pessoa recognised that

'although his personality is not mine, it is not un-alike, it's just a mutilation of it' (Soares, 2003: 15).

Therefore, Bernardo Soares appears as a 'fraction' of the real Pessoa, not as a non-living alternative being, like the rest of the heteronyms. The similarities between Soares and Pessoa himself are certainly more than mere coincidence: the poet needed the employee, as Ferreira (2005) pointed out in a book on how Pessoa 'made a living', where he describes the work and organisational experiences of the poet. Interestingly, an appendix to this book is a chapter called *Organizar* (Organising), originally published in 1926 in the *Revista de Comércio e Contabilidade* (Review of Commerce and Accounting), for which Fernando Pessoa and his brother-in-law Francisco Caetano Dias were responsible for several years.

Bernardo Soares is an assistant-bookkeeper in a commercial firm by day – not very different from Pessoa's professional activity, a clerk responsible for writing commercial letters and translating documents – and an anxious writer by night, when he composes his 'autobiography without facts' (Soares, 2003: 54), the *Book of Disquiet* (*O Livro do Desassossego*). Like Pessoa, he is an introvert living in an inner world much larger than the one where his external actions can be seen. The French biographer Robert Brechon (1996) described Soares as a mediocre man who writes words of genius. This mediocrity reflects what Lourenço (1986) characterised as the most banal and grey life. Bernardo Soares speaks of himself as being similar to

> 'those sorts of men who are always on the periphery of things they belong to – who are oblivious not only to their own numbers, but also to the vast gaps between' (Soares, 2003: 45).

Hence, this semi-fictional *persona* lives in a precarious equilibrium between two very distinct realities, one visible, as a clerk who has to fulfil all his duties and obligations to his boss and the company for which he works, and another, invisible, where he has

> 'to choose what I detest – either the dream, which my intelligence hates, or action, which my sensibility despises; either action, for which I was not conceived, or the dream, for which no one was conceived' (Soares, 2003: 47).

Bernardo Soares recognises this duality, when he notes that

> '…despite the lofty majesty of my many dreams, I'm an assistant bookkeeper in the city of Lisbon. But this contrast does not get the better of me – it frees me; and the irony that lies within is my own blood' (Soares, 2003: 48).

Revealingly, he tries to reconcile these different worlds

> 'with an inward smile [by which] I remind myself that life, which has these pages filled with names of plantations and white owners and money, and its neat, ruled lines and letters, also includes great seafarers, saints and poets of all ages – all of them unaccounted for – a vast category that is not itemised along with these that tally the world's worth' (Soares, 2003: 49).

In bridging his two worlds, the same 'care and indifference' (Soares, 2003: 55) is used by Bernardo Soares in both his daylight keeping of ledgers and his nocturnal writings, thus allowing enough free space for organisational forces, like Boss Vasques, to benefit from his (dis)engagement.

Enters Boss Vasques…

Sharing the same stage as his colleagues, whilst playing his 'visible' role, Bernardo Soares also experiences the same organisational reality, including that of leadership, which is represented by Boss Vasques. Boss Vasques is the owner of the firm – a successful fabrics trading business. He lives in the upper-class suburb of Estoril, 20 kilometres west of Lisbon and he

> 'owns [his employees'] hours and the days of [their] lives' (Soares, 2003: 52).

Bernardo Soares takes the time to describe his boss in some detail as follows:

> 'Boss Vasques … medium height, stocky, coarse in his limits and affections, frank and astute, brusque though not ungentle –

> *chief, aside from his money, of his slow and hairy hands, with bold veins like little coloured muscles, his stout, but not fat, neck, his taut, ruddy cheeks under a dark and well-tended beard ... his deft gestures, his eyes inwardly examining outward matters ... his smile, voluminous and human, like applause from a crowd'* (Soares, 2003: 52)

The sarcasm with which Bernardo Soares tints some of his boss's traits reveals that he is not a subordinate eager to follow his leader or to emulate his character – quite the opposite. Although he compares Boss Vasques to life (Soares, 2003: 53) he does so stressing that

> *'Life, monotonous and necessary, willing and unknown. This banal man epitomises Life's banality'.*

Boss Vasques is not an enticing leader; he is not surrounded by enthusiastic followers, eager to excel under his command. Nevertheless, as we will see in the next section, there appears to be an effective relationship between the leader and his follower Soares, albeit one based on disengagement.

Towards a Typology of Engagement and Disengagement

The case of Bernardo Soares suggests that there may be a positive side in disengagement – an aspect that has not been truly considered in the organisational literature. To contrast this observation with the previous literature, we have built a typology that articulates positive and negative consequences with engagement and disengagement, which is presented in Table 1. The typology suggests three profiles whose existence has already been recognised in the literature (the citizen, the cynical, and the uncivilised), plus the profile of what, inspired by Soares, we called the (dis)engaged organisational member. Below, we briefly mention the first three types, and then dedicate some more attention to the case of the (dis)engaged.

The citizen. 'Citizens' are the organisationally engaged members, whose actions are volitional and positive. Their relevance to organisations has been acclaimed in the literature (Organ, 1988). Their commitment to both organisation and leader paves the way to excellence, which is achieved by high levels of intrinsic motivation and leadership enticement. Companies replete with organisational citizens have been praised for their resilience and collective awareness (Manville & Ober, 2003). Citizens tend to care about their organisations, to think about what they can do for them, and to express extra-role behaviours. They have been metaphorically described as 'good soldiers' (Organ, 1988).

	Positive	Negative
Engagement	The citizen	The uncivilised
Disengagement	The (dis)engaged	The cynical

Table 1: *Positive and Negative forms of engagement and disengagement*

The uncivilised. Some people may be highly engaged with their organisations in a negative way. They may feel mistreated and cheated and they decide to 'pay back'. In Neuman and Baron's (2005) distinction, this profile may correspond to Type D of organisational misbehaviour: *intended to inflict damage*. Some people may thus have developed a tendency to act in ways that have been described as marked by incivility (Pearson, Andersson & Porath, 2000). They tend to provoke a negative impact on their organisations. There are several variations of the uncivilised profile but in general, they tend to damage the organisational environment.

The cynical. The cynical corresponds to the disengaged person who produces negative results. Organisational cynicism has been described as resulting from the lack of trust in the organisation and its leaders by individuals who have witnessed continued contradictions between what is said and done (for more on organisational cynicism see Dean, Brandes & Dharwadkar, 1998). Cynical people may adopt covert tactics of resistance and even appear, on the surface, to be devoted members of the organisation. Fleming and Sewell's (2002) analysis of Svejkism in the workplace represents another possibility for understanding the process and consequences of organisational cynicism: excessive enthusiasm and voluntary obedience may in fact signal covert resistance.

The (dis)engaged. This type corresponds to the less-researched disengaged organisational member who contributes positively to the organisation, thus rendering broadly equivalent results as positively-engaged members. This individual looks inward, as s/he pursues an undisclosed private agenda, important enough to make her or him accept and abide by a set of external rules in which s/he finds no meaning. Given her or his centrality to our discussion we will dedicate the next sections to this type; first, by exposing the advantages associated with disengagement; second, by discussing the conditions that may lead to positive disengagement.

The Positive Side of (Dis)Engagement

Studies on effective organisations tend to portray them as crowded with enthusiastic employees working hard to reach challenging, SMART objectives (Locke & Latham, 1984). Yet, as Bernardo Soares shows, effectiveness can co-exist with concealed, highly prized private objectives. In fact, despite his disengagement from current reality, Soares recognises that Vasques & Co is centrally important to him. Indeed, he reflects on who he would be were he not an assistant bookkeeper at this firm. He then concludes that he would not be able to *be*, that is, he would not be capable of writing of him*self*, his *Book of Disquiet*:

> '*I owe to the fact of being a bookkeeper most of what I can feel and think, such as negation and escape from my job*' (Soares, 2003: 150).

Apart from a high-value personal objective, such as the one presented by Soares, the positive effects of disengagement are more likely to occur when two situations occur. First, when the disengaged member displays an explicit intention to remain in the organisation. Bernardo Soares stresses that he works with Vasques because he wants to, since *'it would be easy to escape from this tedium, were I to have the simple will to just do so'* (Soares, 2003: 133).

In keeping all other options consciously open, as Bernardo Soares does when he emphasises

'To act: behold the true intelligence. I will be whatever I want. But I have to want whatever I am. Triumph lies in being triumphant, not in having the possibility to triumph.' (Soares, 2003: 133)

he carefully avoids retaliatory actions towards the organisation, signalling the distance between the (dis)engaged and the uncivilised. In fact, he has no incentive not to cope with the firm, since he can leave whenever he wants to.

Second, when the disengaged member genuinely knows and accepts the rules of the game. That is what Bernardo Soares reveals when he describes what he calls the 'man of action':

'The world belongs to those who have no feelings. The main qualification for being a practical man is the lack of sensibility. The main thing in life is … will' (Soares, 2003: 286).

He continues, explaining that one must forget about others' individuality, their feelings, their grief and joy in order to act successfully in the real world. After remarking that a man of action is always in a good mood he reflects,

'the one who works even in a bad mood is a tool of action; he can be … a bookkeeper …but he can rule neither things nor men.' (Soares, 2003: 287).

His acceptance of the rules is most explicit when he writes

'Boss Vasques closed a deal today in which he ruined an invalid and his family. [But he] is not a hoodlum, he is a man of action. A person who gets the short end of the stick today can, in fact, count on [Boss Vasques'] charity tomorrow, because [he] is actually a generous man' (Soares, 2003: 287).

Nevertheless he had previously admitted, as a fact, that his promotion from assistant-bookkeeper to bookkeeper would mark one of the most important days of his entire life. By accepting this external reality, he creates enough space for leadership to flow and render the positive effects that eventually lead to organisational effectiveness.

Inspired by the example of the poet, we argue that today's equivalent to Bernardo Soares is the individual who, despite her or his disengagement from the company, is capable of behaving as expected by her/his peers and superiors. The disengaged behaviour is distinct from that of the cynical person since there is no intention of harming the organisation, nor is it the member's intention to pursue her or his objectives *despite* those of the employer. The relationship between the (dis)engaged and the organisation is one of a symbiotic nature, albeit anchored in concealed reasons. S/He will work hard to attain organisational objectives, will be enthusiastic enough to celebrate the organisation's successes, will give room for events to take place, will not argue against the imposed rules, will make an effort to go unnoticed and thus keep the private dream alive. Given this abiding behaviour, leaders do not have to adopt any special measures to deal with the (dis)engaged employee. In fact, leaders will experience some

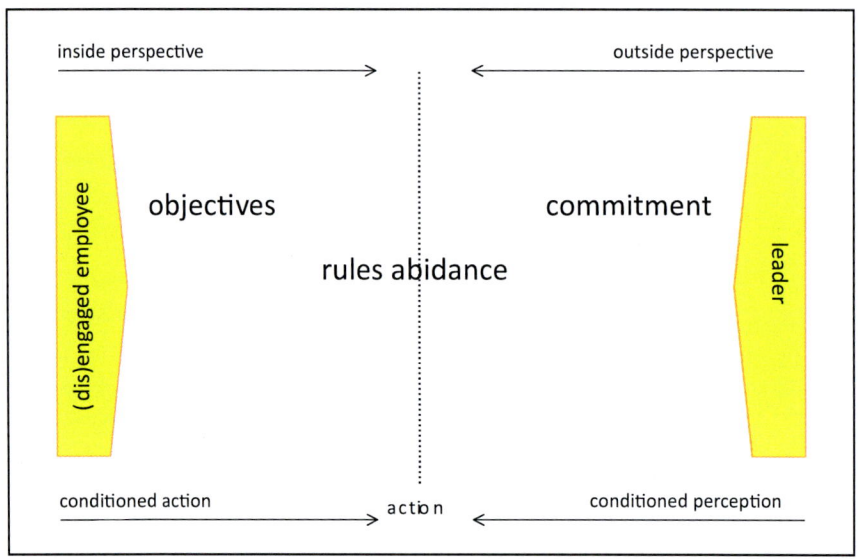

Figure 1: *The (dis)engagement equilibrium*

difficulties when asked to draw out the (dis)engaged person. In some instances, they can even confuse her or him with an organisational citizen, unconscious of the true nature of the glue binding the (dis)engaged to the company.

As can be depicted from Figure 1, the effectiveness of (dis)engagement is anchored in the different perspective each agent – (dis)engaged member and leader – has of the organisational collaborative phenomenon. Whereas the leader sees commitment to the firm in the form of voluntary rule abidance by the employee, the (dis)engaged member is focusing in her or his personal objectives, thus *having* to abide by the rules, eventually (and involuntarily) leading to a resemblance of commitment. As long as the equilibrium between actions conditioned by private objectives and leaders' perceptions of those same actions is maintained, the positive results of disengagement can be secured.

Even being part of the organisation, the (dis)engaged is, above all, an outsider, with no links to superiors or peers. This lonely standing keeps her/him at bay from company politics, both as a source and as a target. S/He will, therefore, be free fully to dedicate to the dutiful performance of the job, unworried about such issues as career paths, wage fairness or political arenas, which commonly take a share of others' work time and tend to create resistance that tempts organisations to develop forms of control and monitoring (Bain & Taylor, 2000). The (dis)engaged is the epitome of the no perks 'organisational man' (Whyte, 1956), a loyal, devoted and self-restrained individual with no need for reward and no necessity of control. S/He, in fact, is working for her/himself only, but in a state of 'fit' with the job and the organisation (Caldwell & O'Reilly, 1990).

(Dis)engagement can thus contribute to the creation of positive organisations, i.e., those able to fulfil both individual and company goals in a highly satisfactory way.

The (dis)engaged adjusts with the organisation in order to fulfil concealed private objectives. Therefore, when the organisation aims at 'excellence' by means of extraordinary contributions from its ordinary employees, (dis)engaged people, provided that their private objectives are compelling enough, will play their part in the overall organisational efforts by continuously acting as expected.

(Dis)Engagement: Not Always an Extreme Case

We argued that there is no need for bonds between leaders and subordinates for leadership to be effective: Soares and his dear Boss Vasques represent this relationship. In this section, we discuss the reasons why effectiveness is attained through such an apparently dysfunctional relationship.

In management, disengagement is often confused with lack of commitment and with negative outcomes or workplace negativity (Topchick, 2001). As we have seen in the previous sections, this is possibly the case of cynical organisational members often fed by extrinsic phenomena, such as inadequate human resources policies, unreasonable goals or faulty leadership examples. However, if Bernardo Soares is taken as an example – or indeed Pessoa, as the projecting source of the 'mutilated' fiction – one is confronted with disengagement rooted in individual and private causes. Soares suggests that organisational detachment may be a result of an inward reflection and monologue with the self. The assistant bookkeeper needs his job, his leader and his organisation to be grounded on reality, thus having a reason to live. It is not a simple *raison d'etre*, or a way to write his *Book of Disquiet*: the organisation is his blood, the only thing keeping him away from schizophrenia. His leader, 'Boss Vasques [,] is Life' (Soares, 2003, 53), not only figuratively someone who shows him how ordinary people carry on their lives without succumbing to existential anguish – Vasques epitomises the possibility of a 'normal life', something Bernardo Soares would want to live but is incapable of.

One can argue that Bernardo Soares is an extreme case of disengagement. But that does not preclude the existence of other – less dramatic – reasons for positive (dis)engagement on the personal process of reflexivity that leads to specific actions. In fact, by simply pursuing one's personal interests – such as a future job opportunity, a hobby, a sport, participation in any kind of social activities – one may already be walking the (dis)engagement path. This is even truer if, as in the case of Bernardo Soares, those interests are not related to one's full time professional occupation. The occupation, in turn, is taken as a mere means for attaining other, actively sought, personal objectives. In cases such as these, the organisation is seen as the supplier of a supportive infrastructure: providing the material wealth and psychological baseline that will set the individual free to pursue other *higher* interests. Given one's job criticality in the pursuit of personal interests, one will behave according to the established rules, avoiding any kind of disruptive confrontation within the organisation. Moreover, familiar to the demanding organisational context, where commitment, passion, and loyalty are common words of order, the likes of Bernardo Soares, the (dis)engaged organisational members, will unconsciously hide their true source of motivation under a cover of positive reactions such as hard and efficient work, external manifestations of *genuine* praise, and rejoice with all the company's successes. Not cynical by nature, their actions will render the same results as if they were truly inspired by the company's objectives and vision.

Final Discussion

The leadership process is often described as implying enthusiastic subordinates enticed by their leaders to excel in every task to which they are assigned, in search of a common purpose, and as involving happy celebrations of collective achievements (Deal & Key, 1998). In many organisations, this view of life seems naive and such a clean and streamlined relationship between leaders and subordinates appears to be missing. Reality is often less bright and engagement may be minimal. Legitimised by the proximity between person (Pessoa) and fictional character (Soares), strong enough to allow for the transformation of the fictional into conceivable reality, we have taken inspiration in Fernando Pessoa's heteronym Bernardo Soares and suggested that Soares may be viewed as a possible archetype for the (dis)engaged yet positive organisational member.

Two main possibilities have been advanced as proxies for leadership effectiveness. First is a high extra-organisational motivation to attain specific and valued personal objectives. This will set the subordinate's tone *vis-à-vis* the organisation and their reaction to it. Second is the necessity of psychological free space that allows the subordinate to seek his/her personal interests. This will imply the need for enough material wealth and, consequently, the need to secure the job, regardless of the level of disengagement. The combination of these 'motivators' will lead to a high degree of compliance with the organisation's rules and practices, including a productive relationship with a fully satisfied, albeit unaware, leader. Depending on the sustainability of personal interest – its persistence over time – positive outcomes may endure, thus allowing a niche for the positively (dis)engaged member.

Having been inspired by the poetry of Pessoa, we realise that our arguments do not portray the common organisational member – at least as pictured in the management textbook. Indeed, the (dis)engaged person may be a special case amongst a multitude of truly engaged members who eagerly follow their effective leaders. We certainly do not deny the importance of leadership and need for a 'truly' committed workforce. Yet, organisations embody other types of relationships that can produce equally good results – or not. In her book on the democratic corporation, Gratton (2004) pointed out the benefits arising from the recognition by the organisation that different employees may have diverse interests. It would then be in the organisation's interest to segment its members according to their needs. The positively (dis)engaged member may correspond to a not-so-well-studied segment. In the age of high commitment/high involvement work practices, however, even those employees who developed a more transactional relationship with their organisation should live under a façade of enthusiasm. This is a prudent attitude considering the thin line separating autonomy/authenticity and coercion (Proença, 2010).

This chapter invites the reader to join the author on a journey exploring the relationship between art and business, taking us across Europe and meeting some of the major artists, curators, dealers and managers in the art business world. The relation between art and business is a dynamic and evolving relationship, and this paper represents a unique and individualistic engagement with it, reflecting on the use of art as a mechanism for reflecting on economic realities. For, as the author suggests, when art and business connect (and collide) some central organisational issues emerge.

Over the last few decades Pierre Guillet de Monthoux has become an intellectual fulcrum for new developments in management thought. He has interjected a dynamic, peripatetic, literary-philosophical and altogether uncategorisable dimension to the study of management and organisations. His attention is on the unpredictable flows of power and ideas between and through art, business and the organisation, usually by looking at the way these flows are registered by art works, through the processes of art making and the forms of dialogue that art generates. The author has made a huge contribution to the collapse of the opposition between 'art and business' so dominant in the minds of students and creative practitioners alike, inherited as it is from a misreading of art's history – and a philosophical misreading of central romantic strains in Western thought. Art has always been business, and creativity has always played a role in organisational development and industry. In some ways, putting art and business together is like re-uniting two torn halves, where these halves have become all too accustomed to living apart.

Masters of Business Art: Visiting Art and Business in Europe 2000-2005
Pierre Guillet de Monthoux

PROLOGUE

What follows is a script I made for a road-movie about 'Art and Business' in Europe between 2000 and 2005. We were then commissioned by the Swedish National Bank to find out more on how art connects to business, and what on earth the role of aesthetics has to do with management. I toured Europe, organised a couple of conferences, curated some art shows, taught seminars and in this process interviewed a number of European key actors in the art and business field. Some artists have become PhDs and some PhDs have turned into artists. Some have become even more famous than they were. Apart from writing books and articles and supervising thirteen Swedish PhDs about all this, I also shot a kind of 'road-movie' where all these guys appear and where you can see the spaces where they acted. Here comes the companion-text I wrote to introduce the documentation about this pioneering work in a field, which is now almost mainstream in both management and art education. Enjoy!

BERLIN

My mission is to show how art mixes with the economy and with management in an ongoing creative process. Let us look at the *flows* between the worlds of contemporary art and the managerial worlds of work, consumption, investment, and the media. Let us meet some old and new *masters of business art*.

Today art is a global visual industry with multitudes of 'mega-venues'. Before 1989, a Berlin wall of concrete re-enforced abstract ideologies of an 'inside and an outside'. After 1989, the living metaphor of the wall no more fenced off 'free' economic markets from socially-grounded acts of organisation, and in Berlin market and organisation, business and politics, began mixing with Art deep inside the new muddle. Those who doubt the power of Art must go to Berlin, where around every corner you'll find traces of totalitarian art like the Volksbühne Theatre – once a playhouse for Nazis and Communists – and next door the Babylon Movie Palace, home of Murnau, Lang, and Riefenstahl, the last of whom typically quoted Hitler, whose main propaganda artist she became, insisting that he wanted 'an artist and not a political movie maker'.

In Berlin in 2005 the gallery *Kunstfabrik* put on a show called 'Product Vision' and featured artists presenting portraits of one single firm – a Berlin Publishing House. In Berlin 2001, I curated a show called 'Art Works Consultant', gathering managers and artists to reflect on the economy. We showed how business connected with art using pink painted machinery from traditional industrial facilities together with art pieces by artists working on the themes of management and business. All was accompanied by seminars with the keynote by Italian master of *business art*, Michelangelo Pistoletto. Opening with the following words in 2001, a couple of month after the terrorist attack of September 11th, he stated:

> 'The moment the Berlin wall fell down, the communist system disappeared. The communist system may have disappeared but the problems are still there. And now after twelve years, and the Twin Towers of New York, we ourselves have an unfolding capitalist drama…'

BIELLA

Michelangelo Pistoletto's home base is Biella in northern Italy. It is to Italian factories here that the English outsourced during the last century, but now industry is declining and Italy now outsources to Asia. Only luxury brands like Zegna or Cerruti remain next door to Cittadellarte, a restored old textile mill where Michelangelo found a place to do his art. He says:

> 'You have to create a place where you can become visible – you become a realization, you become the building, you become a thing. So I, by building this Cittadellarte, I transform the no-place of Utopia into a place.'

Warhol had a pop-art factory, Pistoletto has his Cittadellarte. Here he welcomes young artists in residence linked by global IT to the outside world. Backstage in his space, Michelangelo's *Mirror Art* – the mirror-pieces for which he is world famous – are stored up like batteries of aesthetic energies fuelling the front stage of his centre. Here art students also create thought-provoking work, like the installation by Henrik Schrat using Zegna products, or the work by Leopold Kessler that articulates the sustainable energy balance of suit production. Seeing this latter work, I feel that they are tuned into Master Pistoletto's Arte Povera icons; I saw some of them on show at the 1997 Documenta in Kassel, Germany. Addressing energy balance in art is apposite, as art has a magnetic force, it *attracts*. Art venues like the Biennales and Documenta are places of contemporary modern pilgrimage, in some ways taking the role of churches and religion.

And maybe art then is a sort of spiritual retreat for hard-working business people, people well aware that the Director of the Guggenheim has a business degree, and that many art spaces are run by business school drop-outs. Some years ago, a business student of mine, Peter, painted his self-portrait as a 'free' student and then a second canvas appeared with a scary image of himself as a 'bureaucratised' business man. Could art save MBAs from turning into bureaucrats?

In 2001 in Berlin, we gathered together – management students active in the arts interested in turning a Masters of Business Administration [MBA] degree into a *Masters of Business Art*. One of the participants was Armin Chodzinski – an artist with experience in business, who then acquired a PhD in the field of art and business whilst perusing his career as a performance artist. Armin reflected on being in business:

> 'It's so nice to be in business; it's so really nice, because you enter your office, someone waits for you and says … Good morning, how are you. You say, fine, thank you; no calls this morning please. When you are out working as an artist, most of the time you are in your studio, you work on your own all alone.'

However, artists in business today cannot be alone: there are few lone wolves in the art world today. Daniel Birnbaum – philosopher, critic, ex-director of the Stadelschule in Frankfurt and now head of the Museum of Modern Art in Stockholm – portrays the successful artist Olafur Eliasson as an efficient manager:

> 'Olafur called upon me when I was in Chicago. I was supposed to make a short text for him; I met him in a business class lounge on the top floor of the Swiss Hotel...and he was already answering his 111th email... he is operating like a top manager…'.

Forget about the artist-craftsman idea, art now is high tech. US artist Robert Whitman reflects on new ways of understanding technique:

> 'The curators, and people like that, have gotten over the idea that every little thread, or every little 'sweat-part' of the original art work is not valuable. That's not where the essence of the work lies; it's in what you see. The means of that is irrelevant; it doesn't matter how you make it. They've begun to accept that idea that what they are buying is the image, not the machine or the technique or anything else.'

Thirty years ago, Joseph Beuys, a German artist in a felt hat, began advocating 'flows' between art and business. He said that art was *social sculpture*, like serving your family a good meal. When Maria, Michelangelo's partner, served pasta in Biella, she explained a concept central to his view on business art:

> 'I like the term 'game'... because art is a game. 'The Game' is important to consider because in a game it doesn't really matter if you win or you lose. There is always the winner and the loser, but they're both part of the game. It is not really either something terrible or something overly fantastic.'

Joseph Beuys in the felt hat would have preferred 'play' [spiel] to the word 'game'. He explained that art is captain and that everyone is an artist. Beuys used to preach:

> 'Enlarging the concept of art serves all humans and is useful for changing all societal conditions in urgent need of transformation.'

BEUYS

Beuys was an inspiration for the emergent Green Party in Germany in the 1980s, and turned art into a socioeconomic force – in the vein of ideas from German aesthetic philosophy from Immanuel Kant and Friedrich Schiller. Following Friedrich Schiller, Joseph Beuys saw art as facilitating *the playful*, a liberating movement in German 'schwung', and in that spirit a team of young artists went from Cittadellarte to rescue an old hat factory situated in the Biella region. This was a typical case of an old industry rooted in physical matter and ruled by formal administration. Inside the factory, the informal and immaterial forces of the new global economy threatening the very existence of this hat factory.... seemed so very far away.

What could be more *material* than compressing rabbit hair into a lump of felt? And what could be more *formal* than forcing and forming this raw matter into ways of existence and being? When a hat is made by skillful old fashioned hatters, it's almost metaphorical for how our behavior can be frozen by established standards of doing and thinking. Is this what *managing* should be about? Have the 'traditions' of industry made managers focus solely on better ways of bending and twisting matter into form, until we conceive of only two perspectives, either form or matter? This is precisely where we need artists because they work in the midfield between form and matter – innovating poetically by playing with form *and* matter. The question today is whether the manager is sensitive enough to perceive this gentle play. Professor Robert Austin of Harvard Business School and now at Copenhagen Business School reflects on this:

'What I am most aware of when I talk to executives or MBAs about this stuff is that they very much would prefer a world where what they understand about management transfers seamlessly to the 'new world' (you know, the 'knowledge economy' or whatever hokey phrase you'd like to use for that). And they're disappointed and resistant to the possibility that it doesn't. And suggesting that you need to learn something about the process of how artists do their work, is telling them in essence that what you are expert in is not good enough; you need to learn something else'.

So do we need Masters of Business Administration or Masters of Business Art? Do we need Harvard Business School or *Pistoletto's Cittadellarte*? When old industrialists collected art – and many of the great art collectors of our time were old industrialists – they might have had this intuition that something might change by art. The Grand lady of corporate curating, Marjory Jacobson, who once put the MIT media tech lab on the 'art-track', is aware of the importance of the right feeling for art. She said:

'You may want to act as patron to the visual arts…..but as a company or you as the director of a company, you must have a particular feeling… maybe not knowledge, but a feeling about the art that you're collecting..'

But how does art enter into contact with business? Where does the 'feeling' go? Michael Dawids, now deceased pioneer of Copenhagen Learning Lab, suggested that there are…

'..two distinct issues – whether the artist is just a role model, or whether you actually interact with the artist. If role models, there are two kinds: one involves metaphors like 'jamming' or 'orchestrating' change; these are metaphors we derive from the arts; the other is competencies, which is for example how do we learn how to improvise? Can we learn something from looking at a jazz band about improvising? However – if you actually interact with the artist, you have what we call events or products. Events is where say a theatre company comes into a business corporation and works with them for a day and then they leave, and so forth. When they actually start producing something together, creating an object or entity, we call it 'products', or 'processing'.'

PLAY

When art gets into the reality of business and real action, it can become like a game or play, with many participants as spectators, artists, technicians, and critics, gravitating around the art. As for technicians and technical production, artists are making ever more challenging demands. Just listen to US artist Spencer Finch, who mainly works with light:

'I am going to try to check out the exact light situation of Troy. Yes the light that was there in Homer's time! I am curious to recreate it in a gallery context using artificial light. The company Philips is providing the technical expertise and lighting and the actual equipment is coming from a lighting company in Hartford called CLS, which is owned by this big collector who has bought my work before.'

Paolo Naldini who is working in Cittadellarte, continues with our theme:

'Most businesses have a very short term minor interest in working with us artists, which makes it very difficult for us to intervene... because we are not an advertisement agency whose impact can be recorded and measured. Some are more enlightened, and working with us makes them shift their focus from short term to the long term. Therefore we are dealing with an entrepreneurship that is enlightened and that is able to understand how from art and intellectuals and artistic enterprises you can get very deep and strong stimulus for your business production for your business vision.'

In this context Marjory Jacobson again makes an important remark:

'Art is not made to meet a market... it creates a market by being made. It is not created for a market that's over there; it's a market-maker if you like.'

Philosopher Gernot Böhme, at a conference in small French village Gattières in 2002, explained how he looked upon another art-business interaction effect – atmospheres.

'Actually, atmosphere is something between us, or our soul, our mind and the objects outside, something in between, so it's difficult to talk about, but you know it when you experience it.'

Art also contributes by shaping spaces you dwell in. It does that in intricate ways. Antonio Strati, a pioneer of organisational aesthetics, comments:

'That's the conflict ..... this dialogue is a continuous dialogue, in this epistemology in this perspective, it's continuously there, so we can't specify which sort of dialogue is going on, I cannot see a break between the interpreter and the artefact.'

MAGIC

The spaces of business and management are affected by art in subtle ways. It´s not really the matter of an art work just being beautiful by itself, as Tor Hernes says in defining contemporary beauty:

'And maybe the 'visual' dimension of space is often identified with the physical space, but I think there is a beauty in the social dimension of the space, and also the mental space, the beauty of ideas.'

When art interacts with a place, art-work becomes art-space. To go beyond institutional formal conventions and the limitations of the material is part of the competency of the artist, as well as the technician. Only when art works, when *schwung* becomes a fact, comes the words, the stories.... this could happen anywhere, and why not in my own garden, for which in 2002 I invited Daniel Birnbaum to regularly curate an annual small art show:

'This garden, *Le Jardin*, belongs to Pierre Guillet de Monthoux, but he offers it to artists in order to realise projects. There are a number of things that have already happened. There's a wishing tree by Rivane Neuenschawander, and you can still see the remnants of it. It has been very effective, because people have hung wishes on it, and the wishes have actually come true. So, it's a very good wishing tree.'

Rivane Neuenschawander, who was my invited artist in 2002, explains what she does and thereby alludes to the magical effect of art:

'It's called a wish tree and actually I've developed it from a previous project in Brazil. You have ribbons made out of fabric, *and you put them around your wrist and you make three knots and you state three wishes. When it breaks off, it means that your wishes will come true. So I've collected wishes from friends and different people and also visitors of exhibitions; so I have 50 different wishes and they repeat themselves, so I put them on the tree, sort of for the birds so they can pick them up and build nests. That's like an idea that I know it's gonna help them.'*

Daniel Birnbaum continues explicating in 2003 how art magically, even surreally, transforms the tiny place of my garden:

'There's a piece also hanging in the tree that's by Michelangelo Pistoletto – that's a permanent installation and a homage to Mediterranean culture. And there's a little structure, a house for extra-terrestrials. This region is well-known for its connection to outer space and many people believe that they have seen UFOs. So Spencer Finch built this house for extra-terrestrials, and now it's an interactive piece. Right now it's children that have activated it, but in it you can put up images of things you think extra-terrestrials should know about our civilisation. And the new project, which is not visible at the moment, but which is very visible at certain moments during the day, is by Korean artist, Koo Jeung-a. She did a similar piece for the Venice Biennale in 2003 in the so-called Aperto section, where she used artificial light and diamonds, small artificial diamonds in the wall, and they reflect. But here it's more of a cosmological installation; it's really about the relationship between the earth and sun, and she explains it with just a sentence on the invitation card – it's invisible but then highly visible.'

BRANDING

From my tiny garden – 'transfigured by art', using Arthur Danto's term – we could travel to the big Venice Biennale the day before the opening in 2003. Venice was for a long time the model for visual art events; biennales have now globally mushroomed. Artists have always exposed their work to changing economic realities – once upon a time Arts met Crafts, then Art went into the Factories of Industrial work, (think for instance of Fernand Léger, the Constructivists, the Futurists, later the minimalist artists). Today it's about meeting and interacting with the business world of money and marketing much more than mass-manufacturing. As Barbara Stevini explains:

'In the 1960s we were not talking literally about art and business and organisations......it was very much to do with industry and physical production. The term business only came in much later. It is fundamentally different from industry... it is the whole business of taking responsibility and being motivated, whether you're an artist or anybody outside the white-cube; professional security is a very different matter now.'

So slowly art and industry (the binary relation between the two often carried Marxist undertones), turned into art and business. Artists first opened their doors to the labouring practices and realities of factory workspaces in the 1920s, by the 1980s they made artwork that interconnected with the world of corporate branding; now the doors have opened to marketing magic. One of these artist groups (more concerned with fiddling with the mind of markets than the objects of production) is what Alvar Gullichsen and Richard Stanley call Bonk Business Inc.

Alvar Gullichsen tells the background story of Bonk:

> 'Bonk was the fruit of a creative process where coincidence, megalomania and alcohol are a major part. Bonk Business Inc came out of this, and in the Spring of 1989 I had my first one man show at a gallery in Helsinki, which actually was a trade fair installation. Actually, personally, Bonk I guess reflects some of my family background, an industrial family, the Ahlström family, maybe one of the last family owned companies in Europe. It's an old forest company, now maybe even more with Fi-Tech, but a paper company originally. And I'm a part of the artistic branch of that family. My grandmother was Maire Gullichsen, who was quite an important art collector and a supporter of design and architecture. She was a good friend of Alvar Aalto, who also designed a house for her and my grandfather. Here is one of the clichés we have been exploring from the business world – symbols of success and power – and that's the head of product development being young and fresh. Bonk reflects what happens when industry get branded.'

Richard Stanley, Alvar's partner in Bonk Business Inc. and a commercial film-maker adds:

> 'To me, I'm a filmmaker originally, and I don't see any variation between the creation of Bonk and what I do for companies: I'm writing narratives, except I try to be much more honest than most people who write narratives for companies; I try to persuade companies to take different attitudes, but in the end, you're trying to convey the essence of the company or a product to other people, and the idea of it is actually to persuade people to buy it, and we're doing that with Bonk. Except, in the case of Bonk, people really want to buy it. Many people come and say to us that they wish the Brand was true.'

This focus on marketing and branding (instead of manufacturing) has made cooperation between art and business take very different forms from past interconnections with industry. Billy Klüwer, the initiator of EATS engineering (an arts and technology movement) stated,

> 'There is no possibility for industry and art to meet. That's impossible.'

But now things are different, art is not only regarded as 'form', it is not only 'context', but also *content*. In that respect even that 'Mecca of management education', Harvard Business School [HBS], seems hopelessly old fashioned, for the issues that matters most for them involve merely the physical shape of the graduate students and how MBAs still follow habitual dress codes and old forms of education. The old dichotomy of form and matter… still matters, although old industry is giving way to new business. No one can really guarantee anyone a brilliant and secure career for students anymore, at least by a process of shaping them to fit little standardised boxes. So will MBAs turn to a Master of Business Art when private businesses search for creativity?

Robert Austin, an HBS teacher who made MBAs take art seriously by writing specific cases about art and business, put his finger on the kind of old-fashioned industrial paradigm:

> 'There's this tension always between what we call 'stewards' and what we call 'creators'. The stewards are the people who feel most

strongly that it's their job (assuming everybody's well-intentioned)... sometimes there are other characters around too but... the stewards are the people who really care about spending the shareholders' money well. For example, they are keenly aware that they are spending other people's money and that they should not invest a dollar that won't return a dollar.'

INSIDERS

Having artists mix with managers causes business to reflect on one of its central fixed ideas – *performance*. The search for artistic creativity makes sought after lecturers of violin virtuoso, Miha Pogačnik, on corporate leadership, and Paul Robertson and his Medici Quartet, teaching teamwork at the Center of Art and Leadership of Copenhagen Business School. I was invited by Rob Austin to a Jazz Improvisation at Harvard Law School to improve methods for training negotiation skills involving the *schwung* of jazz. Carl Hegemann – a long time dramaturgic leader of the Berlin avant-garde stage Die Volksbühne – even began explaining his theatre successes in business terms. In a place where one was used to reciting Rosa Luxemburg and Karl Marx, he gave public readings of Tom Peters and Pine & Gilmore, stating that no one can remain a 'critical outsider' in contemporary capitalism:

> 'The capitalist function makes it impossible to remain outside – we don't produce FOR the market – that's no fun; we all know we have to sell what we do – but we say we produce IN the market: we try to sell our stuff to find an audience... my love and devotion has no meaning if no one sees it and buys it.'

Donatella De Paoli who runs one of the successful master programs in art and business in Norway says:

> 'Young artists tend to say that they are not free in any case, because they have to get grants and money from the government, so they apply for money for one project, but then want to change the project but can't and have to do the project that they got the money for. Young artists have a much more pragmatic view of business; they say that it's no problem for us to get used by the business world, because the money I get working for one month for the business world gives me money to do all my crazy projects for the rest of the year; they prefer that than getting money from the government. Some artists are very negative and say that it's like the 'end of art'; but other artists say that art has always, through history, shown that it can escape – you know, when they get pressured they find new ways of escaping and new forms of making art....'

The tendency among young artists that Donatella De Paoli has noted we may call insider art. Artist Philippe Mairesse, now completing his PhD about his own art-business activities, remarks on how some artists still resist this new 'insider' position, for they state

> 'This is not moral, this money is dirty funding; but their public funding or art funding or selling to an art market, is clean money!'

The art-business trend has many roots. Ruth Bereson, a professor of arts management, mentions one such, which is indeed more political than commercial:

> 'Australia designed an economics document in the guise of an arts policy document, entitled *Creative Nation*. New Zealand

changed the name of its arts ministry to Creative New Zealand. Then you see Creative South Africa, and Creative America documents. You start to see that creativity starts to look like technology and starts to enter other worlds, and the nature of the arts are being changed with it. So this thing we've been talking about, Trojan Horses for a while, sort of came in incrementally. One eminent Australian critic, Professor Donald Horne, who was head of The Australia Council [for the Arts] in the late 1980s, sort of said that this was the great Trojan Horse – it changed the nature of the debate about art and of funding and so on, into a language of economic rationalisation, yet still under the guise of creativity. It's creativity with an industrial component, and that's why I and many other researchers started to research the relationship between art and business.'

MARKETS

If business sees an interest in art then it happens in times when art becomes more and more like juggling with brands in business. Listen to Maria Finders of Basel Art Fair on the global art market:

> *'…it starts off with the Moscow Biennale in February, then it continues on with the Venice Biennale in June, then Art Basel finds itself stuck in the middle. So we're negotiating about vernissage dates of the Venice Biennale. So then Basel, after that is Documenta…and then Münster, and then Istanbul and then Lyon, all in one single calendar year. So when I think about 2007…I realise that the Basel Art Fair maybe better off cancelled, you know: where can you put a trade show in the middle of a year like that? We had an interesting discussion in Paris with Sam Keller, who's the Director of the Basel Art Fair, but unfortunately the curator Kasper König wasn't there to help us out to decide on the vernissage dates. And those who come to these things… there was a flock of collectors. Collectors migrate. You really wonder how they actually work to make enough money to buy art – but they're all around, and artists are also migrating around with them. Consider the actual amount of work that can be sold in the first two days of the Basel art show – this year in June everything that could be sold was sold, everything!! (I mean I'm saying everything that could be sold was sold because some things just can't be sold, because they're just not interesting or they're filler pieces or whatever). The show was changed on Thursday 'cause it runs from the Tuesday, which is kind of the preview day for the super-important collectors to the point where a collector will come actually on the Monday dressed up as a worker carrying a log and go into the show and try to buy work before the preview…they actually stopped one three times.…we're going to vary the gallery that always gets viewed in the past. So it's a big thing, this preview day. We have two types of V.I.P's – we have the noon V.I.P.'s and these are the ones who can get in at noon; and then we have the 2 O'clock V.I.P's, and these are the ones that get what's left.'*

The art market also may be focused on our 'form and matter' dichotomy. But people, the collectors, investors, shoppers, also relate through pictures, slides, catalogue price lists and maybe they transcend the matter of mere objects and conventions. In a way Liam Gillick and Rirkrit Tiravanija have suggested doing what French Nicola Bourriaud calls 'relational aesthetics, on which Daniel Birnbaum comments:

'So if the general commoditisation of everything and commercialisation of the entire business that we are talking about produces 'pop' objects, then the relational artist is like a therapist, doing art the way that Wittgenstein claimed that philosophy is doing therapy. It's about loosening up.....once we look at the language game and how it's really built up, we see that these knots and problems disappear ...I see on one level like a therapist of contemporary art situations, and Wittgenstein would say, that the therapy will make obvious the fact that it's all a matter of language; so just let the therapy make language go on holiday.'

So, an Art event is no longer only listening and seeing, it implies traveling to and within spaces, changing perspectives beyond clichés and prejudice, making language go on holiday, and this makes art a highly relevant project for organisational consultants – as Raymond Saner, Professor in Organisation and International Management at the University of Basel, suggests:

'Working as a consultant I think you have to be able to see more or less the phenomena of what is. And you get confirmation by people if they're really interested and that's what you're looking for. If they're interested you get somebody else to help them see what's happening, and they will let you know how you should change. What to do then, is next... how to shape that into something else in order for it to stay it has to be....'

TRUTH

In blind business bureaucracies it might be good to be able to see again. You may be looking for the light, as Hans Henriksen from Nokia, Denmark, suggests:

'We have to use the source of renewal – it is that the new guys coming in here and asking to say what are you actually seeing when you come in here. It does not necessarily have to be an artist, but I do think it would be wonderful to have an artist every now and then to come and see because...'

So in 2005 at the Produkt Vision show in Berlin the question was how do artists go about seeing and learning in a business firm? The CEO who had welcomed the artists and given them a traditional introduction to his company asked,

'Do you think we were right from the beginning, what we told you, did we provide you with accurate information do you think?'

Upon which artist Teike Asselbergs broke out in the following remark really about what sort of things that matter for artists – when they want to know more about an organisation:

'My colleague and I, we need more time, and we need direct experience not descriptions. Yeah... you gave us lots of information – you were very open and we appreciate the gesture, but the actual content of the information is not that digestible for us, because it describes your view or your colleagues view on what they describe as the organisation. But the description is very much in formal terms – that's the way you are used to describing an organisation, and for us this information is just too poor. It is very good information, but it is not the right type...it's a different kind of information than we actually need to make art.'

Businesses are too serious. We need to make them play again. This might be the role of artists in business and make businesses dare show their real face. We want them to take off the formal shroud of success. Philippe Mairesse wants business to use a different aesthetic definition of beauty:

> 'Beauty is linked to failure, to Greek theories about beauty, and the necessity of de-symmetry. Symmetry is too much, too perfect for a 'human' beauty. You always need in theory an attempt to be symmetrical. This is what I'm talking about – the beauty of being human. And the deep beauty is, what does it mean to be human? To behave humanly? It means both an attempt to be perfect and a failure to be perfect. And in that case, you have beauty, success and failure, and all of these things like a circle, a cycle. If you take one part off it's not a cycle anymore.

Ken Friedman, professor of design management and also an artist and art theorist associated with Fluxus, found beauty is linked to truth...

> *When you talk about integrity, what many short-term managers look upon as a beautiful strategy is very bounded, and is not an act of integrity because it functions without justice toward all the colleagues of the company, as well as all the legitimate stakeholders of the company, the company of itself, or the company imbedded in society. It's really 'am I going to make my nuts for this quarter', and often this strategy makes the appearance of making my nut for this quarter to either get me my bonus, or push the stock up, or to get me my new set of shares, or to get me my next job so that I will be somewhere else when the next two years come down the line – I know then what will really happen from this beautiful strategy.'*

Ian King, professor of management and an art-business pioneer, speaks about artist working without constraints that block seeing the truth:

> 'The artist has realised that there's a wall there, but rather than being concerned about this wall, they're playing with the wall and they're going around the wall and they're saying the wall is still there... we're not going to say that it's not there. But managers are unwilling to take that risk because managers are concerned with cultures that are essentially about blame, about power, about control. That's what's great about artists – they say look, we know these things exist, but we're prepared to stretch them, we want to see how much we can test them.'

RESOURCE

Insider artists get under the skin of businesses. Insider art is about aesthetic consulting that demands honest client relations. Once good healthy, wealthy companies paid second-rate artists for embellishing and decorating. Now first class artists are asked to address economic problems when companies and organisations in trouble ask for their assistance. London Banker Dominic Palfreyman recalls how corporations begin taking art seriously:

> '...my experience of art in banking was... it was always kind of an icing on the cake. We work very hard, we make lots of money, we can afford to do a little bit of corporate art sponsorship, or have an art collection. It's very much because we're successful we can do these things, and because they're not that important. Whereas for Unilever, if their share price and business is doing badly and they need to change.....they have artist

residencies, they send people out, they give people leaves of absence to go and do creative or cultural work. They interact with art and artists in a whole range of different ways.'

In 2001 Henrik Schrat talked about his view of a gap between business jargon and art speak. At Product Vision 2005, Ariane Berthoin Antal of Wissenschaftszentrum Berlin asked Schrat if he has been able to narrow that art-business gap over the years. Schrat replied:

> 'They realise that you can speak a bit more relaxed and that you can use lots of personal terms and don't have to be polite and official. But, of course… now… the tone you have found on a personal level doesn't work anymore.'

The one's introducing artists to the art world are the critics. In the business world consultants play similar roles, but rather more complex, as Philippe Mairesse explains:

> 'At the start, the consultant was behaving much more like a sponsor, not a producer, not like a guy who's producing a new piece, financing the production, the research, the development.. But then in this process we were working together. They were not only paying (and we designing), rather we were conceiving the project together. It was much like the movie producer, you know the movie producer pays of course (the financing), but he can be also very close to the author, and can rewrite, or have the script rewritten a few times. He can ask for another actor, he can really affect the creation…

Like an art critic, Bernhard Krusche, a management consultant, judges the role of the artist to the audience, rediscovering the human face of a firm.

> …as for any company or organisation in the world it is very important to be not only a place for people to make profit and profit and profit, but a business is a place where they spend their lives…

CO-CREATION

Typecast as either emotional creators or irrational uncreative managers, both artists and managers actually protest. In reaction to this split picture, the rational versus the irrational, artist Teike Asselbergs exclaims loudly:

> 'What you're saying is like insane, you know, it's like, what is this person talking about?'

And the CEO Feldman also protests:

> 'I do really not agree that people working at a company are paid to be uncreative bureaucrats; I think that's totally nonsense. Sorry.'

Art and business makes artists feel more than being just managers, and at the same time managers are encouraged to leave their typecast roles as rational bean counters, or the like. Art in business perhaps is nothing more just getting better pay for some thrilling experience or experience economy management consultancy. Joseph Pine Jr., who sells his advice on how to set up an 'experience business', sees the limitations of his own instrumentality:

> '… because the second time you have an experience it is not going to be as good as the first. The third time is not going to be as good as that, and pretty soon you have your customers mouthing those immortal words 'been there, done that'. That's the words of a commoditised experience: 'been there, done that.' And so because experiences are going

to be commoditised as well, there's actually a fifth and final economic offering in this progression, when you customise the experience. Think about designing an experience that is so appropriate for a particular person, that is exactly the right experience that they need right now; that no other experience will do. Then you can't help but turn it into what we often call a life-transforming experience.'

Does Pine preach that ideology or religion comes after the consumption of thrilling experiences? Maybe not. Perhaps what he really hovers around is less than religion, although US consultants often act as evangelists of capitalism. Maybe art is what it's really about! If this is so, then it would be better to listen to artists than consultants. Or perhaps we need to consider that artists are the true consultants?

OPENING

In February 2005, one of the classical masters of business art moved his project to the huge Central Park in New York. Christo Javateff has a long history of presenting his art work in terms of free aesthetic enterprise. Christo said in connection with another of his installations in Berlin more than ten years earlier:

> 'I like to make a work of art. A work of art deals with beauty, proportion, color, volumes. The second point: I pay for that. There will be no tax money, the community will benefit. The money will be extended to the community. The third: we will recycle all the materials, there will be no waste, I like to translate the experience of art to the people.'

Let our experiences of Central Park or Le Jardin in Gattières inspire a change in the consulting model. When we talked to Hans-Ulrich Obrist about art and business he immediately referred to an important master of business art person, Kurt Schwitters, who had the same idea and who baptised his art-business movement Merz by extracting the 'com' from 'commerce.' The artist/ insider in business, perhaps acting as a consultant, will no longer not boast about his ability to solve problems or provide turn-key methods for profit and success. As Mairesse pointed out, this would only restore the false idea of perfection that actually not only blocks learning about the truth but also hinders human beauty to blossom. Forget about the knowledge-industry or as Barbara Steveni puts it:

> 'I call art and business a period of not knowing. Capitalists are prepared to pay for not knowing, and that's what artists hope, to all the time try and work with not knowing, and try and get capitalist structures to pay for not knowing.'

Daved Barry professor of organisation and inspirer of the 'Product Vision show' hints at another important aspect of artists as consultants. They will make us see new things and not focus on making managers feel good and powerful:

> 'What this is, is an exercise in discomfort, and in some way what artists do when they are entering into the business realm, into this domain, this strange art/business divide of being, is extending your area of discomfort. I mean, you've gone way beyond, you've said several times you were afraid, you were worried ...

Lindsay Crouse, the famous actress, expands on that theme pointing out at the importance of not blocking learning by clinging to correctness:

> 'It seems to me that in the success/failure model that this refers to… is that it is a result of thinking in terms of measurement. This is where artists begin to train themselves in terms of possibility. To absolutely leave the world of measurement to the greatest extent possible – for this will only result in the world of comparisons and standards, which can only result in success/failure, being included or not included or win/lose. Those are the only outcomes possible from the conversation, "What's in it for me?", and "Will there be enough?" The conversation of possibility is continually exchanging self for others, which is what they mentioned first, which is that your mistakes are moments of learning and adding information as well as what you played yesterday that worked. It's all the same! There is no such thing as "oh my god, the mess is not to be included and everybody's watching." I think that is a very, very important distinction to make here. The greatest actors, the greatest artists, the greatest human beings…*

And finally listen to Philippe Mairesse putting in a nutshell what the meeting of art and business might contribute to opening up for human creativity in both organisations and on markets:

> 'You feel that you could bring more than you bring, but they don't want you to bring what you could, and this is very interesting. This is exactly what I mean. You have to install a situation where people feel free to bring what they decide to think.'

EPILOGUE

Ok friends, this was all from conversations and excursions to the land of art and business five years ago. It is a European vision of course; it rests probably on the old world's views of art as philosophically part of the constitution of human capitalist societies. The new world is perhaps more nature (Wild West-style-management I guess.) than art and culture oriented? What then has happened in the last five years? Well, we have moved onward a little into the mainstream with our art and artist ideas. Aesthetics is now starting to be taken very seriously by management. When I went to the American Academy of Management meeting in 2010, I heard the president of that venerable association for management education state that 'beauty' was of utmost importance to business education. I then read that the Carnegie Foundation (the same one that thirty years ago urged us to become more 'scientific' in management) is about to issue a report advising business educators to turn to humanities and liberal arts. We are on to something guys so let's continue on our journey. Let's educate, find and support our future Masters of Business Art….

In this chapter, one of the key figures in the field of organisational aesthetics ponders the shape of the future, and does so by considering the past. He refers to his own reflection and process of thinking about this chapter, and the writing of it. He situates himself in a nexus of events, ideas, people, theories and publications as he moves through a series of questions on organisations and how they are being 'reconfigured'. The chapter thus begins reflexively: for looking at the changing nature of organisation requires an ever present assessment of how our very processes of 'looking' is conducted. What concepts, what language, what assumptions are we using? Changing organisational contexts will always make our research problematic. Our research can always be contested. We always require an attentiveness to the regimes of knowledge our thought processes inhabit and the hierarchies of value to which they appeal.

The relevance of Organisational Aesthetics must be understood as extending from academia into industry and consultancy, then again outwards to the fields of design and art. This chapter bears testimony to the author's intellectual journey, and his own creative practice in painting and photography. Artistic practice provides the opportunity to reflect on the aesthetic dimension of organisational life and the conceptual limits of organisational thinking: the processes and dynamics of organisation sometimes can only be *shown*, or revealed visually. The chapter also exemplifies how a research interest in organisation provokes entry into a broader exploration of culture, literature, film and philosophy.

Becoming or Process: What Future for Aesthetic Discourse in Organisations?

Antonio Strati

Aesthetic organisational research has fascinated me ever since I wrote the book *Organisation and Aesthetics* (1999). In my article 'Sensations, Impressions and Reflections on the Configuring of the Aesthetic Discourse in Organisations' (which appeared in the very first issue of the journal *Aesthesis* in 2007), I constructed a theoretical background with reference to the contemporary Italian philosopher Emanuele Severino (2006). When reflecting on the big philosophical themes of immortality, finitude and destiny, Severino wondered whether the world, and reality itself, should be understood not in terms of a fixed or stable quantity, but in terms of *becoming*, or as *process*. Becoming and process are, in fact, two very different views on how all the social phenomena we experience assume their form, and these terms struck me as a fruitful way of discussing how art, aesthetics and everyday life were playing an increasing role in changing the configuration of organisations. I still find this line of inquiry stimulating, and I consequently return to it in this chapter. To make it less grandiose and more quotidian, I now start by asking whether this very act of pursuing the same topic should be viewed in terms of a process, or as becoming.

The aesthetics of the artifact and the becoming of its theoretical status

Returning to the themes discussed in 'Sensations…' has given me a subtle and profound pleasure. Firstly, because I have reworked an article already in print and which, therefore, has done (or is doing) its 'work' as a contribution, however modest, to the debate on the current state of organisational aesthetics research. Secondly, and no less importantly, my pleasure has derived from my sense of freedom in sifting, eliminating, smoothing, expanding, rewriting, retouching, or maintaining intact the its words and images. Hence, while reworking 'Sensations…', this article has now become two artifacts instead of just one.

From the literal point of view, the two artifacts are absolutely identical. From an ontological point of view, they are very different. One has the theoretical status of a complete artifact (it has appeared in print), whereas the other (the to-be-reworked version) has the status of an incomplete artifact. Indeed, the latter has changed from being an accomplished and carefully revised text to the raw material for a further one. It therefore had to be scratched, decomposed, or even broken in some of its parts, as one would do with a sculpture when wanting to reconstruct the progressive layers of execution lying beneath its finished beauty.

I have thus worked with pleasure on disarticulating, de-structuring and fragmenting the text, in search of the hidden plots and dissonances, which in part I already knew and in part were surprising. What has become of it? Has it involved a 'process' or a 'becoming'? I shall explain below what precisely is meant by this question later. For the moment we need to consider two other aspects of organisational research: its methods and its objects.

Originality can be a distinctive feature of work practices in general, and of artistic and intellectual ones in particular. It is tied to creativity which, however paradoxical it may be to explain, has acquired mythical, if not salvific, status in contemporary organisational life. *Repetitiveness*, by contrast, often has negative connotations: an

Figure 1: *Antonio Strati*, Untitled, *1979. Polaroid SX-70 – Artificial light/flash.*

author becomes repetitive when s/he has nothing new to say and therefore does not create, invent, innovate, revolutionise, or surprise. In other words, s/he tells 'the same old story'. A commonplace belief concerning the relationship between a work of art and its author is that once a painter, for example, has made his or her artistic 'mark', they then 'paint the same picture', so to speak, for evermore. And a musician can be said always to compose the same music. And an author always writes more or less the same novel again and again. After all, one may ask, what is it that enables us to recognise that the architecture of the Guggenheim Museum of Bilbao in Spain, and that of the

Weatherhead School of Management in Cleveland, Ohio, is the work of the Canadian-American architect Frank O. Gehry, if not the fact that when comparing them we find evident similarities and recurrences? Does not the style that distinguishes an author therefore spring from an ability to repeat himself or herself?

If we move from art to science and take mathematics, for example, can we also say that a mathematician has made his or her 'mark' in the same way? That a mathematician is such that, by and large, they always create and re-create the same theorem? I am not sure that art and science are similar in this respect. I have not found it to be so in my research on the organisational culture of mathematicians (Strati, 2008). What my research instead showed was that the beauty of the mathematician's work consists in articulating a problem to study and solve, that is, a problem which cannot be solved with one's own proof, but which is 'felt' to have profound significance for mathematical research. This 'feeling' of an important problem discovered is shared by other researchers. In the community of pure mathematicians, this posing of a problem for others is regarded as an act of intellectual generosity of which only good researchers are capable.

We are therefore in a dimension of 'doing' very different from that of establishing one's own style. One would not even know how to do what one 'feels' would be beautiful, or be the most significant thing to do. This is a dimension of experience that is present also in the 're-doing' of what has been done, when one imagines making changes to a previously-written text, changes whose essential characteristics are still unexplored.

Both of these very different dimensions of research, the one drawn from art in terms of giving expression to a style, and the one drawn from mathematics in terms of inventing a problem for one's community, both evoke meaningful aspects of what I am calling the self-configuring of aesthetic discourse in organisations.

Organisational aesthetics research and the dominion of becoming

Why is *becoming* (in our case, the emergence and self-configuring of organisational aesthetics) of such great concern? I must make it clear immediately that I am not using the term 'becoming' as synonymous with progress, evolution or improvement, as I shall also specify later. I mean exactly 'becoming'; and when I address the theme of 'self-configuring' I am afraid that I am unavoidably projecting the 'aesthetic discourse on organisations' onto 'becoming'. Among the many analyses of the matter, particularly insightful are those by the philosopher Severino, who conducts his reflections in a manner both close to and different from the philosophical doctrines which I find most congenial, namely phenomenology and existentialism, and the hermeneutic tradition which distinguishes Continental philosophy from analytic philosophy.

Severino writes that the whole of Western civilization is conditioned by *'the way in which the Ancient Greeks established the meaning of becoming'*, or the *'grappling of things between being and nothingness'*, their *'being contested by being and nothingness'* and therefore *'their not being definitively bound to either of them'* (Severino, 2006: 9-10). Therefore, like an image on a background in photography or films, as well

Figure 2: *Antonio Strati, Finitude, 2010. Acrylic on canvas (60x120cm).*

as in metaphor, I would project the self-configuring of the aesthetic discourse on organisations onto this grappling between being and nothingness, without having it settle on either the former or the latter. I could not anyway project it onto *being*, i.e. locate it among eternal things, because in the philosophy of the Ancient Greeks, as interpreted by Severino, this would entail approaching the distinctive and privileged property of being divine.

But here a first question arises. Are we certain that there is nothing in the study of organisational aesthetics that we cannot place among 'eternal things'? I am not so sure, because there is something that I would consider 'eternal', while mindful of performing an arbitrary operation of

Figure3: *Antonio Strati,* Inner Worlds, *1980. Polaroid SX-70 – Artificial light/tungsten.*

aesthetic-symbolic sacralisation, though this gives me a genuine feeling of pleasure. I consider the following to be 'eternal things'. The Standing Conference on Organisational Symbolism (SCOS) in Antibes in 1985 and the discourse that followed. This discourse involved a profound re-definition of the organisation, the actor or individual, and the artifactual-symbolic landscape of organisational life. Following this is the enormous range of publications, projects and scholars that emerged in the 1990s to the present, including Aacorn (Arts, Aesthetics, Creativity & Organisation Research Network). Then there are the 'other voices', other thinkers and writers, with a diversity of tonality, that are contemporaneous with the study of organisational aesthetics. These were heard especially in the course of the cultural (or linguistic) turn of the 1980s. But there also other voices which are much more distant in time.

I note particularly the attention they demanded to the *corporeality of human action* in organisations. They came from gender studies, Foucault's sociology, post-structuralist philosophy, earlier French phenomenology or even past figures like Georg Simmel's and his sociology of the senses.

The term 'sense' can signify many levels of experience and meaning. It brings us to a central theoretical bifurcation. This bifurcation is the relationship between sensory perception and social action via the senses on the one hand, and representation and understanding through language on the other.

I want to illustrate this bifurcation and the theoretical tensions it generates with reference to one of the six mediaeval tapestries, each depicting the senses, displayed in the oval room of 'La Dame à la Licorne' at the Musée National du Moyen Age, Thermes de Cluny, Paris.

À mon seul désir

The six tapestries are all large format. Designed to function as wall hangings, the tapestries are made of wool and silk and are believed to have been woven between 1484 and 1500 (Erlande-Branderburg 1989). In each of them, the setting is an oval island, blue in colour and covered with flowers. At the centre of each island is the principal focus of La Dame. Beside her stands a damsel, (though she is absent from two of the tapestries). There are then the two principal animals, the unicorn and the lion, and others of smaller size, rabbits, apes, cheetahs, dogs and puppies, various birds and a parrot. They stand amid the island's vegetation, which is luxuriant not only with flowers but also trees like pines and oaks, or orange trees loaded with leaves and fruit. Finally, each tapestry has a specific object at its centre: it is the basket of flowers in the tapestry on the sense of smell; it is the cup with small sweetmeats in the tapestry on taste; it is the organ in the one on hearing, and a mirror in the one on sight, and lastly, a jewel casket in the one entitled A MON SEUL DESIR ('To My Only Desire'). Only the tapestry depicting *touch* lacks a specific object.

The balance between open and closed form, and the detachment of one object from another, are, as Michel Serres observes, achieved by colour and by the warp and weft of the tapestry, almost as if they constitute its skin (Serres, 2003: 61-7). There are no men in these tapestries, and no sky. The external senses (sight, touch, smell, hearing and taste) abandon themselves to

Figure 4: A Mon Seul Désir *(detail)*. *Wool and silk tapestry, 378x466cm, woven between 1484 and 1500. Sala* La dame à la Licorne, *Musée Cluny, Paris. Source: Strati, 2010: 110.*

the leaves and the branches, to the rabbits, the young hornless unicorn, open and absorbed in their sensations, that is until (as Serres notes) the 'inner sense finally speaks and, for the first time, the tent is imprinted with fiery tongues and crowned with script' (2003: 65). This is the sixth tapestry, the one depicting *the advent of language*. In this tapestry scene, an inscription on the upper part of the canopy reads A MON SEUL DESIR in large letters. The canopy tent is open, and the lady stands at the threshold. She emerges and drops her jewels in a small casket held for her by a damsel.

These are the only words that appear in the La dame à la licorne tapestry series, and they are significant, for they announce an abandonment of 'the world', fleeing its jewels. The three words of the inscription, as Serres observes (ibid., p. 67), express the 'first cogito', or principle thought on life itself. Here is a situation where a desire for the world departs, leaving only the inscription (and its meaning). The desire 'identifies itself with [the] script'. As a cogito, we see figured the statement 'I exist only in language'.

If we can extrapolate and relate this to our own subject of concern, is it not the *life* in organisations that becomes the 'world' that departs, when the desire for it exists only in the *cogito*, in language. For the primacy of language is the presupposition of almost every contemporary philosophical perspective informing the research of organisations. On this matter Roberto Esposito comments:

> 'From whatever angle you look at the philosophical quadrant of our time – from logic to phenomenology, from pragmatics to structuralism – language is the epicentre of all trajectories of thought, if not indeed 'the home of being', in a perspective that extends beyond Heideggerian ontology to encompass the domains of action (in Apel and Habermas, but also in Austin and Searle), of subjectivity (in Gadamer and Ricoeur), and of the unconscious (in Lacan).' (Esposito 2010: 8)

Language is the place where we live, in which we walk, in which we connect with the world and with others. The assumption of the linguistic nature of all experience and meaning, a primacy in some way transcendental, is at odds with large parts of Italian philosophy. This is especially true of the tradition that began with Machiavelli, Giordano Bruno and Giambattista Vico, which developed a very different approach to the questions of meaning and language. For it is contextualising the latter within the broader interweaving among history, politics and corporeality that characterises human life. Esposito writes of an *'even more specific element, which became an invariable feature of nineteenth-century Italian thought, (was) the corporeal, and therefore vital, characterization that Vico gave to the conceptually unrepresentable dimension'* (2010: 28) of immersion in the senses. In other words, the fact that 'life itself, in all its manifestations, material and ideal, sensory and cognitive, emotional and rational, originates from that corporeal magma from which it can never completely detach itself' (2010: 77).

I shall go no further with these digressions on the Italian difference in European philosophical thought, as it sheds particular and sufficient light on my conception of the 'aesthetic discourse': it can never be entirely detached from the everyday life in organisations, whether individual, social or imagined sensory experience.

Becoming or process: the self-configuring of organisational aesthetics discourse?

Central to the aesthetic discourse on organisations is the question concerning *what is real*, and the cognitive content of the aesthetic. This question arose, as we know, with the Enlightenment, with the reform of academic knowledge, with the opposition to the French rationalism (of Descartes) by the Neapolitan philosopher Giambattista Vico, with Joseph Addison's articles in England's *The Spectator* and, above all, with the work of the German philosopher Alexander Gottlieb Baumgarten who, amongst other things, coined the term 'aesthetics'. What happened, however, Sergio Givone asks (2010: 7-8),

> '[w]hen we turn our gaze to the past and, adopting a perspective that has developed over recent centuries, seek to reconstruct ancient aesthetics, mediaeval aesthetics, renaissance aesthetics, baroque aesthetics (presuming it can be called such), and so on? A certain risk of distortion, if not indeed of historical falsification, seems to prevail over any objectivity.'

In looking at the self-configuration of the aesthetic discourse on organisations, I locate

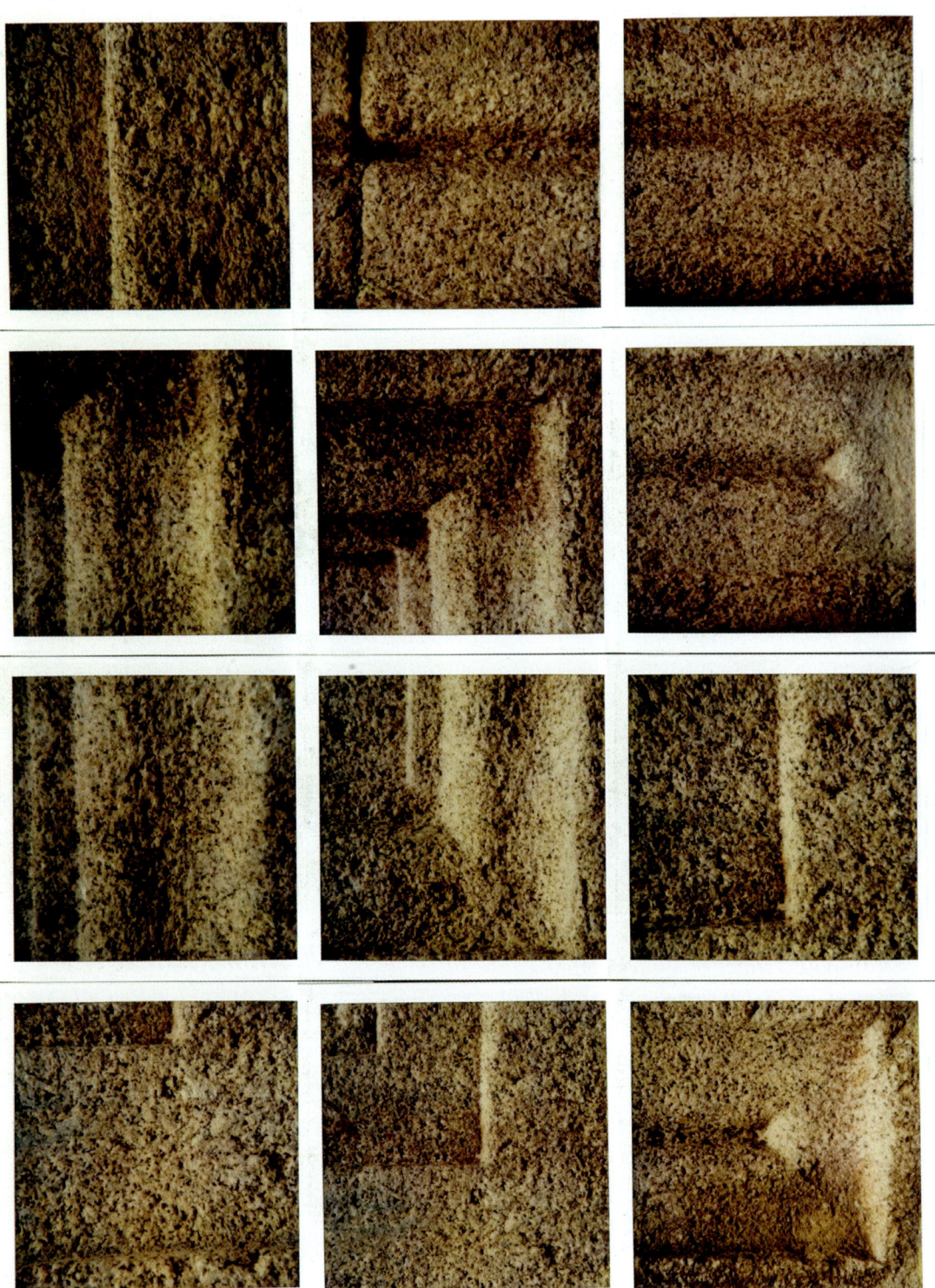

my writings epistemologically in so-called 'weak thought' (Vattimo, 1983). 'Weak' thought denies the reality of absolute or transparent truth, but holds that knowledge is at once created and is pervaded by doubt. I feel at ease when a truth gives rise to other truths (but without losing its own). The 'ultimate truth' is, of course, a paramount theme in Western philosophy, writing and culture, and not only when it is disputed by proponents of 'weak thought', such as postmodernism, constructionism, symbolism, and other currents that formed the so-called cultural turn in social science in the decade of the 1980s. Severino puts it very well, (though not himself belonging to 'weak thought') when he writes:

> *'Undoubtedly, contemporary philosophy destroys every 'definitive and absolute' truth, every 'foundation', every incontrovertible 'principle', every necessary proposition. But it does not perform this destruction arbitrarily; rather […] it does so because, like the whole of Western culture, it posits becoming as absolute 'evidence' and original 'truth'. The scepticism of contemporary philosophy is the inevitable consequence of faith in becoming in the Greek sense.'* (Severino, 2006: 15-16)

With irony, therefore, the *becoming* of 'Sensations …' is now itself absolute. It has not revealed itself as 'being', able to impose itself on the various interpretations of 'sense' to which 'Sensations …' is subject. Rather, it has emerged as a 'becoming'. And paradoxically its becoming has been the reason for the destruction of the ultimate, definitive truth of one of its two identities: it is no longer the same as before, even though it has always been the same as before. Its definitive truth is therefore becoming.

We have thus come to the crux of the self-configuring of the aesthetic discourse on organisations. Becoming is a feature shared by both 'strong thought' and 'weak thought'. As Severino points out, it is *'the dominant dogma, the fundamental faith of our civilization: the faith that the variation of the world is a process'* (2006: 19). In the contest of this 'faith', everything is thrown into question, *'but it remains the undisputed horizon of every discussion'*. This horizon, however, is disputed by Severino's own 'future philosophy', which, along with the issue of becoming *qua* faith, I shall not pursue

I shall pursue, rather, what I see as the crux of the self-configuring of the aesthetic discourse on organisations. I use the term 'self-configuring' to evoke the image of the process and the becoming of that discourse. We will remain distant from the great narratives of academic disciplinary progress, with their improved knowledge-gathering methods and incremental knowledge. I do not see in this 'self-configuring' a transformative force able to revolutionise the theory of organisations from foundations, uprooting it entirely from cognitivism and the logical-analytical process. Not only is such not feasible, it would deny the theoretical and methodological value of knowledge-forms based on reason and intellect, which remain a source of organisational knowledge. I do not discern nor anticipate a paradigm shift able to subsume the dominant theoretical bases of organisational studies under the aegis of aesthetics.

Figure 5: *Antonio Strati*, Flavour of the Truth, *1985/87. Tableau Polaroid SX-70 – Natural light.*

What I like about aesthetic knowledge of organisations is its *dialogic* nature, as I have explained elsewhere (Strati, 1999). But I do realise that by asserting the dialogic nature of aesthetic knowledge I am also affirming the value of the flow of experience and of diversity, the succession of negotiations and interactions. In short, I affirm the variation of approaches in the world of organisational knowledge, as variation is itself process. The question I raise is whether it is possible to disjoin the *process* from the becoming, so that the self-configuring of the aesthetic discourse on organisations maintains its nature as dialogic knowledge, fuelling and valorising the process, without being necessarily dominated by the becoming.

My propensity to disjoin becoming from process and have the latter comprise the self-configuring of the aesthetic discourse on organisations is prompted by my artistic and sociological experience, as well as by my philosophical interests. These factors have led me to appreciate the 'principle of fundamental indeterminacy', which seems to fit well with process, but less so with becoming. This principle was formulated by Howard Becker when discussing art work and seeking an answer to the question 'What does it mean to speak of the work of art itself?' (2006: 21 and 23) Becker replied that it is impossible for a sociologist or a social scientist to analyse and discuss the 'work itself' because the work 'itself' simply does not exist. What one can study and discuss is the variety of occasions on which

Figure 6: *Antonio Strati,* Unfinished Beauty, *1982. Tableau Polaroid SX-70 – Natural light.*

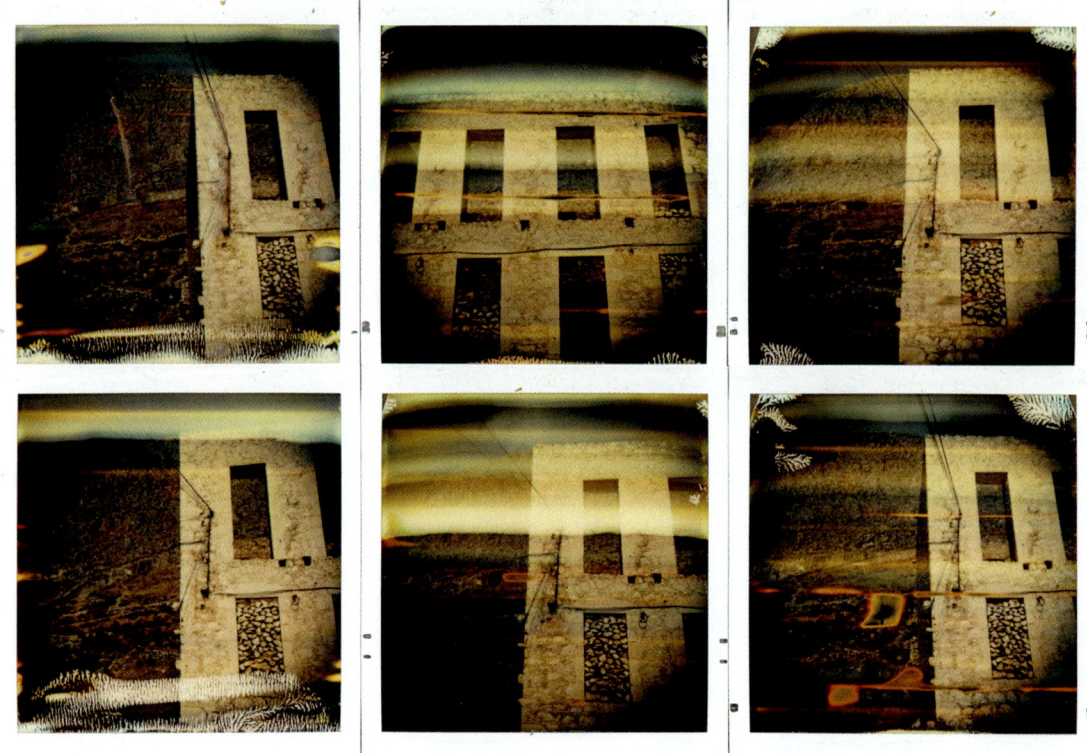

the work of art appears, is exhibited, is performed, is watched, is read, and is noted. Each of these many occasions is or may be different from the others. A work of art, Becker argues, is fundamentally indeterminate: you never know when it is finished, when it exists and when it does not, or what its form or nature are. Nor can one ever know what is being talked about without resorting to:

> '….some convention as to what – which of the many forms it takes from moment to moment – counts as the 'real', 'basic' work and which kinds of variation don't matter, don't interfere with the 'fundamental' or 'essential' character of the 'work itself.' This is the kind of shared understanding social scientists recognize under a variety of names: culture, norm, shared understanding, etc.' (Becker, 2006: 23)

Now, however, I shall leave this dense train of thought to address a lighter issue – that of the awareness among organisation scholars of the aesthetic dimension.

Intermezzo: aesthetic awareness

Our assumption that, since the cultural turn in organisation studies, and with more than twenty years of research and studies on organisational aesthetics, there is a greater 'awareness' among scholars, students, consultants and managers of the knowledge forms and actions of people in organisations, may seem ironic or decidedly presumptuous. The range of influence of studies on art and aesthetics in organisations is actually restricted to organisational theories, which 'fortunately' have always been characterised by a paradigmatic pluralism (and fragmentation) than by the dominance of one paradigm over others.

However, if this paradigmatic pluralism (and fragmentation) contrasts with the intellectual obscurantism so often characteristic of one-paradigm dominance, it entails a certain condition of 'non-communicability' among the plurality or diversity of theoretical frameworks. This obstructs dialogic knowledge in organisation theories and management studies.

I shall illustrate this point: the real is true and untrue at the same time. I shall use as my coordinates the four sociological paradigms of organisation proposed by Gibson Burrell and Gareth Morgan (1979). These are the paradigm of radical humanism, the paradigm of radical structuralism, the interpretative paradigm, and the functionalist paradigm. I acknowledge that these were formulated to make sense of the theoretical complexity of organisation studies from the end of the 1970s, and prior to the cultural turn from which arose organisational aesthetics. So what will I stress? That the aesthetic discourse on organisations actually pertains mainly to two of these paradigms: interpretative sociology and radical humanism. The self-configuring of the aesthetic discourse on organisations belongs to the interpretative paradigm by virtue of its principle that *an organisation is an artifact which can only be explained in terms of symbolic interactions among its members*. It belongs to the paradigm of radical humanism because of its *critical analysis of the factors impeding the full realisation of people in organisational routine*, and in particular their aesthetic-sensory sensibilities, their subjective differences arising from interactions, and their creativity. Moreover, the aesthetic understanding of organisations shares with radical humanism the *priority accorded to the human sciences rather than to the physical ones*, intuition rather than analytical logic, the evocative knowledge-gaining process rather than ones based on causal explanations.

But the reason that the aesthetic discourse on organisations is not confined to a single paradigm is even more general. It consists in the fact that aesthetics exists, but is noticed and unnoticed at the same time, as I shall show with the tale which follows.

The practice of going out for lunch or dinner is frequent among us organisation scholars. Where? With whom? What should we eat? These are everyday questions which we address with careful negotiation! 'No, I don't want to eat anything too rich', I think, 'my digestion would give me hell'; 'no, the food's bad at that restaurant', I remember; 'I want to eat Calabrian food this evening and I know a place where they do it well', I say, and the thought of grilled vegetables steeped in fragrant olive oil makes my mouth water. An aesthetic sensation, therefore, produced by imaginatively foretasting the goodness of the dish; a goodness which is only *evoked*, however. An aesthetic sensation perceived as already experienced, at home perhaps, but now stimulated by the image of a small organisation – the Calabrian restaurant – operating in the catering industry. This aesthetic sensation is therefore stimulated by an organisation's production of aesthetics.

Is this a process experienced by everyone? Certainly not. How, therefore, can we share this aesthetic experience with others? By listing the nutritional properties of the dish of cooked vegetables? But saying that it has so many calories, contains such-and-such fats, such-and-such mineral salts would deprive the dish of its poetry, however irreproachable such discourse might be from a scientific point of view, and however attractive from the logical-analytical one. It is perhaps difficult to grasp the extent of this attraction if we remain with the dish of cooked vegetables. It may become clearer if we consider another organisational artifact of an alimentary nature, situated in another organisational setting.

Imagine that we are in a supermarket and we want to buy a bottle of mineral water. We inspect the label for the water's provenance and for the supervisory body that has tested its quality, and we gauge its organoleptic properties from the percentages of salts and minerals. If we want softer water with less magnesium or more potassium, we look for the label on the bottle of a different brand. What we are trying to understand is whether the water with the characteristics described on the label will do us good, will be suited to our body, will help us digest, and whether or not we will like it. This is in some sense a rigorously intellectual operation, but not devoid of *pathos* because we feel drawn to the terminology on the labels (not so much at the level of cognitive meaning as that immediate and often unconsidered sensitive-aesthetic knowledge and the affectivity connected with it). Our choice of the mineral water that 'we like most' is based on the interaction among several modes of knowledge acquisition by our bodies (cognitive-ratiocinative and sensory-aesthetic) and by the attraction that they both exert on us even before we have actually tasted the mineral water chosen after reading the labels.

What I wish to stress is not that logical-analytical and aesthetic comprehension

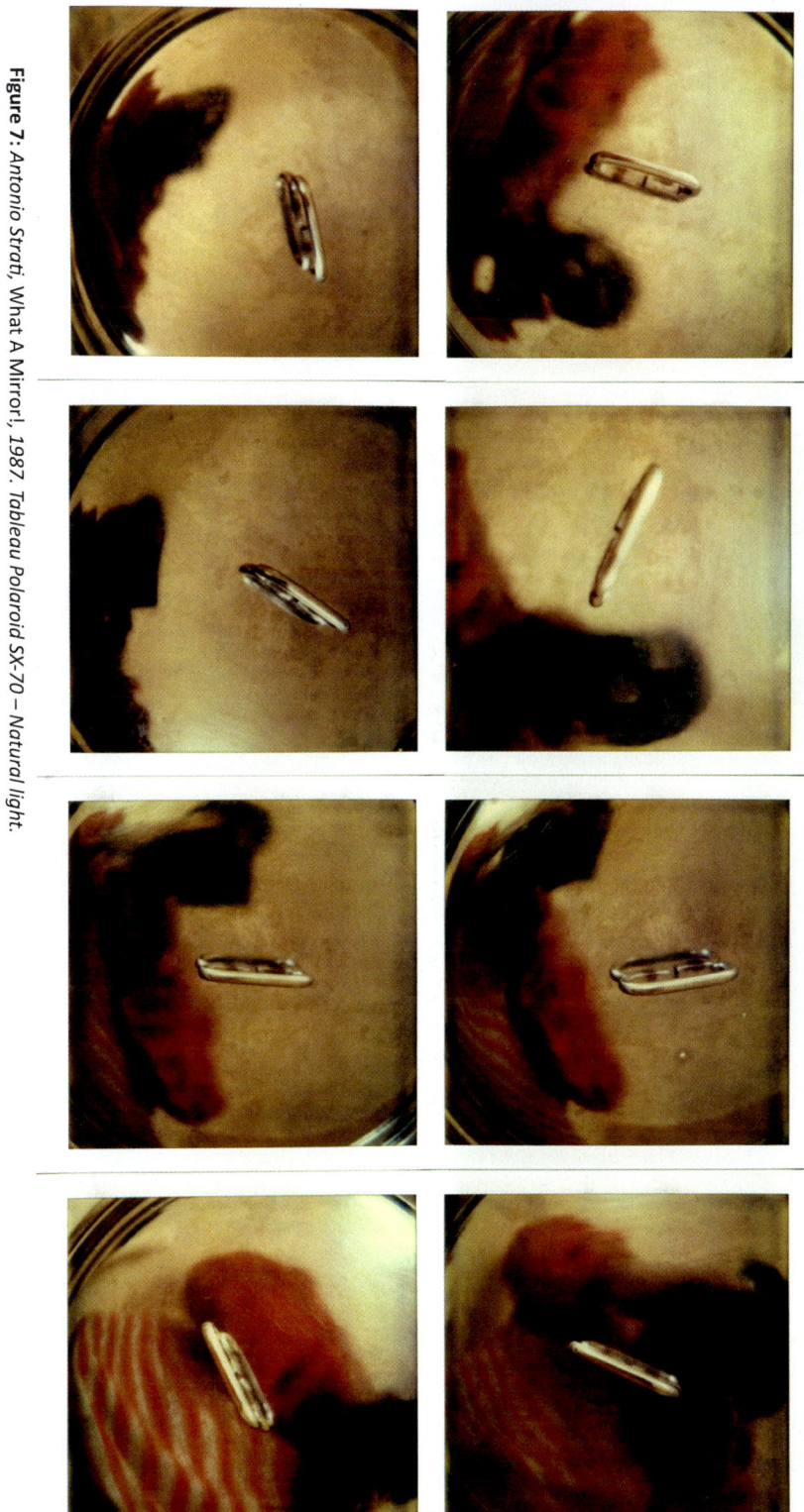

Figure 7: *Antonio Strati, What A Mirror!, 1987. Tableau Polaroid SX-70 – Natural light.*

alternate with each other, but that they overlap, and merge. Of this we are well aware in the aesthetic discourse on organisations, although the polemic against dominance of the mental in organisational theories has often obfuscated this awareness. One cannot exist without the other, although it sometimes happens that one is more appropriate than the other… just as we do not perceive with only one sense at a time. We choose the mineral water by assessing its limpidity with our eyes, listening to the sound that it makes when we pour it into a glass, ascertaining its flavour and texture as we sip it, and smelling its sulphurous or calcareous odour. It is by activating our entire stock of knowledge about this organisational artifact that we determine its impact on our body and protect ourselves against the damage that may be caused by an unsuitable or even harmful product. This is the essential difference – writes Giovanni Matteucci (2010: 120) when discussing Helmuth Plessner's anti-Cartesianism and studies on perception (1975) originally published in 1928 – between the analysis and the experience of the qualitative with respect to the quantitative:

> *'This is an irreducibility due to the total incongruity that exists between calculable elements and phenomenal quantities, as shown by the absolute heterogeneity between the measurement of frequencies and a concrete acoustic or chromatic event. But it is also an irreducibility that is* experienceable, *because it is endowed with a peculiar sensateness and objectivity. The qualitative structuring of the world, that is to say, is no longer imputed to the arbitrariness of mere subjective interiority […] rather, the qualification of the world is made objective and binding by sensoriality.'*

What I wish to stress, in fact, is the aesthetic attractiveness of something that is wrongly evaluated as exclusively cognitive, logical and intellectual. This is an aspect that has distinguished my research on the aesthetic discourse on organisations since its beginnings, when I pointed out that a mathematical theorem may have the beauty of a symphony for the mathematicians working in a particular university department. This is an outright aesthetic pleasure felt by certain actors (the mathematicians) and which was also evidenced by the rigorous philosophical rationale of 'becoming' and 'process' outlined in the previous section. Besides their cognitive meanings, both these concepts possess an imaginative-emotional *pathos* that attracts us to one more than the other. For that matter, it is this that art shows us, in particular Dadaism when Duchamp suggested leafing through the dictionary for abstract words to restore with the energy of pronunciation.

> *'… (along the way to surrealist automatic writing), Dadaism conducted minute examination of linguistic procedures. Thus, whilst on the one hand there came about a decisive rejection of 'literariness' in favour of 'literality' (through automatic and aleatory practices), on the other 'literariness' was taken to exaggerated extremes (through attempts to provoke a chain of logical short circuits in normal utterances).'* (Magrelli, 2006: 125)

Thus produced was a plethora of puns, proverbs, glossaries, idioms, anagrams and charades, rather than verses regulated by the conventions of the poetic tradition, but which were still aesthetically attractive for some, though obviously not for all. As I have repeatedly pointed out, the aesthetic repels just as much as it attracts when it arouses intense, profound and apparently irrational feelings. It joins and differentiates us on the basis of *'I like it'*: some immediately concur, others feel uninvolved, yet others cannot understand how *'it can be likeable'*. To return to the dish of vegetables at the Calabrian restaurant, some may *'re-live the pleasure'* of sampling Calabrian cuisine, others may add the *'displeasure'* that follows pleasure because of poor digestion. Some will deploy their sensibilities to acquire knowledge of a previously unknown cuisine by tasting it. Yet others will give way to socio-emotional group pressure and sample the vegetables through suspiciously gritted teeth, that is, without letting themselves savour with all their senses – smell the perfumes, visually enjoy the presentation of the vegetables, delicately touch them with knife and fork, listen to the crunch and relish the scents and flavours. *'I can't do anything about it'*, they will say, because they must listen to themselves as they decide; they must listen to their senses as they produce sensations of either pleasure, disgust or indifference. In other words, at the core of the decision-making process performed in this small organisation is the corporeality of actors, which is anything but static.

Scientific research tells us that out of the fifty thousand billion cells that make up the human body, 500 billion are replaced every day, with a consequently extremely high rate of organ and tissue regeneration. Indicative of corporeal processes of which we are unaware are the following: we grow a new skin on average once a month; we replace our taste buds (easily damaged on contact with food) every two weeks; our red corpuscles have lifetimes of about three months; our entire skeleton is reconstituted every two years. But there are other bodily processes that are more easily seen and therefore noticed, those, for instance, relative to the corporeality that becomes enriched with colour and fullness as we abandon ourselves to the pleasure of food. This was depicted very well by Gabriel Axel's film, *Babette's Feast* (Denmark, 1987), which showed how the cheek colours, physiognomies and facial expressions of the villagers in a village in the West of Jutland, Denmark, changed with their mood as they consumed the feast prepared by the refugee-housekeeper Babette.

If we return to organisation scholars and the fact that, as such, they often eat in bars, cafeterias and restaurants, we would expect them to be well aware of the value of the aesthetic discourse on organisations. But this is not so, owing to the influence of the mentality that transforms into cognition even the enjoyment of a plate of Calabrian cooked vegetables. A mentality which for analytical purposes separates out the complexity of human knowledge forms so that it is unable to grasp that enjoyment in its totality as sensory perception, cognitive process, aesthetic judgment, culture, symbolism, ritual, organisational phenomenon, material and intellectual nourishment. In sum, one cannot place much reliance on the awareness of organisation scholars in configuring the aesthetic discourse on organisations and aesthetics as a form of organisational understanding and action. Only some of them realise the extent to which decisions taken on the basis of aesthetic knowledge are important for the study of organisations, or the extent to which they influence organisational routine. Instead, the majority of organisation scholars have simply dismissed these organisational phenomena as banalities with no influence on organisational life, or as extraneous to organisations.

It is this that one sees in Axel's film. The feast that Babette prepares is sumptuous, exotic and sensuous for villagers whose Puritan protestant morality dictates they must eschew the pleasures of the table. Fortunately, such moral strictures do not apply to organisation scholars, especially those who took active part in the social construction of the culturist turn in organisation studies. The event that Babette organised as a means to thank the villagers for their kindness to her, was exceptional. Cooking the feast required the deployment of complex gastronomic cultures, the sourcing of rare foodstuffs, and an expert knowledge that Babette alone in the village possessed. But in another Scandinavian village (on the Danish island of Möns) and during a 'Wahlalla' SCOS workshop held in preparation for the 1991 SCOS Conference in Copenhagen, Babette's feast was replicated for the participants as a symbolic event which followed viewing of the film (though not entirely, as the turtle soup was missing from the menu, as some of those present still remember!).

There is irony as well as a taste for controversy in my insistence that aesthetics has been discriminated against and censored in organisation studies, a prejudice due to the fact that in its most general and quotidian form aesthetics is seen and not seen, or experienced and enacted but not adequately valued. Mine is a 'serious' irony, and directed at the banal and routine organisational action whereby, on the basis of their aesthetics, organisation scholars group together and disband, foster the spread of dietary customs, and contribute to the economic success of certain working and organisational practices of the catering industry. It is disillusioned irony as well, though nevertheless affable and accentuating my preference for the self-configuring of the aesthetic discourse on organisations as a 'process' rather than a 'becoming'. I now move to some concluding digressions.

Concluding digressions

The topic of this chapter has been the self-configuration of the aesthetic discourse on organisations. I have addressed it in a way that considers whether the configuring should be located in the domain of 'becoming' or whether it is possible, as I prefer, to treat it in terms of 'process'.

Also, the notion of 'understanding', which I find preferable to 'explanation', should be subjected to a pinch of irony, albeit delicately. This I do by recalling a key moment in the 1955 film *Summertime*, directed by David Lean. The plot of the film is flimsy and hackneyed, but at the same time delicate and poetic. A middle-aged American spinster visiting Venice, Jane Hudson, played by a delightful Katharine Hepburn, falls in love with the city – lushly photographed by David Lean without lapsing into banality or the picturesque – and is attracted to an ageing Venetian art dealer played by Rossano Brazzi. The film is poignant and autumnal (the city, in fact, is the real protagonist). The key moment comes when Jane asks, before Renato seduces her, 'why' they should see each again. She wants to 'understand'. Renato gives the standard reply, but with elegance of delivery and formal rigour:

> *'Understand? Why do you want to understand? The most beautiful things in life are those that we don't understand.'*

The things, that is, which we want to do because we *'feel'* them and they *'make'* us think. Like the call for artistry, which increasingly influences the decisions and methods of aesthetics-based research on organisations.

I have a reputation for paying close attention to fieldwork and for using qualitative methods which draw on current developments in the social sciences as well as on artistic forms (such as performance art) and the multiple aesthetics of artistic language. Art performances are perhaps the most interesting from the viewpoint of organisational research methods, probably because of the predominant level of lived experience in their contribution to the production of organisational knowledge, something which also highlights the insurmountable difficulty of recreating the sense and value of such experience through narration and analytical reflection. Yet what else can one do but try and represent lived experience? A performance of the performance can be made. Or, at least this is what Anna Scalfi, an artist and sociologist, endeavoured to do at the 6th International Conference on *Organisational Learning & Knowledge* (OLK) held at the Faculty of Sociology, Trento University, in 2005, on the theme of passion for knowledge in organisational contexts (Viliani, 2011).

Thus conceived was the performance entitled *Don't Cross the Passion Line*, and whose preparation and staging involved

Figure 8: *Antonio Strati,* Handing Down, *1993. Tempera on canvas (80x120cm).*

243

numerous and diverse protagonists. Some of them knew about the entire project, others were aware of only a very small part of it and were ignorant of what would follow. The majority were completely in the dark and found the performance meaningless until they spontaneously began to play their own part in it. At this point, the performance staged one year previously in Paris during the *2nd Art of Management and Organisation Conference* (Scalfi, 2007), and which in many respects resembled the one in Trento, became comprehensible. Which brings us back to the question asked in the first part of the chapter: could I grasp the sense and value of 'Sensations…' only by reworking it, as shown, indeed proved, to be possible by Anna Scalfi's performance? But how did the performance go?

Imagine that you are in the main lecture hall of Trento University and attending the last plenary session of the Conference. The speaker, Anna Scalfi, has started to read the text of her presentation, while the video of the performance in Paris is being projected on a large screen behind her. After a few minutes, a fit of coughing forces Scalfi to leave the hall, and the chair must continue reading the text in pace with the video projection, so as not to bring the session to a halt.

There ensue numerous interruptions. Leaning against the wall, one of the conference attendees switches off the lights in the hall. Then the projection screen rises and descends. Further disturbances follow. As the audience grows increasingly agitated and annoyed, the imperturbable president continues to read the text while the video projection proceeds. Suddenly a mobile phone rings and its owner hurries out of the hall to answer his call. As he opens the door, a kid goat slips into the hall and wanders among the audience, which, if they have not thus far understood what is happening, no longer have any doubts and explode into noisy laughter. The attendees turn to each other and exchange jocular comments. But not so the chairperson of the session. In the now surreal atmosphere of the conference, he does not relinquish his professional role and solemnly continues reading the text, while the video reveals to the audience what they are experiencing by relating it to what happened likewise in Paris.

What follows is a turmoil of events, surprises, laughs, noises, sounds and lights. First, some children enter with human-shaped toy balloons and run up and down the hall. There then enters a bulky 'bouncer', who chases the children away and starts cordoning off the audience with yellow tape printed with the repeated instruction 'Don't Cross the Passion Line', thus confining the attendees to the theme of the conference. Finally, the lights in the hall are again switched off, being replaced by discotheque lights, while music starts with a rhythm that proves irresistible to the participants, who first rhythmically clap their hands and then get up from their chairs to dance. Not so the chairperson of the session, however. Overwhelmed by the music, lights and noise, he climbs onto the table to make himself heard. The performance ends with the dispensing of *spumante* to the attendees by two waiters, while the lights of the room are switched back on, the music fades away, laughter subsides, the goat is petted, and flowers arrive for Anna Scalfi.

This performance had an intrinsic beauty, as was apparent from the laughing faces of those people who, to various extents and in different roles, took part in it. But its beauty also consisted in its involvement of the audience, catching them by surprise, giving them an opportunity to change and become someone else, in short, a chance to become the authors and actors of the performance. It finally had the merit of giving salience to meaning and language and how these are embedded in the corporeality of human experience, as discussed earlier in the chapter. An organisational performance is recounted badly with the words of a text, or even with images. It is grasped better (and learnt better) if an analogous organisational performance is experienced. After all, does not this happen at work; is this not how working and organisational practices are learnt?

Equally well-known, in fact, is my passion for the practices and micro-practices that abound in the everyday lives of organisations. A passion driven by the findings of the sociological study of art and principally by Georg Simmel's analysis of the art of Rembrandt (1916; Eng. trans. 2005: 155):

> 'The achievements of intellectual history are shot through with a contrast that can be characterized as that between the capacity to create [Schöpfertum] *and the capacity to fashion* [Gestaltertum]. *Given a certain extension of these concepts, there is no human work, beyond pure imitation, that is not simultaneously fashioning and creating.*'

A finding, I believe, corroborated by the Dadaist aesthetic of the ready-made. Consider the *Bottle Rack*, which Duchamp decontextualised from the 'language' to which it belonged and turned into a surrealist sculpture, thereby recontextualising it in the language of art. The *Bottle Rack* remains such aesthetically but not ontologically, in the sense that it is a bottle rack but does not do what bottle racks do.

When I draw this distinction between the aesthetic or *pathos* and the ontological or *logos*, I do so in order to emphasise that the *logos* does not yield the ultimate meaning, the true meaning, of *what is* that which is. Philosophical ontology has been marked by a series of controversies in this regard, and it invites us to bear in mind that we should speak of ontologies rather than of ontology: absolute or relative or pluralist ontologies; descriptive and prescriptive ones. The hermeneutic ontology that denies any value to ontology because it is restricted to a world-reflective model of science; and the realist tradition which conceives of an ontology stratified into levels of reality ranging from the material to the mental and spiritual.

> *All this requires us to acknowledge that when we speak of ontology, neither the coordinates of the discipline nor the methodologies that it should use are entirely clear [...] this basic indeterminacy should be borne in mind, for as matters stand it prevents univocal meaning from being attributed to the term 'ontology'.* (Varzi, 2005: 51)

My polemic against *logos* concerns not descriptive but prescriptive ontology, and I am pleased to report that in certain cases the latter is valueless: a bottle rack is still a bottle rack when it is no longer a bottle rack but a sculpture. Its shapes and features are those of a bottle rack but its capacity for action is that of a sculpture, that is, an artistic discourse reflecting on its own meaning and image.

Figure 9: *Antonio Strati,* Viewfinder Awareness, *2002. Polaroid T809 – Emulsion lift.*

Whence derives the logic of the ready-made, that formidable Trojan horse which Dadaism contrived to introduce into aesthetics by two operations: the first intended to expel taste (consider Duchamp's Bottle Rack, Égouttoir, as a play on words between drips, 'gouttes', and taste, 'goût'), the second to criticise art itself (Magrelli, 2006: 31)

The bottle rack's features have not changed. Indeed, one still witnesses the refined artistic operation of taking a mundane artifact belonging the banality of everyday life and translating it into a different language, that of art, thereby confronting us with the paradox and absurdity of prescribing how reality should be configured, including the reality of the aesthetic discourse on organisations.

Thus outlined is my propensity to reflect upon and discuss the self-configuring of the aesthetic discourse on organisations in accordance with the aesthetic principle of the 'pleasure of doing' (the fact that we cannot avoid doing it, that we are unable not to do it, that it is pleasurable being able to do it) rather than the ethical principle of the 'obligation of doing', and to locate this discourse in the 'process' of dialogic knowledge-acquisition in organisational theory, rather than in the 'becoming' of organisational studies. I do so in the awareness, however, that there are two devices with which to grasp *how* the aesthetic discourse on organisations is configuring itself, both of which interesting but very different from each other. They can be described by returning to the art work and considering two highly influential art movements: Cubism and the Dadaism to which I have just referred apropos Duchamp and his ready-mades.

The Cubist poetic is made up of fragments which, though disconnected, are able to induce interrelations among elements with very different meanings. The aesthetic discourse on organisations is thus configured by fragments which, however disparate, converge on coherence, structuring and constructing it. The Dadaist poetic, by contrast, lets neither convergences nor interrelations of meanings emerge. Perhaps, as Octavio Paz (1985) remarks, more than being art works proper, ready-mades are signs questioning conceptualisations of the art work and of works in general, such as the ongoing work of socially constructing the aesthetic discourse on organisations. Like Duchamp's ready-made *To Be Looked at (from the Other Side of the Glass) with One Eye, Close to, for Almost an Hour*, 'pointless, formless, informal, this product seems to stand at the threshold of history to ratify the definitive disappearance of the aesthetic experience' (Magrelli, 2006: 122). This is a meta-ironic gesture of self-reflection, which in regard to aesthetic discourse on organisations is just as fascinating (if not more so) than that which structures it.

I wish to express my gratitude for the institutional support received both the *Centre de Recherche en Gestion (PREG-CRG) – École Polytechnique-CNRS*, Paris, France, and the *Department of Management Politics Philosophy (MPP) – Copenhagen Business School*, Copenhagen, Denmark, where I was visiting research fellow for my sabbatical year 2010–2011. My thanks also go to the colleagues of both institutions for their insightful comments, and among them, in particular, to Pierre-Jean Benghozi and Pierre Guillet de Monthoux for their encouragement.

This work is dedicated to the memory of Rino Fasol, colleague and friend of the University of Trento.

CONCLUSION

The New Landscape of Organisational Life

Ian W. King
and Jonathan Vickery

This book set out to examine the powerful realms of experience that animate organisational life. We have done this by exploring the following questions, topics and issues:

> How our understanding of the concept 'organisation' is formed. Why do we think about organisations in the way we do? How can organisations think about themselves, or ask themselves questions about their invisible conventions, behaviours, practices and ideals? The shape and structure of organisations seem so logical, pragmatic and even inevitable, and yet are historical, often formed by confused assumptions about productivity and development.

> What is 'de-familiarisation', and how might it promote a means for organisations to develop their self-knowledge? Many organisations assume that their strategy documents give them an accurate picture of their modus operandi, shape and structure. Yet, organisations are not only historical but formed by invisible forces of power and disempowerment. How can organisations develop their self-reflexivity in this area?

> How does *individuality* in management leadership provide a means for developing *collective* thought capacity, or collaborative thought processes?

> How can we understand the organisation as a realm of dense sensate knowledge? The body, its facility for perception, intuition and sensory expression, is the locus of both our individual experience and our shared experience of the motility and decisions of others.

> How do the spaces and environments of the organisation forge the relationships between employees, management and organisational executive? How do space and the design of space determine an employee's horizon of understanding, of their role and potential?

> Why do dominant strategic planning models generate a 'tunnel vision' in organisations through an obsession with fixed objects and measurable objectives? How do they become capable of understanding the broader field of their activity and develop 'peripheral' vision?

> How can organisations adopt (and/or re-create) powerful means of self-reflection and reflexive planning by using design and design methods?

Organisations are usually thought of as entities in themselves, formed by structures, regulations and conventions, boundaries and hierarchies. People work 'in' organisations, and organisations are usually defined (by legal or financial frameworks) in ways that emphasise their objective independence from actual people or any one group of people. People come and go, but the organisation remains as some form of edifice. Organisations are generally seen as specific and determinate entities, whereas people are relative and changing. This, of course, is an empirical observation that can hardly be challenged, but our concern in this book is that this empirical observation is embedded with values, and an implicit valuing of organisations as entities and employers of people. In this book we attempted to uncover the profound human dimension of organisations – the life that characterises an organisation, that is, makes it what it is. It may be perplexing that the 'life' of organisations is not something that most organisations want to acknowledge. In fact, it is all too often ignored. Indeed, the 'life' of organisations is only recognised if it fits into existing frameworks, structures, regulations and conventions, boundaries and hierarchies

The fact that so much of the potential 'life' of organisations is routinely ignored suggests that there is something about the human senses, emotion, ideas and innovation, knowledge and creativity, communication and critique, that threatens the very nature of organisation. The tradition of organisations is built upon rationality and control and allowing those aspects of 'life' to emerge and threaten this status-quo cuts to the very nature of their identity. After all, organisations depend on collective cooperation, uniformity and harmony; it is not surprising that the experience of individuality or originality can become unpredictable or threaten stability. Organisations are therefore faced with a choice. This choice amounts to more than just 'adding' some creativity or individual expression to the everyday tasks of organisational productivity. The choice amounts to the equivalent of a strategic decision, one that challenges the very nature of thinking differently, imagining the organisation as a very different kind of space and place, where individual employees or clients or customers can discover an expanded realm of experience and possibility. Expanded realms of experience can offer all kinds of options and opportunities concerning the way organisations operate, manage (and are managed), and become productive. This book, we hope, explains how productivity is not just a matter of the creation of products and services, but involves the organisation evolving in shape or form, developing knowledge and aptitudes, moving into new spheres of influence, communicating and interacting with other organisations.

One of the reasons why organisations are reluctant to think differently, or imagine radically different options, is because of the value-embedded categories that they use to think. One of the purposes of this book is to show that the words and terms we use about organisations, and assume to be true, are also assumptions about power and value. As such these also trap us into patterns of thought and action that severely limit our understanding and our actions in organisational settings. For example, the terms 'profit' and 'growth' are without doubt widely thought to be essential to understanding and managing an organisation. While few people would contest the way that profit and growth are often important as objectives, to define 'profitability' and 'growing' in terms of the bottom line of the quarterly corporate accounts is to miss huge parts of organisational opportunity. As a consequence, the organisational entity, its products and services, are regarded as the sources of profitability and growth, and the work-force just the means of achieving this.

One reason why organisational 'profitability' and 'growing' is defined financially is the bewitching effect of numbers and the scientific guise of financial data. The apparent invincibility of numerical data has been seriously damaged since the advent of the global recession. Organisations are waking up the fact that numbers or data are often used to obscure judgment and justify mediocrity. Numbers and data can deny opportunity, and reinforce a narrow linearity of action in organisations. The unpredictability of our global economy, rather, demands lateral thinking and people able to respond to unusual circumstances. Organisations are now waking up to the fact that they need a deeper and more philosophical approach to strategy-making. They must develop a sense of honesty, integrity and self-examination. These are the routes to a sustainable future for organisations.

One of the reasons why numerical data assumed a primary role in organisations in the first place was the basic historical scientific distinction between subjective and objective, where the former was infinitely variable and depended on individual interpretation, and the latter universal and incontestable. Numerical data, given its apparent neutrality and universality, was awarded the status of objectivity, and the accounting methods by which data was organised, along with strategic management developed around those methods, all shared the vital condition of objectivity. In short, it assumed the status of truth and those elements unable to justify or provide support were cast out and denigrated as frivolous!

The distinction between subjective and objective, of course, has been a distinction of some consequence throughout the entire history of human civilization (at least in the West). During the late middle ages, the advanced philosophical and scientific thought of the day assumed that the human body and it senses were the source of all wanton desire and moral confusion. The mind, the light of human reason and mathematical logic, were its corrective.

Throughout Western modernity and to this day, the relation between body and mind remains uneasy, in contention, and provides a theoretical field for the battle between subjective and objective. The denigration of the body and elevation of the mind (or certain functions of the mind) still generates a strong sense of mutual exclusivity, which organisations hope to contain. The modern compulsion for objectivity tends even today to repress all forms of meaning issuing from sensory, embodied or expressive agency, or even denigrate in subtle ways the sensory life of individual labouring subjects.

Throughout this volume, however, we have explored the ways in which human experience, feeling and emotion, can take organisational forms, and present a more developed vision for organisational life. The problems with social and organisational life today are all too often rooted in or focused on action at the expense of a willingness to understand basic human experience, the need for inter-subjective communication, a meaningful environment to work in, and the sense of creative individual development. The dichotomy of subjectivity and objectivity can appear in many guises, including dominant ideals of organisation and management itself. 'Organisation' is assumed to be about companies, corporations, businesses or legal-physical entities that stand apart from any person or subjectivity. Management is assumed to be about people and arrangements of power or communication between people, disciplining and refining subjectivity for objective uses. Organisations are widely assumed to be the fixed structure, where 'management' is the enabler of practice. In other words, organisation is the 'container' and management the 'life' or activity. These are traditional assumptions, which clearly make sense and seem obvious. But again, we find the 'subjective and objective' dichotomy driving us to misleading conclusions. The organisation is often invested with 'objectivity' in the way its strategic ambitions are usually determined outside the forms of life created in and around management. The management and its arrangement and formation of a labouring society within the organisational structure, is assumed to be provisional, mutable, simple supporting or actualizing organisational objectives, and ultimately expendable.

This book has painted a different picture – of people and their organisation together, as one realm of 'life. We use the phrase 'paint a picture' deliberately, as this book has not aimed to build a single 'objective' framework for analysis, or set of 'solutions'. Our picture is something akin to a post-impressionist painting, where the *act* of representation (the experimental techniques of expressive description) are in tension with a recogniseable objective reality. Like Cézanne's scenes of Mont Sainte-Victoire (1887), we clearly see a mountain, but at the same time we also see the many different ways of seeing the mountain. It shows us how subjectivity can also be a significant dimension of objectivity. It shows us that 'reality' is formed by subjectivity and objectivity meeting in particular, and powerful, ways.

The dynamic organisation

We hope, therefore, that this book has accomplished three things in bringing together the subjective and objective:

First, we have portrayed the way organisation is bound up with practices and regimes of management, and vice versa. The shape, form and dynamics of management are indissolubly bound up with the shape, form and dynamics of organisation.

Second, we hold that organisation is not a static structure, but a process of thought, feeling and action.

Third, the organisation is a realm of unique possibility, experience and collective interaction. It is a social space, with profound cultural possibility, taking us beyond the limited frameworks of management strategy.

All too often corporate life is forged out of a series of denials of the 'cultural', in a vain attempt to establish professional modes of conduct that are distinct from the world around it. Yet the cultural is the glue that holds organisations together – in other words, take away the glue and the organisation may well fall apart! We point out that culture, art (and even creative forms of leisure) can be a *resource* for organisational life, and not a threat. Artistic culture can also generate significant intellectual capability, as it contains within it ideas and ideals on agency, materiality, space, interaction and the cognitive process.

Our emphasis on experience, perception and emotion, throws into relief the way organisations can repress their members through logical, rational, statistical or fixed structures of order and uniformity. Organisations can exercise a dominant and dominating power simply through following accepted patterns of regularity and linearity. Against these accepted patterns of practice, we do not resort to now anachronistic romantic individualism, or idealistic concepts of creativity (inspiration, genius, imaginative transformation). Yet, individuality is crucial, and there are indeed forms of philosophical romanticism that remain a potent intellectual resource, particularly those that remind us of our ever-evolving potential for self-reinvention and do things differently. If empowered to do so, we possess a natural 'human' tendency towards dissent and change, as well as towards order and domination.

By looking at the broad landscape of experience, what we called, 'organisational life', we identified more clearly the anatomy of organisational domination. Traditional, standardised, and often imposed templates of management are extraordinarily repressive, yet in ways that are not altogether easy to discern. We so easily see their 'logic' and reason, and find it hard to imagine how they could be otherwise. The routine rhetoric of freedom from domination (from the political Right, championing individual liberty; from the political Left, demanding social justice) is not usually armed with a clear understanding of alternatives. For us, 'alternative organisation' begins with understanding the organisation as a form of experience – and the dimensions of that experience in relation to practice. It then proceeds by imagination, and the capacity for thinking otherwise. It is not just a matter of 'freedom from', but 'strategic change', for without an equally pragmatic pathway to organisational freedom, all demands for freedom dissolve in the face of the necessity of production and survival. In an era when the average worker is fortunate simply to hold down his or her job, calls for change need to be as equally determined to meet the present and future challenges of production.

In what follows, we will summarise the main claims our contributing authors have made, so to advance our thinking and re-thinking of the repressive norms that regulate organisational life. We then attempt to set out some pragmatic responses to these claims, whereby some measure of practical development can be advanced. If thought itself is not to remain purely speculative, or simply get drowned in the maelstrom of information and communication around us, what possible way forward can we envisage? These questions need to confront the reader, as they confront us. Our ideas and suggestions are not in any way models or (more) templates for organisational life, rather they attempt to initiate a process of decision-making and action that lead to expertise rather than repetitive experience. They are as much for arguing against, as they are for thinking more, different, thoughts. One of the themes of this book is that 'thought' itself is tied to the corporeal experience of the physical situation in which the subject is located, positioned (and often trapped).

Thought also emerges from the sense and sensibility of space, place, and environment, and the animating dynamics of that environment. One of the unfortunate characteristics of 'how to' management models, and the management consultancy templates that so pervade the corporate world, is that they conceive organisational action in terms of 'a priori' solutions, techniques or abstract 'steps'. Their popularity obviously testifies to a measure of impact. However, our research suggests that solutions, techniques or abstract 'steps' perpetuate the rationalised, abstract and experience-denying patterns of organisational management, which are limited in their ability to effect real progress. In our context, 'progress' would mean the interactive development of the organisation in its social, cultural and economic forms.

Every corporation knows that what goes on outside its boundaries is as important as what happens inside (outside in the markets, in customers homes, in retail spaces; inside in the marketing department, in product design, or sales). Evidently, the emphasis on the economic dimension of production has engendered distorted ideals about the role of management and limited organisational consciousness of the joined-up nature of economic and social life.

So to summarise: what are we saying?

> *Tensions and contradictions are significant*: Life, organisational life, human thought and even human science, is fraught with contradiction and tensions. Organisational leadership and strategic management attempts at all costs to avoid contradiction and tensions, or to 'resolve' them as soon as possible. And yet, while contradiction and tensions may be problematic, they are not necessarily 'wrong' or undesirable. They are often both symptom and source of truth and meaning, offering a means of insight into the relationships between subjects and objects, agencies and structures, employee and employer, organising and organisation, individuals and management, and so on. The critical practice of cultivating *a productive conflict* (a clash of ideas, criticism and critique, visualising radical alternatives, changing positions, and opposing all stable systems of practice and thinking) is the only real means of progress in organisational life.

> *We need possibility as much as reality*: Our understanding of organisations (our standard, inherited, industry-based, concepts, ideas, ideals and basic theories) always seems straightforward, corresponding to a form of 'reality', usually in the form of today's corporate life all around us. The cognitive frameworks that direct our thinking (from regulatory frameworks, to professional norms, codes of conduct, industry standards, benchmarks of innovation) may be necessary, but 'necessity' is never as imperative as it appears. Reality itself is never presented to us in pure empirical form. It emerges from a multi-layered collection of experiences which, incidentally, organisations never master, control or ultimately conquer. We need to maintain our conception of 'reality' in tension with an openness to experience, thereby allowing hybrid conditions of possibility to emerge.

> *Things don't think, people do*: Understanding organisation life is a process. It is as much in need of 'de-familiarisation' and deconstruction as is the setting of models of practice, plans or frameworks. The fixed empirical structures (from management hierarchies to office walls) are entirely relative to the landscapes of experience that move within, around, and outside, them. Within management and organisational structures, with their set patterns of organisational behaviour, there usually lie embedded hierarchies of power that favour 'relations between things' over 'relations between people'. Organisations have a tendency of self-preservation that come down to favouring the structures and mechanisms of production over the intellectual life of their people. This seemingly 'natural' tendency needs to be countered consistently with intellectual activity by its people, who can offer alterative forms of measured development

and self-evaluation. 'De-familiarisation' is a process whereby people and their thought-potential are placed in priority over physical structures and systems, and in turn where physical structures and systems are made more productive and responsive in relation to the thought life of the organisation.

> *The body is a powerful thinking tool*: The role of the senses in organisations, while seemingly contained and disciplined by the regimes of management, are still unchartered territory. Codes of organisational conduct and behaviour are so often predicated on the suppression of, and not the use of, the senses. The senses, however, are not objects, entities or quantifiable resources that can be easily subject to order. Rather they open-up realms of possible synthesis and perception, new ideas and means of inter-relationality, sometimes they can disrupt and become destructive (all manner of depressions have a somatic basis). They remain indelible to the guise of all people-based organisations.

> *Art is life, life is art*: Creativity is a term subject to ludicrous ideals and false promises. Organisations need to conduct their own research into understanding what they mean by (and want from) creativity, and how they might introduce creativity into their own developing understanding of organisational life. There are many phantom versions of creativity – eccentric and even inspiring art works that achieve little for organisations. Can we have real creation without fully understanding creativity? 'Real' creativity needs to withstand and operate within rigorous and pragmatic frameworks of business strategy and work practice, where its ideas and ideals can be tested.

Real creativity is not simply an eccentric form of self-expression and communication. It is a critical comprehension of the current cognitive conditions of labour, and a means of driving disparate forces of change in the experiential landscape of organisational life.

> *Knowledge is one thing, we also need truth*: Industry research and its standard methods have so often echoed the most restrictive aspects of organisations. Research data is often defined in terms of information-gathering, fact-based assertions, single-point recommendations. Its methods copy the natural sciences in their assumption that uniformity, consistency, and delimited problem-solving is the key to the 'truth' of the situation. The nature of truth, however, is the truth of nature, and how human experience forms and is formed by circuits of meaning under certain conditions. The nature of truth is the symbiotic relationship between means and ends, methods and outcomes, labour and its products. This is why 'aesthetics' is fundamental to our understanding of organisational life: it looks at the interrelatedness of subjectivity and objectivity, systems and structures, people and spaces, spaces and places, and how these all make for a realm of unique potential.

> *Value in organisations can often be invisible*: Tomorrow's 'tools' of organisational development, according to current trends in industry, are the technological tools of messaging, information and data transportation. While obviously impressive, they inadvertently strip human labour down to coded instructions and plotted co-ordinations, as oblivious to their origins as to their

implications. Art and art-based activities can be used to activate and draw attention to the missing registers of human agency that new media and technology in organisational life takes out. Art is centrally about interpretation, translation, visualisation, and non-verbal communication in organisational life. Knowledge resources embedded in memory, experience and latent 'know-how' can find a means of, and a more functional role in, developing the whole spectrum of activities that together make for organisational development. The messaging, information and data transportation that are so impressively made possible by our new multi-media technologies, are only productive when leaving the virtual domains of communication, and entering the world of work, and people, and production. It is this 'real world' environment that is often neglected in terms of intellectual development and cultural investment.

With the thoughts above, how then do we approach the world of practice, or the world of 'applied thought'? The categorical distinction between theory and practice (along with subjectivity and objectivity, body and mind) is a third enduring dichotomy in Western thought. In a global context (notwithstanding the globalisation of Western thought) the distinction seems less intractable. After all, is it not the 'global organisation' that has discovered news ways of adapting to complex and multiple social contexts, managing across cultural borders and political jurisdictions, with multiple centres of power and dispersed sites for operations. The global organisation, like the many conglomerates and MNCs that we call global brands, retain an organisational coherence in de-centred, multi-site, networked and irregular compositional form. It seems clear, then, along with the obvious facts of online communication and remote management, that organisations do not need the old straight-jackets of static management hierarchies, single locations and fixed schedules.

In this new context, our aesthetic perspectives on organisations gain a greater sense of pragmatic validity. There is also a wealth of psychological and cultural research pointing out some basic facts about creativity and human freedom in the workplace. For example, organisations are usually plagued by two major disabling factors: employee sickness, and the constant threat of advancing competitors. Creativity, and a personal investment in a self-fulfilling project, without doubt promotes workplace wellbeing which has direct impacts on individual health. Furthermore, creativity (as in art) has always operated through a consistent alertness and peripheral vision, the consistent influence of others and the advancing achievement of competitors. Being 'influenced' by and advancing ideas of competitors has always been a basic characteristic of the artistic personality.

We therefore conclude with some pragmatic suggestions, which are not simply theory or practice, but aimed at bringing both together. Organisations need to find their own ways of 'translating' theory into practice, according to our observations above, and need to develop site-specific and sector-relevant techniques for operationalising theoretical insights and the knowledge accumulated in this book. Nevertheless, we can offer some tentative suggestions in this direction.

Art

The use of art involves the use of a 'media' or medium. The medium is important, as it creates a fresh, open and relatively neutral focal point, neither organisation-centred nor employee-centred. The media of art are not necessarily physical materials or paint, wood or ink, but can be the arrangement of space, the formation of groups or lines of communication, the modulation of rhythm and tempo in working schedules, the use of multi-media and online communication. Some organisations reserve rooms or areas for this purpose. Such rooms can become a barometer for the mood, attitudes or changing social orientations of the organisation. It may be used for a developing installation art, employees' films or white boards requesting anonymous statements, ideas, and perspectives. Each organisation need to locate its own media through which creativity can be conducted.

The characteristics of media, perhaps, are the elements and dimensions of organisations that can be used to stimulate attentiveness to form, colour, light and detail in the very texture of organisational life. Perhaps this will involve the way communication and representation operates, or how alternatives, creative ideas, controversial perspectives or objections are used to form the connections between management and employees? The 'art' of management engages in a self-conscious organisational 'composition', comprehending the aesthetics of organisational life and the 'quality' of that life as it is lived out within the 'frame' of organisational space. Sometimes filming or video is done informally by employees, and then circulated, as a means of generating awareness of this. By attending to the visual, sensory, representational and experiential form of management communication, employees invest in and become active in developing the art of organisational life, with its increasing capacity for individual perception, expression and interpretation.

Design

What does a beautiful organisation look like? Beauty in organisations is more a matter of design than art, but may involve both. What kinds of beauty or ugliness prevail in your organisation? What are the long-term consequences for ugly organisations? Art is good at identifying the spectrum of feeling through which ugliness impacts on the individual. Design is good at forming a language with which to deal with this. Beauty is never simply a visual phenomenon, to do with how fixed entities 'look'. It is also about the flow, processes and rhythm of working life. For the sight of 'mess', for example, like an office with piles of documents on the floor, is usually relative to the nature of the project and its people. 'Mess' is usually about dynamics and stress, rather than office tidiness. An 'art' of organisation is always the generation of a creative energy, and therefore has a high level of tolerance for mess. In fact, certain kinds of messiness can help generate essential energies and an impulse for making new arrangements of things. Design, however, has great resources for extending that impulse into real strategic patterns of action and problem-solving.

Organisations need to develop an understanding of design process, where they can see just how many 'design decisions' are made without knowing it, and with no real understanding of the consequences. Design process is a capability that enables an organisation to places its management and production within a reflexive framework, where each stage and activity can subject to thorough concept development, modeling and prototyping, intelligence and feedback mechanisms, expanding all the while the possibility for a change of track. The 'designed organisation' is aware how all of its activities have consequences for how its employees experience work, and space, and management. Many organisations now use employee briefings, creative mentoring, strategic information through graphics and in-house displays, and develop a 'style' of working life that generates a sense of design consciousness.

Space

A central product of the organisation's design capability is its space. Usually space is designed by default, or simply regarded as a physical manifestation of the production process. This is naive. There is no simple relationship between production processes and spatial design. Organisations have a 'style', expressed through its space, even if that style is random, disheveled or out of date! The organisation is a collection of people with the capacity for designing their own space, as they possess intimate knowledge of it. Organisations can experiment with their own facilities by allowing employees to generate visual ideas on more effective special arrangements, or inviting an independent designer to facilitate dialogue and research on the use and effectiveness of space.

Space may seem empty or just a facility, and yet we all know otherwise. The aroma, 'atmosphere', territorialisation of power and sensory clues on organisational values all have profound impacts on behaviour. Organisations can set about developing a register of free thought within its spaces. Its spaces can become 'epistemic', with areas set aside for critical or reflexive thinking. Some organisations maintain 'brainstorm' rooms, which of course are trendy and can become routine, but can provide wall space for free thought, expression, ideas and critique otherwise censored or sensitive. Generating the organisational capabilities for self-understanding not only increases potential for performance but it undermines those in management positions whose personal interests invest in the under-performance of employees or the denigration of the workforce.

As we noted in our introduction, it is extraordinary the extent to which people in power have benefitted from the calamities of the global recession. Organisational life is perpetually held back and morally sullied by those whose personal interests lie in the organisation *not* developing and its people not extending their capabilities. A designed space is an open, transparent and interactive space, but intelligently provides refuge for individuality and non-conformity. It understands the way every item, piece of furniture, lighting, the shape of the doors, all together make for a symbolic landscape of meaning and stand as the organisational horizon of future possibility.

Creative communication

The space of the organisation is the means by which art, design and the body come together to develop a new 'inner life' of the organisation. This 'inner life' is a life of imagination and possibility, and a capacity for consistent new ideas and visions of future development. Work becomes a place of inspiration, not exhausting routine. Employees are incentivised by feeling that they belong to a project of organisational transformation, giving them a greater purpose and perspective on their everyday tasks and responsibilities. Being part of a collective endeavor enables the individual to reflect on and refine his or her decision-making processes, their work patterns and the ways in which they interact with others. A creative approach to workplace communication mitigates the imposition of necessary regulatory structures, protocols, expectations and hierarchies of power. It can expose the concealed forces of debilitation and unhappiness, and make the hidden dimensions of organisational life an object of reflection. This in itself can be a profoundly liberating activity, where challenges are shared and made a common concern. One of the most powerful impacts of creative communication is the production of empathy, where through the common project of organisation, a collective imaginary emerges, where employees begin to see themselves as part of an interconnected body.

There are direct correlations between the productivity and health of an organisation and the way its spatial economy becomes open to creativity. Some organisations have secondary roles assigned to employees, whereby they become responsible for developing creativity as well as their usual job. The hobbies or cultural skills of employees, in photography, oratory, performance or poetry, can be used to develop a capacity for language and an ability to mobilise diverse skills sets. It can enable people to feel connected and invested in a collective project, where inhibitors to performance and interaction are addressed. And importantly, it can democratise creativity, whereas in organisational life creativity itself can be marshaled as another form of hierarchical power or personal self-advancement.

And finally, the pervasiveness of creativity in an organisation makes for an ethical situation, whereby the experience of organisational life gains a profoundly cultural and reflexive dimension. Members of the organisation know they are working for the 'good', and maintain a conviction in the inherent value of the organisation. Work becomes a project of self-development and collective knowledge, not just a space of command-and-response. The organisational culture of hard work becomes a cultural democracy where work becomes as empowering as art itself.

CONTRIBUTORS

Robert M. Bauer is Associate Professor of Organization and Innovation at Johannes Kepler University, Linz, Austria and a Visiting Professor at the Marcel Desautels Centre for Integrative Thinking, Rotman School of Management, University of Toronto. His research focuses on creative and innovative processes in/between organisations with particular emphasis on (a) complexity and knowledge integration (b) design thinking and epistemological issues in creativity and innovation, and (c) relationships between management and organisation, arts and design. He is also a registered psychotherapist and has extensive experience as a consultant and coach to top executive management. Contact: robert.bauer@jku.at

Robert Chia is Research Professor in Management at the Adam Smith Business School, University of Glasgow. He received his PhD in Organisation Studies from Lancaster University and publishes regularly in the leading international journals in organisation and management studies. He is the author/editor of five books and several international journal articles in a variety of management sub-fields. His latest books include *Strategy without Design: The Silent Efficacy of Indirect Action* (with Robin Holt) Cambridge University Press, 2009 and *Philosophy and Organization Theory* (with Hari Tsoukas) Emerald Group Press, 2011. His research interests revolve around strategic leadership and foresight, complex thinking and decision-making and the impact of contrasting East-West metaphysical mindsets on business practice. Contact: robert.chia@strath.ac.uk

Miguel Pina e Cunha is Professor at Nova School of Business and Economics, Lisbon. He has a PhD from Tilburg University and published in journals such as the Academy of Management Review, Human Relations, Journal of Management Studies, Journal of World Business, Organization, and Organization Studies. His research deals with positive and negative organising, and emergent processes in organisations, such as improvisation, surprise and serendipity. Contact: mpc@fe.unl.pt

Ward M. Eagen is Senior Researcher in Design and Innovation, Institute of Innovation and Technology Management, Ted Rogers School of Management, Ryerson University. His research interest is on design as a moral process of the intuitive unfolding of a solution space from the problem place. Having worked as an architect for ten years with the premier firm of Arthur Erickson, Ward has taught design from a number of perspectives including architecture, film, photography, web design, and new media in North America and Africa. Ward holds degrees in architecture, and philosophy, and is currently working on a PhD in Design Science. Contact: weagen@ryerson.ca

Robin Holt is a Professor at the University of Liverpool Management School, UK. He has enjoyed a serpentine academic career, working in departments of politics and philosophy as well as business and management, and at a number of universities. Throughout he has been interested in investigating our experience of evaluating and valuing things, currently through research work on judgment and the conditions of judgment; on entrepreneurial activity; and on strategic practice. Contact: r.holt@liverpool.ac.uk

Barbara A. Karanian, PhD, is a Professor of Social Sciences at Wentworth Institute of Technology in Boston, USA, and a Lecturer in Mechanical Engineering Design at Stanford University. Founder of the Design Entrepreneuring Studio, she uses storytelling to facilitate project progress from the idea phases to reality. The author of "Entrepreneurial Leadership: A Balancing Act in Engineering and Science"; and "Tell/Make/Engage-Actions for Innovation", Her research focuses on how entrepreneurial leaders create amazing team environments. Barbara makes productive partnerships with industry and creates collaborative research teams with members from the areas of engineering, psychology, and communication. Her recent work examines perceived differences in on-line and off-line lives. Barbara also paints pictures. Contact: karanian@stanford.edu

Ian W. King formerly worked in the theatre and music business, and then turned to academia as a second career. Whilst he was at the University of Essex he co-organised with Ceri Watkins and Steve Linstead the Art of Management and Organization conference series held in London (with the Tate Modern), Paris (Pompidou Centre), Krakow (national museum) and in Canada (the Banff Centre). Ian has published widely and he was also General Editor of international peer-reviewed journal – *Aesthesis* (2007-2010). Ian is presently Professor of Aesthetics and Management at the University of the Arts, London, and is currently organizing a series of colloquia in conjunction with fashion weeks in London, Milan, Paris, New York and Tokyo. Contact: i.king@fashon.arts.ac.uk

Wendelin Küpers presently works at the Department of Management, Massey University, Auckland, New Zealand. Before he has been affiliated to the Chair of Business Administration, Leadership, and Organisation at the FernUniversität Hagen (Distance University), Germany and the Institute for Leadership and Human Resource Management at the University of St. Gallen, Switzerland. Based on an advanced phenomenological orientation, he pursuits research on embodied, emotional and aesthetic as well as integral dimensions of organisational life-worlds and leadership. Contact: W.Kupers@massey.ac.nz

Pierre Guillet de Monthoux. Since the early 1990s, Pierre has focused his management research on aesthetics. In his view, art and what art-worlds achieve help us focus on the aesthetical side of social action. Pierre has published widely including his well received book *The Art Firm: aesthetic management and metaphysical marketing* (Stanford University Press 2004); he has also documented his interest in aesthetics in a variety of media, including his road movie "Masters of business art" (http://www.youtube.com/watch?v=6f698oKcXY0). In this context he also supervised several doctoral thesis presented in *Aesthetic Leadership* (Palgrave Macmillan, 2007). He is presently Chair in Philosophy of Management and Head of the Department of Management, Politics and Philosophy at Copenhagen Business School, Denmark. He holds honorary positions in Finland and Germany, is currently guest professor at St. Gallen University in Switzerland, and research fellow at the Art Management Program, SUNY Buffalo in the US. Contact: pgm.lpf@cbs.dk

Enrico Maria Piras is a sociologist, and holds a PhD in Information Systems and Organization (University of Trento). He is a research fellow at Fondazione Bruno Kessler (www.fbk.eu), since 2008. His research activity focuses on the work with/around the electronic medical infrastructures and information systems of both professionals (physicians, nurses, clerical staff) and laypeople (patient, citizens). He is also a member of the university-based Research Unit on Communication, Organizational Learning and Aesthetics, Trento University (Rucola; http://www3.unitn.it/rucola/) – a group of scholars and researchers collaborating since 1993 on the basis of common professional interests in specific aspects of organisation studies. Contact: piras@fbk.eu

Chris Poulson, PhD Yale. From a Kodak Bullseye to a Nikon D3, he has generated 100,000+ images. Docent at the Museum of Photographic Arts in San Diego, he has exhibited work in solo and group displays and at conferences (primarily Art of Management and Academy of Management) and also in university and community settings. He is Chair, Academy Arts of Academy of Management, Professor Emeritus of Management at Cal Poly Pomona. Chris has taught at the University of Tasmania, Hong Kong University of Science and Technology, Bocconi University, Sun Yat-sen University. He is Visiting Professor (2011–2012) at the new Sampoerna School of Business in Jakarta, and is David L. Bradford Distinguished Management Educator of 1998. Contact: tascat@me.com

Bob Robertson's design focus is visual communications design, design management and planning. His portfolio includes the development of corporate identities, collateral brand elements and the design of wayfinding/signage systems. Bob holds a Bachelor of Fine Arts (Art + Design) degree and a Master of Arts degree in Communications and Technology from the University of Alberta. He has also studied graphic design at post-graduate level at the prestigious AGS School of Design in Basel, Switzerland. He continues to pursue his keen interest in exploring how design thinking works to support people in their daily lives. Contact: ricr@telusplanet.net

Antonio Strati is Professor of Sociology of Innovation at the University of Trento, and is an Art Photographer. His book *Organization and Aesthetics* is published in English (Sage, 1999), in French (PUL, 2004), in Portuguese (FGV, 2007), and in Italian (Mondadori, 2008). He is also author of the book *Theory and Method in Organization Studies* (Sage, 2000) and of a number of essays that have appeared in international journals. Some of his "photopoems" – his artistic research in conceptual photography – are published in books and journals, and are collected by the Bibliothèque Nationale de France (Paris) and the Polaroid Collections (Cambridge, Mass., USA) among a number of Collections. Contact: antonio.strati@soc.unitn.it

Steven S. Taylor is Associate Professor in the School of Business at the Worcester Polytechnic Institute (WPI) in Worcester, Massachusetts, USA. His research focuses on the aesthetics of organisational action and reflective practice. Recently his academic work has involved theorizing the use of arts-based process within organisations and exploring beautiful action within organisations. He is the author of the book *Leadership Craft, Leadership Art*, and is the editor of the journal *Organizational Aesthetics*. Steve is also a playwright whose work has been performed in England, France, Poland, Canada, New Zealand, and the USA. Contact: sst@WPI.EDU

Jonathan Vickery is Associate Professor in the Centre for Cultural Policy Studies, University of Warwick. He has been a Henry Moore research fellow, a director of The Aesthesis Project, editor of the journal *Aesthesis*, and reviews editor and regular contributor to Art & Architecture Journal. He has published articles on aesthetics, urban space and art theory, co-edited with Diarmuid Costello *Art: Key Contemporary Thinkers* (Oxford: Berg, 2007) editor and author of *FLASH@Hebburn* (London: A&AJ). He also works as an art critic. At the moment he is writing a book on art, cultural politics and the public sphere, and developing the Art and Architecture Journal with Jeremy Hunt, involving a new website for urban research and a cultural documentary program. Contact: J.P.Vickery@warwick.ac.uk

Samantha Warren says as an ex-filing clerk, call centre agent and underwear sales rep, she has always been interested in the beauty, fun, disgust and boredom of the workplace, but it was not until she became an academic that she realised these things amounted to an "aesthetic way of being" at work. Her fascination with the aesthetic is primarily methodological and most of her published research focuses on the role and import of the visual as a sensuous mode of knowing, particularly with regard to professional and workplace identities. She is currently researching smell and organisation, and works as a Professor in Management at Essex Business School, UK where she teaches "critical people issues". Contact: swarren@essex.ac.uk

Alberto Zanutto is a sociologist, and holds a PhD in Information Systems and Organization (University of Trento). He is grant researcher at the University of Trento, since 2008, where he is teaching Sociology of Economy, Methodology of Social Sciences and Organization of Social Services. His research activity focuses on different fields, such as the information technology innovation in medical organisations, organisational analysis and methodology. He is also a member of the Research Unit on Communication, Organizational Learning and Aesthetics (Rucola; http://www3.unitn.it/rucola/) founded by Silvia Gherardi e Antonio Strati in 1993. Contact: Alberto.Zanutto@unitn.it

REFERENCES

ABC News Nightline (1999) 'The Deep Dive', July 13, 1999.

Abrahamson, E. and Freedman, D. (2006) *A Perfect Mess: The Hidden Benefits of Disorder*, London: Weidenfeld and Nicholson.

Ackerman, D. (1990) *A Natural History of the Senses*, New York: Random House.

Adler, N. J. (2006) 'The arts & leadership: Now that we can do anything, what will we do?' *Academy of Management Learning & Education*, 5: 486–499.

Agar, M. H. (1980) *The Professional Stranger*, New York: Academic Press.

Akin, O. (1986) *Psychology of Architectural Design*, London: Pion.

Alferoff, C. & Knights, D. (2003) 'We're all partying here: targets and games, or targets as games in call centre management' in Carr, A. & Hancock, P. eds. *Art and Aesthetics at Work*, London: Palgrave Macmillan: 70–92.

Anzieu, D. (1989) *The Skin Ego*, New Haven, CT: Yale University Press.

Appleton, J. (1996) *The Experience of Landscape*, Chichester: John Wiley.

Arts and Business (n.d.) 'Creative Development' available at http://www.aandb.org.uk/render.aspx?siteID=1&navIDs=1,185,319 (accessed May, 2007).

Bain, P. & Taylor, P. (2000) 'Entrapped by the 'electronic panopticon'? Worker resistance in the call centre', *New Technology, Work, and Employment*, 15: 2–18.

Baldry, C. (1999) 'Space – The final frontier', *Sociology*, 33(3): 535–53.

Baldry, C., Bain, P. and Taylor, P. (1998) 'Bright Satanic Offices', in Warhurst, C. and Thompson, P. eds. *Workplaces of the Future*, Basingstoke: Macmillan: 163–83.

Barab, S. A., Thomas, M. K., Dodge, T., Squire, K., Newell, M. (2004) 'Reflections from the Field: Critical Design Ethnography: Designing for Change', *Anthropology and Education Quarterly*, 35(2): 254–268.

Barbaras, R. (2008) 'Life, Movement, and Desire', *Research in Phenomenology* 38, 3–17.

Barnard, C. I. (1938) *The Functions of the Executive*, Cambridge, MA: Harvard University Press.

Baron-Cohen, S. and Harrison, J. (1996) *Synaesthesia: Classic and Contemporary Readings*, Oxford: Blackwell.

Barrell, J. (1993) 'The Public Prospect and the Private View: the politics of taste in eighteenth-century Britain' in Pugh, S. ed. *Reading landscape: country-city-capital*, Manchester: Manchester University Press.

Barry, D. (1996) 'Artful Inquiry: A Symbolic Constructivist Approach to Social Science Research', in *Qualitative Inquiry*, 2(4): 411–38.

Bateson, G. (1972) *Steps to an Ecology of Mind*, San Francisco: Chandler.

Bateson, G. (1979) *Mind and Nature: A Necessary Unity*, New York: Bantam Books.

Bateson, M. (1994) *Peripheral Visions: Learning Along the Way*, New York: Harper Collins.

Baudrillard, J. (1994) *Simulacra and Simulation*, Michigan: University of Michigan Press.

Baudrillard, J. (1998) *The Consumer Society*, London: Sage.

Bauer, R. M. and Eagen, W. M. (2010) 'Designing – Innovation at the Crossroads of Structure and Process' in Shamiyeh, M. ed., *Creating Desired Futures: How Design Thinking Innovates Business*, Basel, Boston, Berlin: Birkhäuser: 145–163.

Bauer, R. M. and Moldoveanu, M. C. (2008) 'Einige Bemerkungen zur Frage: Was ist organisationale Komplexität?' *Die Betriebswirtschaft*, 68: 568–596. [no English translation].

Bauman, Z. (1998) *Work, Consumerism and the New Poor*, London: OUP.

Baumard, P. (1999) *Tacit Knowledge in Organizations*, London: Sage.

Beardsley, M. (1982) 'Some persistent issues in aesthetics' in Wreen, M. J. and Callen, D. M. eds. *The Aesthetic Point of View*, Ithaca: Cornell University Press.

Becker, Howard (2006) 'The Work Itself', in Becker, H. S., Faulkner R. R. and Kirshenblatt-Gimblett, B. eds., *Art from Start to Finish: Jazz, Painting, Writing, and Other Improvisations*. Chicago: The University of Chicago Press: 21–30.

Beckman, S. L. and Barry, M. (2007) 'Innovation as a Learning Process', *California Management Review*, 50: 25–56.

Belova, O. (2006) 'The Event of Seeing: A Phenomenological Perspective on Visual Sense-Making', *Culture and Organization*, 12(2): 93–107.

Berleant, A. (1993) 'The aesthetics of art and nature' in Kemal, S. & Gaskell, I. eds. *Landscape, natural beauty and the arts*, Cambridge: Cambridge University Press.

Beyes, T., and Steyaert C. (2006) 'Justifying Theatre in Organizational Analysis: A Carnivalesque Alternative?' *Consumption, Markets & Culture* 9(2): 100–110.

Biehl, B. (2007) 'The Aesthetics of Emptiness', *Aesthesis*, 1(2): 80–85.

Bishop, C. (2004) 'Antagonism and Relational Aesthetics', *October* 110 (Fall 2004): 51–80.

Bloom, H. (1994) *The Western Canon*, London: Chaptermac.

Boland, R. J. and Collopy, F., eds. (2004) *Managing as Designing*, Stanford, CA: Stanford University Press.

Borthwick, F. (2000) 'Olfaction and Taste: invasive odours and disappearing objects', *The Australian Journal of Anthropology*, 11: 127–140.

Bothwell, L. (1983) *The Art of Leadership: Skill-building techniques that produce results*, Englewood Cliffs, NJ: Prentice-Hall, Inc.

Bourdieu, P. (1984) *Distinction: A Social Critique of the Judgement of Taste*, Cambridge: Harvard University Press.

Bourdieu, P. (1990) *The Logic of Practice*, Stanford: Stanford University Press.

Bourdieu, P. (1998) *Acts of Resistance: Against the New Myths of Our Time*, Cambridge: Polity Press.

Bourdieu, P., and Haake H. (1995) *Free Exchange*, Stanford: Stanford University Press.

Bourriaud, N. (2002) *Relational Aesthetics*, Dijon-Quetigny: Les presses du réel.

Brechon, R. (1996) *Estranho estrangeiro: Uma biografia de Fernando Pessoa*, Lisboa: Quetzal.

Brewis, J. & Warren, S. (2001) 'Pregnancy as Project: Organizing reproduction', *Administrative Theory and Praxis*, 23(3): 383–406.

Bronwen, M. and Ringham, F. eds. (2003) *Sense and Scent: An Exploration of Olfactory Meaning*, London: Philomel.

Brown, S. and Eisenhardt, K. M. (1997) *Competing on the Edge*, Boston: Harvard University Press.

Brown, T. (2008) 'Design Thinking', *Harvard Business Review*, Reprint R0806E, Boston, Massachusetts: 85–93.

Bryman, A. (2008) *Social Research Methods*, Oxford: Oxford University Press.

Buchanan, R. (1992) 'Wicked Problems in Design Thinking', *Design Issues*, 8: 5–21.

Buchanan, R. (1995) *The Idea of Design: A Design Issues Reader*, Cambridge, MA: MIT Press: 82.

Burgelman, R. (1991) 'Intraorganizational ecology of strategy making and organizational adaptation: Theory and field research', *Organization Science*, 2: 239–262.

Bazerman, M. H. (2001) *Judgment in Managerial Decision Making* (5th ed.), New York: John Wiley and Sons.

Becker, F. and Steele, F. (1995) *Workplace by Design: Mapping the High-performance Workscape*, San Francisco: Jossey-Bass.

Brookes, M. and Kaplan, A. (1972) 'The office environment: space planning and affective behavior', *Human Factors* 14: 373–391.

Burgelman, R. (2002) 'Strategy as vector and the inertia of coevolutionary lock-in', *Administrative Science Quarterly*, 47: 325–357.

Burke, E. (1790) *Reflections on the French revolution*.

Burrell, G. and Morgan, G. (1979) *Sociological Paradigms and Organizational Analysis*, London: Heinemann Educational Books.

C. Greene, Myerson, J. (2011) 'Space for thought: designing for knowledge workers', *Facilities*, 29(1/2):19

Cairns, G. (2002) 'Aesthetics, morality and power: design as espoused freedom and implicit control', *Human Relations*, 55: 799–820.

Cairns, G., McInnes, P. and Robertson, P. (2003) 'Organization space/time: from imperfect panopticon to heterotopian understanding', *ephemera*, 3: 126–132.

Caldwell, D.M. & O'Reilly, C.A. (1990) 'Measuring person-job fit using a profile comparison process', *Journal of Applied Psychology*, 75: 648–657.

Campbell, C. (1987) *The Romantic Ethic and the Spirit of Modern Consumerism*, Oxford: Blackwell.

Canetti, E. (1976) 'The writer's profession' published in *Art and Thought*: http://www.qantara.de/uploads/496/fwf77_16canetti.pdf (accessed May 2007)

Carlile, P. R. (2002) 'A Pragmatic View of Knowledge and Boundaries: Boundary Objects in New Product Development', *Organization Science*, 13: 442–455.

Carlson, A. (2002) 'Appreciation and the Natural Environment' in Neill, A. & Ridley, A. eds. *Arguing about Art: Contemporary philosophical debates*, London: Routledge.

Carmona, S., Ezzamel, M. and Gutierrez, F. (2002) 'The Relationship Between Accounting and Spatial Practices in the Factory', *Accounting, Organisation and Society*, 27: 239–74.

Carr, A. and Hancock, P. eds. (2003) *Art and Aesthetics at Work*, Basingstoke: Palgrave Macmillan.

Carr, H. (2009) *The Verse Revolutionaries*, London: Jonathan Cape

Casey, C. (2000) 'Sociology Sensing the Body: Revitalizing a Dissociative Discourse', in Hassard, J., Holliday, R. and Wilmott, H. ed. *Body and Organisation*, London: Sage: 52–70.

Chan, W-T (1963) *A Source Book in Chinese Philosophy*, Princeton: Princeton University Press.

Chi, M. T. H., Glaser, R., & Farr, M. eds. (1988) *The nature of expertise*, Hillsdale, NJ: Erlbaum.

Chong, D. (2003) 'Revisiting Business and the Arts', *Journal of Nonprofit & Public Sector Marketing*, 11(1) (January 1): 151–165.

Chu, S. & Downes, J.J. (2002) 'Proust nose best: odors are better cues of autobiographical memory', *Memory and Cognition*, 30: 511–518.

Clair, R. P. (1998) *Organizing silence: A world of possibilities*, Albany, NY: SUNY Press.

Classen, C. (2005) *The Book of Touch*, Oxford: Berg.

Classen, C., Howes, D. & Synnott, A. (1994) *Aroma: The Cultural History of Smell*, New York, London: Routledge.

Clegg, S., and Kornberger, M. (2006.) 'Organising space', in *Space, Organizations and Management Theory*, ed. S. Clegg and M. Kornberger: 143–62. Copenhagen: Copenhagen Business School Press.

Clough, P. with J. Halley eds. (2007) *The Affective Turn: Theorizing the Social*, Durham, NC: Duke University Press.

Cohen, W. A. (1990) *The Art of the Leader*, Englewood Cliffs, NJ: Prentice Hall.

Constable, J. (1835/1951) 'Papers' in Leslie, C.R., *Memoires of the life of John Constable*, London: Phaidon Press.

Coopperrider, D.L. & Whitney, D. (2001) 'A Positive Revolution in Change', in Cooperrider, D. L. Sorenson, P., Whitney, D. & Yeager, T. eds. *Appreciative Inquiry: An Emerging Direction for Organization Development*, Champaign, IL: Stipes: 9–29.

Corbett J. M. (2003a) 'Sound organ-isation: a brief history of psychosonic management', *Ephemera: critical dialogues on organization,* 3: 261–272.

Corbett, J. M. (2003b) 'I sing the body (in)corporate: identity, displacement and the radical priority of reception', in Brigham, M., Brown C. and Associates, eds. *Critique and Inclusivity: Critical Management Studies, 3,* Lancaster: AMS Press.

Corbett, J. M. (2006) 'Scents of identity: organisation studies & the cultural conundrum of the nose', *Culture and Organisation,* 12: 221–232.

Courtney, R. (1995) *Drama and Feeling: An Aesthetic Theory*, Montreal: McGill-Queen's University Press.

Cross, N. and Dorst, K. (1998) Co-evolution of Problem and Solution Spaces in Creative Design: Observations from an Empirical Study' in Gero, J. and Maher, M. L. eds. *Computational Models of Creative Design IV*, Sydney: University of Sydney.

Cross, N. (1982) 'Designerly Ways of Knowing', *Design Studies*, 3: 221–227.

Cross, N. (2006) *Designerly Ways of Knowing*, London: Springer.

Crossley, N. (1996) *Intersubjectivity: The Fabric of Social Becoming*, London: Sage.

Csikszentmihalyi, M. and Robinson, R. (1990) *The Art of Seeing: An interpretation of the aesthetic*, Malibu, CA: Getty.

Czarniawska, B. (2008) *A Theory Of Organizing*, Cheltenham: Edward Elgar Publishing.

Dale, K. and Burrell, G. (2000) 'What shape are we in? Organization theory and the organized body' in Hassard, J., Holliday, R. and Willmott, H. ed. *Body and organization*, London: Sage: 15–30.

Dale, K. & Burrell, G. (2003) 'An-aesthetics and architecture' in Carr, A. & Hancock, P. eds. *Art and Aesthetics at Work,* London: Palgrave: 155–173

Dale, K. (2005) 'Building a social materiality: spatial and embodied politics in organizational control', *Organization,* 12: 649–678.

Dale, K., and Burrell, G. (2008) *The Spaces of Organisation and the organisation of space: Power, identity and materiality at work*, Basingstoke: Palgrave.

Darke, J. (1978) 'The Primary Generator and the Design Process' in Rogers, W. E. and Ittelson, W. H. eds., *New Directions in Environmental Design Research*, Proceedings of EDRA 9: 325337. Washington: EDRA.

Davel, E., Vergara, S.C. and Ghadiri, D.P. eds. (2007) *Administração com arte: Ensino e aprendizagem*, São Paulo: Editora Atlas.

Dawson, R. (2000) *Developing knowledge-based client relationships: the future of professional services*, Woburn, MA: Butterworth-Heinemann: 12, 43.

Day, G. and Schoemaker, P. (2004) 'Peripheral vision: sensing and acting on weak signals', *Long Range Planning*, 37: 117–121.

Day, G. and Schoemaker, P. (2004) 'Driving through the fog: managing at the edge', *Long Range Planning*, 37: 127–142.

de Bono, E. (1967) *The Use of Lateral Thinking* [Dt.: *Serious Creativity*, Stuttgart: Schäfer-Poeschel] London: Jonathan Cape.

De Certeau, M. (1984) *The Practice of Everyday Life*, Berkeley: University of California Press.

de Cock, C. (2006) 'Questioning Consensus, Cultivating Conflict', *Journal of Management Inquiry,* 15(1): 18–30.

Deal, T.E. & Key, M.K. (1998) *Corporate Celebration: play, purpose and profit at work*, San Francisco: Berrett-Koehler.

Dean, J.W., Brandes, P. & Dharwadkar, R. (1998) 'Organizational Cynicism', *Academy of Management Review*, 23: 341–352.

Dégot, V. (1987) 'Portrait of the Manager as an Artist', in *Dragon* 2: 13–49, (reprinted in *Aesthesis*, 1(2): 6–42.

Deleuze, G. and Guattari, F. (1988) *A Thousand Plateaus*, London: Athlone Press.

Denhardt, R., Denhardt, J. (2006) *The Dance of Leadership*, New York: Sharpe.

Denzin Y. and Lincoln, N.K. (2005) *Sage Handbook of Qualitative Research* (3rd ed.), London: Sage.

Denzin, N. K., Lincoln, Y. S. (2000) *Handbook of Qualitative Research* (2nd ed.), Thousand Oaks, CA: Sage Publications.

DePree, M. (1989) 'Leadership is an Art', *Human Resource Development Quarterly*, 2(4): 409–412.

DePree, M. (1989) *Leadership is an Art*, New York: Dell.

DePree, M. (1992) *Leadership Jazz*, New York: Dell.

Detienne, M. and Vernant, J.P. (1978) *Cunning Intelligence in Greek Culture and Society*, Sussex: The Harvester Press.

Diaconu, M. M. (2005) 'Tasten, Riechen, Schmecken. Eine Ästhetik der anästhesierten Sinne', Wuerzburg [The Rebellion of the Lower Senses: A Phenomenological Aesthetics of Touch, Smell, and Taste] in *Essays in Celebration of the Founding of the Organization of the Phenomenological Organisations*, eds. Cheung, C.-F., Chvatik, I., Copoeru, I., Embree, L, Iribarne J., & Sepp, H.R.: web-published at www.o-p-o.net, 2003

Diaconu, M. M. (2006) 'Secondary Senses', entry for *Handbook of Phenomenological Aesthetics, ed. by* Embree, L. and Sepp, H.R., The Hague: Kluwer: 6.

diMaggio, P. (1987) 'Managers of the Arts', Washington, D.C.: Seven Locks Press.

Dewey, J. (1930/1988) *Qualitative Thought,* in Boydston, J-A. ed. *The Later Works, 1925–1953* (vol. 5), Carbondale: Southern Illinois University Press.

Dewey, J. (1934) *Art as Experience*, New York: Perigee Books.

Drobnick, J. (1998) 'Reveries, Assaults and Evaporating Presences: Olfactory Dimensions in Contemporary Art', PARACHUTE #89, (Winter): 10–19

Drobnick, J. (2006) *The Smell Culture Reader*, Oxford: Berg Publishers

Duke, D. L. (1986) 'The aesthetics of leadership', *Educational Administration Quarterly*, 22: 7–27.

Eastman, C. M. (1970) 'On the Analysis of the Intuitive Design Process' in Moore, G. T. ed., *Emerging Methods in Environmental Design and Planning*, Cambridge, MA: MIT Press.

Eastman, C., McCracken, M. and Newstetter, W. eds. (2001) *Design Knowing and Learning: Cognition in Design Education*, Oxford: Elsevier.

Eco, U. (1990) *La definizione dell'arte* [The Definition of Art]. Milano: Mursia [1st ed 1968].

Edwards, D.J.A. (1984) 'The experience of interpersonal touch during a personal growth', *Human Relations*, 37(9): 769–780

Ehrenzweig, A. (1965) *The Psychoanalysis of Artistic Vision and Hearing*, New York: George Braziller.

Ehrenzweig, A. (1967) *The Hidden Order of Art*, Berkeley: University of California Press.

Einhorn, R. (1980) *Judgment and Choice: The Psychology of Decision*, Chichester: John Wiley and Sons.

Eoyang, E. (1989) 'Chaos misread: or, there's wonton in my soup!', *Comparative Literature Studies*, 26: 271–84.

Erlande-Brandenburg, A. (1989) *La dame à la licorne*, Paris: Éditions de la Réunion des musées nationaux.

Esposito, Roberto (2010) *Pensiero vivente: Origine e attualità della filosofia italiana* [Living Thought: The Origin and Present State of Italian Philosophy] Torino: Einaudi.

Fawcett, W. and Chadwick, A. (2007) 'Space-time management and office floorspace demand: Applied experience and mathematical simulations', *Journal of Corporate Real Estate*, 9(1): 5–24

Featherstone, M. (1991) *Consumer Culture and Postmodernism,* London: Sage.

Feng, G. and English, J. (1972) *Lao Tsu: Tao Te Ching*, New York: Alfred Knopf.

Ferreira, A.M. (2005) *Fazer pela vida. Um retrato de Fernando Pessoa, o empreendedor*, Lisboa: Assírio & Alvim.

Flecker, J. and Hofbauer, J. (1998) 'The New Model Worker', in Thompson, P. and Warhurst, C. eds. *Workplaces of the Future*, Basingstoke: Palgrave.

Fleming, P. & Sewell, G. (2002) 'Looking for the good soldier Svejk: Alternative modalities of resistance in the contemporary workplace', *Sociology*, 36: 857–873.

Fleming, P. & Spicer, A. (2004). 'You can checkout anytime, but you can never leave: spatial boundaries in a high commitment organization', *Human Relations,* 57(1): 75–94.

Flyvbjerg, B. (2001) *Making Social Science Matter*, Cambridge: Cambridge University Press.

Foucault, M. (1977, 1991) *Discipline and Punish*, London: Allen Lane.

Freud, S. (1911) 'Formulations on the Two Principles of Mental Functioning' in *The Standard Edition of the Complete Psychological Works of Sigmund Freud*, Volume XII (1911–1913): The Case of Schreber, Papers on Technique and Other Works: 213–226.

Fry, L.W., Vitucci, S. & Cedillo, M. (2005) 'Spiritual leadership and army transformation: Theory, measurement, and establishing a baseline', *Leadership Quarterly*, 16: 835–862.

Fuller, J. B., Simmering, M. J., Marler, L. E., Cox, S. S., Bennett, R. B., & Cheramie, R. A. (2011) 'Exploring Touch as a Positive Workplace Behaviour', *Human Relations*, 64(2), 231–256.

Gabriel, Y. (2000) *Storytelling in Organizations: Facts, Fictions, and Fantasies*, Oxford: Oxford University Press.

Gagliardi, P. ed. (1990) *Symbols and Artifacts: Views of the Corporate Landscape*, Berlin: Walter de Gruyter.

Gagliardi, P. (1996) 'Exploring the Aesthetic Side of Organizational Life', in Clegg, S. R., Hardy, C. and Nord, W. R. eds. *Handbook of Organizational Studies,* Sage: London: 565–580.

Gagliardi, P. (2006) 'Exploring the Aesthetic Side of Organizational Life', Clegg, S. R. et. al., eds. *The Sage Handbook of Organization Studies* (2nd ed), London, Thousand Oaks and New Delhi: Sage: 701–724.

Gendlin, E. T. (1992) 'The Primacy of the Body, not the primacy of perception: How the body knows the situation and philosophy', *Man and World*, 25(3/4): 341–353.

Gherardi, S. (2006) *Organizational Knowledge: The Texture of Workplace Learning,* Oxford: Blackwell publishing.

Gibson, J (1986) *The Ecological Approach to Visual Perception*, Hillsdale, NJ: Lawrence Erlbaum.

Gieryn, T. (2000) 'A space for place in sociology', *Annual Review of Sociology*, 26: 463–496.

Gieryn, T. (2002) 'What buildings do', *Theory and Society*, 31: 35–74.

Gilmore, S. & Warren, S. (2007) 'Unleashing the power of the unconscious: a case of craft, graft and disputed premises', *Tamara: Journal of Critical Postmodern Organization Science*, 6(1): 106–122.

Glindemann, D., Dietrich, A., Staerk, H. J. & Kuschk, P. The Two Smells of Touched or Pickled Iron – (Skin) Carbonyl-Hydrocarbons and Organophosphines (2006) *Angewandte Chemie Int*, 118(42)

Golembiewski, R.T. ed., *Handbook of Organizational Behavior* (2nd ed.), New York: Marcel Dekker: 611–629.

Goodsell, C. T. (1992) 'The Public Administrator as Artisan', *Public Administration Review*, 52: 246–53.

Gordon, G. L. (1973) *The Science of Design*, Cambridge: Cambridge University Press.

Goshal, S. (2005) 'Bad Management Theories Are Destroying Good Management Practices', *Academy of Management Learning and Education*, 4 (1): 75–91.

Gratton, L. (2004) *The Democratic Enterprise*, London: Financial Times/Prentice Hall.

Gray, R. T. (1993) 'The Dialectic of 'Enscentment': Patrick Suesskind's 'Das Parfum' as Critical History of Enlightenment Culture', PMLA 108 (1993): 489–505.

Greenfield, A. (2008) T*hink Tank*. http://www.adobe.com/designcentre/thinktank/greenfield.html

Griffin, J. (2000) *Fernando Pessoa – Selected Poems (introduction)*, London: Penguin Classics.

Grint, K. (2001) *The Arts of Leadership*, Oxford: Oxford University Press.

Grove, A. (1999) *Only the Paranoid Survive: How to Exploit the Crisis Points that Challenge Every Company*, New York: Doubleday.

Guba, E. G., and Lincoln, Y.S. (1994) 'Competing Paradigms in Qualitative Research'. In Denzin, N. K. & Lincoln, Y.S. eds., *Handbook of qualitative research,* London: Sage: 105–117.

Guillet de Monthoux, P. (2004) *The Art Firm: Aesthetic Management and Metaphysical Marketing*, Stanford: Stanford University Press.

Guillet de Monthoux, P. (2006) 'The Oppression Blues – Or the Aesthetics of a Critical Theorist', *Consumption Markets & Culture*, 9(2): 145–146.

Guillet de Monthoux, P., Gustafsson, C. and Sjöstrand, S-E. eds. (2007) *Aesthetic Leadership: Managing Fields of Flow in Art and Business*, Basingstoke: Palgrave Macmillan.

Hagen, U. (1973) *Respect for Acting*, New York: MacMillan.

Halford, S. (2005) 'Hybrid workspace: re-spatializations of work, organization and management', *New Technology, Work and Employment*, 20: 19–33.

Hambrick, D. and Frederickson, J. (2001) 'Are you sure you have strategy?' *Academy of Management Executive*, 15 (4): 48–59.

Hamel, G. and Välikangas, L. (2003) 'The quest for resilience', *Harvard Business Review*, September: 52–63.

Hancock, P. (2002) 'Aestheticizing the world of organization: Creating beautiful untrue things', *Tamara: Journal of Critical Postmodern Organization Science*, 2(1): 91–106; reprinted as Hancock, P. (2003) in Carr, A. & Hancock, P. eds. *Art and Aesthetics at Work,* London: Palgrave: 174 – 94.

Hancock, P. (2005) 'Uncovering the Semiotic in Organizational Aesthetics', *Organization*, 12(1) 29–50.

Hancock, P. and Spicer, A. (2011) 'Academic architecture and the constitution of the new model worker', *Culture and Organization*, 17 (2), March: 91–105.

Hassard, J., Holliday, R. & Wilmott, H. (2000) *Body and Organ-isation*, London: Sage.

Hatch, M. J., Kostera, M. and Kozminski, A. K. (2004) *The Three Faces of Leadership: Manager, Artist, Priest*, London: Blackwell.

Hatch, M.J. (1990) 'The Symbolics of Office Design', in Gagliardi, P. ed., *Symbols and Artifacts*, New York: Aldine de Gruyter.

Heaney, S (2007) 'The Pathos of Things', Manchester: *Guardian Newspaper*, Saturday 24th November.

Heaney, S. (1995) *The Redress of Poetry*, London: Faber and Faber.

Heidegger, M. (1953/1959) *An Introduction to Metaphysics* (trans. Ralph Manheim), New Haven: Yale University Press.

Heidegger, M. (1962) *Being and Time.* (trans. John MacQuarrie and Edward Robinson), Oxford: Blackwell.

Heidegger, M. (2004) *On the Essence of Language: The Metaphysics of Language and the Essencing of the Word*, New York: SUNY.

Hein, P. (2003) *The Man Who Wrote 10,000 Grooks.* www.powerweb.net/playandlive/piethein.htm

Herbst, P. H. (1976) *Alternatives to Hierarchies*, Leiden: Martin Nijhoff.

Herrigel, E. (1953/85) *Zen in the Art of Archery*, London: Arkana.

Hertz, R. (1997) 'Introduction: reflexivity and voice', in R. Hertz, r ed. *Reflexivity and Voice*, Thousand Oaks, CA: Sage.

Hertz, R. (2007) *The Scent of Desire: Discovering Our Enigmatic Sense of Smell*, New York: William Morrow.

Hockey, J. (2009) 'Switch On': sensory work in the infantry', *Work, Employment and Society*, 23(3): 477–493.

Hoffman, D. (1998) *Visual Intelligence: How We Create What We See*, London: W.W. Norton.

Holstein, J.A., Gubrium, J.F. (2009) *Handbook of Constructionist Research*, New York: Guilford Press.

Howes, D. (2003) *Sensual Relations: Engaging in the Senses in Culture and Social Theory*, Ann Arbor: The University of Michigan Press.

Hickson, D. (1986) *Top decisions: Strategic decision-making in organisations*, Chichester: John Wiley and Sons.

Hockney, D. (2001) 'Secret Knowledge: Rediscovering the lost techniques of the Old Masters', London: Thames and Hudson.

Ihde, D. (2007) *Listening and Voice: Phenomenologies of Sound*, Albany: SUNY Press.

Inkpen, A. and Choudhury, N. (1995) 'The seeking of strategy where it is not: towards a theory of strategy change', *Strategic Management Journal* 16: 13–32.

Isenburg, D. (1984) 'Top decisions: Strategic decision-making in organisations', *Harvard Business Review*, Dec/Jan, 81–90.

Jacobs, C. & Coghlan, D. (2005) 'Sound from Silence: On listening in organizational learning', *Human Relations*, 58(1): 115–138

Jacobs, C. (2003) *Managing Organizational Responsiveness – Toward a Theory of Responsive Practice*, Wiesbaden: DUV.

Jacobson, M. (1996) Art and Business in a Brave New World, *Organization*, 3: 243

Jacques, R. (1995) *Manufacturing the Employee*, Thousand Oaks, CA: Sage.

James, W. (1890) *The Principles of Psychology*, New York: Henry Holt & Co.

James, W. (1911/96) *Some Problems of Philosophy*, Lincoln and London: University of Nebraska Press.

Janik, A. and Toulmin, S. (1973) *Wittgenstein's Vienna*, New York: Simon & Schuster.

Jimenez, M. (2005) *La querelle de l'art contemporain*, Paris: Gallimard.

Jobs, S. (2005) 'Stay Hungry. Stay Foolish', Stanford University Website: http://news-service.stanford.edu/news/2005/june15/grad-061505.html (accessed April, 2007).

Johnson, B. (1989) *A World of Difference*, Baltimore: Johns Hopkins University Press.

Johnson, M. (2007) *The Meaning of the Body: aesthetics of human understanding*, Chicago: University of Chicago Press.

Jones, M., Moore, O., Michael, D. and Snyder, R.C. eds. (1988) *Inside Organizations: Understanding the Human Dimension*, Newbury Park: Sage.

Jossey-Bass. Schrage, M. (2000) *Serious Play: How the World's Best Companies Simulate to Innovate*, Boston: Harvard Business School Press.

Journal of Business Strategy, 56 (5) 2005 (Special Issue on Arts-based learning for business).

Jullien, F. (2000) *Detour and Access: Strategies of Meaning in China and Greece*, New York: Zone Books.

Jullien, F. (2004) 'In Praise of Blandness: Proceeding from Chinese Thought and Aesthetics', Korsmeyer, C. *Making Sense of Taste, Food and Philosophy*, Cornell: Cornell University Press.

Jullien, F. (2004) *A Treatise on Efficacy: Between Western and Chinese Thinking*, Honolulu: University of Hawaii Press.

Jung, C. G. (1921) *Psychologische Typen* [trans. *Psychological Types*, Bollingen Series XX (6) Princeton: Princeton University Press].

Jütte, R. (2005) *A History of the Senses: from antiquity to cyberspace*, Cambridge, UK: Polity Press.

Kant, I. (1781) *Kritik der reinen Vernunft* [(1999) Critique of Pure Reason, Cambridge: Cambridge University Press.

Kaczmarczyk, S. and Murtough, J. (2002) 'Measuring the performance of innovative workplaces', *Journal of Facilities Management*, 1(2): 163–76.

Kant, I. (1952) *Critique of Judgement* (trans. J. C. Meredith), Oxford: Clarendon Press.

Karanian, B. (2007) *Entrepreneurial Leadership: a balancing act in engineering and science*, ASEE June meeting, Honolulu, HI.

Käser, P. (2007) 'Quiet Time: A Positive Organizational Intervention?', paper presented at the European Academy of Management (EURAM) Paris (France) 16.-19.05.2007.

Katz D, (1989 orig.1925) *The World of Touch*, (trans. by L E Krueger) Hillsdale, NJ: Lawrence Erlbaum Associates.

Keats, J. (1817/2002) 'Letters to G. and T. Keats, 21st December 1817', in G.F. Scott, ed. *Selected letters of John Keats*, Cambridge, MA: Harvard University Press.

Kelley, T. (2001) *The Art of Innovation*, New York: Random House.

Kelley, T. and Littman, J. (2004) *The Art of Innovation: Lessons in Creativity from IDEO, America's Leading Design Firm*, London: Profile Books Ltd.

Kets de Vries, M. F. R. (2001) 'Creating authentizotic organizations: Well-functioning individuals in vibrant companies', *Human Relations*, 1(54): 101–111.

King, I.W. (forthcoming) 'Epistemological positions and Kant's Copernican Revolution' forthcoming *Management Learning*.

Knights, D. and Willmott, H. (1989) 'Power and Subjectivity at Work', *Sociology*, 23(4): 535–58.

Koivunen, N. (2006) 'Auditive Leadership Culture. Lessons from Symphony Orchestras', in Hosking, D.M. and McNamee, S. eds.*The Social Construction of Organization*, Oslo: Liber: 91–111.

Koivunen, N. and Rehn, A. eds. (2009) *Creativity and the Contemporary Economy*, Copenhagen: Liber-Copenhagen Business School Press.

Kolodner, J. L. and Wills, L. M. (1996) 'Powers of Observation in Creative Design', *Design Studies*, 17: 385–416.

Kornberger, M. and Clegg, S. (2004) 'Bringing space back in', *Organization Studies*, 25: 1095–1114.

Kuhn, J. W. (1996) 'The misfit between organization theory and processional art: A comment on White and Strati', *Organization*, 3: 219–24.

Küpers, W. (2002) 'Phenomenology of Aesthetic Organising – Ways towards Aesthetically Responsive Organ-isations' in *Consumption, Markets and Cultures*, 5(1): 31–68.

Küpers, W. (2004) 'Art and Leadership' in Burns, J. M., Goethals, R. R. & Sorenson, G. J. (2004) *Encyclopaedia of Leadership*, Thousand Oaks, CA: Sage: 47–54.

Küpers, W. (2005) 'Embodied Implicit and Narrative Knowing in Organizations' in *Journal of Knowledge Management*, 9(6): 113–133.

Küpers, W. (2005a) 'Envisioning a Refined Existence between the Sense of Reality and the Sense of Possibility through a Responsive Encounter between Art and Commerce' in Brellochs, M. & Schraat, H. eds. *Sophisticated Survival Techniques - Strategies in Art and Economy*, Berlin KADMOS: 372–397.

Küpers, W. (2009) 'Perspective on integral 'Pheno-Pragma-Practice' in organizations', *International Journal of Management Practice*, 4(1): 27–50.

Küpers, W. (2010) 'Inter-Places" Embodied Spaces & Places of and for Leader-/Followership - Phenomenological Perspectives on relational localities & tele-presences of leading and following' in *Environment, Space, Place,* 2(1): 79–121.

Küpers, W. & Edwards, M. (2008) 'Integrating Plurality – Towards an Integral Perspective on Leadership and Organ-isation' in Wankel, C. ed. *Handbook of 21st Century Management*, London: Sage: 311–322.

Ladkin, D. (2006) 'The enchantment of the charismatic leader: Charisma reconsidered as aesthetic encounter', *Leadership*, 2: 165–179.

Langer, S. (1957) *Philosophy in a New Key,* Buckingham: Open University Press.

Lash, S. & Urry, J. (1994), *Economies of signs and space,* London: Sage.

Lawson, B. (1972) *Problem Solving in Architectural Design*, Doctoral Thesis, University of Aston, Birmingham.

Lawson, B. (1979) 'Cognitive Strategies in Architectural Design', Ergonomics, 22: 59–68.

Lawson, B. (1994) *Design in Mind*, Oxford: Architectural Press.

Lawson, B. (1997) *How Designers Think: The Design Process Demystified* (3rd ed.) London: Architectural Press.

Lawson, B. (2004) *What Designers Know*, Burlington, MA: Architectural Press.

Leder, D. (1990) *The Absent Body*, Chicago: University of Chicago Press.

Levin, D. M. (1989) *The Listening Self: Personal Growth, Social Change and the Closure of Metaphysics*, London, New York: Routledge.

Levin, D.M. (1985) *The Body's Recollection of Being: phenomenological psychology and the deconstruction of nihilism*, London: Routledge & Kegan Paul.

Lefebvre, H. (1991) *The Production of Space*, Oxford: Blackwell.

Libet, B., Freeman, A. and Sutherland, K. (2004) *The Volitional Brain: Toward a Neuroscience of Free Will*, Thorverton, UK: Imprint Academic.

Lincoln, Y.S. and Guba, E.G. (1985) *Naturalistic Inquiry.* Sage, Beverly. Hills, CA.

Linstead, S. (2002) 'Organizational kitsch', *Organization,* 9(4), 657–682.

Linstead, S. (2002) 'Organizational Kitsch', *Organization*, 9(4): 657–682.

Linstead, S. and Höpfl, H. eds. (2000) *The Aesthetics of Organization*, London: Sage.

Littlefield, D. (2009*)* *Good Office Design*, London: RIBA Publishing.

Lloyd, P. and Scott, P. (1995) 'Difference in Similarity: Interpreting the Architectural Design Process', *Planning and Design*, 22: 383–406.

Locke, E.A. & Latham, G.P. (1984) *Goal Setting: a motivational technique that works*, Englewood Cliffs, NJ: Prentice-Hall.

Loomis, J. & Lederman, S.J. (1986) 'Tactual Perception' in Boff, K. R., Kaufman, L. and Thomas, J. P. eds. *Handbook of Perception and Human Performance*, New York: Wiley & Sons.

Lopes, M.P. & Cunha, M.P. (2005) 'All that Glitters is not Gold: A critically-constructive analysis of positive organizational behavior', paper presented at the *4th Conference of the Iberoamerican Academy of Management,* Lisbon, December.

Lourenço, E. (1986) *Fernando, Rei da nossa Baviera,* Lisboa: Imprensa Nacional Casa da Moeda.

Lupton, D. (1996) *Food, the Body and the Self,* London: Sage.

Macmurray, J. (1957) *The Self as Agent,* London: Faber.

Magrelli, V. (2006) *Profilo del dada* [A Profile of Dada], Bari: Laterza.

Mangham, I. L. (1993) *Organizzazione come teatro,* Milano: Raffaello Cortina Editore.

Manville, B. & Ober, J. (2003) *A Company of Citizens,* Boston, MA: Harvard Business School Press.

March, J. (1994) *A Primer on Decision Making: How Decisions Happen.* New York: The Free Press.

Mariampolski, H. (2006) *Ethnography for Marketers: A Guide to Consumer Immersion,* London: Thousand Oaks, CA: Sage.

Marmot, A. and Eley, J. (2000) *Office Space Planning: Designing for Tomorrow's Workplace,* New York: McGraw-Hill.

Martin, P.Y. (2002) 'Sensations, Bodies, and the 'Spirit of a Place': Aesthetics in Residential Organizations for the Elderly', *Human Relations,* 5(7): 861–885.

Martin, R. L. (2007) *The Opposable Mind – How Successful Leaders Win Through Integrative Thinking,* Boston, MA: Harvard Business School Press.

Matteucci, G. (2010) *Il sapere estetico come prassi antropologica. Cassirer, Gehlen e la configurazione del sensibile* [Aesthetic Knowledge as Anthropological Praxis: Cassirer, Gehlen and the Configuration of the Sensible]. Pisa: Edizioni ETS.

Maturana, H. R. and Varela, F. J. (1984) *El árbol del conocimiento* [English translation: The Tree of Knowledge, Boston MA: Shambala].

Mayer, J. D., Salovey, P. and Caruso, D. R. (2004) 'Emotional Intelligence: Theory, Findings, and Implications', *Psychological Inquiry,* 15: 197–215.

McKinlay, A. & Starkey, K. (1998) *Foucault, Management and Organization Theory: from Panopticon to Technologies of Self,* London: Sage.

McGrath, J. (1982) 'Dilemmatics, The study of research choices and dilemmas', in McGrath, J.E. , Martin, J., and Kulka, R.A. eds. *Judgement calls in research,* Newbury Park, CA: Sage: 69–102.

McGregor, W. (2000) 'The future of workspace management', *Facilities,* 18(3/4): 138–143.

Merholz, P., Schauer, B., Verba, D. and Wilkens, T. (2008) *Subject to Change: Creating Great Products for an Uncertain World,* Sebastopol, CA: O'Reilly Media, Inc.: 27, 81.

Merleau-Ponty, M. (1945) *Phénoménologie de la Perception* [trans. (1962) Phenomenology of Perception, New York: Routledge].

Merleau-Ponty, M. (1960) *Signs,* Evanston: Northwestern University Press.

Merleau-Ponty, M. (1962) *Phenomenology of Perception,* trans, Colin Smith. London: Routledge.

Merleau-Ponty, M. (1964) 'Eye and Mind', reprinted in *The Merleau-Ponty Aesthetics Reader,* ed. Johnson, G., Evanston, IL, Northwestern University Press.

Merleau-Ponty, M. (1964) *Sense and Nonsense,* Evanston, IL: North-western University Press.

Merleau-Ponty, M. (1968) 'The Intertwining the Chiasm', in (1995) *The Visible and the Invisible,* Evanston, IL, Northwestern University Press: 130–155.

Merleau-Ponty, M. (2004) *The World of Perception,* London: Routledge.

Minahan, S. and Wolfram, J. Cox, eds. (2007) *The Aesthetic Turn in Management,* London: Ashgate.

Mintzberg, H., Raisinghani, D., and Theoret, A., (1976) 'The Structure of 'Unstructured' Decision Processes, *Administrative Science Quarterly* 21, 246–275.

Morgan G. (1980) 'Paradigm, metaphors, and puzzle solving in organization theory', in *Administrative Science Quarterly* 25: 605–22.

Morgan, G. (1981) 'The schismatic metaphor and its implications for organizational analysis', *Organization Studies,* 2(1): 23–44.

Morgan, G. (1996) *Immaginizzazione,* Milano: Franco Angeli.

Myerson, J., and Ross. P. (2003) *The 21st century Office,* London: Lawrence King.

Nahavandi, A. (1997) *The Art and Science of Leadership,* Upper Saddle River, NJ: Prentice Hall.

Nathan, M. & Doyle, J. (2002) *The State of the Office: The politics and geography of working space,* London: The Industrial Society.

Nehamas, A. (2001) 'The Sleep of Reason', *Representations,* 71: 37–54

Neuman, J.H. & Baron, R.A. (2005) 'Aggression in the Workplace: A social-psychological perspective' in Fox, S. & Spector, P.E. eds., *Counterproductive Work Behavior: Investigations of actors and targets,* Washington, DC: American Psychological Association: 13–40.

Nonaka. I. (2000) *Enabling Knowledge Creation: how to unlock the mystery of tacit knowledge and release the power of innovation,* Oxford: Oxford University Press: 292.

Norem, J.K., & Chang, E.C. (2002) 'The Positive Psychology of Negative Thinking', *Journal of Clinical Psychology,* 58: 993–1001.

Novitz, D. (1992) *The Boundaries of Art,* Philadelphia: Temple University Press.

O'Reilly, C. & Pfeffer, J. (2000) *Hidden Value: How great companies achieve extraordinary results with ordinary people*, Boston, MA: Harvard Business School Press.

Oldham, G. R., Cummings, A., Mischel, L. J., Schmidtke, J. M. & Zhou, J. (1995) 'Listen while you work? Quasi-experimental relations between personal-stereo headset use and employee work responses', in *Journal of Applied Psychology*, 80(5): 547–564.

Organ, D.W. (1988) *Organizational Citizenship Behavior: The good soldier syndrome*, Lexington, MA: Lexington Books.

Oswick, C. (1996) 'Insights into diagnosis: an exploration using visual metaphor' in Oswick, C. and Grant, D. eds. *Organization Development: Metaphorical Explorations*, London: Pitman.

Owen, C. L. (1998a) 'Design Research: Building the Knowledge Base', *Design Studies*, 19: 9–20.

Owen, C. L. (1998b): 'Design, Advanced Planning and Product Development', 3o Congresso Brasileiro de Pesquisa e Desenvolvimento em Design, October 1998, Rio de Janeiro, Brazil: Institute of Design, Illinois Institute of Technology.

Pareyson, L. (1996) *Estetica. Teoria della formatività* [Aesthetics: Theory of Formativity], Milano: Bompiani (1st ed 1954).

Paterson, P. (2007) *The Senses of Touch: Haptics, Affects and Technologies*, Senses and Sensibilities, Oxford: Berg.

Paulson, W. (1991) 'Literature, complexity, interdisciplinarity', in Hales, N. ed. Chaos and Order, Chicago: University of Chicago Press.

Paz, O. (1985) *Aparencia desnuda. La obra de Marcel Duchamp*. México: Ediciones Era.

Pearson, C.M., Andersson, L.M. & Porath, C.L. (2000) 'Assessing and Attacking Workplace Incivility', *Organizational Dynamics*, 2(29): 123–137.

Pelzer L. (2002) 'Disgust and Organization', *Human Relations*, 55(7): 841–860.

Perrow, C. (2000) 'An Organizational Analysis of Organizational Theory', *Contemporary Sociology*, 29(3): 469–476.

Pfeffer, J. and Fong, C. T. (2002) 'The End of Business Schools? Less Success Than Meets the Eye', *Academy of Management Learning and Education*, 1 (1): 78–95.

Pine, B. J., and Gilmore, J. H. eds. (1999) *The Experience Economy: work is theatre & every business a stage*, Boston, MA: Harvard Business School Press.

Pink, D. (2005) *A Whole New Mind – Why Right-Brained Thinkers Will Rule the Future*, New York: Penguin Group – Riverhead: introduction.

Plessner, H. (1975) *Die Stufen des Organischen und der Mensch* (3rd ed.), Berlin & New York: de Gruyter.

Polanyi, M. (1962) *Personal Knowledge*, New York: Harper and Row.

Polanyi, M. (1966) *The Tacit Dimension* [Dt.: Implizites Wissen, Suhrkamp: Frankfurt am Main], New York: Doubleday.

Popper, K. R. (1934) *Logik der Forschung*, Wien: Springer.

Rittel, H. W. J. and Webber, M. M. (1973) 'Dilemmas in a General Theory of Planning', *Policy Sciences*, 4: 155–169.

Postrel, V. (2003) *The Substance of Style: How the Rise of Aesthetic Value Is Remaking Commerce, Culture, and Consciousness*, London: Harper Collins.

Pound, E (1947) *A Guide to Kulchur*, New York: New Directions.

Prahalad, C. K. (2004) 'The blinders of dominant logic', *Long Range Planning*, 37: 171–180.

Prahalad, C. K. and Ramaswamy, V. (2004) *The Future of Competition,* Boston, MA: Harvard Business School Press: 10.

Proença, T. (2010) 'Self-managed Work Teams: An enabling or coercive nature', *International Journal of Human Resource Management*, 21: 337–354.

Proust, M. (1913) *A la recherche du temps perdu*, Paris: Grasset.

Rafaeli, A. and Pratt, M.G. eds. (2005) *Artifacts and Organizations: Beyond Mere Symbolism*, Mahwah, NJ: Lawrence Erlbaum Associates Inc.

Ramirez, R. (1991) *The Beauty of Social Organization*, Munchen: Accedo.

Oseland, N. (1999) 'Environmental Factors Affecting Office Worker Performance: A Review of Evidence', CIBSE, London: Palgrave: 104–23.

Perrow, C. (1991) 'A Society of Organizations,' *Theory & Society*, 20(6): 725–762

Postrel, V. (2003) *The Substance of Style: How the Rise of Aesthetic Value Is Remaking Commerce, Culture, and Consciousness*, London: Harper Collins.

Price, I. and Akhlaghi, F. (1999), 'New patterns in facilities management: industry best practice and new organisational theory', *Facilities*, 17(5/6):159–66.

Rafaeli, A. and Pratt, M.G. eds. (2006) *Artifacts and Organizations: Beyond Mere Symbolism*, Mahwah, NJ: LEA.

Ramirez, R. (2005) 'The aesthetics of cooperation', *European Management Review*, 2: 28–35.

Raphals, L. (1992) *Knowing Words: Wisdom and Cunning in the Classical Tradition of China and Greece*, Ithaca, New York: Cornell University Press.

Raudenbush, B. (2005) 'Positive Effects of Odorant Administration on Humans'. A Review prepared for the Sense of Smell Institute: http://www.senseofsmell.org/papers/B_Raudenbush_pos_effects.pdf

Reid, T. (1764) *An Inquiry into the Human Mind on the Principles of Common Sense*, Edinburgh: Kincaid and Bell.

Reinarz, J. (2003) 'Uncommon Scents: Smell and Victorian England' in Ringham, F. and Martin, B. eds. *Sense and Scent: An Exploration of Olfactory Meaning*, London: Philomel.

Ridderstraåle, J. and Nordström, K. (2000) *Funky Business: talent makes capital dance*, Harlow: Pearson Education.

Ridderstraåle, J. and Nordström, K. (2000) *Funky Business Forever: how to enjoy capitalism*, Stockholm: BookHouse Publishing.

Rittel, H. W. J. (1972) 'On the Planning Crisis: Systems Analysis of the First and Second Generations', *Bedrift Sokonomen*, 8: 309–396.

Ropo, A. & Parviainen, J. (2001) 'Leadership and bodily knowledge in expert organizations: epistemological rethinking' in *Scandinavian Journal of Management*, 17(1): 1–18.

Rowe, P. G. (1987) *Design Thinking*, Cambridge, MA London, UK: MIT Press.

Rowland, G. (2003) *Shall We Dance? A Design Epistemology for Organizational Learning and Performance*, Ithaca, New York: Ithaca College: 20–21

Rüedi, P. (1996) 'The audible landscape' in *ECM: Sleeves of Desire*, Baden: Lars Müller.

Ruskin, J. (1903) *Modern Painters*, London: George Allen.

Ruskin, J. (1927) *The Complete Works*, London: Nicholson and Weidenfeld.

Sackett, P.R. and Larson, Jr. J. A., (1990) 'Research strategies and tactics in industrial and organisational psychology', in Dunnette, M.D. and Hough, L.H., (9th edition.) *Handbook of industrial and organisational psychology*, Palo Alto, CA: Consulting Psychologists press: 419–489.

Samier, E. A. and Bates, R. J. eds. (2006) *Aesthetic Dimensions of Educational and Administrative Leadership*, New York: Routledge.

Sandelands, L. E. (1998) *Feeling and Form in Social Life*, Lanham, MD: Rowman & Littlefield.

Sartre, J.-P. (1943) *L'Être et le néant: essai d'ontologie phénoménologique*, Paris: Gallimard [trans. Hazel E. Barnes, *Being and Nothingness: An Essay in Phenomenological Ontology* (2nd ed.) London: Routledge, 2003].

Sawyer, K. (2007) *Group Genius: The creative power of collaboration*, New York: Basic Books.

Sawyer, R. K. (2006) *Explaining Creativity: The science of human innovation*, New York: Oxford University Press.

Scalfi A. (2007), Untitled 2004 # Paris, in *Aesthesis*, 1(1): 46–47 + CD [00:20:38].

Scandura, T. and Williams, E.A., (2000) Research Methodology in Management: Current Practices, Trends, and Implications for future Research, *Academy of Management Journal*, 43(6): 1248–1264.

Schön, D. A. (1983) *The Reflective Practitioner*, New York: Basic.

Schön, D. A. (1988) *Educating the Reflective Practitioner*, San Francisco: Jossey-Bass.

Schreyögg, G., and Geiger, D., (2007) 'The Significance of Distinctiveness: A Proposal for Rethinking Organisational Knowledge', *Organisation*, 14(1):77–100.

Schwartz, D. (1994) 'Visual Ethnography: Using photographs in qualitative research', *Qualitative Sociology*, 12 (2): 119–154.

Schuler, D. and Namioka, A. eds. (1993) *Participatory Design: Principles and Practices*, Hillsdale, NJ: Lawrence Erlbaum Associates.

Seifter, H. (2005) 'Surfacing Creativity: An interview with Terry McGraw', *Journal of Business Strategy*, 56(5): 6.

Serres, M. (1995) *Angels: A Modern Myth*, Paris: Flammarion Press.

Serres, M. (2003) *Les cinq sens* (1st ed. 1985), Paris: Hachette.

Severino, E. (2006) *La filosofia futura: Oltre il dominio del divenire* [Future Philosophy: Beyond the Dominion of Becoming] Milan: Biblioteca Universale Rizzoli (1st ed. 1989).

Shilling C. (1993) *The Body and Social Theory*, London/Newbury Park/New Delhi: Sage.

Simmel, G. (1916) *Rembrandt, Ein kunstphilosophischer Versuch*, Leipzig: Kurt Wolff Verlag (trans. A. Scott and H. Staubmann, *Rembrandt: An Essay in the Philosophy of Art*, New York: Routledge].

Simon, H. A. (1955) 'A Behavioural Model of Rational Choice', *Quarterly Journal of Economics*, 69: 99–118.

Simon, H. A. (1969) *The Sciences of the Artificial*, Cambridge, MA: MIT Press.

Singer, L. (1993) 'Merleau-Ponty on the concept of style' in Johnson, G. A. ed., *The Merleau-Ponty Aesthetics Reader*, Evanston IL: Northwestern University Press.

Sloterdijk, P. (1988) *Critique of Cynical Reason*, Minneapolis: University of Minnesota Press.

Smith, A. (1776/1991) *An Inquiry into the Nature and Causes of the Wealth of Nations*, London: Everyman.

Smithson, R. (1966/2004) 'Entropy and new monuments' in Foster, H., Krauss, R., Bois, Y-A, and Buchloh, B. eds. *Art Since 1900*, London: Thames and Hudson.

Snowden, D. (2002) *Complex Acts of Knowing-Paradox and Descriptive Self-Awareness*, Basingstoke, England: IBM United Kingdom Limited: 6, 9.

Snyder, E. (1990) *Persuasive Business Speaking*, New York: American Management Association.

Soares, B. (2003) *O livro do desassossego*, Lisboa: Assírio & Alvim.

Soja, E. (1996) *Thirdspace: Journeys to Los Angeles and other real-and-imagined places*, Oxford: Blackwell.

Soper, K. (1995) *What is Nature?* Oxford: Blackwell.

Spang, R. L. (2001) *The Invention of the Restaurant: Paris and modern gastronomic culture*, Cambridge: Harvard University Press.

Spencer Brown, G. (1969) *Laws of Form*, London: Allen and Unwin.

Stacey, R. (2001) *Complex Responsive Processes in Organizations: Learning and Knowledge Creation*, London: Routledge.

Stake, R. (1998) 'Case Studies' in Denzin, N. & Lincoln, Y. eds. *Strategies of Qualitative Inquiry*, London: Sage: 86–109.

Stanislavski, C. (1936) *An Actor Prepares*, New York: Routledge.

Steele, F. (1973) *Physical Settings and Organizational Development*, London: Addison-Wesley.

Sterman, J. D. (2001) *Business Dynamics: Systems Thinking and Modeling for a Complex World*, New York: McGraw-Hill.

Sternberg, R. J. (2003) *Wisdom, Intelligence, and Creativity Sythesized*, Cambridge: Cambridge University Press.

Steyaert C., Hjorth D. (2002), "Thou Art a Scholar, Speak to It…" – on Spaces of Speech: A Script', in *Human Relations*, 55(7): 767–97.

Stokes, L. and Logan, R. (2004) *Collaborate to Compete: Driving Profitability in the Knowledge Economy*, Toronto, Canada: Wiley: 8.

Strati, A. (1992) 'Aesthetic Understanding of Organizational Life', *Academy of Management Review*, 17(3): 568 – 581.

Strati, A. (1996) 'Organizations viewed through the lens of aesthetics', *Organization*, 3(2): 209–218.

Strati, A. (1998) 'Organizational symbolism as a social construction: A perspective from the sociology of knowledge', *Human Relations*, 51(11): 1379–1402.

Strati A. (1999) *Organization and Aesthetics*, London: Sage.

Strati, A. (2000) 'The Aesthetic Approach in Organization Studies', in Linstead, S. and Höpfl, H. eds. *The Aesthetics of Organization*, London, Thousand Oaks, New Delhi: Sage: 13–34.

Strati, A. (2001) *Theory and Method in Organization Studies*, London: Sage.

Strati, A. (2007a) 'Sensations, Impressions and Reflections on the Configuring of the Aesthetic Discourse in Organizations', *Aesthesis*, 1(1): 14–22.

Strati, A. (a cura di) (2007b) *La ricerca qualitativa nelle organizzazioni, la dimensione estetica*, Roma: Carocci.

Strati, A. (2009) 'Do You Do Beautiful Things?' in *Aesthetics and Art in Qualitative Methods of Organization Studies*, in Buchanan, D. and Bryman, A. eds. *The Sage Handbook of Organizational Research Methods*, London: Sage: 230–45.

Strati, A. (2010) *Che cos'è l'estetica organizzativa* [What is Organizational Aesthetics?], Roma: Carocci.

Strati, A., & Montoux, P. G. D. (2002) 'Organizing Aesthetics', *Human Relations*, 55(7): 755–766.

Styhre, A. (2004) 'Rethinking Knowledge: A Bergsonian Critique of the Notion of Tacit Knowledge', *British Journal of Management*, 15(2) (June): 177–188.

Sull, D. (2005a) *Made in China: What Western Managers Can Learn from Trailblazing Chinese Entrepreneurs*, Boston, MA: Harvard Business School Press.

Sull, D. (2005b) 'Strategy as Active Waiting', *Harvard Business Review*, September 2005: 121–129.

Sutton, R. I. and Hargadon, A. (1996) 'Brainstorming Groups in Context: Effectiveness in a Product Design Firm', *Administrative Science Quarterly*, 41: 685–718.

Swan, J. (2007) Knowledge, In Clegg, S. and Bailey, J. eds. *International Encyclopaedia of Organisation Studies*, London: Sage: 750–753.

Swann, C. (2002) 'Action research and the practice of design', *Design Issues*, 18(1): 57

Synnott, A. (1993) *The Body Social: Symbolism, Self and Society*, London: Routledge.

Taleb, N. N. (2007) *The Black Swan: The Impact of the Highly Improbable*, London: Allen Lane.

Taylor, S. (2002) 'Overcoming Aesthetic Muteness: Researching organizational members aesthetic experience', *Human Relations,* 55(7): 821–840.

Taylor S. (2004) 'Presentational Form in First Person Research. Off-line Collaborative Reflection Using Art', *Action Research*, 2(1): 71–88.

Taylor, S. & Hansen, H. (2005) 'Finding Form: Looking at the Field of Organizational Aesthetics', *Journal of Management Studies*, 42 (6): 1211–1231.

Taylor, S. and Spicer, A. (2007) 'Time for space: A narrative review of research on organizational spaces', *International Journal of Management Reviews*, 9(4): 325–346.

Taylor, S. S. & Carbone I. (2008) 'Technique & Practices from the Arts: Expressive Verbs, Feelings, and Action', in Barry, D. and Hanson, H. eds. *New and Emerging Approaches to Management and Organization*, London: Sage: 220–228.

Taylor, S.S., and Hansen, H. (2005) 'Finding Form: Looking at the Field of Organizational Aesthetics', *Journal of Management Studies* 42(6): 1211–1231.

Tester, K. (1994) *The Flaneûr*, London: Routledge.

Thackara, J. (2006) *In the Bubble – Designing in a Complex World,* Cambridge, Massachusetts: The MIT Press: 8.

Thomas, J. C. and Carroll, J. M. (1979) 'The Psychological Study of Design', *Design Studies,* 1: 5–11.

Thrift, N. (2005) *Knowing capitalism,* London: Sage.

Toadvine, T. (2004) 'Singing the World in a New Key: Merleau-Ponty and the Ontology of Sense', *Janus Head,* 7(2) (Winter): 273–283.

Topchick, G.S. (2001) *Managing Workplace Negativity,* New York: Amacom.

Tsang, D. (2009) *Space Office,* Hong Kong: Pace Publishing.

Tuan, Y-F. (1990) *Topophilia: A study of environmental perceptions, attitudes and values,* London: Prentice Hall.

Uhl-Bien, M. (2006) 'Relational leadership theory: Exploring the social processes of leadership and organizing', *Leadership Quarterly,* 17: 654–676.

Urry, J. (2002) *The Tourist Gaze,* London: Sage.

Vaihinger, H. (1927) *Die Philosophie des Als Ob* [English translation (2000): The Philosophy of As if, London: Routledge].

Vaill, P. B. (1989) *Managing as a Performing Art: New ideas for a world of chaotic change,* San Francisco, CA: Jossey-Bass.

Varela, F. J., Thompson, E. and Rosch, E. (1991) *The Embodied Mind,* Cambridge London: MIT Press.

Varzi, A. (2005) *Ontologia* [Ontology], Bari: Laterza.

Vattimo, G. (1983) 'Dialettica, differenza, pensiero debole' [Dialectic, Difference, Weak Thought], in Vattimo, G. and Rovatti, P. A. eds., *Il pensiero debole.* Milano: Feltrinelli: 12–28.

Verbrucken, M. (2003) 'Towards a New Sensoriality' in *The New Everyday,* Arts, Emile. et al. Philips Design.

Vickery, J. (2006) 'Organising Art: Constructing Aesthetic Value', *Culture & Organization* 12(1): 51–63.

Vidiella, A.S. (2008) *Atlas of Office Interiors,* Beverly, MA: Rockport Publishers.

Viliani, A. ed. (2011) *Anna Scalfi Eghenter: KataLogos,* Milano: SilvanaEditoriale.

Waldenfels, B. (1994) *Antwortregister,* Frankfurt/M: Suhrkamp.

Waldenfels, B. (2007) 'The Question of the Other', Hong Kong: Chinese University of Hong Kong.

Waldenfels, B. (2008). 'The Role of the Lived-Body in Feeling', *Continental Philosophy Review,* 41(2): 127–142.

Warren, S. (2002) 'Show me how it feels to work here: the role of photography in researching organizational aesthetics', *Ephemera: theory and politics in organization,* 2 (3): 224 – 245: available at www.ephemeraweb.org

Warren, S. (2005a) 'Exploring Excess: five challenges of an aesthetic research agenda', paper presented to the 23rd Standing Conference on Organizational Symbolism, Stockholm, Sweden, July (unpublished).

Warren. S. (2005b) *Consuming Work: An exploration of organizational aestheticization,* PhD thesis (unpublished), Portsmouth: University of Portsmouth.

Warren, S. (2005c) 'Photography and Voice in Critical, Qualitative, Management Research' *Accounting, Auditing and Accountability Journal,* 18 (6): 861–882.

Warren, S. (2006) 'Post-modern Synaesthesia: Paul Klee and 'The Nature of Creation', *Culture & Organization,* 12(2) 191–198.

Warren, S., and Rehn, A. (2006) 'Oppression, Art and Aesthetics', *Consumption Markets & Culture,* 9(2): 81–85.

Warren, S., and Rehn, A. (2007) 'Messing up organizational aesthetics', Jones, C., ten Bos, R., eds. *Philosophy and Organization,* New York: Routledge: 157–168.

Warren, S. & Fineman., S. (2007) 'Don't get me wrong but… ambivalence and paradox in a 'fun' work environment' in Rhodes, C. & Westwood, B. eds. *Humour, Organization and Work,* London: Routledge: 92–112.

Wasson, C. (2000) 'Ethnography in the Field of Design', *Human Organization,* 59(4):377– 388.

Watkins, C. (2005) 'Representations of space, spatial practices and spaces of representation: An application of Lefebvre's Spatial Triad', *Culture and Organization,* 11(3): 209–20.

Welsch, W. (1997) *Undoing Aesthetics,* London: Sage.

Wettlaufer, A. (2000) 'The sublime rivalry of word and image: Turner and Ruskin revisited', *Victorian Literature and Culture,* 28 (1): 149–169.

Whincup, T. (2004) 'Imaging the Intangible' in Knowles, C. & Sweetman, P. eds. *Picturing the Social Landscape: Visual methods and the sociological imagination,* London: Routledge.

Whitehead, A. N. (1929) *Process and Reality,* Cambridge: Cambridge University Press.

Whyte, W.H. (1956) *The Organization Man,* Philadelphia: University of Pennsylvania Press.

Wilber, K. (2000) *One Taste,* Boston: Shambhala.

Willmott, H. (1993) 'Strength is ignorance; slavery is freedom: managing culture in modern organizations', *Journal of Management Studies,* 30(4): 515–552.

Wilson, A. (1992) *The Culture of Nature,* Oxford: Blackwell.

Witz, A., Warhurst, C. and Nickson, D. (2003) 'The Labour of Aesthetics and the Aesthetics of Organization', *Organization,* 10(1): 33–54.

Wright, S. (1994) 'Culture in Anthropology and Organizational Studies', in Wright, S. ed. *Anthropology of Organizations*, London: Routledge: 1–31.

Yanow, D. (2000) Seeing Organizational Learning: A "Cultural" View', *Organization*, 7(2):247–268.

Yin, R. (2003) *Case Study Research: Design and Methods,* London: Sage